THE FUTURE OF FINANCIAL SYSTEMS AND SERVICES

Also by Edward P. M. Gardener

COMPETITION AND REGULATION OF BANKS (*with Christopher Barclay and Jack Revell*)
CAPITAL ADEQUACY AND BANKING SUPERVISION
UK BANKING SUPERVISION – EVOLUTION, PRACTICE AND ISSUES (*editor*)
INTEREST RATE RISK AND BANKS (*editor*)
SECURITISATION: HISTORY, FORMS AND RISKS (*with Jack Revell*)
STRUCTURE AND REGULATION OF UK FINANCIAL MARKETS (*with P. Molyneux*)

John Robert Stephen Revell
Emeritus Professor, University of Wales

The Future of Financial Systems and Services

Essays in Honour of Jack Revell

Edited by
Edward P. M. Gardener
Professor and Director of the Institute of European Finance
University College of North Wales, Bangor

M
MACMILLAN

First published 1990

Published by
THE MACMILLAN PRESS LTD
Houndmills, Basingstoke, Hampshire RG21 2XS
and London
Companies and representatives
throughout the world

Printed in Hong Kong

British Library Cataloguing in Publication Data
The future of financial systems and services: essays in honour of Jack Revell.
1. Financial services
I. Gardener, Edward P. M. II. Revell, Jack
332.1
ISBN 0-333-47321-3

Contents

List of Figures

List of Tables

Preface

Financial systems and services have changed at an unprecedented pace since the start of the 1970s. The early 1970s heralded the beginning of a new era in financial systems. Traditional compartmentalisation in national financial systems began to erode significantly. Financial institutions began to enter new fields. Some of these new fields were the historical preserve of specialist financial institutions, but others represented completely new activities. Financial innovation helped to spawn new competitors and new forms of competition.

Structural deregulation, allowing financial institutions and markets to compete more freely, has brought new challenges and issues. The redrawing of historical institutional boundaries has taken place in an environment of financial turbulence; the risks and uncertainties facing financial institutions and regulators have burgeoned. Periodic crises have characterised this new environment. Supervisory (or prudential) reregulation has been a concurrent trend alongside structural deregulation.

During the 1970s the growing internationalisation of banking weakened the national sovereignty of domestic financial systems. Domestic financial markets were increasingly penetrated by foreign banks and other institutions. Technology and globalisation trends operated to link increasingly important financial centres and systems into a single financial market that spans the globe. The swaps market and other innovations have been important in this process. The ubiquitous nature of technology has helped to reduce further the traditional comparative advantage of banks in many important financial activities.

Securitisation trends have questioned the longer-term role of traditional financial intermediation, or institution-based intermediation. Market-based intermediation has grown rapidly from the early 1980s. Many domestic financial systems have moved correspondingly towards a stronger 'market orientation'. Bank-type finance has been displaced increasingly by securitised forms of financing.

These are just a sample of the challenges and issues that confront students and practitioners in modern financial systems. All of these changes have accelerated during the 1980s. In the wake of the stock market crash of October 1987 and the approach of 1992 in Europe, we now face a renewed surge of changes in financial systems and services. Many would argue that contemporary changes represent a 'watershed era' for the future of financial systems and services. We are now moving rapidly into new and untried territory from which a return will probably be impossible.

This is an opportune time to present a collection of essays from a group of distinguished students and practitioners on the general theme of change in financial systems. It is also an appropriate moment to honour a distinguished student of change in financial systems, Professor Jack Revell. The present volume attempts to do both. This collection of essays has been compiled as a token of our respect for a student who has made a singular contribution to the study of financial systems and services; Chapter 1 of the book discusses Jack Revell's contribution in some detail.

The 22 papers contributed to this volume have been organised into the following sections:

I Introduction
II Evolution and Development of Financial Systems
III Money and Capital Markets
IV International Banking and Finance
V Managerial and Micro Aspects of Financial Institutions
VI Regulation

Part I by the editor comprises a chapter on Jack Revell's academic contribution and its place in mainstream economics. Part II comprises four papers and it sets the scene for the rest of the book. The theme in Part II is on competition, innovation, risk and structural change; part III contains three papers that focus more specifically on money and capital markets. Part IV comprises four papers devoted to international banking and finance. More specific, but selective managerial and micro aspects of financial institutions are covered within the four papers that comprise Part V of the volume. Part VI contains the largest number of contributions: six papers focus specifically on regulation.

Authors were given a free choice on their contributions, and the editor compartmentalised them into Parts I–VI: there is some inevitable overlapping of papers into different sections (parts) of the volume, but this is unavoidable. For example, two of the papers (Eisenbeis and Montanaro) in Part II discuss regulation and risk in some detail, and this is the focus of Part VI. Nevertheless, the editor has taken the view that the main thrust of these two papers is on stuctural change; it is for this reason that they are included in part II. In short, the editor has exercised some subjectivity in these allocations, but this has been tempered with (hopefully) logical methodological reasoning. The reader must judge the success of this selection process. However, it is the papers themselves that are, of course, more important than the way they are compartmentalised.

The collection of papers has an interesting 'global focus'. Case studies on individual countries are provided alongside more general surveys. Contemporary theory is discussed and evaluated in many of the papers. The thread that runs throughout the volume is the future of financial systems and services; all of the contributors have responded positively to this invited theme. The variety and richness of the ground covered by these essays attest to the quality of the contributors' responses. This volume should, as a result, prove interesting to both students and practitioners.

Many acknowledgements are in order. First of all, the individual contributors who have responded so well to the numerous requests and deadlines imposed by the editor. It should be added that each of the papers is mutually exclusive. There is no presumption that individual contributors necessarily agree (or disagree) with other contributions to this volume. I thank Macmillan for their enthusiasm and help with the volume. I am also especially grateful to Chris Owen and Maureen Simmons who played important roles in the initial proof-reading and editing; Lesley Prendergast also proof-read corrections for the volume. Chris Owen also had the unenviable task of co-ordinating and managing the 'Festschrift project'. She carried out these tasks with her usual efficiency. I thank Helen Treece, Linda Jeavons and Karen Hickson who all typed many drafts. Finally, I thank my wife Ann Christine and our children – Michael, Emma, John and Peter – for their support and tolerance. Any errors, or omissions, are assumed by the editor.

EDWARD P. M. GARDENER

Notes on the Contributors

Jean-Paul Abraham is Executive Vice President at Banque Paribas Belgique, Brussels. He is also Professor of Financial Economics and former Dean, Faculty of Economic and Social Science in the University of Namur, Belgium, and an Honorary Director of the EEC Commission in Brussels. He is co-author of *Les Institutions Financières Belges* and author of many articles in European journals. Professor Abraham is Chief Editor of *Revue de la Banque*, Brussels.

Phil Bourke is Irish Banks' Professor of Banking and Finance at University College, Dublin. Prior to taking up this appointment in Dublin, Dr Bourke was a member of the School of Banking and Finance in the University of New South Wales in Sydney. His research interests include bank management, cognitive aspects of lending and regulation theory.

Cesare Bisoni studied at the Università Bocconi, Italy and the Harvard Business School. He is currently Professor of Banking at the Università di Modena, Italy and a Senior Faculty Member of Scuola di Direzione Aziendale, Università Bocconi. He is also Deputy Director, Dipartimento di Economia Aziendale, Università di Modena and a Member of the Board of Auditors, Cassa di Risparmio di Modena, Italy. His publications include four books.

Roger Buckland studied economics at Cambridge and at York University. Following graduate study at York in 1974–5, he was appointed Ellis Hunter Research Fellow working on the economics of technical change. He joined the Aston Management Centre as a Lecturer in 1978. His published research covers technical change in the steel industry, equity capital markets, and techniques of the privatisation of nationalised industries.

Claudia Campbell has studied for a PhD (forthcoming in 1989) at Washington University. She is an Assistant Professor of Economics and Finance at St Louis University and co-author (with Hyman P. Minsky) of *How to Get Off the Back of a Tiger*. Her doctoral research is on *Federal Deposit Insurance Risk Exposure in Commercial Banks*.

Robert Carter is Norwich Union Professor of Insurance Studies in the Department of Industrial Economics, Accounting and Insurance at the University of Nottingham. He is the author of *Economics and Insurance*, *Reinsurance*, *Success in Insurance* (with S. R. Diacon) and *Barriers to*

Trade in Insurance (with G. M. Dickinson). Professor Carter is heavily involved in the educational work of the UK Chartered Insurance Institute. He is at present a government nominee on the Insurance Brokers' Registration Council and is a member of the Council of the Insurance Ombudsman Bureau. His current research interests are the financial aspects of risk management and international insurance problems.

Francesco Cesarini is Professor of Banking and of Stock Exchange Financing at the Catholic University of Milano, Italy. He is also Chairman of the Board of Directors of Banca Agricola Milanese, and a Member of the Scientific Committee of '*Banca Impresa e Società*', '*L'industria*' and '*Finanza Impresa e Mercati*'. He was a member of the Treasury Commission which reported on the structure of the Italian financial system (1982).

Peter Cooke retired from the Bank of England, where he had been Associate Director since 1982, in November 1988 after a Central Banking Career of 33 years. He was Chairman of the City EEC Committee from 1973 to 1980. From 1976 to 1985 he was Head of Banking Supervision at the Bank of England. In 1977 he became Chairman of the Committee on Banking Regulations and Supervisory Practices of the Group of 10 Countries meeting in Basle, Switzerland, which post he held until his retirement in October 1988. From the beginning of 1989 he moved into the private sector where his principal involvement is with the international accounting firm, Price Waterhouse, as Chairman of their World Regulatory Advisory Service.

Richard Dale graduated from the London School of Economics and read for the bar at Lincoln's Inn. Subsequently he spent five years with merchant bankers NM Rothschild and Sons Ltd. More recently he was a Rockefeller Foundation International Relations Fellow at the Brookings Institution in Washington DC and is currently Professor of International Banking and Financial Institutions at the University of Southampton. Professor Dale is the author of *Anti-Dumping Law in a Liberal Trade Order*, *Bank Supervision Around the World*, *Managing Global Debt* and *The Regulation of International Banking*.

Edward Davis was educated at St Andrews and after research at Aberystwyth and Cambridge, took the Lloyds Bank Chair of Business Finance at Aston in 1971. He is co-author of *The London Clearing Banks*, *Company Finance and the Capital Market* and *Finance and the Firm*. His current research interests include the efficiency of privatisation issues, together with a major study of the Unlisted Securities Market in collaboration with R. Buckland, to be published in 1989. In addition to academic and financial articles on business finance, he has broadcast on taxation on several occasions and has worked as a financial consultant for both British and US companies.

Robert Eisenbeis is currently Associate Dean for Research and Wachovia Professor of Banking in the UNC Business School at Chapel Hill. In addition he is a member of the Shadow Financial Regulatory Committee and is a former member of the Federal Savings and Loan Advisory Council. Prior to going to Chapel Hill, Professor Eisenbeis was Senior Deputy Associate Director in the Division of Research and Statistics at the Federal Reserve Board in Washington, DC; he also has held positions at the FDIC. He has published many articles in professional journals and is co-author of five books.

Edward P. M. Gardener is a Professor at the University College of North Wales (UCNW) in Bangor, Gwynedd, Wales. Previously, he held senior finance posts with Shell-Mex and BP Ltd. He has been Director of the Institute of European Finance at UCNW since 1985 and a member of the London Board of D.C. Gardner Group plc from 1984. He has directed research projects for a wide range of bodies like the Social Science Research Council, HM Treasury, the British Bankers Association and many leading banks. His publications include *Capital Adequacy and Banking Supervision* (editor), *UK Banking Supervision: Evolution, Practice and Issues* and many articles. His current research interests include bank strategy, capital adequacy and supervision.

Charles Goodhart is the Norman Sosnow Professor of Banking and Finance at the London School of Economics. Before joining LSE in 1985, he worked at the Bank of England for seventeen years as a monetary adviser, becoming a Chief Adviser in 1980. Earlier he had taught at Cambridge, where for a couple of years he was one of Jack Revell's colleagues, and at LSE, and was an Economic Adviser in the Department of Economic Affairs (1965–6). He has just revised his graduate monetary textbook, *Money, Information and Uncertainty*. He earlier published a collection of papers on monetary policy, *Monetary Theory and Practice*, and an institutional study on *The Evolution of Central Banks*, which has just been revised and reprinted; plus a large number of articles and papers on monetary and banking issues.

Richard Harrington currently lectures in economics at the University of Manchester. In 1979 he was consultant to the Building Societies Association. He has lectured widely and produced a number of books and articles on money and banking. During 1982–6 he was consultant to the OECD and author of a monograph on asset and liability management by banks.

Mervyn Lewis is Midland Bank Professor of Money and Banking at the University of Nottingham, Co-director of the Nottingham Institute of Financial Studies, and Visiting Professor in Economics at the Flinders University of South Australia. In 1986 he was elected a Fellow of the Academy of the Social Sciences in Australia. He was a Consultant to the Australian Financial System Inquiry and Visiting Scholar at the Bank of England. Professor Lewis has published six books on monetary economics, the last being (with K. T. Davis) *Domestic and International Banking*.

David T. Llewellyn has held appointments at Unilever in Rotterdam, HM Treasury in London, the University of Nottingham and the International Monetary Fund in Washington. He is the Professor of Money and Banking at Loughborough University and Chairman of the Loughborough University Banking Centre. He is currently Consultant Economist to money brokers Butler Harlow Ueda and a member of the London Board of the Halifax Building Society. As well as many articles he is the author of *International Financial Integration, Framework of UK Monetary Policy, Evolution of the British Financial System,* and *Regulation and Supervision of Financial Institutions.*

Hyman Minsky has been Professor of Economics at Washington University, St Louis since 1965. He is the author of many articles on money, banking and finance. His publications include *John Maynard Keynes*, *Can 'It' Happen Again* and *Stabilizing an Unstable Economy*.

Joël Métais is Professor of Economics at the Universities of Grenoble and Paris Dauphine. He was formerly consultant with the UNIDO (United Nations Industrial Development Organization) on financial problems of the industrial development (1981–2). From 1985 to 1988 he was attached with the French Ministry of Economy and Finance as a consultant on the financial and banking sector matters. He has published widely and his publications include *Le marché des eurodollars et des euroobligations and Les mutations du système financier français* (co-author). His main research interests are in international capital markets, comparative banking systems and the industrial economics of the financial sector.

Elisabetta Montanaro is a full Professor in Banking at the Faculty of Economics and Banking at the University of Siena, Italy. She has been Director of the University of Siena from 1981. Elisabetta Montanero is also Professor of Banking Management at the University of La Plata (AR), which has been promoted by the Department of International Cooperation of the Italian Government. She is the author of many articles and seven books on banking.

Neil Murphy is Professor of Finance at the School of Business, Virginia Commonwealth University, USA. He has held appointments on the research and policy staffs of the Federal Reserve Bank of Boston, the Federal Deposit Insurance Corporation, and the President's Commission on Financial Structure and Regulation (Hunt Commission). He was also a Faculty Member at the Universities of Maine, Oklahoma and Connecticut, and has been a Senior Vice President of Payments Systems Inc., then a research and consulting subsidiary of the American Express Co. He has also held visiting academic assignments in Israel and the Netherlands. He has written several books and articles for professional periodicals. He has served as an associate editor of the *Journal of Finance*, a member of the editorial board of the *Journal of Bank Research*, and was a founding co-editor and first executive editor of the *Journal of Financial Services Research*.

Marco Onado is Professor of Banking in the University of Bologna and he has been Visiting Professorial Fellow at the University College of North Wales. He is a member of the Scientific Committee of Prometeia (Association for Econometric Research) and a member of the Editorial Committee of the journals *Bancaria* and *Banca Impresa Società e l'Industria*. He has written many articles and book contributions.

Leo Schuster is Chair Professor in Banking and Director of the Institute of Bank Research at the University of Saint Gallen, Switzerland. From 1964 to 1971 he held academic posts at the University of Nuremberg; he came to St Gallen in 1971 where he completed his habilitation in 1975. He was Dean of the Business Administration Department at Saint Gallen from 1983 to 1985. He is a member of the advisory board to the Marketing Association of Cooperative Banks, Stuttgart, Germany; of the German Federation of University Professors in Business Administration; and of the Société Universitaire de Recherches Financières, Tilburg, The Netherlands. He is co-editor of the *Zeitschrift für das gesamte Kreditwesen* (*Bankers Magazine*) Frankfurt, Germany and of the *Bankwirtschaftliche Forschungen* (*Research in Banking*); editor of *Schriftenreihe Bankrevision* (*Auditing in Banks*) and of the *Beiträge zur Bankbetriebslehre* (*Research Papers in Banking*). He has published some 20 books and more than 120 articles in German, French, Italian and Spanish in banking, business finance and corporate strategy.

Ray Shaw is a Senior Executive of TSB Group working as a management consultant to Group companies. He was formerly Director of the TSB Group Management College from 1983 to 1987 and Director of Banking

Studies at the University of Loughborough. He is the author of the *London Money Market* and (with J. B. Howcroft) *Banking Law*. He is also TSB Senior Visiting Fellow at the University College of North Wales, Bangor and an advisor to University Paris-Dauphine.

Synopsis of the Contributions

Chapter 1 is devoted to an examination of Jack Revell's contribution to the study of banking and financial systems. Ted Gardener examines this contribution from a number of different perspectives. Charles Goodhart – in the summary of his paper for the Festschrift – summarises succinctly Jack's methodological stance:

> Theoretical analysis, and policy advice, should be underpinned by thorough empirical knowledge of institutions and history, as Jack Revell has always emphasised.

Ted Gardener suggests that in one sense Jack has carried forward the methodological torch carried for many years by Professor Richard Sayers. Nevertheless, Jack has also emphasised strongly the importance of applied industrial economics and micro aspects of banking in his studies on financial systems. These and other related characteristics are discussed in Chapter 1.

In Chapter 2 David Llewellyn considers the recent structural developments in the British financial system which have changed the system from its historical structured and specialised basis to one of financial conglomeration. In particular, emphasis is given to competition which has been the major factor behind structural change. A series of propositions are made about the likely effect on an industry subject to more competition and these are found in many recent examples in the financial system. The chapter concludes with a review of how structural change might have contributed to increased efficiency in the financial system.

Chapter 3 takes as a starting point that in banking the process of change is at least as important as change itself. Jean-Paul Abraham analyses the processes of internationalisation, (de)regulation and automation in Belgium under the small open economy hypothesis. In Belgian banking, international and domestic markets interact very strongly; the importance of tax incentives and tax deterrents is striking. Financial deregulation has occurred mainly by undermining or eroding the existing regulations, but he argues that this process requires stronger stimuli. Finally, he suggests that the problem of adequate scale becomes crucial in the context of 'Europe 1992'.

Recent proposals to reform the US financial system arising from concerns about bank and thrift failures, increased competition and narrowing spreads appear to be rooted in assumptions about the nature of banking which may no longer be valid or relevant in today's international banking environment. In Chapter 4 Robert Eisenbeis emphasises that market developments are eroding the imperfections which gave US commercial banks their advantages over intermediation in direct credit markets such that they no longer perform their same unique functions in the nation's payments system. Moreover, because of globalisation and the ability of financial institutions to engage in structural arbitrage, one can no longer ignore the international considerations in financial engineering. The thesis is developed that regulation can no longer restrain domestic institutions without stimulating various distortions. Additionally, it is argued that concerns for maintaining the safety and soundness of the dollar payments system differ significantly now from those that were relevant when the present US regulatory structure was put in place. These structural considerations suggest that US policies designed to insulate domestic institutions and markets from those of the rest of the world, or to insulate affiliates or subsidiaries from risk taking in the rest of the institution, are doomed to failure.

In Chapter 5 Elisabetta Montanaro analyses the various phases of the present banking crisis in Argentina from 1981 until 1987. This crisis is one of the most sustained in banking history, but it lacks rigorous study. The argument advanced is that the crisis is the unavoidable epilogue of banks' operating inefficiencies. These inefficiencies are largely the result of many different policies of monetary and credit control against inflation and hyper-inflation. The enormous quantity of financial national resources destroyed in the course of the protracted banking crisis, together with the consequential mounting loss of credibility in the solvency of the banking system (the central bank and commercial banks) in the eyes of national savers and foreign lenders, are amongst the main determinants of the dramatic problems posed by Argentina's external debt.

In Chapter 6 Charles Goodhart is concerned with a general theoretical issue, i.e. why practitioners have usually been opposed to indexation (whereas academics have favoured it), in the context of a particular historical decision, that of the UK authorities to introduce indexed gilts in 1981. Theoretical analysis, and policy advice should be underpinned by thorough empirical knowledge of institutions and history, as Jack Revell has always emphasised. In this chapter Goodhart seeks to contribute by providing a more detailed historical account of the various arguments, pro and con, influencing the authorities' decision in this case.

Ray Shaw in Chapter 7 reviews – in the wake of the 'Big Bang' – the changes which have occurred in the London money markets since 1983. He emphasises the developing role and changing structure of the discount market, the various aspects of monetary policy and the resulting market and institutional relationships with the Bank of England.

Chapter 8 examines the behaviour of new entrants to the Unlisted Securities Market in the 1980s with specific reference to bank borrowing.

Roger Buckland and Ted Davis consider in particular the question whether such firms use the new issue market to raise new equity in order to reduce excessive bank borrowing and whether such an effect is more pronounced for smaller firms. The authors find the variability of entrants by gearing ratios dominates the size effect which can be observed. But the authors conclude that if alternative methods of raising capital were available from the banking sector, then such firms might not have sought quotation at all, or done so at a later stage of their growth and at inevitably lower costs.

A theme of Chapter 9 is that the theoretical understanding of the functioning of banks and banking systems outside the United States is comparatively underdeveloped. Phil Bourke examines the theory and expirical evidence on the determinants of international bank profitability. He discusses the results of research that he conducted on large banks in fifteen countries or territories around the world. Within this survey he examines market structure, regulation and several of the internal determinants of profitability.

From the 1970s onwards the financial sectors in the main industrial countries entered an internationalisation process, the outcome of which will probably be the emergence of a global financial industry along the lines already experienced by other industries. In Chapter 10 Joël Métais provides, first, an overview of developments during the past fifteen years. Two important sub-periods are identified from this overview. A tentative theoretical analysis is developed which stresses the importance of analytical tools and the framework of industrial economics in order to interpret important features of the contemporary financial industry like innovations, deregulation, the emergence of financial conglomerates, the entry of non-financial actors in the sector, and mergers and acquisitions (especially between banks and non-bank financial intermediaries). In this respect special attention is devoted to key areas like the existence of economies of scale and/or scope, the production and cost functions, the pricing of the multiproduct financial firms and barriers to entry in the financial sector.

In Chapter 11 Leo Schuster examines the role of Swiss banks in international finance. He emphasises the importance of the globalisation phenomenon to Swiss banks, and he discusses the role of Switzerland as an international financial centre; the 'strategic success' position of the Swiss financial centre is examined. In his conclusion he identifies the future challenges for the Swiss financial centre and discusses the modern role of innovation compared to tradition.

The first part of Chapter 12 explains the two ways in which insurance and reinsurance operations are conducted internationally, the reasons why governments have sought to restrict such trade and the variety of measures that have been adopted to achieve that objective. In the second half of the chapter, Robert Carter outlines briefly the moves that have taken place within the OECD and the GATT to reverse the trend of protectionism and initialise the liberalisation of international trade in insurance. After examining the case for liberalisation, the steps taken in the European Community towards the creation of a single market in insurance are discussed as providing a framework for negotiations on a wider plane. The chapter ends with a suggested programme for liberalisation.

In market economies, a series of institutions has evolved for sharing and shifting risks. Firms providing insurance services come immediately to mind. But the financial system as a whole performs a risk sharing function, and the management of risk lies at the heart of all financial intermediation. Mervyn Lewis explores in Chapter 13 the idea that banking can be viewed as a form of insurance. This conception provides a framework which enables him to compare retail banking, wholesale banking, international and off-balance sheet banking, and explore the implications for bank safety and deposit insurance.

During the past 20–30 years, banking has become more complex as banks have diversified by product, by currency and by geographical area. Such diversification has contributed to and, in turn, benefited from the growth of financial markets. Banks, nowadays, regularly bid for funds in, and offer funds to, a range of such markets. But rates of interests and other conditions can change fast and banks operating in a wide range of markets need to manage carefully their balance sheet in order to control any gaps or mismatches which could lead to unforeseen losses. In Chapter 14 Richard Harrington describes how banks' awareness of the new risks has grown and how they have responded by developing the technique of asset and liability management.

In Chapter 15 Ted Gardener examines the strategic challenges of financial conglomeration in London. A primary aim is to explore important strategic dimensions of these challenges that are apparently neglected in the contemporary literature on the microeconomics of banking. He uses Porter analysis as a framework to discuss the competitive challenges of investment banking in the deregulated London market. Chapter 15 emphasises the managerial challenges associated with the 'organisational design' of bank financial conglomerates. Selected macro and general regulatory implications are also highlighted. The subject matter of this chapter is closely related to Chapter 10 (Joël Métais), but the emphasis is more on managerial and strategic aspects of bank financial conglomerates.

In recent years bankers in the United States have encountered the problem of paying depositors a competitive, deregulated rate of interest while simultaneously maintaining a costly delivery system of branch offices. The branch office system was established in part as a substitute for explicit interest payments when the latter were constrained by regulation. One approach to this dilemma is the more intensive use of the branch system to market more services, i.e. spreading the cost over expanded product lines. However, a parallel trend is the development of automatic teller machines (ATMs), effectively pulling customers out of the branch offices. In Chapter 16 Neil Murphy investigates the behaviour of a sample of households in the United States. In particular, the characteristics of those customers who use the branch intensively are compared with those who are active ATM users. It is concluded that those customers most likely to be candidates for more financial services are also most likely to avoid using the branch office, preferring the convenience and flexibility of ATMs.

The global stock market crash in October 1987 has intensified the debate over regulation of the financial services industry in general and stock market activity in particular. Richard Dale in Chapter 17 addresses the various regulatory issues raised by the prospect of increased stock market volatility and examines the implications for the stability of the banking system.

In Chapter 18 Peter Cooke provides a detailed, 'insider-view' narrative of the intensive international discussions over the last few years which led ultimately in the summer of 1988 to an international agreement between the Group of Ten major industrialised countries on the measurement of the capital adequacy of international banks and on a minimum international capital standard. He describes the reasons why a momentum developed to achieve this agreement and sets out the major issues and national circumstances which had to be reconciled in order to arrive at a framework which was at the same time practicable and intellectually coherent and credible to the banking and regulatory community worldwide. Chapter 18 outlines the main stages in the debate which began seriously around the time of the Mexican debt crisis in 1982 and which concluded with the publication of the Basle Supervisors Committee paper of July 1988, which sets out the agreed international framework of capital adequacy measurement and standards which countries round the world are currently being encouraged to put into effect by the end of 1992.

It is explained in Chapter 19 that deposit insurance in the United States is not insurance in the sense of an actuarial sound policy as issued by private insurers. There are reasonable contingencies in which the assurance of deposits involves a pledge of the full faith and credit of the Federal government. The financial instability hypothesis interpretation of Keynes details the endogenous processes of capitalist economies through which the integrated financial and real market structures become incoherent, and intervention by lenders-of-last-resort whether by the central bank, the Treasury, or through the instrumentality of deposit insurance is necessary. The financial instability hypothesis holds that environments change and the structure of regulation and intervention needs to evolve in order to adapt to the changes. Throughout the 1970s and 1980s the deposit insurance agencies as the agent and the federal government in the principal in the pledge of the full faith and credit in support of deposits, failed to adjust to the new risk environment. As a result the problem of funding the government's guarantee has become ever greater, so that major Treasury spending, which grows with every delay, will be necessary to fulfil the guarantee. If poorly done this spending can be disruptive of the relative relaxed inflation we have enjoyed. Claudia Campbell and Hyman Minsky suggest that the regulatory agents are astride a Tiger and getting off not only requires care but also knowledge and understanding.

All financial systems currently show an urgent need to redefine their overall framework. In Chapter 20 Marco Onado points out the necessity for a uniform regulatory structure, taking the Italian case as a leading example of a country where barriers between intermediaries have crumbled and where it is necessary to strengthen prudential controls instead of structural regulation.

Francesco Cesarini analyses the structure and rationale of the regulations of large loans exposures in the Italian banking system, with a view to measuring their distance from the standards set out in the EEC Recommendation of 22 December 1986, to which Italian regulators are expected to comply within a relatively short period of time. He explains in Chapter 21 that the control of large loans exposures is a field of prudential regulation in which Italian banks are subject to rules far more permissive than those usually applied in other industrial countries. His analysis of the several sets of available data on large loans exposures – in order to get an idea of the dimension of the concentration problem and of its intrinsic riskiness – leaves little doubt that Italian regulations currently in force would need to be revised.

Economic doctrine has dealt extensively with the capital of credit institutions and the related problem of capital adequacy. During recent years the supervisory authorities of various countries have designed instruments – mainly balance sheet ratios – to ensure that banks maintain their capital at required levels. In Chapter 22 Cesare Bisoni discusses recent Italian supervisory experiences with capital adequacy. The Italian authorities refrained until March 1987 from imposing compulsory ratios. The two ratios that have been introduced are described, and some of their possible effects are examined.

Glossary

CHIPS	Clearing House Interbank Payments System
EC	European Community
FDIC	Federal Deposit Insurance Corporation
FHLBB	Federal Home Loan Bank Board
FSLIC	Federal Savings and Loan Insurance Corporation
GATT	General Agreement on Tariffs and Trade
OECD	Organisation for Economic Co-operation and Development
OPEC	Organisation of Petroleum Exporting Countries
SOFFEX	Swiss Options and Financial Futures Exchange
TSA	The Securities Association
UNCTAD	United Nations Conference on Trade and Development

Part I
Introduction

This opening chapter is devoted to a discussion of Professor Jack Revell's contribution to the study of financial systems. 'Revell' and 'financial systems' have virtually become synonymous. The editor explores how Revell's work has fitted into mainstream economics and finance. It is explained that, in some sense, Revell has successfully carried forward the approach developed by earlier distinguished students like Sayers. In other respects, however, Revell's contribution has been singular and distinctive.

1 Jack Revell

Edward P. M. Gardener

John Robert Stephen Revell was born on 15 April 1920 in Tunbridge Wells. He was educated at Skinners' School, Tunbridge Wells, and the London School of Economics (LSE), where he read for a BSc (Econ.) degree. Before going up to LSE in 1947 he spent ten years in the Civil Service and Army: during this time he became an Associate of the Institute of Linguists (French and Spanish). These language skills were put to good use in some of the academic work for which he was later to acquire a wide European reputation.

Following his graduation in 1950 from LSE Jack worked as a research economist for a commercial organisation. In 1957 he joined the Department of Applied Economics (DAE) at the University of Cambridge: this was a time of new initiatives at the DAE. Jack was a Research Officer at the DAE from 1957 to 1963 and a Senior Research Officer from 1963 to 1968. He was also Director of Studies in Economics at Selwyn College, Cambridge from 1960 to 1965. From 1964 to 1967 he held the post of Director of Studies in Economics at Fitzwilliam College, Cambridge. He was a Fellow of Fitzwilliam College from 1965 to 1968, and also Tutor (1965–7) and Senior Tutor (1967–8) in Economics at Fitzwilliam.

Jack left the University of Cambridge in 1968. He took up the Chair in Economics at the University College of North Wales, Bangor in 1969, which he held until 1983 when he took 'early retirement', a misnomer in his case. He was made Professor Emeritus of the University of Wales in 1983. Following his early retirement he moved back to Cambridge. He continues to maintain close working links with Bangor as a Consultant Director of the Institute of European Finance, which is based in the University College of North Wales.

The work for which Jack was to become internationally recognised began in earnest during his years at Cambridge. His research on national balance sheets was conducted within a unit headed by W. B. Reddaway. From 1963 to 1966 Jack's work on national balance sheets became an integral part of a wider research project at Cambridge under the direction of Professor Richard Stone to study the financial implications of growth in the British economy. The Bank of England, the Committee of London Clearing Bankers, the British Bankers Association, the Building Societies Association and other important City institutions provided funds for this wider project.

Revell in the United Kingdom, and Goldsmith and Lipsey in the United States, became the internationally respected experts on national balance sheets and the associated structural aspects and workings of financial systems. Jack's main contribution to this field is summarised in *The Wealth of the Nation* published in 1967. This research, assisted by Graham Hockley and John Moyle, was directed at producing the national balance sheet of the United Kingdom for 1957–61.

During this period Jack also published two other papers that are of particular contemporary interest; the first with John Moyle, *The Owners of Quoted Ordinary Shares: A Survey for 1963* (1966) and, secondly, *Changes in British Banking: The Growth of a Secondary Banking System* (1968). The 1966 paper drew attention to the decline in personal sector shareholdings on the Stock Exchange and the corresponding rise of institutional investors. In a 1972 monograph *Financial Structure and Government Regulation* he explored these trends further and examined the phenomenon of 'privileged financial circuits' in the post-war development of the British financial system. The taxation system has now been recognised widely as a particularly important influence on the modern evolution of the British financial system. The present government has also set out to restore personal sector shareholdings on the Stock Exchange.

Jack's 1968 paper identified the emergence of a new banking system, the secondary banking system, that had grown up in the United Kingdom during the 1960s alongside the primary, or traditional, banking system. This 1968 paper began a more formal exploration of the principles and implications of wholesale banking. In the September 1968 issue of *The Banker* he published an article entitled 'A secondary banking system', which was subsequently reprinted (1972) in H. G. Johnson (ed.), *Readings in British Monetary Economics* (London: Oxford University Press).

The rapid development of the secondary banking system and its associated parallel money markets in the United Kingdom were indicative of an important and more general break in the historical evolution of banks and banking systems. The rise of wholesale banking and the wider internationalisation movement in banking and finance helped to mark the emergence of an era of profound changes in the industrial structure of banking and finance. Jack began to turn most of his research attention towards banking and other financial institutions. Thus began in earnest the 'Bangor period' in his academic work.

Jack's work at Cambridge had given him a unique set of skills in order to apply his brand of research towards identifying, analysing and commenting on the rapidly developing changes in banking and financial systems. In one sense he took over the torch carried so valiantly and for many years by Professor Richard Sayers at LSE. Sayers was internationally recognised as the doyen of the so-called 'institutional approach' for studying banking and financial systems.

In 1967 Tobin (p. 509), commenting on a famous paper by Meltzer (1967) on the regulation of financial institutions, recommended:

> I have no conclusions or recommendations to offer, only perplexity. I hope that those who continue to work on this fascinating and important subject will not hesitate to take from time to time a fundamental and radical look at the institutions they are appraising.

Sayers had adopted this kind of approach as his *modus operandi*, and Jack's work at Bangor extended and developed it, but in a distinctive way. This approach to research became very unfashionable during the 1970s and 1980s in mainstream economics. The emphasis had shifted more towards theoretical developments, computer-based modelling and statistically orientated research. This era in economics was characterised by an increasing emphasis on more formal 'scientific method' in economic reasoning and related empirical work.

Jack's work, however, continued to emphasise the need for a closer understanding of the practical workings of financial institutions and systems: his style of research was an explicit reflection of these professed needs. Students like Hyman Minsky and others within the corpus of so-called 'institutional economics' possessed a great (at least implicit) methodological affinity with this approach, but Jack's style and contributions remained separate, distinctive, committed and often largely isolated from much of mainstream economics. Even the so-called 'institutional economists' in Veblenian vein retained and developed potential compatibility with important parts of mainstream monetary economics.[1] Jack, however, was not concerned primarily in his work with forging links with mainstream money and banking that had, to some extent, distanced itself from the kind of more practical, institutional considerations that interested him. In recent years, however, there has been a resurgence of interest and concern by monetary economists in the structure and practical details of the workings of financial systems; new tools have been forged to combine institutional studies with more formal theoretical and empirical work.

During the 1970s and 1980s Jack was increasingly recognised as a leading student of the institutional structure and workings of financial institutions and markets. His 1973 book *The British Financial System* – it is now being updated – is generally regarded as a classic. Revell and 'financial institutions' became increasingly synonymous in British academe and the City. Although his institutional approach is unique in the context of much of modern monetary economics, it is also reflective of a broader and well-accepted methodological approach that was once, at least, a feature of studies in industrial economics. Let us explore this statement.

Jack's approach is unique in two respects. Firstly, it was not the approach that was generally being pursued by mainstream banking and financial researchers in the United Kingdom at that time. Sayers was really the last of a distinguished line of institutional students of this genre. Jack's methodology was also unique in that he invariably adopted the criterion that a researcher should be able to explain his or her theories and views in 'plain English' to practitioners. He prided himself on the fact that he was able to 'speak the language of practitioners'; he is critical of theories and models that assume away important parts of practical reality. Jack's view is that the best way to understand the workings of financial institutions and markets is to communicate effectively with the relevant practitioners.

Revell's methodological approach is distinguished by two other characteristics that reflect some linkages to early mainstream industrial economics. First, his work is invariably characterised by a detailed study of the actual workings of the particular institutions or sector under study. Second, a careful analysis of the role of history in shaping contemporary and possible future developments is given a high priority. This approach is typified in his (1987) monograph *Mergers and the Role of Large Banks*, the so-called 'Revell Report' in Spain. Early industrial economists, like Mason and his followers, were also distinguished by their use of this methodology. Jack follows Kindleberger in emphasising the importance of history in shaping the development of financial systems.

In recent years students like Ballarín have added the strategies of individual financial institutions to these two methodological pillars. Ballarín builds on the important work of Michael Porter (1980) in competition analysis. Jack's contribution to our understanding of the evolution and structure of financial institutions and financial systems bears a close methodological similarity to this modern research.

Jack's adherence to his institutional approach naturally did not make him popular in all academic circles. He sees his approach as a kind of 'applied commonsense' model in tackling specific research questions. In researching a specific decision strategy, for example, his proclivity is to ask individual practitioners why and how they make the decision rather than seeking to make inferences from more aggregated data. In this respect it is interesting to note the recent resurgence of interest by accounting and management researchers – like Tomkins and Groves (1983) – in so-called naturalistic research and the increasing concern with the practical foundations of much of the modern finance research – see Findlay III and Williams (1985).

Jack, however, is certainly not a modern Luddite. He uses a computer for his own work where it will help. His 1980 and 1985 work (assisted by Christine Owen of the Institute of European Finance) on costs and margins for the Organisation for Economic Co-operation and Development (OECD) required extensive computer-based data manipulation. He was also a keen advocate of word processing at a very early stage. I can confirm the 'annoyance' of Bangor's Department of Economics with 'Jack's toy', our first experiments with word processing in the 1970s. I hasten to add that the annoyance was of the more friendly variety, but we were practically all potential Luddites to a man and woman. Jack, of course, is the proud possessor of his own (hard disk) personal computer!

Nevertheless, Jack has not been a researcher who has made wide use of more advanced statistical techniques and computer modelling. His explanation of this apparent omission is again pragmatic. Jack's comparative advantage simply does not lie in fields like econometrics. Unlike some researchers he recognised this law of comparative advantage at an early stage of his career.

Jack's research approach combines a long maturation in the practical details of financial systems with an ability to process within his own mind a vast amount of detailed financial information and data. His impressive mental dissemination skills are evidenced in his Euclidean, no-nonsense presentation of complex financial issues and systems. The 1983 OECD publication *Banking and Electronic Fund Transfers* is an example of the wide range of mental versatility encompassed by his work.

Although Jack was very much an 'academic island' in British academe during his early Bangor years, some US and many continental European financial economists had long adopted a similar 'institutional approach': this is especially evident in continental Europe. Nowadays, researchers into financial systems sometimes distinguish between the so-called US and continental approaches, although any such labelling of schools is bound to be a little misleading in particular instances. The US approach emphasises the role of regulation (especially taxation) in shaping financial flows and systems: it is derived in large part from the path-breaking Modigliani-Miller theorems. Within this 'US school' broader attempts to explain financial innovation have been formalised in models like the Kane-Eisenbeis regulatory dialectic.

The so-called Continental approach, like that of Jack, emphasises a close and detailed study of the practical workings of financial systems, together with a study of the role of history in shaping evolutionary changes. The 'Continental approach' alternative for explaining financial innovation is the kind of eclectic apparatus typified by the Bank for International Settlements (BIS) supply and demand framework: see BIS (1986, ch. 8).

The methodological congruence between Jack's work and the Continental approach found expression at an important level in the European aspects of Bangor's development in banking and finance. In 1973 he founded the Institute of European Finance at Bangor. The Institute is a non-profit-making organisation that is closely associated with the (then) Department of Economics, now the School of Accounting, Banking and Economics (SABE) in the University College of North Wales (UCNW). It became a vehicle for applied research and researchers in financial institutions and financial systems generally.

Revell's reputation, and a close friendship developed over the years, attracted Jim (James) Maycock as his first Co-director of the Institute. Jim Maycock was formerly Economic Adviser to Midland Bank and a Visiting Professor at Georgia State University in the United States. Jim is a well-respected figure internationally within bank economists' circles. His 1986 book *Financial Conglomerates: The New Phenomenon* exemplifies his methodological affinity with Jack.

Revell, with Maycock, established the Institute's reputation and they started to build up its Information Centre, which is now one of the most comprehensive university archives of banking and financial systems in a European university. The extent and depth of the Centre's material is evidenced in the bi-monthly publication *World Banking Abstracts*, which is produced entirely from Bangor's own library resources. From very small beginnings the Institute has established itself as an important research and information facility within the British and European university system.

Jack's publications (listed at the end of this book) reflect the level of activity and European focus of the Institute's work at Bangor. Good examples include his various OECD works, his 1978 *Savings Flows in Europe* and his widely publicised works on the Spanish banking system. He has also published many articles in a wide range of banking and financial journals. Jack has had many prestigious academic appointments and served on the editorial boards of several well-known journals. Since 1981 he has been an Academician of Accademia Italiana di Economia Aziendale. During 1985–6 he was Deputy Chairman of a scientific steering committee for the EEC colloquium on Europe and the Future of Financial Services, a good reminder of the theme of the present collection of essays within this volume.

A particularly important innovation by Jack was his energy, vision and commitment in forming the European Association of University Teachers of Banking and Finance, the so-called 'Wolpertinger Club'. The Wolpertinger Club was formed in 1982. It is an informal organisation of University academics in Europe who have a common interest in the institutional and pragmatic aspects of banking, finance and financial systems. Many of the Wolpertinger Club are contributors to his volume of essays; Jack is generally regarded as the important 'founding father' of the club.

Once a year the Wolpertinger Club holds a seminar in a different European university to present research and discuss recent developments in members' respective systems. The Club has produced close friendships and strong working relationships between the University groups involved. Bangor, for example, regularly receives banking students from Namur (Belgium), Gothenburg (Sweden) and Siena (Italy). In 1987 Bangor and Siena were awarded an Erasmus grant by the European Commission.

The Wolpertinger Club is indicative of Jack's vision. He has frequently been an innovator in identifying areas that were later to become important within mainstream banking and finance. A good example is his early 1970s work on banking supervision and risk. His 1975 monograph *Solvency and Regulation of Banks* was an innovatory commentary from a British university group. Money and banking specialists and banking practitioners had barely begun to recognise issues like capital adequacy and supervision at that time. It is a recognition of Revell's single-mindedness and commitment to his beliefs that he has preserved and extended the 'Sayer's tradition' in the practical study of banks and financial systems. History figures highly in much of Jack's recent research, and it is interesting to reflect on his strong links with Bangor. In fact Bangor has a long tradition of practical links with banks and bankers. One may be forgiven for a little licence here in reflecting on the 'accident of events' that often forms an apparent logical, historical pattern.

In 1902 George Rae endowed the sum of £1500 to the University College of North Wales (see Gardener, 1988):

> in order to assist in the establishment of a Lectureship in the subjects of Banking and Finance, as forming part of the larger subject of Political Economy, of which I trust the study may eventually be established by the University.

A number of lectures were given on banking in the immediate years following the establishment of this fund, but this innovatory yearly lecture series stopped in 1919–20. Rae was a famous country banker and a prolific writer: he wrote under the pen name of Thomas Bullion. George Rae was Chairman of the Wales Bank, which was later to form an important part of the modern Midland Bank group.

In an historical context Jack was instrumental at Bangor in building a bridge back to the aspirations of an earlier age of innovative and distinguished banking thinkers. It is interesting to note that this earlier age was also characterised by many of the features in banking and financial systems that we regard today as innovations. Multinational banking, for example, was well established in Rae's day.

But the period in which Rae endowed his lecture series at Bangor, and the start of the modern banking build-up at Bangor associated with the arrival of Jack, were both characterised by marked changes in banking and financial systems and corresponding high rates of innovation. The intervening historical period was distinguished correspondingly by its several decades of comparative stability. During its modern phase of development Bangor has established itself as one of the leading European University Schools of Banking and Finance. Major financial institutions fund student sponsorship schemes and several academic posts at Bangor, including two Chairs.

Revell's contribution to the development of the University College of North Wales was recognised in his appointment as Vice Principal from

1979 to 1983. He was greatly respected in College and admired for his energy and drive. Not only did he establish (or, more correctly, re-establish) banking and finance at Bangor, but he also initiated new degrees in banking, insurance and finance and accounting and finance within SABE (the School of Accounting, Banking and Economics), the former Department of Economics. SABE is now a rather unique and widely respected inter-disciplinary group of academics. It is a tribute to Jack's vision that in an emerging age of vocational studies he emphasised the need to retain financial economics as the underlying thread of our banking, insurance, finance and accounting degrees. He saw a university banking degree as equipping graduates with the mental skills and flexibility to cope with the complex and rapid changes in modern banking and finance, together with some vocational affinity towards more practical banking and financial issues. This strong economics tradition has been retained at Bangor. The current Chairman of SABE is Professor Alan Winters, himself a former DAE man from Cambridge. Alan told me that he 'inherited Jack's office carpet' at Cambridge, but I do not intend to weave Alan's Bangor appointment into my preceding 'historical tapestry'!

A fine tribute to Jack's energy and scholarship is contained in the essays collected within this volume; the response to this Festschrift reflects the high esteem in which he is regarded. Raymond Goldsmith was too infirm to write and he asked me to include a congratulatory note to Jack. I thank Professor Goldsmith for this note and we all acknowledge his splendid contribution to the field. I hope that this volume will be a reminder to Jack that 'in his retirement' we will all continue to read with interest his informed commentaries, analyses and views on banking and financial developments. The volume is also, of course, a tribute to a student who has made a distinctive and important contribution to our understanding of financial systems.

Note

1. Keller (1983, p. 1087), for example, argues the case that 'the development of post-Keynesian macroeconomics has expanded the sphere of compatibility between Keynesian and institutional thought'. Wilbe (1985) explores the related philosophical issues associated with the possibility of a new synthesis of economic science that involves an architectonic of economic theories from '(1) institutional, post-Keynesian, and neo-classical economics and (2) pragmatism and contemporary philosophy of science'. In a more practical context Luckett (1981) has suggested how the institutionalist economic theory of Thorstein Veblen may be used to help explain broader structural changes in US banking.

References

Ballarin, Eduard (1986) *Commercial Banks Amid the Financial Revolution* (Cambridge, Massachusetts: Ballinger Publishing Company).
Bank got International Settlements (1986) *Recent Innovations in International Banking*, April (Basle: BIS).
Findlay III, M. Chapman and Edward E. Williams (1985) 'A post Keynesian view of modern financial economics: in search of alternative paradigms', *Journal of Business Finance and Accounting*, vol. 12, no. 1, Spring, pp. 1–18.
Gardener, E. P. M. (1988) *Banking: Thomas Bullion Revisited*, Inaugural Lecture Series (Bangor: University of Wales).
Goldsmith, R. W. and R. E. Lipsey (1963) *Studies in the National Balance Sheet of the United States* (Princeton: Princeton University Press).
Johnson, H. G. (ed.) (1972) *Readings in British Monetary Economics* (London: Oxford University Press).
Keller, Robert F. (1983) 'Keynesian and institutional economics: compatibility and complementarity?', *Journal of Economic Issues*, vol. 17, no. 4, December, pp. 1087–95.
Kindleberger, Charles P. (1984) *A Financial History of Western Europe* (London: George Allen & Unwin).
Luckett, Dudley G. (1981) 'The future of banking in the United States: an application of institutionalist economic theory', *Nebraska Journal of Economics and Business*, vol. 120, no. 2, pp. 25–36.
Mason, E. S. (1957) *Economic Concentration and the Monopoly Problem* (Massachusetts: Harvard University Press).
Maycock, James (1986) *Financial Conglomerates: The New Phenomenon*, Gower Studies in Finance and Investment (Aldershot: Gower).
Meltzer, Allan H. (1967) 'Major issues in the regulation of financial institutions', *Journal of Political Economy*, part 1, vol. 75, no. 4, August, pp. 482–500.
Minsky, H. 'Financial resources in a fragile financial environment', *Challenge*, vol. 18, no. 3, August, pp. 6–13.
Porter, Michael E. (1980) *Competitive Strategy: Techniques for Analysing Industries and Competitors* (London: Macmillan).
Revell, J. R. S. (1968) 'A secondary banking system', *The Banker*, vol. 118, no. 1, September, pp. 798–804, reprinted in H. G. Johnson (ed.) (1972) *Readings in British Monetary Economics* (London: Oxford University Press).
Sayers, R. S. (1970) *Modern Banking* (London: Oxford University Press).
Tobin, James 'Comment', *Journal of Political Economy*, part 1, no. 4, vol. 75, August, pp. 508–9.
Tomkins, Cyril and Roger Groves (1983) 'The everyday accountant and researching his reality', *Accounting, Organisations and Society*, vol. 8, no. 4, pp. 361–74.
Wilbe, J. R. (1985) 'Institutional economics, positive economics, pragmatism, and recent philosophy of science: reply to Liebhafsky and Liebhafsky', *Journal of Economic Issues*, vol. 19, no. 4, December, pp. 984–95.

Part II
Evolution and Development of Financial Systems

Part II comprises the logical starting point of a volume devoted to the future of financial systems and services: the evolution and development of financial systems. The nature and extent of the evolutionary changes in financial systems since the start of the 1970s have been unprecedented in modern times. The process of change has tended to accelerate during the 1980s. Chapter 2 examines competition and structural change in the British financial system, and David Llewellyn emphasises that competition is the dominant pressure inducing structural change. Chapter 3 focuses on the process of change in Belgian banking; Jean-Paul Abraham uses Belgian experiences as a small open economy to show that the process of change in financial systems is at least as interesting as change itself. Chapter 4 discusses the impact of securitisation and internationalisation on market imperfections with particular reference to the United States. Robert Eisenbeis explores the implications of these developments for regulatory reform and the structure of the payments system. Chapter 5 is a case study on the history of the banking and financial system crisis in Argentina: Elisabetta Montanaro analyses the development and nature of a crisis which is one of the most protracted in the history of world financial crises.

2 Competition and Structural Change in the British Financial System

David T. Llewellyn

INTRODUCTION

No scholar has contributed a more systematic analysis of the British financial system than Jack Revell, and the breadth of his work is indicated in the wide range of contributions to this volume from academic economists and practitioners. It is a tribute to the power and authority of his work that he has been uniquely successful in integrating the different perspectives of each. In countless books and articles he has analysed all the major dimensions of the financial system: the role of competition, structural change, regulation, efficiency and profitability, and the business operations of financial institutions.

The focus of this contribution is the nature and causes of structural change in the financial system with particular emphasis being given to a constant theme of Jack Revell: the role of competition. This is currently a particularly apposite topic as never before has the pace of structural change and financial innovation in the British financial system been as intensive and extensive as over the past few years. It would be a brave (perhaps even foolhardy) scholar who would seek to replicate Revell's seminal work *The British Financial System*, for it demonstrates the characteristics of the 'Forth Bridge syndrome': by the time the final strut has been painted the first needs repainting. Similarly, the pace of structural change in the financial system is currently such that by the time the last chapter had been written the first would need to be radically re-written!

HISTORIC STRUCTURE

For most of this century the structure of the British financial system has been remarkably stable; historically it has been a highly structured system based on specialist financial institutions with clear functional demarcations between them (Revell, 1973). In particular, and in common with many other financial systems (most notably the United States, Canada, Japan and Australia) but in contrast to many in Europe, there has been a clear functional distinction between the major business areas of commercial banking, investment banking, housing finance, insurance, fund management and securities trading. However, this structured system has not been predominantly a product of official regulatory limits on the range of business activities, but more a function of restrictive practices, anti-competitive mechanisms, and self-imposed constraints.

On the other hand, the regulatory authorities have been sympathetic to this structured approach. It was viewed as one way of dealing with potential conflicts of interest that can arise in institutions conducting a wide range of business. It also made regulation easier in that if the objective was to regulate *functions* there was a clearly defined set of *institutions* performing each function. It also meant that to a large extent regulation could be 'sub-contracted' to the sectors themselves. The authorities also took the view that risks are reduced through limiting the range of business activities, and that systemic risk is lowered by, for instance, reducing the danger of contamination of one part of the business, say banking, by risks in other parts, e.g. insurance. Thus separation has been viewed in part as a means of containing potential systemic risk. However, this risk argument is open to challenge on the same grounds as an efficiently diversified portfolio of assets is less risky than a concentrated one. In practice, enforced demarcations may increase risk.

A US study by Heggestad (1975) finds that commercial banking is one of the most risky activities, when risk is measured in terms of the variability of profits. He also found that the returns on some activities that might be conducted by banks, such as real estate agency, insurance broking and so on, are negatively correlated with banking and hence banks could reduce their risk exposure by diversifying. Wall and Eisenbeis (1984) also conclude that had banking organisations been passive owners of some prohibited activities, their earnings might have been less volatile during the 1970s. In fact several activities that *prima facie* appear more risky than banking have returns that are negatively correlated with those of banking, suggesting that such activities and more diversified business would reduce risk for banks. Carron (1983) also finds that the lack of portfolio diversification at thrift institutions in the United States has caused lower and more volatile earnings compared with banks.

Competition has been limited by powerful pressures in the British financial system. There has been a strong strand in the history of regulation based upon the alleged dangers of excessive competition inducing both excessive risk-taking by institutions and resultant systemic dangers (Llewellyn, 1986). There is a trade-off between the objectives of regulation and the benefits to be derived from competition, and the chosen mix varies over time (Bain, 1981; Llewellyn, 1987). It is also the case that monetary policy was operated in a way (e.g. through direct credit controls) that had the effect of limiting competition in banking for decades.

However, regulation has not been the most powerful force constraining competition in finance. In fact, throughout the 1970s and 1980s the process of deregulation was largely a response to competitive pressures and financial innovation rather than to dramatic policy changes designed to force the pace of change, competition and innovation. Thus, the policy of *Competition and Credit Control* (see Bank of England, 1971) and the pressure on the clearing banks' cartel, were a product partly of the competitive thrust introduced by the entry of foreign banks, and the abolition of direct controls on lending was induced by a steady process of circumvention.

The abandoning of the building societies' interest rate cartel followed increased competition in the hitherto virtual monopoly position of building societies in the mortgage market. The recent substantial changes in the securities industry were motivated not so much by the threat of referring of the Stock Exchange rule book to the Restrictive Trade Practices Court but by the force of international competition in the securities industry. The recent diversification allowed by building societies developed largely because, in the new competitive environment, building societies were placed at a competitive disadvantage through being substantially restricted in the range of allowable business. Thus deregulation has been as much a product of competitive pressures as a factor creating a more competitive environment in the financial system (Bank of England *Quarterly Bulletin*, 1983). For an excellent review of regulation in the United Kingdom see Gardener (1986).

There have been many self-imposed restrictive practices and anti-competitive mechanisms in the financial system which have fixed prices and limited the range of business activities of different sub-sectors. The structured nature of the British financial system has been as much a product of self-imposed constraints and restrictive practices as official regulation. Nevertheless, such restrictive practices and self-imposed constraints would not have survived had they not been condoned, if not positively encouraged, by the regulatory authorities. They were condoned partly because they were viewed as an alternative to explicit regulation and as performing the same role as regulation in limiting risk by constraining competition.

STRUCTURAL CHANGE IN THE FINANCIAL SYSTEM

In this historical context, the major structural changes that have dominated the recent evolution of the British financial system relate to competition, the process of diversification, the undermining of the historic structured system, the form and extent of regulation, the increasing internationalisation of finance, and the acceleration in the pace of financial innovation. Overwhelming all other forces has been the role of competition; the competitive environment has intensified both within and between sub-sectors of the system. In the process the specialist basis of financial institutions has been eroded as diversification has produced a trend towards financial conglomerates. This has been a comparatively easy process as historic demarcations have been largely self-imposed, rather than forced by legislation. At the same time, competitive pressures have undermined most of the traditional features of self-imposed regulation based upon restrictive practices.

The dominant change has been the process of diversification and the erosion of the historic structured basis of the financial system (Llewellyn, 1985). This has occurred across the full range of financial institutions and markets. The clearing banks have bought securities trading firms and merchant banks, and they also own unit trusts, thus merging four areas of finance that have traditionally been kept separate. One bank (the TSB) has also bought an insurance company. At the same time the process of diversification into a limited range of financial services includes non-finance companies such as BAT Industries, Marks and Spencer (which holds a banking licence), and moves by several retail stores into financial services. Thus conglomeration has come to straddle both financial and non-financial companies.

There have been particularly major and far-reaching changes in the securities industry. Historically, this sector has been highly regulated through practices enforced by the London Stock Exchange (Goodhart, 1987). In particular:

1. a strict division was enforced between market-makers (jobbers) and brokers;
2. brokers were required to deal exclusively with jobbers rather than matching customer deals between themselves;
3. minimum commission charges were established so as to remove the incentive to by-pass the jobbers which, it was alleged, would have undermined the market-making role to the eventual detriment of all users of the Stock Exchange;
4. the extent of external ownership (e.g. by banks) was substantially limited.

As a result of deregulation in the securities industry, British and foreign banks have become major elements in the securities industry as part of integrated financial groups comprising banking, merchant banking, securities broking and market-making, together with fund management components. In October 1986 fixed commissions for securities trading in London were ended following the agreement between the government and the Stock Exchange. In March of the same year Stock Exchange rules were changed to allow 100 per cent outside ownership of stock broking and jobbing firms. The abolition of minimum commissions would inevitably undermine single capacity, but the industry as previously constituted was undercapitalised for dual capacity. This required a change in the rules to allow a capital injection via banks buying securities firms. The resulting capital injection by a wide range of British and foreign banks has changed the UK market in two major respects: the hitherto separate and specialist role of jobber (market-maker) and broker which had been enforced by internal regulation since 1908, has been abandoned, and the major securities firms have become parts of integrated financial institutions.

Building societies have also been diversifying. From being a set of highly specialised institutions whose business was exclusively to collect retail savings deposits to finance mortgage loans, they are emerging as diversified retail banks encompassing consumer lending, insurance underwriting, stock exchange brokerage services, portfolio management and money transmission services which have hitherto been the monopoly of a small number of clearing banks.

Structural change in a financial system is not a random process and, as in any industry, it can be analysed in terms of the factors undermining existing arrangements and creating pressure for change. The substantial changes in the British financial system evident in the 1980s are a product of several factors operating simultaneously. Llewellyn (1989) has identified the major factors inducing structural change in the financial system as competition, changes in regulation, technology, changes in the market environment, changes in relative efficiency and the dynamics of financial innovation. In this chapter the focus is upon the first of these factors; the dominant pressure of competition.

A simple model

But before considering the role of competition, a simple representation of the financial firm is presented which will be used to illustrate aspects of the argument.

A financial institution is a firm in the standard sense. Its role is to take deposits and make loans or otherwise acquire assets. A grossly simplified representation of the financial institution (ignoring the fact that it is a multiproduct firm) is represented in Figure 2.1. The demand curve represents customers' demand for loans, related to the rate of interest. The supply of deposits to the institution (S_D) is assumed to rise as the institution's deposit interest rate rises relative to all other interest rates which, for purposes of analysis, are held constant. The firm's supply of loans (S_L) is correspondingly also a rising function of the rate of interest. The lending margin *LM* (which might be termed the 'supply price of financial intermediation') covers the firm's non-interest costs, the contribution to capital from profits, allowance for risk and bad debts, tax liabilities, and requirement to earn a rate of return on equity capital. In another sense *LM* is also a measure of the firm's efficiency and the cost to the consumer of financial intermediation services; the wider the margin, the less the depositor receives and/or the more the borrower is charged. In general the margin widens as costs rise, internal efficiency decreases, risks rise, required capital ratios are increased, and as the cost of capital rises. In various ways, regulation can have the effect of raising the supply price of financial intermediation. On the assumption that the market clears, equilibrium is at a volume of business *OA* where the deposit rate paid is i_0 and loan rate charged is i_1. This representation is used later when considering the impact of competition.

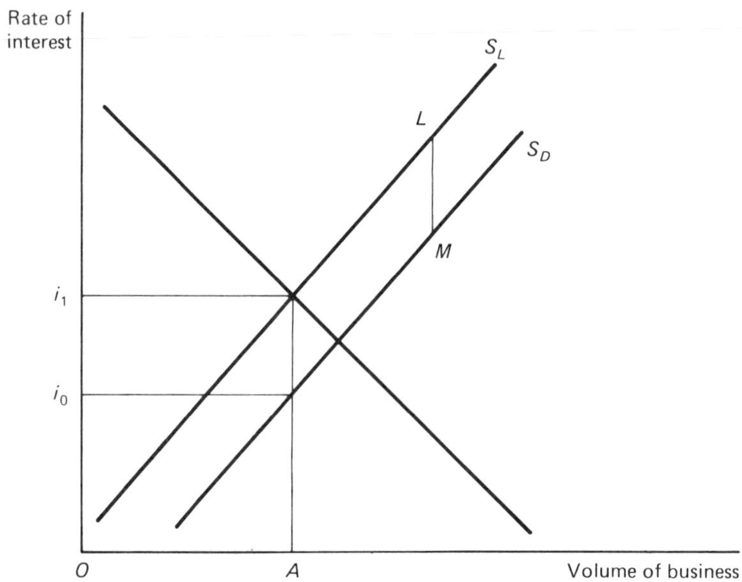

Figure 2.1 The financial firm

ANALYSIS OF COMPETITION

The dominant pressure inducing structural change in the financial system has been competition and the greatly intensified competitive environment that has been such a feature of the 1980s. The financial system has been an industry subject to increased competitive pressures both from within and between sub-sectors. It is therefore instructive to consider what would normally be predicted in any industry that is subject to more competition. This is summarised in Table 2.1 and it is the experience of the recent evolution of the financial system that this framework applies as much to the finance industry as to any other.

Table 2.1 Impact of competition

(1)	The most efficient firms would become yet more efficient, and the average efficiency of the industry would rise.
(2)	The pricing of the product would tend to eliminate any excess demand that might previously have existed.
(3)	Internal cross-subsidies, and pricing structures not based on cost or risk considerations, would tend to disappear under the pressure of competition.
(4)	The industry would be likely to experience more mergers as the less efficient firms find the competitive environment too demanding.
(5)	There would be considerable pressure towards the elimination of any cartel that might exist over the fixing of the industry's prices.
(6)	Restrictive practices would be competed away through circumvention.
(7)	Overall profitability is likely to decline.
(8)	The overall risk characteristics of the industry are likely to increase.
(9)	Firms seek to diversify.
(10)	Exits.

(1) Efficiency

The first proposition, though perhaps the most important, is the most difficult to test in practice. Certain indications, however, suggest that the basic efficiency of the system has increased. Domestic and international competition has eroded lending margins in wholesale banking, and the abolition in 1983 of the building society cartel (where the margin used to be set at a level sufficient to maintain the less efficient societies in business) has increased pressure on less efficient building societies. Across the board clearing banks are also under increased pressure to control their operating costs.

One particular aspect of efficiency associated with competitive pressures has surfaced in the mortgage market, with the emergence of securitised mortgages and partnership arrangements. In both cases overall efficiency is raised because institutions concentrate on that part of the lending process in which they have a comparative advantage. In the securitisation process, a finance vehicle or institution raises funds via the issue of a capital market instrument and the proceeds are used to buy a block of mortgages from an institution which had previously made such loans. The mechanism is based upon there being three functions in a loan: an initiating procedure where the loan is made, administration of the loan, and the holding of the asset. Traditionally all three functions have been performed by the same lending institution which seeks a borrower and makes the loan, administers the loan contract, and holds the loan as an asset on the balance sheet. There is no reason, however, why the functions should not be split if different institutions have different comparative advantages in different functions. A building society or a retail bank may have a comparative advantage in the first two functions in that it has a branch network which gives access to customers, and may have excess administration capacity such as computers. It would therefore be efficient at initiating and administering mortgages. On the other hand, because of funding or capital constraints, it may be less efficient than some other institution, such as a wholesale bank with no retail branches, at holding the asset because it can not fund the asset as cheaply, or because its balance sheet is constrained by a shortage of capital. In this case, overall efficiency is increased if each institution exploits its comparative advantage: the first institution initiates and administers the loan, while the second buys the mortgage from the initiating institution, as it is able to finance the holding of the asset at a lower price. This particular innovation raises efficiency through a process of decomposing the lending process and exploiting the different comparative advantages.

The partnership arrangment is designed to exploit the same comparative advantages and has also been developed in the mortgage market in a way that has enabled foreign institutions without UK branch networks to reach retail customers. Foreign institutions have no advantage in the *origination* of mortgages, though building societies do. A combination of a change in the pattern of interest rates (the mortgage lending rate has risen relative to wholesale money market rates through which foreign institutions fund their sterling business), and regulation (which in the early 1980s limited the extent to which building societies could fund in wholesale markets rather than the more expensive retail deposit market), meant that some foreign institutions developed a comparative advantage in holding mortage *assets*. An obvious strategy, and one that has been adopted, is for both to exploit their particular advantages, with the foreign institution funding a loan that has been originated by a British institution, which in turn is paid a fee for the origination. A recent example is the Skipton Building Society marketing mortgages in the United Kingdom for the Société Générale of France, which pays the building society fees and commissions.

(2) Elimination of excess demand

The second proposition in Table 2.1 states that competition normally has the effect of eliminating any excess demand that might exist. This implies that the price is set below the market clearing level at i_0 in Figure 2.2. The building society cartel operated in this way with varying queues for building society mortgages being the norm prior to 1983. In Figure 2.2 at i_0 the supply of loans is OA but, at that rate of interest, the demand would be OB. The market clearing mortgage rate would be i_1. This was sustainable in the mortgage market for two reasons, both associated with an uncompetitive mortgage market; firstly, the building societies were part of a cohesive, co-operative industry which operated a collective cartel and, secondly, they were not subject to external competition until banks entered the mortgage market in a significant way in 1981 (Llewellyn, 1983). If competition develops, either internally or from outside, competitors bid away the excess demand by raising the rate of interest to the market-clearing level (i_1 in Figure 2.2). Thus the effect of competition in this case is to raise the mortgage rate, eliminate excess demand, and increase the supply of loans. The same dynamics would apply in the case where new entrants were less efficient than existing suppliers; this is indicated with the supply curve of loans of SL_1, compared with SL_0 for existing suppliers. In practice, excess demand has been eliminated in the mortgage market since the entry of banks in the early 1980s.

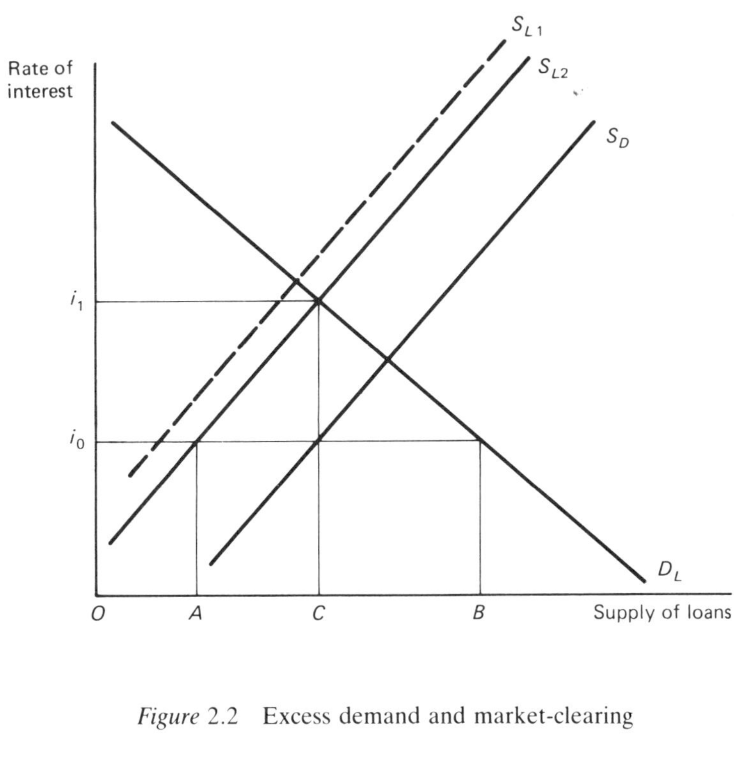

Figure 2.2 Excess demand and market-clearing

(3) Cross-subsidies

Proposition 3 in Table 2.1 relates to the pricing policies of the firms in the industry. When competitive conditions vary between the different business areas of an institution, there is scope for 'cross-subsidising'. This implies a pricing policy which does not fully reflect differences in cost and risk, and frequently means that prices are set high in one market, where competition is less, and low in another such that the former effectively 'cross-subsidises' the latter. As competition intensifies such cross-subsidies are normally competed away as, in effect, new entrants concentrate on the 'subsidising' component of competitors' business which undermines their ability to price the 'subsidised' component at a low level.

A particular example of how competition has eroded 'cross-subsidies' is again in the mortgage market. Traditionally, and when not subject to external competition, building societies charged higher interest rates on large mortgages compared with smaller mortgages, even though they were in practice less risky and cheaper to administer. This implied a perverse pricing strategy with low-risk and large mortgages cross-subsidising higher-risk and more costly mortgages. This would not be sustained in a highly competitive market as new entrants would secure a high risk-adjusted rate of return through competing away the large mortgages, by slightly under-cutting building societies, and leaving building societies with the less profitable business. This is how the banks behaved when they entered the mortgage market in the early 1980s, and it had the effect of forcing building societies to reverse their pricing policies; it is now more common for large mortgages to be offered at a lower rate of interest.

The position becomes more complex when a particular product performs several services simultaneously, and when it is difficult to unbundle the components. In this case it is difficult to identify and price separately the subsidising and subsidised components. An example is free banking on current accounts, which are both deposits and a part of the money transmission service offered by banks. Generally, banks do not charge for the use of current accounts while they remain in credit, but similarly they do not pay interest on credit balances. This implies a cross-subsidy from those who hold large average balances (effectively an interest free loan to the bank) to those who make many transactions with their current account and hence impose costs on the bank which are not recouped from the customer. This implicit cross-subsidy would be eliminated if the market rate of interest were paid on all outstanding balances while the economic cost was charged for all services. This would induce customers to maintain higher average balances and at the same time seek to reduce their costs by, for instance, greater use of credit cards so as to minimise the number of transactions.

Leaving aside the question of tax-efficiency (i.e. interest received is taxed while the subsidy received through no charges is not) the problem arises because consumers are using both 'services' of a current account and everyone is a subsidiser and a recipient of subsidy. The position is therefore not as clear-cut as when the subsidising and receipt of the subsidy involve different customers who can be targeted by competitors.

However, although it is more difficult in practice to identify the subsidising and subsidised customers, the pricing arrangement makes it potentially attractive for competitors to bid for transactions balances. With the regulation changes in the 1986 Building Societies Act several building societies have done this. Banks have also begun to pay interest on current accounts with large average or minimum balances though without simultaneously levying charges. In a competitive market, with building societies now able to compete for money transmission business, it is doubtful whether the clearing banks will be able permanently to avoid the logic of paying interest on credit balances and charging economic prices for all services, most especially as the latter can be avoided by increased use of credit cards. The thirteen building societies which were offering current account facilities in 1988 all paid interest on outstanding credit balances.

(4) Mergers

Proposition 4 has been a feature of the building society sector during the 1980s, with the number of societies declining from 273 in 1980 to 138 by the end of 1987. These have included mergers within the ten largest societies. It is likely that there will be substantial pressures for a further concentration in the industry. Both the absence of the cartel and the competitive environment have created pressure on the less efficient societies. To the extent that scale is a factor in market success, for example in computer facilities and the managerial ability to offer a wider range of services, this will be reinforced in the medium term. Regulation could also emerge as a future pressure on smaller societies since they do not have the same range of powers, either on asset or liability diversification, as the larger societies.

It is likely, therefore, that the number of societies will continue to decline and the industry will become yet further concentrated. In practice, future concentration will more likely involve a merging of medium-sized societies; in effect, the 20 per cent of business undertaken outside the ten largest societies will be undertaken by considerably fewer societies.

(5) Cartels

Competitive pressures undermine non-market-clearing pricing structures. Similarly, if a cartel fixes prices at a level that creates excessive profits competition may develop from outside the cartel. It was competitive pressure from the New York Stock Exchange, where large UK investors could transact at lower dealing charges, that was the major factor undermining the minimum commission charges enforced by the London Stock Exchange. For a cartel to be effective the industry needs to be cohesive and not subject to external competition. This was true of the building societies and the Stock Exchange price-fixing arrangements until the early 1980s. The building societies' cartel was abandoned in 1983 after the entry of banks into the mortgage market. Competition from New York, after technology developments made it feasible for UK investors to trade in New York, was the dominant factor undermining the price-fixing arrangements on the London Stock Exchange.

(6) Restrictive practices

The argument above is a particular example of a more general proposition that competition undermines all forms of restrictive practices through circumvention. If it is technically possible to do so, customers seek to avoid restrictions by dealing outside the cohesive group maintaining them. The Stock Exchange is a major example. An earlier section outlined the various restrictive practices, such as single capacity operation, contained in the Stock Exchange rule book. However, the London market became increasingly by-passed by big institutional investors: not only were British investors using foreign securities firms for their purchases of overseas securities but securities firms operating in other countries were also creating markets in British securities. This development was associated with a decline in the competitive position of the Stock Exchange (most especially compared with New York) as a result of fixed minimum commissions, the government's stamp duty of 1 per cent payable by buyers of securities (which could be avoided by trading in New York in American Depository Receipts), and the limited capital base of the British industry compared with large securities firms based in New York. As the costs for large institutional investors dealing in New York were lower, the London Stock Exchange came to be by-passed.

(7) Erosion of profitability

A normal expectation is that competition has the effect of eroding profitability most especially as new firms enter the industry. This has clearly been the case in international banking, wholesale banking generally, and in securities trading in the United Kingdom since 'Big Bang' in October 1986.

It is not, however, invariably the case, and the outcome depends upon how the industry operated before the competitive environment intensified, and specifically upon whether it was previously seeking to maximise profits. An instructive case study is provided by building societies, whose profitability both absolutely and in terms of the rate of return on assets and capital has risen in the 1980s, notwithstanding the more competitive climate (Llewellyn and Drake, 1987). This is associated with the operation of the building society cartel prior to 1983 which had the result of maintaining the mortage rate below the market clearing level. The effect of this, and of subsequent competition, is shown in Figure 2.3 where the relevant curves prior to competition from banks have subscripts '1'. Under the cartel; the volume of mortgages was *OA* at a mortgage rate i_1 and deposit rate i_0. If the cartel is abolished, but with no external competition, the equilibrium position is a volume of *OB* at i_3 and i_2 rates of interest. Profits rise as the same margin is earned on an increased volume (*AB*) of mortgages. However, as competition has the effect of taking demand away (the demand curve shifts to D_2) and eroding the previous lending margin (S_{L1} shifts to SL_2) the net effect upon profits is indeterminate: while the effect of the narrower margin (i_5i_4) and the shift in the demand curve is to reduce profits, the volume of mortgages may still be higher (*OC*) than that prior to the abolition of the cartel (*OA*), and by an amount that offsets the effects of the narrower lending margin. Thus profits can be increased due to the stock-adjustment effect of moving to a market-clearing, profit-

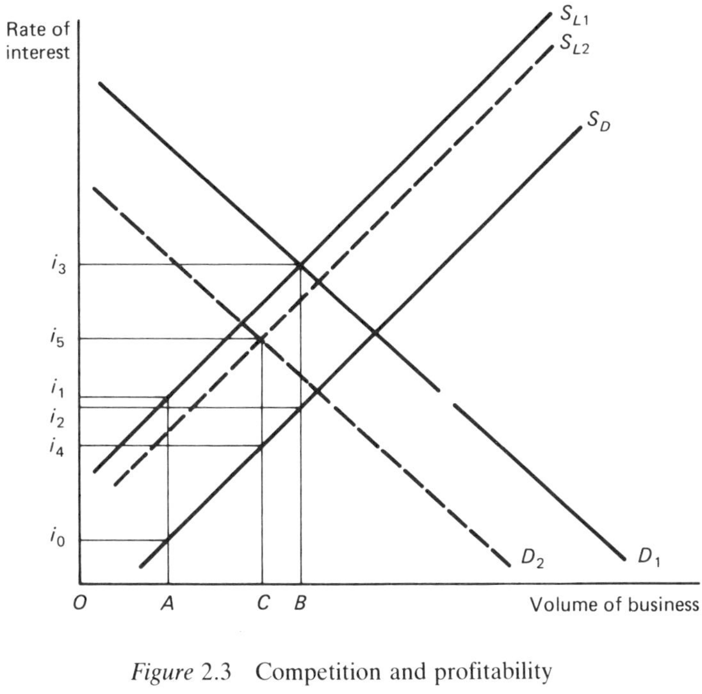

Figure 2.3 Competition and profitability

maximising position. The rise in building society profitability during the 1980s is due in part to this effect. However, profits have also benefited from the very sharp rise in the total demand for mortgages which means that although building societies have lost market share, the actual volume of their mortgage lending has expanded.

(8) Risk

Competition may have the effect of increasing risk in two ways: firstly by increasing the variability of profits, and secondly by inducing lending criteria to be relaxed. This latter seems to have been the case in international lending during the 1970s, and the evidence indicates that the risks on building society mortgage lending increased in the early stages following the entry of banks. This was associated, in part, by lending bigger multiples of borrowers' income and a high proportion (sometimes 100 per cent) of the value of the property. The former makes the borrower more vulnerable, and the latter means there is no equity margin in the event that the society needs to take possession of the property should the borrower default. It is also the case that risks also increased because, by previously maintaining excess demand, building societies had rationed-out less credit-worthy borrowers. Overall, there is evidence that competition induces institutions to take bigger risks, perhaps in order to maintain market share or profits.

(9) Diversification

Competition developing in a firm's existing market is likely to induce diversification. This has been true throughout the financial system as has been described. For instance, a major competitive influence on building societies has been a strategic decision adopted by their banking competitors during the 1980s to target the personal sector for retail deposits, loans and the provision of financial services generally. This represents a switch in priority from wholesale to retail banking. The effect is seen by comparing the proportion of the value of outstanding sterling loans of the clearing banks. In 1980 the company sector was more important with 55 per cent of the banks' outstanding loans to this sector. By 1986 this had fallen to 32 per cent while loans to the personal sector had risen from 41 per cent to 57 per cent of the total.

The dominant factor in this strategic shift was competition. Competitive pressures towards the end of the 1970s and into the 1980s were considerably greater in wholesale markets and lending to the corporate sector than in retail and personal sector markets. This was visible in terms of the finer margins on on-balance sheet loans to the corporate sector, and the profitability of some wholesale business had become very low. There are several reasons for this: firstly, firms in the corporate sector have traditionally had access to a larger number of banks than has the personal sector; secondly, for corporate business the capital market is a potential competitor to banks, and the securitisation process indicates that shifts can be made when conditions are conducive; and, thirdly, it is also the case that the capital market has been particularly innovative in the 1980s. The corporate sector also has international banking and capital market options which further intensifies competitive pressures for the corporate sector business of UK banks. For these reasons the strategic shift of the banks towards the personal sector during the 1980s has been a response to competitive pressures. This represents a stage of diversification designed to maintain overall profitability.

(10) Exits

In the final analysis, and failing other strategies, the ultimate effect of competition is to induce exits from the industry as the industry becomes overcrowded and the more efficient force the exit of the less efficient. In practice this has not been a common reaction in the financial system although there has been an example in the securities industry. One of the features of 'Big Bang' was a substantial rise in the number of 'market-makers' both in the gilts and equity markets. Prior to 1986 there were only four jobbers (market-makers) in the gilts sector, but this rose to twenty-eight in 1986. New entrants were anticipating a sharp rise in turnover following the abolition of minimum commissions, as had previously been the effect in New York following similar reforms in 1975. In practice the increase in turnover required to enable the much larger number of market-makers to remain profitable was not a realistic proposition, and some firms have ceased to be market-makers.

In the event, and especially after the stock market collapse in October 1987, the volume of equity transactions actually declined sharply. This caused several equity market-makers to withdraw within the first two years of the new market structure. At the same time several firms announced that they will no longer service personal accounts below a certain figure.

INTERNATIONAL DIMENSION

Competition has been a major impetus to structural change in the British financial system during the 1980s. It is also evident that these competitive pressures have had an increasingly powerful international dimension (BIS, 1986; Llewellyn, 1988).

Although the bulk of world financial intermediation and the provision of financial services is conducted through national mechanisms, finance has increasingly become global. National financial systems are losing some of their traditional 'efficiency' such as transactions costs, access to customers and information advantages, and 'imposed' competitive advantages, such as exchange control. In practice this amounts to domestic institutions and markets being subject to competitive pressures from foreign financial systems.

The process of *globalisation* is emerging in several dimensions. The most obvious is in securities trading where shares and other national capital market instruments are now traded in several national markets. A second dimension is location; there has been an increasing trend for banks and other financial institutions to enter foreign markets, not only to conduct international business but also to develop domestic business. Thirdly, cross-border business has become more important for financial institutions; borrowers are able to arbitrage and increasingly have international financing options. This is reflected in the growing use of international as opposed to domestic funding instruments and the effect is that domestic financial institutions face competitive pressures emanating from a global financial system.

In the provision of financial services arbitrage would tend to eliminate the differences in supply prices which can vary between countries for three general reasons: firstly, differences in basic efficiency, secondly, different regulatory taxes, and thirdly, differences in the competitive environment sustaining a higher level of costs or profits in one system compared with another. In principle a high price in one national system (as measured, for instance, by the margin between deposit and lending rates of financial intermediaries or issuing costs in securities markets) would be competed away either through the entry into the domestic system of foreign firms, or by the users of financial services using foreign mechanisms. Although it varies considerably between countries and for different users, this process can be impeded by exchange control, location costs, regulation, and entry barriers, together with information and transaction costs. In practice these impediments are becoming less powerful, with significant implications for the evolution of national financial systems. A specific European dimension will be added with the ambition to complete the EEC 'internal market' by 1992.

However, competitive pressures are not equal for all sectors of business. The competitive environment in wholesale and corporate sector banking has intensified more than in retail banking, though the latter has not been immune. The net result is that market conditions in much wholesale and corporate banking business approaches the characteristics of perfect competition in many countries, while profit margins in general are wider in retail business. In the process, a two-tier structure of banking has emerged in which the corporate sector increasingly has global options while the financial intermediation of the retail/personal sector is still limited, mainly within national financial systems. This is partly because, despite developments in technology, servicing the retail sector still frequently requires a branch network, and the size of individual transactions is small. It is largely through the corporate sector that global competition has developed between national financial systems.

DYNAMICS OF COMPETITION

Reaction times in financial markets are short and hence adjustments can often be made quickly. The financial system, most notably the banking segment, is characterised by oligopolistic competition. One implication of this is that competitive pressures frequently force firms to move together in a fashion sometimes described as 'herd instinct'. This is especially the case when the trend is towards a more comprehensive offer of services. As a consequence, collective action is likely to be considerable as all institutions and competitors move together, the net result of collective change is likely to be substantial, and the fallacy of composition applies since the collective change can undermine the calaculations made by each firm individually as the force of the collective change is to change market conditions.

The concept of overshooting is well-established in financial markets, most especially in the foreign exchange market. Adjustments are made to shocks which take the portfolio position beyond the longer-run equilibrium position. Evidence also suggests that to some extent this is true also of the portfolio behaviour of financial institutions. This is partly associated with the oligopolistic structure of the industry, as the equilibrium position is determined partly by the behaviour of competitors. This implies substantial potential for instability when the environment is changing.

These characteristics can be related specifically to the effect of deregulation, which frequently implies a significant change in the market environment. The thesis is based upon three propositions: (i) financial institutions choose their portfolio position based upon current regulatory requirements even though they might prefer a different position; (ii) they have a view about a desired portfolio in the absence of regulation; but (iii) if regulations change they move substantially and quickly to the new desired position. Reaction times are short, in that institutions move quickly to a desired position which they would have arrived at over a longer period in the absence of prior regulation. In effect, if portfolio selection is impeded by regulation and those regulations are suddenly removed, the adjustment is likely to be quick, substantial, potentially unstable and difficult to moderate.

There are several examples in the financial system of this effect. *Competition and Credit Control* produced a dramatic rise in bank lending in the early 1970s and some banks and secondary banks clearly made big mistakes and had to be rescued. Sterling bank lending rose by 70 per cent in the first year after CCC and by 145 per cent in the first two years; property lending rose by 250 per cent. The response was so substantial and speedy that a major reassessment of the policy was made and the Corset was introduced. The sharp response made to the new unregulated environment also produced bank failures and the most serious banking crisis in the United Kingdom since the 1930s, which forced the substantial lifeboat operation in 1974. This episode has been interpreted by some (e.g. Moran, 1984) as a failure of regulation and supervision.

There is also the example of the initial over-adjustment that banks made in the mortgage market when the Corset was abandoned in 1981 (see Llewellyn, 1983). The abolition of hire purchase controls produced a similar effect. The same phenomenon is currently unfolding in the securities industry as more market-makers entered the market than could be sustained in the long run.

It would appear that a characteristic of the competitive structure of the financial system is a bias towards overreaction. An analogous point has been made by Barclay (1978) who argues that financial crises are often associated with competitive pressures. The entry of new firms disturbs the position of existing producers. The additional point being made here is that deregulation itself intensifies the competitive environment, most especially in the early stages of an initial stock-adjustment to portfolios.

A current example relates to competitive pressures in the retail financial services. There is a danger that the provision of retail financial services is becoming an overcrowded industry. A whole range of institutions (clearing banks, insurance companies, foreign banks, building societies and even non-financial firms) have targeted the personal sector simultaneously. In their own ways, and for reasons associated with competitive pressures and deregulation, all are seeking to diversify as the traditional specialist distinctions between sectors in the financial system are eroded. There are many reasons why financial institutions or firms generally seek to diversify. They do so in order to maintain profitability when there is more competition in traditional markets, to reduce risk by less concentration, to reap economies of scope, to reduce excess capacity, because of high profitability of existing suppliers or because competitors have higher costs, to compete away cross-subsidies, and so on.

The profitability of diversification, however, depends in part upon what is happening to the demand for the product. If demand is rising strongly a particular institution might find an area profitable which might not have been profitable before. The demand can be met by a new institution without taking business from others. If, on the other hand, demand is static the net result is that all have a smaller volume of business and it is almost certain that profitability is lowered.

Given the extent and magnitude of the shift towards selling financial services to the personal sector, it is difficult to avoid the conclusion that strategies are being built on optimistic assumptions about the size and profitability of the market. Competition, both domestic and international, eroded the profitability of parts of the wholesale banking sector in the 1970s as more firms (often foreign banks) entered the market. The same is likely to happen in the retail sector in the 1990s.

STRUCTURAL CHANGE AND EFFICIENCY

The structural changes in the financial system that have been the focus of this chapter do seem, on the face of it, to have contributed to enhancing the *structural efficiency* (as defined by Revell, 1983) of the system. There is now considerably more choice in the provision of financial services and the range of available instruments and markets. All financial institutions offer a wider range of products and services than a decade ago, and a process of product differentiation has meant that there are fewer discontinuities in the range and types of services and instruments available. One of the most basic of products – the bank account – has also been subject to the same process, with banks now offering accounts ranging from the basic current account (with or without the payment of interest) to accounts based upon wholesale money market rates of return, and accounts specifically targeted at particular types of customer.

A theme of this chapter has a direct bearing on a second aspect of structural efficiency: the competitive environment. This element of efficiency has clearly been enhanced as, through the process of diversification, all services are now provided by a wider range of suppliers rather than by specialist institutions. The most obvious example in the retail sector is the mortgage market where building societies had a virtual monopoly for decades. Basic household mortgages are now supplied also by clearing banks, foreign banks, insurance companies and specialist mortgage institutions funded entirely in the wholesale markets. In many services the corporate sector increasingly has international options. Competition and financial innovation has had the effect of widening the range of customers who can access particular services, products and instruments. Although it remains the case that large customers have access to more instruments and facilities than small ones, the trend has been for the minimum size both of customer and transaction to decline. A particular example is with respect to risk capital to finance new businesses which, historically, has not always been readily available. A new group of venture capital companies (some established by the clearing banks) has had the effect of making risk capital more readily available to small firms.

There is a presumption that competition, both domestic and international, and the wider range of choice in financial services, has contributed positively to *structural efficiency*. Competition has had the predictable effect of eliminating excess demand, most especially in the mortgage market, and of undermining cross-subsidies, restrictive practices, and cartels such as building societies and the Stock Exchange. The allocation of finance is now more dominated by the price mechanism than by rationing. To the extent that many of the structural changes in the financial system that have emerged are associated with the abandoning of restrictive practices and the undermining of self-imposed anti-competitive mechanisms, then the presumption is that efficiency has increased, however difficult in some areas it is both to identify and measure.

References

Bain, A. D. (1981) *Economics of the Financial System* (Oxford: Martin Robertson).

Bank for International Settlements (1986) *Recent Innovations in International Banking* (Basle: BIS).

Bank of England (1971) *Competition and Credit Control.*

Bank of England (1983) 'Competition, innovation and regulation in British Banking', *Quarterly Bulletin*, September.

Barclay, C. (1978) 'Competition and financial crises: past and present', in C. Barclay *et al.*, *Competition and Regulation of Banks* (Cardiff: University of Wales Press).

Carron, A. (1983) 'Political economy of financial regulation', in R. E. Noll and B. M. Owen (eds), *The Political Economy of Deregulation* (Washington: American Enterprise Institute).

Gardener E. P. M. (ed.) (1986) *UK Banking Supervision* (London: Allen & Unwin).

Goodhart, C. A. E. (1987) 'Structural change in the British capital markets' in Goodhart *et al.*, *Operation and Regulation of Financial Markets* (London: Macmillan).

Heggestad, R. (1975) 'Riskiness of investments in non-bank activity by bank holding companies', *Journal of Economics and Business*, June, pp. 80–93.

Llewellyn, D. T. (1983) 'Banks in the mortgage market', *Building Societies Institute Journal*, November.

Llewellyn, D. T. (1985) *The Evolution of the British Financial System* (London: Institute of Bankers).

Llewellyn, D. T. (1986) *The Regulation and Supervision of Financial Institutions* (London: Institute of Bankers).

Llewellyn, D. T. (1987) 'The Competition and the regulatory mix', *National Westminster Bank Review*, August.

Llewellyn, D. T. (1988) 'Financial intermediation and systems: global integration', in D. E. Fair and C. de Boissieu, *Integration: European Dimension* (The Hague: Martinus Nijhoff).

Llewellyn, D. T. (1989) 'Structural change in the British financial system', in D. T. Llewellyn (ed.), *Reflections on Money* (London: Macmillan).

Llewellyn, D. T. and L. Drake (1987) 'Profitability: case study of the Halifax Building Society', Loughborough University Banking Centre *Research Monograph No.2.*

Moran, M. (1984) *The Politics of Banking* (London: Macmillan).

Revell, J. R. S. (1973) *The British Financial System* (London: Macmillan).

Revell, J. R. S. (1983) 'Efficiency in the financial sector', in D. Shepherd and A. Silbertson (eds), *Microeconomic Efficiency and Macroeconomic Performance* (Oxford: Philip Allan).

Wall, L. and R. Eisenbeis (1984) 'Risk considerations in deregulation of bank activities', Federal Reserve Bank of Atlanta *Economic Review*, May, pp. 1–15.

3 The Process of Change in Belgian Banking

Jean-Paul Abraham

INTRODUCTION

The starting point of the present chapter is the contradiction – apparent or not – between the conventional wisdom about the Belgian financial system and the author's own experience in Belgian banking. The conventional wisdom classifies Belgium among countries like Germany and Switzerland, where change and financial innovation are slow because the authorities are conservative and financial institutions are averse to risk and competition. The author's experience in a middle-sized Belgian bank is to the contrary. Continuous change has meant that few people do the same things in the same way now as they did fifteen years ago; new units have been set up to produce and to sell new products; some traditional departments have been trimmed and their product mix has been changed; automation combined with telecommunication has penetrated everywhere. Of course, these developments have been taking place in banking all over the world. Maybe the 'continuous change' which impresses the author is only part of an adjustment to innovations, which had been initiated elsewhere and had to be integrated in each individual banking firm in order to stay in the market.

Apart from this adjustment hypothesis, the relevance of which is quite obvious, two other theses are developed in this chapter. Firstly, we suggest that the current literature on financial innovation, after having concentrated too much on the circumvention of regulation, now focuses too heavily on 'bubbles' and 'gadgets' in the product mix, neglecting more fundamental, if slower, changes and – above all – ignoring the fact that the process of change is at least as important as the change itself. Secondly, we believe that the small open economy hypothesis, which has been used quite extensively in recent macroeconomic analysis of Western European countries, can be usefully applied to the process of change in Belgian banking since the beginning of the 1970s. Consequently the chapter focuses on the analysis and the explanation of the process of change in the financial sector of a small open economy such as Belgium.

Several publications over the last two years have highlighted the 'facts and figures' on past and prospective changes in the Belgian financial system, so no attempt will be made to restart and extend the fact-finding procedure. Tables 3.1 and 3.2 summarise some relevant data, which will be

Table 3.1 Changes in Belgian banking over the period 1970–86

	Banks	*Savings banks*	*Public credit institutions*
In billion BEF			
Total variations	+2.407	+875	+2.231
of which due to:			
1. Global expansion of financial system	+2.196	+811	+2.596
2. Product mix	−79	−3	+73
3. Residual competitiveness	+380	+67	−438
In % of total			
Total variations	100	100	100
of which due to:			
1. Global expansion of financial system	+88.0	+92.7	+116.4
2. Product mix	−3.2	−0.4	+3.3
3. Residual competitiveness	+15.2	+7.7	−19.7

Table 3.2 Changes in Belgian banking over the period 1980–86

	Banks	*Savings banks*	*Public credit institutions*
In billion BEF			
Total variations	+1.374	+470	+996
of which due to:			
1. Global expansion of financial system	+1.150	+417	+1.287
2. Product mix	−22	−12	+23
3. Residual competitiveness	+246	+65	−314
In % of total			
Total variations	100	100	100
of which due to:			
1. Global expansion of financial system	+83.7	+88.8	+129.3
2. Product mix	−1.6	−2.7	+2.2
3. Residual competitiveness	+17.9	+13.9	−31.5

Source: Computations by Y. Lacroix-Destrée on the basis of data of table 7 in 'Le marché monétaire et le marché des capitaux en Belgique de 1970 à 1987', *Notes Economiques Paribas*, no. 74, July 1987. Updating in June 1988.

discussed within the following analysis. We simply refer to the recent literature on the subject, as mentioned in the bibliography of the present essay.

The two first sections of this chapter will be devoted to methodological remarks on financial innovation and on the small open economy hypothesis. In the three subsequent sections we will try to apply briefly our methodological approach to three processes of change which have been active in the Belgian financial system: internationalisation, (de)regulation, and automation.

FINANCIAL INNOVATION; A MULTIFORM PROCESS

In a recent paper on 'Financial innovation and economic growth' (Abraham, 1986), we argued that Schumpeter's definition of (industrial) development could more easily and more usefully be applied to financial innovation than other more recent approaches in innovation theory. Schumpeter included under 'development' not only new products, but also new methods of production, new markets, new sources of supply, and new forms of organisation of industry. He clearly saw development or innovation as an economic phenomenon with many aspects; a multiform process.

The literature on financial innovation tends to neglect this characteristic of multiformity. In the later 1970s and early 1980s it concentrated unduly on the circumvention of regulation as the primary source of financial innovation. Now the rapid emergence (but also disappearance) of new products in globalised international or domestic markets are first on the agenda.

It goes without saying that the present approach is, in many respects, less narrow than the original one; it integrates factors of demand pull and supply push in one global analysis and it no longer reduces the influence of regulation on innovation to circumvention, but admits that financial innovation can be induced by public or private regulation and intervention. But the current literature, especially in its popularised versions in magazines and newspapers, seems to be utterly fascinated, if not obsessed, by the bubbles of new products emerging everywhere and often disappearing after a few years: FRNs, NIFs, FRA, CATS, TIGERS, ZEROS, PARTLY PAIDS. As Dufey and Giddy (1981) had already pointed out in the early 1980s, products of this kind are new variations – bundling or unbundling – on old themes: yield, risk, maturity, commitment, currency, jurisdiction, and so on. They open up new markets, but these highly specialised, highly professional, highly international markets remain marginal to traditional customer-orientated ones, unless their products spill over into these traditional markets. Some disappear before doing so.

Under these circumstances, financial innovation theory, like exchange theory, should not be impressed too much by these bubbles in new markets, but should (re)turn to fundamentals: to the determinants and the process of permanent, irreversible changes in the financial system.

What is to be considered as 'permanent, irreversible change' is, of course, subject to discussion. We have three obvious candidates with solid arguments for nomination: technological change, consisting of much research and development 'embodied in capital and skilled labour', multiform applications, up-and downstream linkages, continuous processes of change; internationalisation, which is a combination of (international) deregulation changes in portfolio choices and technological change – in other words a combination of demand pull, supply push and institutional change; (de) or (re)regulation, which are institutional changes, usually slow to be decided, but penetrating in their effects, with a direct effect on innovation as a stimulator, accelerator, multiplier or as a brake on change.

In our opinion, the Belgian question of change or no change has primarily to be considered from this threefold point of view.

THE CASE OF THE SMALL OPEN ECONOMY CASE

The small open economy has received much attention in recent macroeconomic analysis, especially as far as exchange rate policy and monetary policy are concerned. This approach concentrates on the idea that it is very difficult to isolate a small economy from economic and monetary developments abroad, even through a system of flexible exchange rates. In these circumstances, the exchange rate is no longer an instrument but becomes an (intermediate) target of economic policy, which links up national monetary aggregates, national interest rates, national prices and national wages with the corresponding parameters in dominant foreign countries. Because the country is not only open but small, it is a price taker on international markets, which means that it is not only influenced but determined by developments abroad. Dependence, not independence, and not even interdependence, prevails.

This argument can easily be extended and applied to the financial sector. In a small open economy, both banks and their customers can do on foreign or international markets what they are unable or unwilling to do on domestic markets. Foreign or international bonds become substitutes for domestic bonds; deposits or credits in foreign currencies replace deposits or credits in national currency; foreign or international markets give access to financial instruments not available on domestic markets. Operations on these markets are particularly attractive when:

1. returns are higher;
2. transaction costs are lower;
3. taxes are low or non-existent;
4. operations are less regulated and more anonymous, especially with respect to national monetary and fiscal authorities;
5. the absorption capacity, the 'surface' of these markets, is larger.

Hence, internationalisation will be particularly attractive when the domestic market is small, slow-growing and overbanked. In these conditions, internationalisation is the obvious way for a financial institution of a small open economy to relax the constraints on the growth of its balance sheet and of its income and to profit from returns to scale. It is also the obvious way for the bank customer to diversify his/her assets, to maximise the after-tax return on these assets and to hedge against a depreciation of the national currency.

But on foreign and international markets the financial institutions of the small open economy are price takers on very competitive markets. As their national currency is not widely used, they rarely have privileged access to cheap financial resources: interest rates, spreads and fees are dictated by the market. As the predominant part of the international business takes place on highly professional and competitive markets, interest margins are rather low. The expansion of business volume must compensate for the small spreads and fees. But the expansion of assets and liabilities, due to internationalisation, very soon destabilises the balance sheet and financial structure of the bank, lowers its capital ratios and attracts the critical attention of supervisory authorities. To circumvent prudential control, off-balance sheet operations are launched, which seldom escape prudential control for very long.

The latter part of this story is, of course, not specific to the financial institutions of small open economies, but it concerns them most as the expansion of their international business is likely to contrast more with the sluggishness of their domestic base of assets and liabilities, and the margins of a price taker are usually much lower than those of a price setter.

Last but not least, most of the small open economy models include a *secteur abrité*: a domestic market, where international competition and the law of one price do not penetrate, where often producers are price setters and not price takers. In this sector, prices are often flexible because of public or private regulation. The higher margins in the *secteur abrité* not infrequently subsidise operations in the highly competitive sector.

As the services sector is often quoted as the archetype of the *secteur abrité*, the link with banking is is immediate. In the protected domestic financial sector, interest rates and commissions are traditionally fixed more by government regulation or private agreement than through the working of the market. These markets are more directly subject to monetary rescue requirements, withholding taxes and prudential control; stability is often preferred to allocative efficiency through competition. However, when applying the 'sheltered market' concept to the financial sector in small open economies, two specific remarks must be added.

Firstly, in most sectors the protection of the domestic market is determined by the nature of the product (that is, ponderous and/or perishable products; strictly personal services) or the geographical limitation of the market by distance, absence of transport facilities, absence of information, and so on. Geographical limitation no longer applies to the financial sector in a significant way; communication technology has significantly reduced the impact of geographical distance on financial operations. The protection in the financial sector is much more usually secured by regulation, both public and private, than in most other sectors. It is regulation which decides whether the domestic financial market will continue to be isolated from the foreign or international markets. It is regulation which decides where financial innovation from abroad will spill over into the domestic markets. Finally, it is regulation which decides whether the 'parochial' system in the financial system, which we describe below, will be or remain institutionalised. These factors increase the importance of the deregulation issue for the financial system of small open economies.

Secondly, the number of market participants in the domestic markets of small open economies tends to be small, especially on the supply side. Often these markets constitute a 'parochial system' where everyone knows everyone else, where competition is not anonymous, where the behaviour of parishioner 'A' directly affects parishioner 'B', and where contacts between market participants and the authorities are frequent and intensive. This makes for tensions, but also for some sense of solidarity. Cut-throat competition is out of order in a parochial system. This feeling of solidarity is increased when the parish is under international pressure. As the authorities are concerned for the stability of the system and the financial institutions for the profitability of their operations, regulation is expected to promote stability through profitability, by fixed margins and commissions on the sheltered domestic market.

If this policy is carried to the extreme, the financial sector of a small open economy looks like the industrial sector of many developing countries. It is a kind of dual economy with, on the one hand, a highly competitive internationalised sector, with a sophisticated product mix, intense competition, narrow margins, no fixed commissions and intense growth of business and, on the other hand, a domestic sector, sheltered by 'defensive' regulation, with a limited and unchanging product mix, high margins, fixed commissions and a slow growth of business. However the case of Belgium (and of other small open economies) will show that this extreme hypothesis loses some of its relevance because the internationalised markets exercise a demonstration effect on the domestic ones, and because authorities are gradually changing their preferences as to the balance between stability and allocative efficiency.

THE PROCESS OF INTERNATIONALISATION

Without being a real international financial centre, Belgium has, after Luxembourg and the United Kingdom the most internationalised banking system in Western Europe. Out of the *Vade-mecum Statistique du Secteur Bancaire 1987* we extract the following figures:

— external assets amount to 57 per cent of the gross total assets of the banking system
— external operations (outstanding operations in foreign currency and operations in BEF with non residents) made up no less than 67 per cent of the 1987 total balance sheet, 27 per cent of customers' deposits, 47 per cent of customer credits, 94 per cent of interbank operations.

Of the 84 banks operating in Belgium at the end of 1987, 31 were branches and 29 were subsidiaries of foreign financial institutions. These 60 banks with links abroad represent 49 per cent of the total balance sheets, 64 per cent of the balance sheets in foreign currency, 67 per cent of total interbank operations, 36 per cent of customer credits, but only 18 per cent of customers' deposits in the Belgian banking system. On a world scale the share of Belgium in total external banking assets amounts to only 3.9 per cent against 22.2 per cent for the United Kingdom, 5.8 per cent for France, and 4.4 per cent for Luxembourg, but it is only one point smaller than those of Germany (4.9 per cent) and larger than Switzerland's (2.0 per cent), the Netherland's (2.7 per cent) and Italy's (1.8 per cent).

These figures relate to banks only, which represent 69 per cent of the total balance sheet but only 43 per cent of customers' deposits of the whole Belgian banking system. The savings banks and public credit institutions are much less internationalised. In this respect, the figures overstate the degree of internationalisation of the Belgian financial system as a whole. On the other hand, they understate the importance of internationalisation, because they do not reflect adequately the operations on capital markets and off-balance sheet operations.

To our knowledge, the literature on the subject has always underlined the importance of internationalisation but has seldom analysed the process of internationalisation to its full extent. This process appears as a scenario where portfolio choices to the customers, interbank operations derived from them, and autonomous expansion of the interbank operations combine and reinforce each other under the influence of factors such as tax incentives and tax deterrents, fear of depreciation of the national currency, interest differentials, overbanking of the internal market, and so on. The main components of this internationalisation movement can be listed as follows:

On the customer's side

The 'Belgian dentist syndrome'

Well-to-do Belgian people – especially of the professional type – want to avoid simultaneously the disclosure of part of their income and wealth, the imposition of a 25 per cent withholding tax on income from investments and the (expected) depreciation of the national currency. They invest in eurobonds, especially in Luxembourg-based eurobonds, where subsidiaries of Belgian banks are very active on the primary and secondary market. In Belgium itself public offerings of eurobonds are not allowed by the authorities, because the national capital market has to be reserved for long-term financing of the budget, but private, over-the-counter dealings flourish. Coupons are cashed abroad in order to avoid disclosure and the 25 per cent withholding tax. This situation particularly favours the ECU bond market where Belgian banks, whose national currency is not an international currency, feel themselves on an equal footing with their colleagues abroad. In this way, Belgian banks became the main promoters of the ECU on the investors' side.

This process gives rise to some interesting factors.

1. The combination of tax and currency deterrents creates and maintains an important outflow of capital. Since 1987, however, this movement has been at least temporarily reversed as a consequence of the obligation of Dutch banks to disclose the interest payments to their resident customers, and also because Belgian public authorities permitted the public offering of tax-exempted SICAVs (*Société d'Investissement à Capital Variable*), set up according to Luxembourg law by Belgian financial institutions in Luxembourg. The decision to introduce a 10 per cent withholding tax in West Germany from 1 January 1989 onwards works in the same direction.
2. There is an 'upstream' linkage between portfolio decisions of customers and the important participation of Belgian banks in eurobond business on the primary and secondary market. The placement capacity of Belgian banks has been a rather significant factor in the expansion of the eurobond market in Western Europe.
3. The ECU has been successful among Belgian investors because the characteristics of ECU-denominated bonds corresponded exactly to what Belgian investors were looking for: an average, tax-free interest income and a shelter against the depreciation of the Belgian franc.

Logically, the preference for ECU investment should diminish in Belgium as the Belgian franc is becoming stronger against other European currencies and tax deterrents are being partly removed.

Internationalisation of the Belgian franc through triangular operations via Luxembourg and the Netherlands

In Belgium, small customers' deposits are regulated by private agreement and do not follow the rise of market rates in periods of strong rate increases. Besides, they are subject to the withholding tax of 25 per cent, except for the tax-favoured savings deposits on the *livret d'épargne*. In periods of high market rates, even the small Belgian investors turn to Luxembourg or the Netherlands in order to earn more market-orientated interest and escape the 25 per cent withholding tax. Because the Belgian franc is not an international currency, Luxembourg and Dutch banks have to re-export this flow of funds through the interbank market. The economic effect is that Belgian banks are ultimately paying on these funds the market rate they are refusing to pay directly to their clients.

Currency diversification of deposits

In periods of pressure on the Belgian franc, enterprises and households acquire or keep a significant part of their banking assets in the form of foreign currency items. Belgian firms no longer insist absolutely on being paid in national currency for their exports. Their proportion of exports being invoiced in Belgian francs has been reduced from 52 per cent in 1974 to 35 per cent in 1987. However, this movement slows down when the Belgian franc becomes stronger. Customers' bank deposits in foreign currencies amounted to 9 per cent of total customer deposits in 1970 and 15 per cent in 1980, increased to a record level of 25 per cent in 1984 and reduced to 22 per cent in 1987.

On the banks' side

Autonomous interbank operations

Belgian banks not only supported the internationalisation movement because of the change in portfolio choices of their customers, but also expanded their interbank operations all over the world in a spectacular way. In most cases they joined the different interbank markets but rarely shaped them. The only exception was the ECU market where Belgian banks were very influential in developing the interbank deposits market, including the compensation system. As already mentioned, in the ECU market they are on an equal footing with the large international banks of the countries of which the national currency is also a eurocurrency.

Foreign credits

Belgian banks joined the movement of syndicated credits to developing countries and to the Eastern countries in the 1970s. They were mostly underwriters, less frequently managers, of these credits. Foreign credits in general are favoured by a generous tax system called QFIE (*Quotité Forfaitaire d'Impôt Étranger*), which provides for a tax deduction of 15 per cent on income from foreign credits and other assets, in order to compensate for withholding taxes abroad. The system is, of course, very favourable in the case of credits or assets in countries with less than 15 per cent withholding tax. It has been argued that QFIE is the only reason why a significant number of foreign banks have an establishment in Belgium. Some international banking groups located part of their foreign credits portfolio in Belgium to enjoy the QFIE system. However, the intervention of Belgian banking on the international credit markets never attained the same importance as their activities on the bond markets. Hence, their exposure never reached the level of American banks towards Latin American countries or German banks to the Eastern bloc. They were not in the front line in the restructuring procedures.

Overlooking the points discussed above, we can conclude that many features of the small open economy appear in the internationalisation movement of Belgian banking. Belgian banks joined the expansion of international banking in the last 25 years but they did not shape the movement, except in the ECU market where they were on the same footing as the international banks of larger countries. Domestic markets in Belgium were under constant external pressure for tax, currency and interest differential reasons. The shift of customer choices to international operations reinforced the position of Belgian banks on the international markets, especially on the eurobond and ECU markets.

THE PROCESS OF (DE) OR (RE)REGULATION

The experience of the last few years has confirmed our thesis that the relation between regulation and innovation in the financial sector should not be limited to the innovation-through-circumvention hypothesis. At least three main cases can be distinguished: regulation leads the market and induces financial innovation (the Big Bang case); market developments lead (de)regulation (the 1980 Deregulation Act in the United States); market developments occur beside or by non-enforcement of regulation (the 'erosion' case).

Financial innovations and new market developments in Belgium were mainly of the 'erosion' type. Formal regulation of the domestic markets was not changed very much but has been undermined by the development of new markets outside the regulated areas and the erosion of regulation in regulated areas. The most important examples of undermining in various markets can be listed as follows:

The deposits market

1. the payment of market-orientated rates on sight deposits of some size, especially on sight deposits of companies and professionals;
2. the creation in 1968 of a market of large time deposits (5 million BEF) with market-orientated rates; these large deposits now represent 75 per cent of the total customer time deposits.

The money market *stricto sensu*

The development of an important market-determined interbank market in BEF, which also absorbs most of the supply of BEF by Luxembourg and Dutch banks. This market was the most important segment of the money market in the late 1970s and is still the connecting interface of the domestic market with the international markets. Its importance has now been topped by the market of T-bills.

The credits market

The development of market-orientated straight loans (overdraft for fixed amounts and fixed durations), mainly up to three months, with an interest rate made up by the interbank offered rate plus a spread, which originally amounted to between 0.50 and 1 per cent and now has been reduced for larger companies to a 0–0.25 per cent spread. At present, straight loans make up 27 per cent of total payment-related credits to customers.

The capital markets

As already mentioned, euromarket instruments are not admitted for public offering, but private dealings have been tolerated so that the sophisticated public get access to all the new financial instruments in foreign currency, especially in ECU and also in Luxembourg francs.

Erosion and undermining of formal regulation have been the predominant feature of the regulation problem in Belgian banking. Formal regulation, such as private regulation on the interest on customers' deposits, and regulated markets, such as the official call market and the rediscount market, look more and more like monuments of the past. They are not, however, abolished nor destroyed because of inertia or of an environmental sense of conservation which is typical of the Belgian financial system.

Besides the erosion phenomenon, three other less important developments must be noted.

In a few cases regulation leads the market. This was the case for the innovations induced by government tax legislation which aimed, firstly, at promoting risk capital (1962) and afterwards at favouring private pension schemes (1987). This was also more or less the case with regulation on (de)specialisation in 1967 and 1975, which allowed the different categories of financial institutions to operate in a larger field of transactions. This despecialisation favoured the banks whose market share grew significantly, in spite of changes in the product mix which were not to their advantage (see the constant market share computation in the appendix to this chapter). But in this case, there was clearly interaction between market and regulation developments, which allows classification of this development under case 2 (the Deregulation Act Type of development).

Secondly, there are a few important instances where regulation, even reinforced regulation, has put a brake on innovation and change; in these respects Belgium deserves the label of a country where little or no change occurs. In the area of short- and long-term financing instruments of the public debt in national currency, while the government participated in all innovations in the international markets to finance its debt in foreign currency, the standard government bond in BEF is still the 7-8 year loan with fixed interest, underwritten by a consortium of banks and reimbursed according to traditional provisions. Only recently call options were introduced in new issues, and some experiments are being made with a tender system for underwriting. The market for T-bills is still largely a market for financial institutions, although the secondary market has been recently opened to institutional investors. Belgium has not participated in the international movement to find new financing instruments of the public debt in national currency.

Thirdly, the regulation on tax-favoured savings deposits (called *livrets d'épargne*) has not been relaxed, but reinforced. Tax-free premiums above the base rate are now restricted to a maximum 35 per cent of the base rate. Here, tax legislation and financial regulation intermix in a dangerous way.

The present government seems to favour a more rapid formal financial deregulation of the Deregulation Act type. An example of this action is the admission of SICAVs for public offerings. Attempts to isolate the domestic markets from international influence are no longer popular. Finally, the plan for a single European financial market by 1992 spurs both the authorities and the financial institutions to liberalise, to deregulate and to reorganise the Brussels Stock Exchange. In August 1988 the Minister of Finance officially announced his determination to open the access of the

Exchange to financial institutions and abolish the 'privilège du bordereau' enjoyed by the stockbrokers corporation.

THE PROCESS OF AUTOMATION

Data processing and telecommunications have revolutionised the functioning of banks and other institutions in Belgium as they have elsewhere. Some features are distinctively Belgian and are to be associated with the small open economy hypothesis:

1. Since Belgium is a small open country with a closely knit financial system, interbank automation has been favoured, both domestically by the CEC (*Centre d'Echange des Opérations à Compenser du système financier Belge*) network and internationally by active participation in the Society for Worldwide Interbank Financial Telecommunication (SWIFT).
2. The investment costs and the possible returns to scale are so large that customer-orientated payment systems have to be set up on a co-operative basis among financial institutions. When different systems are created (Eurocheque, Bancontact, and Mister Cash), they are merged or made compatible after some time, such as Bancontact and Mister Cash in 1987.
3. Customer-orientated interactive systems are being developed for enterprises, but far less so for home banking in private household. The latter development would be a direct threat to the extensive branch network in Belgium.
4. Automation and dematerialisation are lagging behind in the field of securities. Automation does not follow quickly enough the international movement towards capital market operations and securitisation. On the Brussels Stock Exchange, however, things are on the move and the CATS (computer assisted trading systems) automated system, already at work in Toronto and Paris, will permit continuous trading.

   As everywhere else, the back-office problem has become crucial. Organisation, data processing and telecommunication problems often put a brake on the development of new products and new markets. As in many countries, banks in Belgium have experienced the fact that automation is not so easy to adjust and to change as the product mix of banks. Hence, a constant tension exists between the operational departments which sell the products and the administrative departments which are in charge of the current process of production and accounting.

CONCLUSIONS

It is obvious that the various points which have been raised in the present chapter deserve a more rigorous and a more quantified analysis than has been effective in this contribution. But we believe that our discussion has shown that the process of change is at least as interesting and as important as change itself.

Out of this discussion a number of conclusions emerge. Firstly the Belgian financial sector reflects the characteristics of a small open economy with an important, highly competitive international segment and some sheltered areas in the domestic market. However, it is an oversimplification to identify the international segment with the competitive sector and the whole domestic market with the sheltered one. As international and domestic markets interact, some very important competitive and mobile areas have developed on the domestic market. This helps to explain why bankers, mainly active in the international segment and/or in the competitive areas of the domestic market, are experiencing a far greater feeling of 'continuous change' rather than inertia in the Belgian financial system.

Secondly, the importance of tax incentives and tax deterrents in the internationalisation of the Belgian banking system is striking. An important part of international transactions has nothing to do with some glamorous worldwide movement of globalisation of financial markets, but simply with cross-border tax distortions between neighbouring countries. They do reflect the fact that fiscal harmonisation has not followed economic and monetary integration in the framework of the Belgo-Luxembourg Economic Union and the European Economic Community. This aspect should be given priority in working out a realistic plan for unifying the European market of financial services by 1992.

Finally, the predominant practice of Belgium of financial deregulation by limitations of (small) scale are being felt in many respects. Internationalisation can be seen as an attempt to overcome the limited scale of the domestic market. The association of various financial institutions in payment systems and in the setting-up of mutual funds and other SICAVs can also contribute to relax the constraints of scale. At the present level of globalisation of international money and capital markets, and at the present degree of internationalisation of Belgian banking, the problem of adequate scale has become crucial for many financial institutions. More than ever, the challenge for a Belgian bank is to have a sufficient size on the international market, without acting as a ponderous pachyderm on the domestic scene.

Appendix

Splitting increases in deposits of various categories of financial institutions into components according to constant market share analysis

Basic formula

$$X'_i - X_i = rX_i + (\Sigma_k r_k X_{ik} - rX_i) + (X'_i - X_i - \Sigma_k r_k X_{ik})$$

where

$X'_i - X_i$	total variation of deposits of category *i* during the period
rX_i	variations due to global expansion of the financial system
$\Sigma r_k X_{ik} - rX_i$	variations due to changes in the product mix of products
$X'_i - X_i - \Sigma r_k X_{ik}$	variations due to residual factors (e.g. competitiveness)

Selected Bibliography

Abraham, J. P.)1985) 'Les contraintes monétaires d'une petite économie ouverte', *La Question Monétaire au Luxembourg* (Luxembourg: Editions Letzeburger-land).

Abraham, J. P. (1986) 'Financial innovation and economic growth', Symposium on Europe and the future of financial services, mimeo, Brussels EEC Commission.

Abraham, J. P. and F. Lierman (1987) 'De Belgische geld- en kapitaalmarkt 1970–1987–2000: continuiteit of breuk?, Festschrift R. Vanes, *Tijdschrift voor Economie en Management*, no. 4, pp. 359–79.

Acx, R., O. Lefebvre, E. Perée, M. Quintyn and R. Schreurs (1986) *Le marché monétaire belge dans dix ans* (Institut de Réescompte et de Garantie (IRG)) 187.

Association Belge des Banques, *Annual Reports*.

Association Belge des Banques (1988), *Vade-Mecum Statistique du Secteur Bancaire 1987*, May.

Bex, M., R. Ceyssens, L. De Corel, W. Huysmans, A. Swings and W. Vanden Eynde (1986) 'De Belgische geldmarkt overr tien jaar: een uitdaging voor het Herdiscontering- en Waarborginstituut', *Revue de la Banque*, May, pp. 7–40.

Dufey, G. and I. H. Giddy (1981) 'The evolution of instruments and techniques in international financial markets', *Société Universitaire Européenne de Recherches Financière* (SUERF) Series 35A.

Lierman, F. (1987) 'Le marché monétaire et le marché des capitaux en Belgique de 1970 à 1987', *Notes Economiques Banque Paribas Belgique*, July, pp. 2–25.

Matthieu, M., A Roggemans, J. P. Straet and P. Van Roy (1986) 'Révolution informatique et marché monétaire: Esquisse de l'image du marché monétaire belge dans dix ans', *Reveue de la Banque,* May, pp. 43–73.

Reding, P. (1987) 'The Belgian experience in money and capital markets: recent developments', Conference 'Interrelationship between Money and Capital Markets', mimeo, not published (Namur: Facultés Notre-Dame de la Paix).

4 The Impact of Securitisation and Internationalisation on Market Imperfections: Implications for Regulatory Reform and the Structure of the Payments System

Robert Eisenbeis

INTRODUCTION

The United States and the international banking system have changed radically in the past decade. Competition has increased as entry barriers to markets have eroded. Internationally, more and more institutions have expanded abroad and markets have become increasingly global. On domestic fronts, new non-bank competitors have begun to provide alternative services, products permitted to existing institutions have expanded, and in the United States, barriers to interstate expansion have finally begun to crumble.[1] These changes have narrowed spreads, reduced profitability and altered the way payments are made. In the United States, the failure rate of banks and thrift institutions is at an all-time high, raising important concerns about threats to the viability of banking institutions and to the stability of financial markets and the payments system.[2] These problems, fuelled by frustrations with the current regulatory structure, which many believe is outmoded in today's competitive environment, and the perceived competitive inequities resulting from differential regulation of competitors, have become major sources of pressure for regulatory reform. Similar pressures operate in other nations as well.[3]

However, many reform proposals designed to deal with these problems start from assumptions about the nature of banking which may no longer be valid or relevant.[4] For example, it is commonly argued that banks and financial intermediaries are unique and play a special role in the economy as providers of transaction services and as sources of liquidity.[5] Furthermore, government is thought to have a fundamental responsibility to assure the safety and soundness of financial markets. Finally, at least with regard to US proposals, the implicit view is that it remains possible to keep the domestic financial system essentially insulated from international markets.

This chapter argues, firstly, that market developments are eroding the market imperfections which gave commercial banks their advantages over intermediation in direct credit markets. Hence, bank liabilities no longer perform their original unique functions in the nation's payments system. Secondly, because of the internationalisation of financial markets and the ability of financial institutions to engage in structural arbitrage, no one can ignore international considerations when designing new reform proposals. It is no longer possible to constrain domestic institutions through regulation without:

1. creating opportunities for non-domestic institutions to achieve a competitive advantage in domestic markets;
2. providing incentives for domestic customers to seek lower cost alternatives abroad; or
3. driving domestic financial institutions abroad where they may be less constrained.

Thirdly, concerns for maintaining the safety and soundness of the dollar payments now differ significantly from those that were relevant when the present US regulatory structure was created. They have evolved into assuring the integrity of the flow of payments through the payments system as financial assets are exchanged, rather than protecting the stock of money. Finally, forward-looking reform proposals, if they are to be successful, must take into account not only the existing financial and regulatory structure but also how regulated institutions will respond to changes in regulations and regulatory burdens. For these reasons US policies, for example, designed to insulate domestic institutions and markets from those of the rest of the world, or to insulate affilitates or subsidiaries from risk-taking in the rest of the institution, are doomed to failure.

The remainder of the chapter discusses these issues in detail. The second section examines recent changes in financial markets, and the third section considers whether banks may no longer be unique and examines the payments system issues. The last section consists of a summary and conclusions.

RECENT DEVELOPMENTS IN FINANCIAL MARKETS

In the perfect markets world of finance theory, there is no room for financial intermediaries. The rationalisation for the existence of financial intermediation includes monitoring costs, asymmetric information and/or imperfect markets.[6] Recent technological and financial innovations, however, have served to reduce information costs and to increase competition. Kareken (1987) observes that not only have the costs of processing information declined, but also the costs of acquiring and disseminating information have decreased relative to bank lending costs. Similarly, Miller (1986, p. 463) argues almost by definition that, 'Any surviving, successful innovation must have reduced dead-weight transactions costs and expanded the reach of the market, otherwise, it wouldn't have been successful, let alone significant'. These breakdowns represent potentially significant erosions in the advantages to financial intermediaries and have important potential implications for the future viability of financial intermediaries as presently structured.[7] Particularly important developments have been:

1. the explosive growth of asset securitisation and contingent claims; and
2. the internationalisation of financial markets.

Developments in the application of options and asset pricing theory, securitisation and the growth of contingent claims and guarantees have led to an unbundling of the services traditionally provided by depository intermediaries into their component parts.[8] These elementary services can now be tailored to suit individual investors and can often be provided at lower cost in the direct credit markets than in indirect markets. For example, stripping coupons from bonds segments the interest stream from the principal thereby creating a zero coupon bond, and changes the interest rate and price risk characteristics of the security. The spread of pass-through securities has resulted in a segmentation of the origination, servicing, credit evaluation and pricing of credit risk from the credit intermediation function. Standby letters of credit have become pure insurance contracts. Interest rate futures contracts segment the interest rate risk component from the other components of a financial transaction. The growth of foreign exchange options and the introduction of CEWs (consumer exchange warrants) enable corporations and individuals to take an interest in foreign exchange movements without having to take positions in the currencies themselves.[9] Finally, because of the growth in asset securitisation, formerly non-traded or illiquid assets can be valued, and most importantly, new derivative securities can be created which divide up the long-term, intermediate-term and short-term credit and intermediation risks imbedded in longer-term securities.

Growth in securitisation implies a potential decline in demand for the services provided by traditional depository financial intermediaries. High quality credits will become increasingly attractive to creators of derivative securities and the lower rates will atract competition for these high quality credits, traditionally the major source of business for banks. Moreover, the design, underwriting and distribution of securitised assets is not an activity in which banks have traditionally been engaged because of Glass-Steagall restrictions on securities activities. Faced with an erosion of their traditional borrowers, banks have sought to exploit their existing securities powers more intensively and to engage in securities activities through their bank holding company subsidiaries or abroad.[10]

This move by borrowers from the indirect to direct credit markets has already happened in the corporate credit market since large, high quality corporate borrowers now rely significantly on access to the US domestic and eurocommercial paper market for short-term funds.[11] High-quality, middle-market corporate customers are also benefiting from the growth of direct credit market alternatives. Junk bond financing doubled in 1986 and the use of credit enhancements in the form of standby letters of credit and other types of guarantees has increased the acceptability of lesser known borrowers to investors.

As a result of these developments there has been a shift in the institutions who are participating in these markets away from traditional intermediaries towards securities firms and investment bankers skilled in the creation, design and distribution of these new derivative securities. Today, other financial service firms are almost as important as banks and thrifts in the United States, holding about 45 per cent of the total private financial assets held by all financial service firms.[12]

A second development has been the internationalisation and integration of financial markets as both borrowers and lenders increasingly are able to obtain funding or engage in cross-border transactions.[13] A number of forces have contributed to this integration, and these include freer trade flows, reductions in regulatory barriers both in the US and abroad, the recent opening of foreign securities markets to US banking organisations, and the freer flow of information, making it easier for lenders to assess the risks of dealing with offshore borowers. The result is that prices and availability of funds in US markets are no longer insulated from those prevailing in the rest of the world as both borrowers and lenders arbitrage spreads and terms as the opportunities arise. The stock market crash of 19 October 1987 only served to highlight this interdependence among equities and futures markets. Because of increased volatility and the fact that many contracts and equities were traded on more than one exchange around the world, borrowers and portfolio managers had to follow continuously changes in prices on overseas markets, since the value of their positions changed, even when domestic markets may have been closed.

Internationalisation has made it increasingly difficult for individual countries to maintain regulatory structures or regulations different from those in the rest of the world. Through innovation, financial institutions can easily and relatively cheaply avoid the regulatory restrictions of various countries.[14] Moreover, Kane points out that this regulatory avoidance is encouraged by regulatory bodies in individual countries who seek, by providing accommodating regulatory climates, to attract and expand institutions doing business in their country.[15] The inescapable conclusion is that it has now become extremely difficult, if not impossible, to pursue domestic regulatory policies without the co-operation of foreign regulators as well. The recent BIS recommendations on uniform capital standards are a clear illustration of this.[16]

In this environment, it seems increasingly clear that banks are no longer unique or special.

THE UNIQUENESS OF BANKS

The regulation of banks rests on the supposedly special role that banks play in the financial system.[17] A well-functioning financial system enhances the efficiency of production and expands the wealth and income of society. In contrast, financial instability reduces income and can result in recession and economic depression. The fear of the externalities associated with cumulative bank failure have provided the rationale for public regulation of banking.[18] The arguments in the United States that banks are special rest on:

1. the role that banks play as sources of liquidity;
2. the importance of bank liabilities as money;
3. the inherent liquidity problem which banks face because certain bank liabilities are redeemable at par on very short notice or upon demand, whereas their assets are not.

These arguments may however, have been rendered obsolete by market developments.

Bank liabilities as money

In the early US history, individual banks issued their own bank notes to the public, promising to redeem these notes at par for specie.[19] It was not uncommon for notes issued by out-of-area banks to trade below par. The resulting discounts reflected several factors, including transportation and transaction costs, lack of information on the issuing bank and uncertainties about the creditworthiness of the issuing bank. This lack of par clearance in no way affected the ability of state bank notes to function as money.

Since note issues typically were not backed 100 per cent by specie, periodic liquidity problems arose whenever note holders became concerned that a bank might not be able to honour its redemption commitment. Runs on individual banks and the system sometimes occurred, and these resulted, albeit infrequently, in cumulative contractions in the money stock. Suspension of convertibility was a common way for early banks to deal with temporary liquidity problems. This resulted in a decline in purchasing power and shifted the cost of nonconvertibility, at least temporarily, to bank creditors (depositors), giving all liability holders an important incentive to worry about bank solvency.

For these early banks, avoidance of runs meant maintenance of public confidence that the institution could convert notes into specie in sufficient amounts to avoid the need to suspend convertibility.[20] Indeed, the first forms of public regulation dealt with the problems of suspension of convertibility and involved the imposition of reserve requirements specifying permissible ratios of notes to specie. Maintenance of public confidence was assured by engaging in minimal maturity intermediation,[21] by maintaining sufficient specie reserves, and by having adequate capital and liquidity.[22]

Although creation of the national banking system resulted in the elimination of state bank notes, state banks remained viable and prospered because demand deposits, and not currency, had become the principal bank financial liability that was traded and used in making transactions. As had been the case with state bank notes, not all cheques cleared at par, yet these liabilities were accepted and were readily used as a medium of exchange. This experience with both state bank notes and non-par clearance suggests, contrary to the assertions of some authors, that par clearance was never a necessity as far as the public was concerned for bank liabilities to serve as money.[23] Rather, the key attributes were related to value determination and acceptability attributes that are becoming increasingly important today for the liabilities of other financial itnermediaries.

Liquidity considerations, safety and soundness, and bank runs

With the advent of demand deposits as the principal component in the US money supply, liquidity concerns changed from focus on specie convertibility to the ability to meet demands for either withdrawals of currency or payments of cheques to other banks. This was accomplished by maintaining sufficient volumes of reserve balances, demand notes, government securities or other marketable assets in a bank's portfolio.

In the case of national banks before passage of the Federal Reserve Act in 1913, legal reserves included not only cash in vault but also deposits at Reserve City and Central Reserve City banks. Subsequent history showed this to be a structural flaw in the national banking system and a source of financial instability. In a fractional reserve banking system with the pyramiding of reserves, it was easier for a run on an individual bank to have systemic, system-wide effects.

Creation of the Federal Reserve System dealt with the fundamental instability of the fractional reserve system in two principal ways. It eliminated the use of interbank deposits as legal reserves. Additionally, the Federal Reserve was to serve as a temporary source of liquidity by providing emergency credit through the discounting of eligible collateral. In this way, institutions could avoid the technical insolvency that resulted from having to sell otherwise good assets in markets at distressed (fire sale) prices due to a temporary glut on the market and the high costs of quickly seeking out buyers. Unfortunately, during the Great Depression, the Federal Reserve failed to provide the needed liquidity, and it is estimated that the money supply collapsed by as much as one-third.[24]

This failure of the Federal Reserve to provide adequate reserves during the Depression contributed to the institution of Federal Deposit Insurance.[25] Deposit insurance effectively made bank failures independent events by breaking the link between the value of a bank's assets and the ability of insured depositors to obtain their funds when a bank's net worth became negative. Insured depositors had no reason to be concerned about their ability to receive their deposits, regardless of the value of the bank's assets or of the value of the assets of any other bank in the financial system.[26]

It is important to digress for a moment to discuss more precisely what is meant by 'confidence' as it pertains to bank runs because the concept has sometimes been abused. Confidence is not a subjective or ephemeral concept. It does not relate to the management or to intangible attributes of the firm, rather the role of confidence is most easily understood if it is related to depositors' assessment of the market value of the institution's assets relative to its liabilities. As long as the market value of the institution's net worth (including the value of any conjectural guarantees) is positive, then there is no need for a depositor to be concerned about being able to redeem his deposits for currency. With negative net worth, it makes perfect sense for uninsured creditors to attempt to obtain their funds, because some creditors in line will not be paid. Thus, the way for an institution to establish (or to reaffirm) confidence, is to reveal to existing as well as potential depositors and other uninsured creditors, the true quality (market value) of its assets. Convincing the market that it had a positive market-value net worth is what Continental Illinois and most of the state-sponsored insured S&Ls in Ohio were, in the end, unable to do, precisely because they were insolvent, but what Manufacturers Hanover was able to do.

It is also important to note that the runs on the Continental and in the Ohio S&L cases were not runs on the financial system or flights to currency. Funds withdrawn were redeposited at other institutions who did have positive market-value net worth. In the case of the S&L crisis in Ohio, funds were withdrawn from institutions insured by the state-sponsored fund and deposited in federally insured banks and thrifts.[27] These withdrawals took place because depositors perceived the state-sponsored fund to be under-funded, and the state demonstrated that it was unwilling to provide adequate funding after the crisis began.

The public also demonstrated its ability to distinguish between solvent and insolvent institutions insured by the state-sponsored fund. Not all experienced runs, and there is no evidence of runs on federally insured institutions. In fact one non-insured institution remained open throughout the crisis. It is this link between the market value of a depository institution's net worth and public confidence that has led some reformers to argue strenuously for market-value reporting for depository institutions.

Runs to currency are less likely today than in the past. Currency runs are impractical for large dollar depositors.[28] Withdrawing tens or hundreds of millions of dollars from a large bank in cash would be physically impossible. The volumes of currency would not be readily available, even from the Federal Reserve, and transportation and storage would be difficult and costly. In addition, most small dollar depositors' accounts are insured, so there is no need to engage in a currency run. In fact, despite the fears of the Federal Reserve that failure of Continental would cause creditors, especially foreign creditors, to lose confidence in the entire system (or in significant components thereof) a currency run is a very unlikely event.[29,30] Firstly, Federal Deposit Insurance, as it has been implemented, has broken the link among institutions, making failures independent events.[31] Secondly, it is less costly and much easier to demonstrate solvency to the public nowadays than it was during the Depression. We now have public disclosure requirements, and income and balance sheet information on individual institutions are now readily and publicly available. Rating firms now monitor continuously and rate the CDs and debt of many banks and thrifts. In addition, with the rise of pass-through securities and securitisation in general, it is becoming easier to price formerly hard-to-value assets on bank balance sheets. Finally, with the advent of modern communications, dissemination of the relevant information is easier and less costly.[32]

Deposit insurance was created partly in response to the failure of the Federal Reserve to liquify sufficient assets of banks during the Depression. It was specifically structured to safeguard the wealth of small depositors by protecting them from loss of their deposits when a bank failed. Similar protection was afforded the wealth holdings of small depositors in Savings and Loan Associations. The problems of the present structure of the Federal Deposit Insurance system and the risk-inducing elements associated with the flat rate premium structure as net worth goes to zero has been well described elsewhere and will not be discussed here.[33] However, it is important to reconsider the structure and function of deposit insurance in a world where numerous financial liabilities, other than those issued by banks and thrifts, can function as money, where most abodes of purchasing power are held in the form of liquid financial assets other than demand deposits, and where insured transactions accounts may only have non-zero balances in the process of liquidating a financial asset to make a transaction.

These issues arise because the payments system and medium of exchange have changed significantly since the Federal Reserve was created and deposit insurance established. Protecting the payments system no longer means protecting the money supply or protecting competitors because of fundamental changes that have occurred in the way payments are made and in what constitutes the money supply.

Reductions in market imperfections and changes in money and the way payments are made

Not only have financial innovations significantly changed financial instruments, they have also affected the way payments are typically made. Moreover, those institutions whose liabilities are now important elements in the payments system have expanded significantly, and hence the liabilities that serve the function of money have increased.[34] Cheques are routinely written on savings (NOW) accounts at both banks and S&Ls, S&Ls and mutual savings banks offer chequeing accounts, and credit unions offer share drafts. Cheques are also written on cash management accounts at brokerage houses and on money market mutual funds (accounts that are marked to market each day). Debit cards are the technological equivalent of a cheque and automatic transfers and Automated Clearing House (ACH) transactions are being used for predictable and large volume payments, such as social security payments, dividend payments, etc. Less attention has been given to credit card transactions, which now play an important role in the payments system as far as individuals are concerned. This use of credit substitute transactions mediums enables individuals to economise on traditional transactions balances, and even finance transactions through instantly approved credit if sufficient funds are not available. The distinctions between credit transactions and regular demand deposit transactions have become blurred because of the use of automated credit evaluation systems and lines of credit which serve to reduce the costs of credit evaluation.

More important than these new close substitutes for demand deposit payments are methods that have evolved to reduce the need for large dollar balance holders to hold funds in transaction accounts. A host of cash management devices, such as the use of zero balance accounts, deposit scanning and lockbox arrangements, are employed to collect funds that would otherwise be held in the form of idle balances and to channel them into instruments yielding a positive rate of return. When payments need to be made, these interest-earning assets are liquidated, the proceeds temporarily deposited in a transactions account, and immediately disbursed over Fedwire or CHIPS. Upon receipt, funds are immediately converted into an interest-bearing asset, even if it is only to earn interest overnight. Today most large dollar depositors (and increasingly small depositors as well) find that computers and the ease and reduced costs of converting interest-bearing financial assets into demand deposits mean that the traditional function of money balances as a source of liquidity is becoming less and less unique or important. A demand deposit is evolving into an account which at any particular instant in time has a zero balance. The account only has balances for the brief time that it takes to make a transaction while funds are swept into and out of the account in the process of clearing and settlement.

With the continued evolution of asset securitisation and the development of easily divisible securities (i.e. mutual fund shares) as well as the increasing use of computer technology, it is likely that more and more transactions will be taking place without even the temporary use of a transaction account. Once there is low cost convertibility of assets into easily valued securities or shares in mutual funds, it is a small step to bypass traditional transactions accounts when assets are exchanged. Electronic financial barter and exchange of ownership of almost any financial instrument are as easy, and involve fewer steps, than first converting the assets into funds in a transaction account and then exchanging ownership of a demand deposit. All that is needed is a message and switching system and a means to ensure that orders are carried out (settled).

In fact, the key attributes and policy issues associated with an electronic barter system are already in place with CHIPS, Fedwire, and the methods used for large dollar transactions. Changes in the way that large dollar payments are made has focused attention on payments system issues as part of regulatory reform proposals and these are discussed in the next section.[35]

Payments system changes

When the Federal Reserve System was created and Federal Deposit Insurance was established, most payments were made by cheques drawn on demand deposits with the remainder made in currency. Demand deposits were the dominant bank liability and the source of funds to support lending activity. There were not close substitutes for bank liabilities or the functions they performed, nor were the financial markets sufficiently deep enough to provide ready markets for the assets on bank balance sheets. Within such a structure, protecting the payments system meant preventing the cumulative collapse of the money supply. And since the money supply consisted of currency and demand deposits, this meant that preventing bank failures would prevent destruction of demand deposits.

Today the payments system is larger, has many more components (both private and public), and is subject to different risks than in the past. The cheque/demand deposit system, which accounts for the bulk of individual payments, and the one that the present regulatory structure was primarily designed to protect, is actually small in terms of the dollar volume of payments made today. While about forty billion cheques, amounting to some thirty-six trillion dollars, are written on average each year, cheques account for only about 12 per cent of the nation's payments in terms of value today.[36] The balance is made up of computerised transfers of reserve balances on the Federal Reserve's Fedwire system and the privately owned CHIPS (Clearing House Interbank Payments) system, and in the form of Automated Clearing House Transactions. Payments on Fedwire and CHIPS account for about 85 per cent of the transactions made today.[37]

Fedwire's 200 000 daily transactions average $2.5 million per transaction, producing an average daily turnover of $500 billion.[38] About 99 per cent of these transactions are computerised, originating on terminals or through computers at over 7500 depository institutions directly connected to Federal Reserve computers.

Over 90 per cent of the dollar payments between countries throughout the world take place on CHIPS. The volume of transactions on CHIPS is nearly as large as those on Fedwire. Average daily volume is $425 billion for about 114 000 transactions; the average transaction size of more than $3.75 million is even larger than on Fedwire. As with Fedwire, all CHIPS transfers are on-line, electronic payments initiated by settling banks, sent directly to the CHIPS computer.

All of these payments systems consist of two components. The first is a notification and accounting element in which orders to debit and credit certain accounts are routed electronically to the appropriate institutions. The second is the actual transfer of funds among institutions. For reasons of economy, funds are not transferred with each transaction; rather the electronic system keeps track of the net position which each institution has with the other participants, and only the net differences are 'settled' at the end of the day by transferring ownership of reserve balances held at the Federal Reserve.

Payments system risks

The structure of these payments systems determine the risks to which they are subject, who bears that risk, and how vulnerable the systems are to certain kinds of shocks. In the case of Fedwire, once a payment is initiated and in the system, the receiving bank is guaranteed by the Federal Reserve that the funds will be delivered. Thus, failure of the sending institution will not affect the receiving bank. Another convention of the system is that transactions result in immediately available funds for the receiving bank, but settlement by the sending bank with the Federal Reserve is at the end of the business day on a net basis, rather than on a transaction-by-transaction basis. In effect, the Federal Reserve interposes itself between the sending and receiving banks to guarantee the transaction. The Federal Reserve absorbs during the day the credit risk (for a zero return) that a sending institution will not be able to settle its net debit position at the end of the day.

Because of its structure, risks on Fedwire are mainly credit risks borne by the Federal Reserve and the participating banks. These credit risks arise because of the way the settlement and clearing of transactions are structured, and not because they are inherently risky. The sending institution runs the risk that the customer (which may be a corporate customer or a financial institution with an account at a clearing bank) requesting a payment to be made over Fedwire may not be able to cover the transaction. At present this risk is controlled through the establishment of customer overdraft limits which the clearing banks monitor on a real-time basis. The Federal Reserve has significant risk exposure due to the convention of providing immediately available funds to the receiving bank, but not requiring settlement by the sending institution until the end of the business day. This policy encourages sending banks to make payments early, creating large daylight overdrafts in order to obtain free credit from the Fed, and then to borrow Fed funds or otherwise cover its net debit position just before the close of business. Daylight overdrafts grew significantly during the 1980s, and in many cases amounted to several times the invested capital of clearing banks.[39]

The arguments against not allowing overdrafts pertain to the supposed disruptions to confidence that individual institutions would experience when payment orders were rejected.[40] This concern, however, would seem to be of little merit. First of all, institutions faced with the prospects of having payments rejected would have incentives to monitor and control their own risk exposure rather than seeking to take free credit from the system. This would introduce a desirable element of market discipline into the system. Secondly, little instability would be introduced. Because the Federal Reserve provides finality of settlement, there is no systemic risk on the system. Thirdly, immediate settlement would reduce the risks of the Federal Reserve, a particularly important concern, since many of the risks to which it is exposed arise from international transactions initiated by institutions outside the Fed's regulatory jurisdiction. Finally, with automation of the clearing and settlement system and value dating of transactions, it would be a simple matter to establish a queue for payments from individual banks. Those with adequate clearing balances would have transactions that would be cleared more rapidly than those that did not, again adding an element of market discipline to the system.

Risks in the payments system are presently greatest in the private systems which have net settlement and do not have finality of payment. In Chips, for example, payments are not considered final until settlement has occurred. No third party guarantees payments that have been put into the system, as the Federal Reserve does with Fedwire. Thus, if an institution participating in the system were to fail, all payments made by and to that institution during the day would be reversed, and settlement for the rest of the system would be recalculated minus the failed institution. Such systems are subject to systemic risk, since the removal of one failed institution from the system may affect the positions of one or more other institutions and could make them unable to settle.[41] In the case of CHIPS, if the clearing banks are unable to cover the credit, then it must either be covered by clearing bank borrowings from the Fed, or else the system cannot settle. Thus, the Federal Reserve is faced with the prospects of having to rescue the private systems for which it provides the settlement services, and it is the ultimate source of credit and bearer of risk for both the publicly run and privately run clearing systems.[42]

The large dollar volumes of transactions involved with the dominant components of the nation's payments system approach an average volume of a trillion dollars daily. This far exceeds both the capital of the banking system or its potential ability to deal with systemic problems in the payments system. These systemic problems, as described, would not appear to be affected significantly by the governmental support structure put in place to protect the cheque clearing system. Deposit insurance, for example, is essentially irrelevant, since the accounts transferred are not federally insured; moreover, most demand deposit accounts are evolving into zero balance accounts. The systemic problems in the large dollar payments system relate to possible disruptions to the flows of funds through the payments system and not to the stock of funds in the payments system or in clearing institutions.

Maintaining the integrity of payment flows is a substantially more complicated and difficult problem than protecting the stock of demand deposits, for a number of reasons. First, given the large size of the transactions in the system and the size of the system itself, the resources required to support an unwinding of even a short-run problem may be very large, and could exceed the capacity of the private participants, either individually or collectively, to self-insure themselves. The overnight extension of $22.6 billion to the Bank of New York is an example of the sums that could be involved. Second, because the transactions are electronic and occur instantaneously, monitoring the transactions and the net position of each participant is critical to controlling credit risk exposure by participants and the Federal Reserve who is presently the ultimate creditor in both the private and public systems. Third, many of the risks which the Federal Reserve faces in its payments system activities are derivative risks which flow into the system because bank customers may be initiating transactions for which they suddenly may not be able to pay, and which only become obvious when the clearing banks would be unable to settle. These derivative risks might be domestic or international in origin, and, in the case of foreign risks, are beyond the jurisdiction or control of US authorities. Fourth, because of the international character of CHIPS, failure of non-US banks to be able to settle could cause its collapse, which in the process of unwinding transactions could also affect the domestic payments system as well. In such circumstances, the inability for the ultimate creditor to control or monitor the risks posed by non-domestic institutions, except by limiting net exposure to the system at any one time, puts the Federal Reserve in a difficult position. Fifth, when the international activities of US banks and the links between the US payments system and foreign banking organisations are recognised, it becomes difficult to conceive of ensuring domestic financial stability without also ensuring international financial stability. Sixth, many of the present risks integral to the large dollar payments system are in large part functions of system structure and design. Putting the system on a real-time basis and eliminating net settlement policies, which is becoming feasible with current technology, would eliminate the large overdraft and credit risk problems that are the core of the payments system risks today. Eliminating the credit features of the payments system would make its function similar to that of futures markets, where the operator of the system has virtually no risk exposure. If this were to be done for the payments system, then the question arises as to whether operating the switching and accounting mechanism is a proper governmental function.

Some deposit insurance reform issues

It has been argued that deposit insurance may become less relevant as a mechanism to ensure the safety and soundness of the financial system. As the costs of converting financial assets from one form to another decline, then it becomes less and less certain what a transaction account is. In the extreme, if electronic barter becomes prevalent, then there is really little need to maintain a transaction account at all, and it is not at all clear what assets, financial or non-financial, should be insured. In such circumstances, the function of deposit insurance becomes one of providing a risk-free asset for those individuals who do not have access to a diversified portfolio or for whom transaction and information costs remain high. Arguably, this is the very function that deposit insurance was to address when it was instituted during the Depression. However, it is difficult to argue, especially in the present financial environment, why the US government should provide wealth insurance in this way. Granting a government guarantee to a private institution today is potentially discriminatory and could introduce distortions into the financial system. When the guarantee is mispriced, as it is at present, then the contract increases the risk in the financial system and requires a costly system of regulation and monitoring. Even if the insurance were properly priced, theoretical research suggests that regulation would still be required, and this would tend to differentially handicap and favour competitors in financial service markets.[43] Finally, if it is determined that wealth insurance is a proper governmental function, then offering small denomination government debt instruments or infinitely divisible Treasury obligations to the public would be a much less costly, and more effective, way to accomplish the same purpose.

CONCLUSIONS

This chapter argues that financial innovation and technological change have significantly altered the structure and character of the US financial system. In the short term, there is little reason to believe this process can be slowed or that the fundamental underlying economic forces driving those changes will be less important in the future than they have been in the past.[44] Several important observations are made. First, the key attribute of the changes we have observed is the continued erosion of transactions costs, information costs, and market imperfections which have been the basis of financial intermediaries' profitability over the direct credit markets. As the result of these changes bank liabilities are no longer performing the same unique functions in the nation's payments system. Second, because of internationalisation and the integration of the US and foreign financial sectors, new risks are introduced and these cannot be ignored in designing regulatory reform proposals. Moreover, the ability of financial institutions to engage in structural arbitrage means that it is no longer possible to constrain domestic institutions through regulation without:

1. creating opportunities for foreign institutions to achieve a competitive advantage in domestic markets;
2. providing incentives for domestic customers to seek lower cost alternatives abroad; or
3. driving domestic financial institutions abroad where they may be less constrained.

Third, concerns for maintaining the safety and soundness of the payments system differ significantly from those that were relevant when the present regulatory structure was created. Deposit insurance, in its present form, is becoming less and less relevant to ensuring the safety and soundness of the financial system, and these problems will not be solved by simply changing the methods by which deposit insurance is priced or capital adequacy is determined. Fourth, the primary concern in maintaining the safety and soundness of the payments system is in assuring the integrity of the flow of payments through the payments system rather than stabilising the stock of a particular financial asset. The principal risks that the payments system faces are uncontrolled credit risks, which arise primarily because of the way public and private systems operate. Net settlement policies and lack of finality of settlement are the chief sources of credit and systemic risks in the system. These could be eliminated by requiring continuous monitoring and settlement. Such changes, which would reduce the role of the Federal Reserve and lower its exposure to derivative credit risks flowing from international markets, also raise the question of whether there is a role for the Fed in operating what would then amount to an electronic switching and accounting system.

Notes

1. See, for example, Kane (1981), Eisenbeis (1986).
2. See Eisenbeis (1986).
3. For discussions of financial restructuring in several other countries, see Freedman (1987) and Suzuki (1987).
4. Many of these are discussed in Huertas (1987).
5. See Corrigan (1986), Litan (1987), Tobin (1987), Federal Deposit Insurance Corporation (1987).
6. For discussions of imperfect market models of banking, see Pringle (1972), Baltensperger (1980), Klein (1971) and the review paper of Santomero (1984). Benston and Smith (1979) discuss the role of transactions costs in explaining financial intermediation. See also Jacklin (1984).
7. See Fama (1980), Baltensperger and Dermine (1987), and Black (1970) who discuss the general services banks provide.
8. See Greenbaum and Thakor (1987) and Greenbaum (1986).
9. See Forde (1987).
10. See Kaufman (1985, 1987) or Eisenbeis (1988) for descriptions of the securities activities of banking organisations.
11. Rose (1987).
12. The data are dated 1983 and the source is *Blueprint for Reform: The Report of the Task Group on Regulation of Financial Services*, 1984.
13. For a perspective on globalisation, see Corrigan (1987).
14. See Board Staff (1986) for a discussion of the foreign activities of US banks.
15. See, for example, Kane (1981) or Eisenbeis (1986). For a discussion of the international overtones of this process, especially how international structural arbitrage works, see Kane (1986).

16. See Bank for International Settlements (1987).
17. For discussions of the history and forms of the regulation of banking, see Huertas (1983) and Benston (1983).
18. For a summary of the arguments, see Aharony and Swary (1983).
19. Corrigan (1986) indicates that a large modern economy requires the existence of an asset that is both highly liquid and readily transferable at par. This asset has been provided by currency and bank demand deposits.
20. For a discussion of bank runs, see Kaufman (1986) or Bryant (1980).
21. Clearing houses and other banks in the region also provided temporary credit to institutions experiencing liquidity problems (see Kaufman, 1986).
22. Kaufman (1986) notes that bank capital ratios during this period were substantially higher than they were subsequent to the introduction of deposit insurance.
23. See Corrigan (1986).
24. See Friedman and Schwartz (1963).
25. Friedman and Schwartz (1963) regard Federal Deposit Insurance as the single most important reform in the 1930s.
26. Implementation of the failure resolution provisions of the FDI Act resulted in *de facto* 100 per cent insurance for depositors for most of the period since 1933. See Kane (1985) for a discussion.
27. See Kane (1987).
28. Kaufman (1986) provides a useful discussion of the historical evidence pertaining to bank runs.
29. Meltzer (1986) argues that the methods used by the Fed in the Continental case actually increased the risk of loss of public confidence. The failure of the Fed to provide emergency credit itself and, instead, the putting together of a group of US banks to provide credit to Continental, signalled to the market concern by the Fed about the quality of Continental's assets.
30. Runs, other than runs to currency, result in the shifting of deposit accounts from weaker to more sound banks. This type of run creates a recycling problem, the effects of which can be mitigated by a properly functioning discount window.
31. For arguments for reducing insurance coverage, see Kane (1986) or Benston, Eisenbeis, Horvitz, Kane and Kaufman (1986).
32. A welcome and needed addition would be the ready availability of market-value accounting data.
33. See Kane (1985).
34. There is, of course, a voluminous literature on the demand for money and the effects of financial innovation on monetary control, but such a coverage is beyond the scope of this chapter. For references see Tobin (1983), Lindsey (1977), Kareken (1984), Santomero and Siegel (1985).
35. See Corrigan (1986).
36. See Huertas (1986).
37. Huertas (1987).
38. See Mengle, Humphrey and Summers (1987).
39. See Ireland (1986).
40. See Ireland (1986).
41. See Huertas (1986) and Humphrey (1986).
42. As Huertas (1987) points out, the principal risks in these private systems stem from the net settlement policy and lack of finality which places the receiving bank in the position of extending credit to the sending bank until settlement occurs. To attempt to control these risks, CHIPS has established a net debit cap on the amounts that one bank can owe to other banks in the

system. In addition, individual banks establish limits on the net amount of payments to accept from any one sending bank.

43. See Kahane (1977) and Koehn and Santomero (1980).
44. Miller (1986) argues that as transactions costs fall and market imperfections disappear, then the process of financial innovation will slow down.

References

Aharony, J. and I. Swary (1983) 'Contagion effects of bank runs: evidence from capital markets', *Journal of Business*, 56.

Baltensperger, E. (1980) 'Alternative approaches to the theory of the banking firm', *Journal of Monetary Economics*, 6 January.

Baltensperger, Ernst and Jean Dermine (1987) 'Banking deregulation', *Economic Policy*, April.

Bank for International Settlements (1987) 'Proposals for international convergence of capital measurement and capital standards', Committee on Banking and Supervisory Practices, Consultative Paper, December.

Benston, George G. (1983) 'The regulation of financial services', in *Financial Services: The Changing Institutions and Government Policy*, George Benston (ed.) (Englewood Cliffs, NJ: Prentice-Hall).

Benston, George G. and Clifford W. Smith, Jr (1979) 'A transactions cost approach to the theory of financial intermediation', *Journal of Finance*, vol. 31, May, pp. 215–31.

Benston, George G. and George Kaufman (1988) 'Risk and solvency regulation of depository institutions: past policies and current options', Federal Reserve Bank of Chicago Staff Memorandum Series.

Benston, George G.,Robert A. Eisenbeis, Paul M. Horvitz, Edward J. Kane and George G. Kaufman (1986) *Perspectives on Safe and Sound Banking* (Cambridge: MIT Press).

Black, Fischer (1970) 'Banking and interest rates in a world without money', *Journal of Bank Research*.

Board Staff (1986) 'Board staff memorandum responding to questions raised in letter on April 3, 1986 from Chairman Doug Barnard of the Commerce, Consumer and Monetary Affairs subcommittee of the House Committee on Government Operations', *Structure and Regulation of Financial Firms and Holding Companies, Part I.* Hearings before a Subcommittee of the Committee on Government Operations, House of Representatives, 99th Congress, second session, 22 April, 11 June and 23 July.

Bryant, J. (1980) 'A model of reserves, bank runs, and deposit insurance', *Journal of Banking and Finance*, vol. 4.

Corrigan, E. Gerald (1982) 'Are banks special?', *Annual Report*, Federal Reserve Bank of New York.

Corrigan, E. Gerald (1986) 'Financial market structure: a longer view', *Annual Report*, Federal Reserve Bank of New York.

Corrigan, E. Gerald (1987) 'Corrigan offers perspective on globalisation', *American Banker*, 30 July.

Eisenbeis, Robert A. (1985) 'Inflation and regulation: effects on financial institutions and structure', in *Handbook for Banking Strategy*, Richard C. Aspinwall and Robert A. Eisenbeis (eds) (New York: John Wiley & Sons Inc).

Eisenbeis, Robert A. (1986) 'Regulatory policy and financial stability', Proceedings of a Symposium on Debt, Financial Stability, and Public Policy, Sponsored by the Federal Reserve Bank of Kansas City, Jackson Lake Lodge, Wyoming, 27-29 August.

Eisenbeis, Robert A. (1988) 'Banking organisation securities activities and Glass-Steagall', forthcoming.

Fama, Eugene (1980) 'Banking in the theory of finance', *Journal of Monetary Economics*.

Federal Deposit Insurance Corporation (1987) *Mandate for Change: Restructuring the Banking System* (Washington DC: Federal Deposit Insurance Corporation) October.

Forde, John P. (1987) 'Exchange-rate betting hits retail market', *American Banker*, 17 July.

Freedman, Charles (1987) 'Financial restructuring: the Canadian experience', in *Restructuring the Financial System*, a symposium sponsored by the Federal Reserve Bank of Kansas City, Jackson Hole, Wyoming, 20–22 August.

Friedman, Milton and Anna Schwartz (1963) *A Monetary History of the United States* (a study for the National Bureau of Economic Research, New York) (Princeton University Press).

Greenbaum, Stuart I. (1986) 'Securitisation, asset quality and regulatory reform', BRC working paper no. 147, Northwestern University.

Greenbaum, Stuart I. and Anjan V. Thakor (1987) 'Banks funding nodes: securitisation versus deposits', *Journal of Banking and Finance*, 11, pp. 379–401.

Hall, R. E. (1983) 'Optimal fiduciary monetary systems', *Journal of Monetary Economics*.

Huertas, Thomas (1983) 'The regulation of financial institutions: a historical perspective of current issues', in George Benston (ed.), *Financial Services: The Changing Institutions and Government Policy* (Englewood Cliffs, NJ: Prentice Hall).

Huertas, Thomas (1986) 'Risk in the payments system' Appendix D to the Statement by Hans H. Angermueller before the Commerce, Consumer and Monetary Affairs subcommittee of the Committee on Government Operations, US House of Representatives, Washington DC, 17 December.

Huertas, Thomas (1987) 'Redesigning regulation: the future of finance in the United States', in *Restructuring the Financial System*, a symposium sponsored by the Federal Reserve Bank of Kansas City, Jackson Hole, Wyoming, 20–22 August.

Humphrey, David B. (1986) 'Payments finality and the risk of settlement failure', in Anthony Saunders and Lawrence J. White, *Technology and the Regulation of Financial Markets: Securities, Futures and Banking* (Lexington, Mass: Lexington Books).

Ireland, Oliver I. (1986) 'Payments system risk', Appendices to the Statement by Paul A. Volcker, Chairman of the Board of Governors of the Federal Reserve System before the Subcommittee on Commerce, Consumer and Monetary Affairs of the Committee of Government Operations of the United States House of Representatives, Papers prepared by the Federal Reserve Board Staff, June.

Jacklin, Charles (1984) 'Demand deposits, trading restrictions and risk sharing', Working paper 139, University of Chicago, Graduate School of Business.

Kahane, Yehuda (1977) 'Capital adequacy and the regulation of financial intermediaries', *Journal of Banking and Finance*, 1, pp. 207–18.

Kane, Edward J. (1981) 'Accelerating inflation, technological innovation, and the decreasing effectiveness of bank regulation', *Journal of Finance*, May.

Kane, Edward J. (1985) *The Gathering Crisis in Federal Deposit Insurance* (Cambridge, Mass: The MIT Press).

Kanes, Edward J. (1986) 'Competitive financial regulation: an international perspective', College of Business, The Ohio State University, Working paper series 86–11, November.

Kane, Edward J. (1987) 'Who should learn what from the failure and delayed bailout of the ODGF?', Proceedings of a Conference on Bank Structure and Competition, Federal Reserve Bank of Chicago.

Kareken, John (1984) 'Bank regulation and the effectiveness of open market operations', *Brookings Papers on Economic Activity*.

Kareken, J. H. (1987) 'The emergence and regulation of contingent commitment banking', *Journal of Banking and Finance*, 11.

Kaufman, George G. (1985) 'The securities activities of commercial banks', in Richard C. Aspinwall and Robert A. Eisenbeis (eds), *Handbook of Banking Strategy* (New York: Wiley & Sons).

Kaufman, George G. (1986) 'Banking risk in historical perspective', Proceedings of a Conference on Bank Structure and Competition, Federal Reserve Bank of Chicago, May.

Kaufman, George G. (1987) 'Securities activities of commercial banks: recent changes in the economic and legal environments', 31 July, Paper prepared to accompany statement before the Committee on Banking, Housing and Urban Affairs, US Senate, Washington DC, 6 August.

Klein, Michael (1971) 'A theory of the banking firm', *Journal of Money, Credit and Banking*.

Koehn, Michael and Anthony M. Santomero (1980) 'Regulation of bank capital and portfolio risk', *Journal of Finance*, December.

Lindsey, David (1977) 'The implications of removing the demand deposit rate prohibition for monetary control and the conduct of monetary policy', Special Studies Paper.

Litan, Robert (1987) *What Should Banks Do?* (Washington DC: Brookings Institution).

Loehnis, Anthony D.(1987) 'Financial restructuring: the United Kingdom experience', in *Restructuring the Financial System*, A symposium sponsored by the Federal Reserve Bank of Kansas City, Jackson Hole, Wyoming, 20–22 August.

Meltzer, Alan H. (1986) 'Financial failures and financial policies', in George Kaufman and Roger C. Kormendi (eds), *Deregulating Financial Services: Policy in Flux* (Cambridge, Mass.: Ballinger Publishing Company).

Mengle, David L., David B. Humphrey and Bruce J. Summers (1987) 'Intraday credit: risk, value and pricing', *Economic Review*, Federal Reserve Bank of Richmond, vol. 73/1, January/February.

Miller, Merton H. (1986) 'Financial innovation: the last twenty years and the next', *Journal of Financial and Quantitative Analysis*, vol. 21, no. 4, December, pp. 459–71.

Pringle, John (1972) 'An imperfect markets model of the banking firm', *Journal of Money, Credit and Banking*.

Rose, Sanford (1987) 'Random thoughts', *American Banker*, Tuesday 7 July.

Santomero, Anthony M. (1984) 'Modelling the banking firm', *Journal of Money, Credit and Banking*, 16 November.

Santomero, Anthony M. and J. J. Siegel (1985) 'Financial deregulation and monetary policy', paper prepared for the Carnegie-Rochester Public Policy Conference.

Suzuki, Yoshio (1987) 'Financial restructuring: the Japanese experience', in *Restructuring the Financial System*, A symposium sponsored by the Federal Reserve Bank of Kansas City, Jackson Hole, Wyoming, 20–22 August.

Tobin, James (1983) 'Financial structure and monetary rules', *Kredit and Kapital*.
Tobin, James (1987) 'The case for preserving regulatory distinctions', in *Restructuring the Financial System*, A symposium sponsored by the Federal Reserve Bank of Kansas City, Jackson Hole, Wyoming, 20–22 August.

5 The Banking and Financial System in Argentina: The History of a Crisis

Elisabetta Montanaro

INTRODUCTION

The financial crisis in Argentina exploded in March 1980 with the failure of the country's main private bank, the Banco de Intercambio Regional. By the middle of 1982, sixty-eight banks and financial institutions had failed, amongst which were the Banco de los Andes, the Banco Oddone and the Banco International, the third, seventh and ninth banks respectively in the country (Feldman, 1983).

The Argentinian government spent a sum estimated at 3 per cent of GDP and 20 per cent of deposits to cover depositors' insurance in the first year alone of the crisis. The losses which the Banco Central de la Republica Argentina (BCRA) had to sustain to make good credits to the liquidated or rescued banks were valued at $6.6 billion by the end of 1981 (ADEBA, 1987). In just the first two months of the crisis, the additional liquidity pumped into the system, reflecting the extraordinary rediscounts to the banks in trouble, was of the order of $2.6 billion, 27 per cent of the country's monetary base. A large part of this liquidity infusion 'encouraged' capital flights (Fernandez, 1985).

The decrease in the BCRA's reserves, which amounted to $7.2 billion between 1980 and 1982, highlighted a paradoxical reality: the monetary authorities 'financed' the collectivity in as much as it allowed it to transfer the credit supplied abroad, by changing balances in pesos into hard currency.

The Argentinian insolvency *vis-à-vis* its international creditors, which was officially declared in 1981, made it obvious that the internal banking crisis had become a general financial crisis. The Argentian banking crisis, unlike those which took place in Europe in the same period, and in many ways similar to the one which started in the United States after deregulation in 1980, is still in full swing. It is therefore surprising that so little should be known about it and its study is so limited even today. Moreover, there was never any explicit recognition on the part of the Argentine government of the crisis, nor is any trace to be found in the *Memoria Anual* of the BCRA of 1980/81 (BCRA, 1980–81). What research has been done is, however, unanimous in considering it to be the most serious financial crisis ever experienced in Argentina, and in relative terms it can be considered one of the most traumatic episodes in the history of world financial crises on account of its intensity and length (Feldman, 1983).

FINANCIAL REPRESSION AND DEREGULATION

What makes the Argentinian financial crisis particularly interesting emerges from an analysis of the circumstances in which it has developed, exploded and been consolidated. In the first place the banking crisis occurred after a period in which the policy of 'financial repression', which had held sway for the thirty years from 1946 to 1976, was replaced by a radical deregulation of the credit market and the capital market. In the second place the management of the crisis and the consequent re-regulation have generated important changes in the structure of the Argentinian banking system. The present-day reality of the intrinsic vulnerability of the country's economy results from the enormous problem of foreign debt and, at least in part, the historical evolutionary process which has had a determining influence on the efficiency of its banking institutions.

'Financial repression', as defined by Shaw (1973) and McKinnon (1981), was used in many Latin American countries in the 1950s, together with foreign trade protectionism, to promote import-substituting industrialisation through a forced transfer of savings towards protected sectors of manufacturing industry (Shaw, 1973; McKinnon, 1981; Canavese and Montuschi, 1985). Credit policy, through a combination of high reserve requirements, interest rate restrictions on both deposits and loans, and special loan tranches, singled out low costs of financing as the precondition for industrial development. This should also have favoured the flow of investments from abroad, thus compensating for the scarcity of capital on the domestic market. The guiding principle of 'financial repression' was, in short, to 'reward' productive investments and 'punish' the hoarding of liquid assets. This model was designed for economic systems of the LDC type; predominantly agricultural, with low per capita income, non-existent financial markets, scarcely evolved banking systems and with largely export-led development (McKinnon, 1985).

Argentina was rather different from this model in many ways. Whilst it is true that after the Second World War its rate of development had rapidly declined for a number of economic and political reasons, both national and international, which had slowed down exports and stimulated the growth of inflation, its banking system did not differ greatly from that of most industrialised countries. It had developed at the end of the nineteenth century by means of large infusions of foreign capital and was regulated by the Banking Act of 1935, which also established the Banco Central (Canavese and Montuschi, 1985). The financial market was reasonably developed, especially as regards mortgage paper and bonds (Diáz-Alejandro, 1985).

It was thanks to a stable and efficient financial structure and a prudent monetary policy that the Argentinian economy managed to escape almost unscathed from the 1930s crisis; that is with relatively low costs in terms of recession and unemployment (Alhadeff, 1985). Argentina was the only Latin American country to wipe out punctually its entire foreign debt accumulated in the 1920s, converting it into domestic credit with the help of investors and the banks.

The financial history of Argentina, which runs from the middle of the 1940s up until today, is the history of a dramatic 'backward development' of a country for which the normal definition of 'developing country' should in fact read 'de-developing country'.

The strategy of financial repression, which was practised in Argentina from the beginning of the Peronist regime in 1946, was no different from that used in many other countries of South America. The BCRA, which had been nationalised on 25 March 1945, had become to all intents and purposes the organ of the public administration. It took upon itself, on the government's behalf, the monopoly of decision-making about the sectoral division of financing, the cost of credit and the reward for saving.

'Credit planning' between 1947 and 1956 brought about a *de facto* nationalisation of the banking system, through the nationalisation of deposits; from 1957 to 1972 this policy was substituted by a policy of direct control over bank interest rates with high fractionary reserve requirements; and in 1973 the nationalisation of deposits was again put into force until 1977 (Canitrot, 1981). During the periods of deposit nationalisation, banks worked as agencies of the central bank, on whose behalf they raised funds for which they were paid a commission.

The costs of debt interest and depositor's insurance, which was free of charge and with 100 per cent coverage, were taken on by the BCRA. The financing of loans was organised through BCRA rediscounts whose rates – increased by the sum of the commission given to the banks – determined the interest rates paid by borrowers.

The credit risk in this system was in theory charged to the banks which insured the refund of rediscount credits with the refund of agreed loans. In actual fact the certainty of receiving commission for every loan and the fact that the BCRA gave rediscounts almost automatically, with the sole condition of distributing them according to a sectoral plan, made the selection process of borrowers excessively expensive for banking management. Credit rationing in favour of privileged borrowers freed them from making investment decisions which compared expected returns and the cost of capital. All this brought about an inefficient allocation of resources in the production system and a loss of entrepreneurial capacity in the banking system. The growth of intermediation ensured a growth of returns without liquidity risks and, in practice, without credit risk.

Under these conditions the volume of intermediation by banks may remain unchanged or even increase until the propensity to consume does not increase and/or the demand for money decreases on account of negative real returns. This happened in Argentina between 1947 and 1950, when the value of the ratio M2/GDP increased from 0.463 to 0.472, that is with similar values to those seen at the beginning of the 1980s in the mature industrial economies (McKinnon, 1981). The increase in the propensity to consume, accentuated by the growth in inflation in the second half of the 1950s, is shown in the M2/GDP ratio value of 0.317 in 1957; the decrease in importance of the ratio of bank deposits to GDP was even greater, from 0.136 in 1950 to 0.081 in 1957.

The passage to a system of fractionary banking reserves, remunerated at rates which were correlated with the official discount rate, in a regime of deposit and lending rates controlled wholly or partially by the BCRA, did not increase the relative weight of credit intermediation – which in 1975 reached 0.083 – but influenced greatly the structure of the banking system (Canavese and Montuschi, 1985; Epstein, 1987).

The failure of the automatic guaranteed fund-raising from the rediscounts of the BCRA, while a progressive demonetisation of the economy was taking place, was an incentive for banks to compete for savings. Since competition on interest rates was not feasible, the 'hunt' for savings was undertaken:

1. by an increase in the number of branches;
2. with the creation of forms of uncontrolled fund raising, mainly in the form of acceptance which in 1975 represented 40 per cent of interest yielding liabilities;
3. with the creation of non-banking institutions (the so-called *financieros*) which henceforth became a stable, parallel, albeit semi-clandestine, part of the Argentine credit system. Many financial transactions at uncontrolled rates and black market operations in foreign exchange took place in these institutions (Fernandez, 1985; Gaba, 1981).

Territorial enlargement as a direct consequence of financial repression led to an increase in operating costs for Argentinian banks which was much greater than the volume of intermediation and with a consequent loss of operating efficiency. This phenomenon was particularly serious for the state banks and for the smaller private banks of the interior, for which both legitimate and clandestine forms of financial innovation were off limits for institutional or market reasons. The larger private banks of the province of Buenos Aires and the foreign banks felt this much less, due especially to their capacity to reduce the incidence of costs through more profitable uncontrolled financial intermediation (ADEBA, 1987).

The segmentation of the banking system into different categories of banks with different levels of efficiency and stability became, from then on, a constant feature of the Argentinian credit market. This characteristic was accentuated in 1973 when the balance of payments crisis stiffened financial repression, bringing back *de facto* nationalisation by deposits, by making the reserve requirement 100 per cent. Banking once again put on its old 1950s face. Despite the 1969 reform whereby all non-bank financial intermediaries were put under the control of the BCRA, the black market in money and foreign exchange developed enormously (Feldman, 1980).

DEVELOPMENTS FROM 1976 TO 1980

The military junta which seized power in 1976 inherited a country with several economic problems dating from the Perón administration. These included a rate of hyperinflation of around 382 per cent, compared with an average of 25 per cent between 1960 and 1974, and a high rate of foreign debt due to the insufficient and inefficient mobilisation of domestic credit (Gaba, 1981).

The financial deregulation which the new regime implemented was part of a plan to free the economy by improving the allocative efficiency of the banking system and increasing productivity in nationalised industries. The salient features of this programme were the abolition of foreign trade and financial protectionism, and control over capital movements; the relinquishing by the State of the privilege of interest-free financing by the BCRA; the favouring of competition and *laissez-faire*.

The Banking Act of 1977 decentralised deposits, whilst keeping 100 per cent guaranteed, free public insurance (later reduced to 90 per cent for very large deposits); it abolished direct control over interest rates, with the exception of the ban on the remuneration of demand deposits; it enlarged the range of permitted banking transactions, including consumer credit and those in exchange rates which had so enriched the *financieros*; it re-established a minimum, homogeneous, 45 per cent reserve requirement for all categories of deposits. In order to avoid the high reserve requirement causing an excessive increase in the spread between bank rates on loans and deposits, a mechanism of interest equalisation was introduced (the so-called *Cuenta de Regulación Monetaria*) through which the required reserves were remunerated at a rate of interest equal to the current average on interest yielding deposits, with an expiry date over thirty days. At the same time a rate was imposed on the banks, the volume of loanable funds corresponding to the quota of demand deposits exempt from the reserve.

This rate was at the same percentage as that on returns on required reserves. The net remuneration of required reserves for a given percentage of the same on total deposits was therefore positive for the banks when the ratio between interest yielding deposits and demand deposits was greater than the credit multiplier (Gaba, 1981).

Between 1977 and 1980 the value of M2/GDP increased from 0.12 to 0.245. This increase, stimulated partly by the liberalisation of interest rates, was concentrated almost exclusively on the profit-making component: time deposits, acceptances certificates of deposit and later thirty-day Treasury bills. Demand deposits and bills continued to decrease. This led to the increase in the cost of deposits for the banks, and the impossibility of the State doing without BCRA credit as it had originally planned to do.

The control of liquidity through banks' required reserves became unworkable because of the constant deficit recorded by the *Cuenta*, which was the main source of creation of the monetary base for sums which varied between 30 per cent and 70 per cent of the total (Gaba, 1981). The inflation rate was thus transferred from the public to the banks and thence to the BCRA and the Treasury. The correction of the mechanism of interest equalisation, with the radical decrease in the minimum reserve requirement to 10 per cent of deposits in 1980, was largely useless because it came too late.

The *Cuenta* deficit, on account of the interest matured over the years, remains even today among the BCRA's liabilities, accounting for no less than 40 per cent of the total (Morgan Guaranty Trust, 1986). Between 1977 and 1978 the 'almost fiscal' deficit of the BCRA compensated amply for the decline in the government deficit. Its expansionary effects on liquidity were added to the balance of payments surplus and the rediscount credits given by the banks. From the beginning of the 1980s, in addition to the reversal in the balance of capital movements, the new expansion in government deficit and the cost of financing the crisis put severe limits on the effectiveness of monetary controls. From then on these controls were carried out through open market operations, often together with the imposition on banks of portfolio requirements on claims on government (Morgan Guaranty Trust, 1986). The monetary policy of the BCRA became increasingly determined by public deficit management goals. Thus in real terms the BCRA gradually lost its independence with respect to the government.

A further destabilising factor was the unsuccessful exchange manoeuvre of 1978 which aimed at reversing unsound inflationary expectations (Fernandez, 1985). Capital movements to and from the country were almost completely liberalised; the official conversion rate of the peso with respect to the dollar was established with a form of the 'active crawling peg' system, through the so-called *Tablita cambiaria*. This established the future quotations of exchange rates for a certain period, which would be binding for the monetary authorities, on the basis of a plan for diminishing devaluation; this was soon revealed to be completely utopian.

Between 1978 and 1980 there was an explosion of banking euphoria due to the following circumstances: the freedom to contract rates; the possibility of financing and/or investing in hard currency because of the differential between real domestic and international rates of interest; and the enormous opportunities to make money out of arbitrage on exchange rates caused by the growing gap between the official and the effective rate of exchange – the *retraso cambiario* (Epstein, 1987; Fernandez, 1983). Growth of the Argentinian financial system and above all the private banks burgeoned. In the three years which preceded the beginning of the crisis, deposits grew in real terms by 86 per cent and credit by 110 per cent, absorbed in the main by private citizens and firms (Canitrot, 1981). The spread between rates on banking loans and deposits generally remained very high, with an annual average in real terms estimated at between 13 and 15 per cent (Gaba, 1981). This trend was due, at least initially, to the high incidence of required reserves on total yielding assets. But it reflected at the same time the inefficiency of a banking system which during thirty years of financial repression had been deprived of its entrepreneurial resources and discouraged from developing an aptitude for correct risk evaluation.

The high gross earnings margin of banks undoubtedly accounted for a growth in profits, but to a great extent this was utilised to pay for a large increase in staff and investment costs sustained by the banks in the euphoria of liberalisation. Between 1977 and 1979, 100 new private banks were founded in Argentina (ADEBA, 1987). Some of these were set up using capital transferred to the more profitable financial sector from the agricultural and industrial sectors, where the worsening of terms of trade and the overvaluation of the exchange rate had brought about a lower rate of earnings (Caballo and Petrei, 1983). Others emerged from the transformation and concentration of the non-bank financial intermediaries born in the years of financial repression and progressively reabsorbed into the official system after liberalisation.

During the same period 868 banking subsidiaries were inaugurated, of which 817 were private banks. The number of employees remained stationary in the public (state) banks, whose share of the market had been declining. Employees in foreign banks went down, due to the introduction of technological innovations on a large scale, undertaken because of the favourable future prospects which the Argentinian economy seemed to offer. Private banks increased their labour force by over 30 per cent.

THE BUILD-UP TO 1980 AND BEYOND

At the beginning of 1980 the structure of the Argentinian banking system had undergone profound changes compared with 1977. The private banks – especially those with local capital – had increased their share of deposits from 54.2 per cent to 60.7 per cent and, to an even greater extent, their share of assets from 49.2 per cent to 58.6 per cent. The degree of concentration in the banking system had decreased considerably, due to the slower rate of development of large banks, for the most part public (state-owned). The importance of the five largest banks, in terms of deposits, declined in little more than three years from 37.8 per cent to 27.7 per cent, whilst the smaller banks increased their deposits from 31.4 per cent to 43.4 per cent (ADEBA, 1987)

The rapid growth of the private banking sector was, to a large extent, the consequence of an increased demand for financing both by households intent on covering increased expenses for consumer durables (especially imported ones) and by firms for whom the real negative cost of bank debt permitted a rapid increase in real rates of return on equity in the expansionary phase of industrial output in 1977 (Petrei and Tybout, 1985). From 1978, with the reduction of the inflation rate, the real lending rate increased to positive values. During this period when the real rate on dollar loans was between −40 per cent and −100 per cent, opportunities existed for firms to engage in profitable arbitrage on domestic and foreign interest rates as allowed by the *Tablita* in its initial form.

The recourse to financing in pesos became increasingly the means by which to acquire financial assets, particularly government bonds, whose market was just beginning to expand during this period, to use as collateral for dollar debts. The proceeds of the speculation on exchange rates constituted an essential component of the increased earnings of firms until 1979, and it fuelled the euphoria of the later 1970s (Petrei and Tybout, 1985). The popular story of the *bicicleta* – with which pesos, changed into dollars and then once more into pesos, were transferred from one bank to another – shows with dramatic immediacy the rapid transformation of this euphoria into the collective irrational 'overestimate of prospective returns' which Charles Kindleberger calls 'manias' or 'bubbles' (Kindleberger, 1978).

Even for foreign financiers Argentina became one of the most popular markets, due also to the recession under way in most developed countries. Speculative euphoria infected the large multinational banks where the high differential between interest rates in Argentina compared to those on the dollar and the overvaluation of the peso opened handsome profit opportunities.

In the last months of 1979 the domestic lending rate became positive and increased to levels of over 50 per cent in real terms (Petrei and Tybout, 1985). On the one hand, this increase discounted unfavourable forecasts on the government's ability to maintain the exchange rate schedule – which in the 1979 edition of the *Tablita* established a diminishing monthly rate of devaluation with respect to 1978 – and was thought to be incompatible with the sharp increase in government deficit. On the other hand, it also reflected the reduction in elasticity compared to the cost of the demand of firms for financing due to the progressive worsening of cash flow because of a growth in both wages and interest repayments greater than prices and earnings. The beginning of the economic recession, which was consolidated in 1980, and the growing political and social chaos further worsened the earnings of firms.

The banks did not use the increase in the lending rate as an instrument for selecting the most risky borrowers perhaps because, as has been argued above, public depositor's insurance reduced the incentives for a careful evaluation of liquidity and insolvency risks inherent in a qualitative deterioration of loans. It is more likely that the banks did not understand the real nature of such risks (Fernandez, 1983). The demand for credit continued to grow nevertheless, stimulating aggressive policies of liability management for the acquisition of deposits, which for the first time in decades obtained a real positive remuneration (Epstein, 1987). The BCRA rediscount was also used to a large extent.

The growth of leverage by firms was accentuated in 1980, when profits declined still further (Caballo and Petrei, 1983). The vicious circle of 'growing indebtedness, falling earnings' which often precedes the beginning of the financial crises was by now well-established. The spread of cases of insolvency along the chain of debts obtained to cover other debts, transferred the crises from the firms to the banking system and from the banking system to the government and the BCRA.

When the crisis exploded, the BCRA did not intervene quickly enough in favour of the troubled banks in its role of lender-of-last-resort, but tried mainly to fulfil its duties as regards depositor's insurance. The conditions of the banks in trouble would presumably not have allowed any other alternative. This behaviour, however, emphasised the lack of faith in the banks and in the BCRA itself, making the grave defects in contemporary banking supervision visible to both public opinion and international finance (Diáz-Alejandro, 1985). The expectation that when controls became more stringent the number of banks declared insolvent would increase, showed itself to be well founded. Panic spread amongst small and large depositors, triggering the *corrida bancaria* and massive flights of capital (Canitrot, 1981). The 'dollarisation' of the economy was enormously accentuated (Dornbusch, 1986).

THE NEW REFORMS

The management of the banking crisis was not the explicit objective of the new phase of financial repression which began in 1982, after the South Atlantic war, and which was included in the Austral Plan of 1985. The most important problem for the new government was inflation, which by this time had reached 700 per cent. It was not realised that the country's financial crisis was, to a large extent, the consequence of the, by now, chronic banking crisis.

Financial protectionism was not, as in 1946, directed to the import-substituting industries but to the State and, to a lesser degree, to the agricultural exporting sector and the large corporations both private and public. The instruments used were those already experimented with between 1957 and 1975: the increase in the minimum reserve requirements and the distribution of BCRA rediscounts at rates much lower than market rates. The discretionary margins of BCRA controls over the various parts of the banking system were, however, much more stringent on this occasion.

The banks were allowed to acquire a gradually increasing percentage of term deposits at an uncontrolled rate, which up until 1987 were also exempt from reserve requirements. These did not carry public insurance, which was reserved for deposits at a controlled rate (ADEBA, 1987).

This reform, passed in 1982 and still in force, probably had two objectives: on the one hand that of limiting the shift of risks of bank insolvency (the consequence of ill-considered policies of liability management) on to the BCRA. The other objective was that of encouraging growth in the efficiency of the banking system through keeping an area of potential competition alive within it.

These objectives would have been carried out more efficaciously by putting depositor's insurance under conditions of more rigorous banking supervision. This was deemed impracticable in Argentina. Continual changes in banking regulations caused by institutional and economic instability absorbed enormous resources in terms of manpower and time at the BCRA (BCRA, 1985). Controls over banking activities were, therefore, on the whole bureaucratic and administrative. Even the required solvency and liquidity ratios were often waived with the BCRA's consent (Diáz-Alejandro, 1985).

The 1982 reform aimed at delegating control over banking stability and efficiency to the selection of depositors, who might choose uncontrolled interest rate deposits only if the higher return compensated for the greater risk involved in the lack of public depositor's insurance. If this risk were judged too high, the depositors would have put a sort of credit rationing into practice with respect to the less solvent banks. Experience between

1982 and 1987 showed this hypothesis to be false. The search for depositors continued to be carried out by banks generally who saw their liquidity threatened both by firms' failure to pay back loans in a period of severe economic recession, and by the growing drains on the monetary base through reserve and portfolio requirements.

Bank operating costs increased owing to the growth of idle productive capacity caused by the reduction in intermediation and the domonetisation of the economy (BCRA, 1985). Depositors rationed the supply of funds to the banking system, promptly moving from uncontrolled deposits to controlled ones, and in particular from private banks to public ones when new explosions of the crisis were anticipated. The instability of monetary flows led to a high degree of variability in the monetary multiplier, in balances in the *Cuenta de Regulación Monetaria,* and in the demand for BCRA rediscount by the banks (Ground, 1984).

From 1985 to 1986 the management of rediscount policy became a formidable instrument for discretionary intervention in the banking system: it was used by the BCRA to further financial protectionism. The state banks whose credit was, to a large extent, traditionally reserved for the 'privileged' sectors – the State, large firms, the agricultural sector – were the principal recipients of the BCRA rediscount at facilitated rates (Epstein, 1987).

Consequently, not only were private companies 'crowded out' owing to the growing State absorption of resources, implemented mainly through the increase in the required reserves on deposits (on average around 40 per cent between 1982 and 1987), but the private banks were also crowded out by State banks. The latter increased their share of deposits from 39.3 per cent to 52.8 per cent between 1979 and 1986. The increase in their share of loans was even greater, from 41.4 per cent to 68.6 per cent, financed for over 35 per cent by the BCRA facilitated rediscount (Morgan Guaranty Trust, 1986).

The new banking crisis, unlike that of 1980–82 which was, to a large extent, the result of this radical structural change in the Argentinian financial system, led to the suspension of banking licences or the liquidation of 52 private banks despite costly salvage operations by the BCRA between 1985 and 1987. Among these casualties were some of the oldest and most prestigious banks in the country, such as the Banco de Crédito Argentino, the Banco Español, the Banco de Italia y del Rio de La Plata (ADEBA, 1987).

THE FUTURE

It is difficult from the data we have at our disposal to evaluate whether this change improved banking efficiency and stability. The support of a healthy and efficient banking system is indispensable today to Argentina in order to overcome, even in the long run, the foreign debt crisis without causing it to lose its independence and freedom to choose its own social and economic policies. The Argentinian banking system has declined from $15.5 billion in deposits in 1979 to $6.5 billion in 1987 and relies today, for almost 50 per cent, on state banking institutions. These in turn base their operations on the backing of the BCRA, thanks to which their loan/deposit ratio reached the figure of 110 per cent at the end of 1986 (BCRA, 1987). But this financial crisis, which has been an insolvency crisis of the entire country, can by no means be considered finished even today.

References

ADEBA (1987) *Saneamento de Bancos* (Buenos Aires: Lanus de la Serna y As.).

Alhadeff, P. (1985) 'Public finance and the economy in Argentina, Australia and Canada during the depression of the 1930s', in D. C. M. Platt and G. Di Tella (eds), *Argentina, Australia and Canada. Studies in Comparative Development, 1870–1965* (Oxford: Macmillan) pp. 161–74.

BCRA (1980–85) *Memoria Anual* (Buenos Aires: Banco Central de la República Argentina).

BCRA (1987) *Estado de las Entidades Financieras*, Julio (Buenos Aires: Banco Central de la República Argentina).

Caballo, D. F. and A. H. Petrei (1983) 'Financing private business in an inflationary context: the experience of Argentina between 1967 and 1980', in P. B. Aspella, R. Dornbusch and M. Obstfeld (eds), *Financial Policies and the World Capital Market: The Problem of Latin American Countries* (Chicago: University Press).

Canavese, A. J. and L. Montuschi (1985) 'Inflation and the financing of alternative development strategies', in A. Gutowski, A. A. Arnaúdo and Scharrer Hans-Eckart (eds), *Financing Problems of Developing Countries* (London: Macmillan) pp. 115–36.

Canitrot, A. (1981) 'Teoria y practica del liberalismo. Politica antiinflacionaria y apertura economica en la Argentina', *Desarollo Económico*, 21 Julio-Setiembre, pp. 131–88.

Diáz-Alejandro, C. (1985) 'Good-bye financial repression, hello financial crash', *Journal of Development Economics*, 19, pp. 1-24.

Diáz-Alejandro, C. (1984) 'Latin American debt: I don't think we are in Kansas anymore', *Brookings Papers on Economic Activity*, 2, pp. 335–403.

Dornbusch, R. (1986) 'A new chance for Argentina', *Challenge*, January-February, pp. 15–20.

Epstein, E. C. (1987) 'Recent stabilization programs in Argentina, 1973–86', *World Development*, vol. 15, no. 8, pp. 991–005.

Feldman, E. V. (1980) 'Empleo, succursalismo y repression financiera en el sistema bancario argentino', *Ensayos Económicos*, no. 15, Setiembre, pp. 5-28.

Feldman, E. V. (1983) 'La crisis financiera Argentina: 1980–1982. Algunos comentarios', *Desarrollo Económico*, vol. 23, Octobre-Diciembre, pp. 449–55.

Fernandez, R. (1983) 'La crisis financiera Argentina: 1980–1982', *Desarrollo Económico*, vol. 23, Abril-Junio, pp. 79–84.

Fernandez, R. (1985) 'The expectations management approach to stabilization in Argentina during 1976–82, *World Development,* vol. 13, no. 8, pp. 871–92.
Gaba, E. (1981) 'La reforma financiera Argentina. Lecciones de una experiencia', *Ensayos Económicos*, no. 19, Setiembre, pp. 1–50.
Ground, R. L. (1984) 'Orthodox adjustment programmes in Latin America. A critical look at the policies of the International Monetary Fund', *Cepal Review*, no. 23, August, pp. 45–82.
Kindleberger, C. P. (1978) *Manias, Panics and Crashes. A History of Financial Crises* (London: Macmillan) chapter 3.
McKinnon, R. (1981) 'Financial repression and the liberalisation problem within less developed countries', in S. Grassman and E. Lundberg (eds), *The World Economic Order. Past and Prospects* (London: Macmillan) pp.365–86.
McKinnon, R. (1985) 'How to manage a repressed economy', in A. Gutowski, A. A. Arnaúdo and Scharrer Hans-Eckart (eds), *Financing Problems of Developing Countries* (London: Macmillan) pp. 182–209.
Morgan Guaranty Trust (1986) 'Growth and financial market reform in Latin America', *World Financial Markets*, April-May, pp. 1–11.
Petrei, A. U. and J. Tybout (1985) 'Microeconomic adjustments in Argentina during 1976–81: The importance of changing levels of financial subsidies', *World Development*, vol. 13, no. 8, pp. 949–67.
Shaw, E. S. (1973) *Financial Deepening in Economic Development* (New York: Oxford University Press) chapter 4.

Part III
Money and Capital Markets

A great deal of change in financial systems has been concerned specifically with money and capital markets. Developments in monetary policy, competition, deregulation and technology have been amongst the factors that have altered institutional structures and policies in many developed financial markets. During the 1980s attention has also focused on capital markets with Big Bang in London and a sequence of 'Little Bangs' around the globe. Part III addresses some of these changes, with a particular emphasis on the United Kingdom. Chapter 6 examines the issues associated with financial indexation using UK indexed gilts as a case study. Charles Goodhart opens Chapter 6 by referring to indexation as a change in market practice virtually unanimously recommended by the world's greatest economists, but firmly resisted by practical men in authority (notably central bank governors). The following Chapter 7 is a wide-range survey of recent developments in the money markets. Ray Shaw examines the new UK monetary arrangements and the implications (especially regulatory and supervisory) of Big Bang for achieving stable and competitive markets. Chapter 8 reports some recent empirical research on the motives of small firms in using the USM (Unlisted Securities Market) in the United Kingdom. Roger Buckland and Ted Davis suggest that the image of a 'financing gap' – first popularised in the 1931 Macmillan Committee – is now a simplified view of reality.

6 UK Indexed Gilts: A Case Study of Financial Indexation

Charles Goodhart

WHY ACADEMICS AND CENTRAL BANKERS HOLD DIFFERENT VIEWS

What change of market practice has a whole series of the world's greatest economists, such as Jevons, Marshall, Irving Fisher, Keynes and Milton Friedman, virtually unanimously recommended; a change which practical men in authority, notably Central Bank Governors, have generally firmly resisted as far as they could and have only adopted with the utmost reluctance? The answer is a move to index contracts, especially long-term contracts, for example wages, tax brackets and financial contracts.

Economists consider that there are only very limited costs in a fully anticipated inflation, to which all expectations and institutional arrangements (such as accounting practices) had fully adjusted. They reduce to the so-called menu costs of having to change prices more frequently (the higher is the known rate of inflation), the informational costs of working out the appropriate price adjustments and the costs arising from the supposed technical inability to pay interest on currency.[1] The latter cost induces the public to economise on cash holdings, thereby increasing transaction costs (shoe-leather costs), and imposes a tax on their existing currency holding, thus reducing their wealth. Against this, the increase in government revenue from seignorage (that is from the inflation tax) may allow some reduction in other distortionary taxes and the substitution out of currency into other assets may marginally reduce real interest rates, the so-called Tobin effect.[2]

The fact that *fully* anticipated inflation would be relatively painless is, perhaps, less paradoxical than it seems, since if the authorities really could *control* the continuing pace of inflation so exactly, they could also reduce it to a zero rate by a fairly simple currency reform, as Leijonhufvud has pointed out.[3] Accordingly it is fair to regard any inflation as occurring because the authorities are not fully in control – a key point whose implications will be further considered at a later stage. Since inflation is, by assumption, not under full control, equally it cannot be perfectly forecast or anticipated.

In contrast to the limited cost of anticipated inflation, the costs of unanticipated inflation are large. These have been tabulated at some length in the paper by Fischer and Modigliani: 'Toward an understanding of the real effects and costs of inflation'.[4] Although in many cases the losses from unanticipated inflation (for example to lenders) are matched by unexpected windfalls (for example to borrowers), the additional uncertainty is disliked by risk averse agents. Agents should, however, be able to avoid such additional uncertainty by agreeing to write their contracts in indexed form. After all, rational agents should be concerned with real outcomes. Why then are contracts not written in indexed form, which would allow the bargain to be established in a real form, undisturbed by nominal shocks to the price level? In practice, we observe relatively few indexed contracts except in countries suffering from extremely high inflation running into three figures. Why should this not occur when the advantages seem so obvious?

One argument is that the uncertainty about inflation over the next few months, perhaps as far as a year ahead, is relatively low in most countries not subject to war, political crisis or continuing hyperinflation, so that the benefits from indexation would be too few to make it worthwhile drawing up a more complicated contract.[5] Such administrative costs would be greatest where indexation was unfamiliar and the main institutional arrangements, such as taxation and accountancy, were all maintained on a nominal basis.[6] But as McCallum (see note 5) notes, 'this argument does not predict that there will be no linkage [of contracts to price indices] or indexation. On the contrary, it suggests that the benefits of linkage would outweigh the costs in the case of large contracts of long duration – mortgages for instance'.

A reason why one might have expected indexation to be most prevalent in long-term financial instruments is that these are the vehicle primarily used by savers to accumulate wealth over the earning period of their life-cycle in order to finance their consumption, for example out of pensions, in old age. In practice, the wage earner has the power to adjust wages fairly closely to inflation; in addition, tax rates, even when not formally indexed, have been generally adjusted discretionally in reasonable conformity to inflation. But the old have had no such protection. The case in equity for providing the pensioner with a safe asset which protects savings against the ravages of inflation has always been strong.

Yet, prior to the recent issue of indexed instruments by the UK authorities in the form of National Savings 'Granny bonds' in 1975 and indexed marketable gilts in 1981, the number of examples of such indexed financial instruments, other than in countries suffering extremely high inflation, has been remarkably limited.[7] The most extensive usage of index-linked bonds, other than in countries with hyperinflation, was in Finland from 1947 onwards, comprising some three-quarters of all government bonds and most of the outstanding bonds of financial institutions by the end of the 1960s. In France during the politically and financially disturbed period of the 1960s, there was fairly extensive indexing of public and private fixed interest securities. By 1957 about 55 per cent of outstanding French public bonds were index-linked while index-linked issues accounted for 80 per cent of all private bonds issued in 1954. In 1958, however, when the New Franc was created under the stabilisation programme introduced after the devaluation of that year, the government banned most forms of indexation.[8] Indeed it has been common for the authorities to draw back from all forms of indexation, including indexation of financial instruments, as a component of a determined, counter-inflationary stabilisation programme. Following their experience of hyper-inflation in the 1920s and again after the Second World War, the German authorities became adamantly opposed to any form of indexation. Even in cases where the inflation rate was so high that some form of indexed protection became unavoidable, the authorities generally looked on its adoption with regret and reluctance.[9]

One reason why the private sector has not introduced index-linking has been the opposition of the authorities to such contracts. On other occasions, the absence of inflation adjustments in the tax system has served as a barrier. Thus, the ability of borrowers in the United Kingdom to treat all nominal interest payments as a business expense, chargeable against tax even if much of such interest payments merely offset the effect of (anticipated) inflation in eroding the real value of the principal, has served as a disincentive to the issue of standard forms of indexed debt.[10]

This once again serves to draw attention to the question of why the authorities have been so opposed to indexation in practice, even including indexation of financial instruments where the equity argument is particularly strong. The argument has rested partly on historical experience. There are, however, a number of more analytical considerations. Firstly, standard models (see Fischer, 'Wage indexation and macroeconomic stability') show that indexation protects output and employment in the face of nominal shocks but destabilises them in the face of real shocks.[11] Academic economists, especially monetarists, tend to perceive and to criticise nominal shocks induced by misguided government policies. Governments naturally tend to believe that their policies are optimal and often see the fluctuations in nominal magnitudes as largely resulting from a (passive) reaction to external (real) shocks. Thus, the perceptions of the authorities and of academic economists about the relative incidence of real and nominal shocks on the economy are likely to be markedly different.

Secondly, just as academic economists often accuse the monetary authorities of adopting time-inconsistent policies, so the authorities may tend to believe that the private sector would pursue time-inconsistent preferences. Thus, inflation is frequently perceived by the public as a more serious problem than unemployment but the short-term costs of disinflation deter them from being prepared to accept the necessary medicine. Fischer and Huizenga in their paper 'Inflation, unemployment and public opinion polls'[12] note 'the apparently inconsistent result that inflation is generally supposed to be the more serious problem, while it is preferred that policy be directed at reducing unemployment'. If the short-run costs of inflation are made less by indexation, the temptation would be enhanced for the private sector and the electorate to vote for, and to support, policies aimed at short-run reductions in unemployment at the expense of the longer-term, and much worse, combination of unemployment and inflation. Central bankers' fear of indexation may, therefore, be partly due to a belief that the private sector often expresses a myopic and irrational preference for the soft option, and that indexation is a recipe for making that soft option seem softer yet.

Thirdly, as noted earlier, the occurrence of inflation does represent some loss of control by the authorities, whether due to a real shock, such as the oil shocks in 1973 and 1979, union power, or to a failure to operate monetary policy effectively. The effect of indexation is to reduce the inertia, owing to wage/price stickiness, whereby shocks are only passed onto prices in partial form with the remainder of the effect falling on real output. If there are adverse shocks tending to increase inflation, whether nominal or real, the effect of indexation is to exacerbate the purely inflationary effects of such shocks. Without indexation, and in conditions of wage/price stickiness, the inflationary impulse is moderated by declines in real wealth, by falls in real wages, and so on. Now, if the government did have *complete control* over events, it could induce deflationary nominal shocks (for example by reducing the money stock) with a minimal impact on real output; indexation would then enhance the desired effect in reducing inflation. Following this line of reasoning, Milton Friedman advocated indexation plus monetary restriction as an appropriate counter-inflationary policy. But the very existence of inflation reveals that conditions, perhaps a series of adverse supply shocks, perhaps political circumstances, have weakened the power of the authorities to control events. Adverse shocks likely to exacerbate inflation must therefore be seen as more probable, and the ability of the government to maintain a disinflationary policy more doubtful. If inflation is seen as a symptom of loss of governmental control, then the case for a policy such as indexation, which exacerbates the adverse effects of such control failures and depends for its beneficial effects on the authorities regaining full and appropriate control, must be called into question. The academic argument for indexation seems to depend in part on the academic's view that the same government could and would simultaneously be able and willing to introduce those demand management policies and/or rules that the academic believes appropriate.

In reality, governments are subject to 'political' pressures that constrain their actions. Central bankers are painfully aware of this and of the corollary that indexation can be a highly dangerous instrument.

The most extreme example of circumstances when political pressures tend to constrain governments occurs during wartime or civil strife. Lack of power and doubts about the government's future viability may make it harder for the authorities to borrow or to raise taxes. Resort to the printing press may then provide their only, or best, alternative source of finance. Indexation reduces the opportunity for governments to benefit from an inflationary tax by reducing the volume of additional real resources the government can attract from the private sector through printing an additional nominal value of currency and by pushing inflation rapidly up to such a level that the flight from currency will offset the inflation tax gains. Some right-wing commentators believe that the common dislike of governments for indexation is due to the fact that it blunts their ability to manipulate such an inflation tax. I believe that this is wrong. Given the public's vociferously expressed dislike of inflation, it would rarely be in any government's interest consciously to choose to inflate. Instead, circumstances place weak governments in positions where they cannot avoid inflationary shocks. This may seem a fine distinction but it lies, I believe, at the root of the difference of view between academics advocating indexation and the authorities, notably central bankers, resisting it.

The above arguments are directed against indexation in general. The authorities in the United Kingdom have usually tended to assess the various benefits of, and the strengths of the arguments against, indexation as differing depending on the particular contract under consideration. As already noted, the argument in equity, that is for need for protection from unanticipated inflation, seems strongest in the case of the provision of inflation-hedged financial instruments for pensioners and conversely weakest in the case of wage earners, who are in a much better position to protect themselves from the ravages of inflation. Again, concern about indexation reinforcing adverse inflationary shocks was greatest in the case of wages and less so in the case of financial instruments, especially since actual nominal interest payments would be lower in the early years of the life of an indexed instrument and so could not be held to have increased input costs or the need for additional borrowing. This dislike of wage indexation was much enhanced by the disastrous experience with Prime Minister Edward Heath's policy of indexing wages beyond a threshold in 1973. The subsequent oil price shock triggered the thresholds and so an external, real shock generated an internal wage/price spiral that was worse than in virtually any other country.

The authorities in the United Kingdom have tended to prefer those forms of indexation that eased their own financial management problems and disliked those that added to government expenditures. Thus, they have implicitly created a decreasing order of merit for indexation which, in the early 1980s, could be ranked approximately as follows:

1. Financial instruments restricted to old-age pensioners
2. Long-term financial contracts
3. Taxation
4. Pensions
5. Government expenditures
6. Wages

The extent of difference between the cases for indexation in these separate contracts was felt to be sufficiently marked that, during the early 1980s, the Conservative government was taking steps to try to *de-index* government expenditures by forcing departmental programmes to return to a nominal, in place of the previous real, basis and to limit the indexation of public sector pay; at exactly the same time, it was extending the range of indexation on financial instruments and taxation.

This was not illogical; it was simply that the strength of the arguments, pro and con, varied depending on the contract or market under consideration. Nevertheless, a primary concern in each case for any further step to extend indexation to contracts or markets at the top of the merit table was that it should not weaken the case for restricting and withdrawing indexation for contracts or markets at the bottom of the table. This was known as the 'contagion' or 'spreading' argument. Faced with a choice between a fully indexed system and a completely unindexed system, the authorities throughout the 1970s and 1980s (up to the present, at least) in the United Kingdom would have chosen the latter. However, in those cases where 'contagion' was thought to be a remote danger and the benefits of indexation were greatest, the authorities were prepared to consider such cases favourably.

I shall not deal further with the arguments relating to indexation of items 3-6 of the merit table but, in the following section, I shall concentrate on the discussions concerning financial indexation in the United Kingdom over the last two decades.

THE UK EXPERIENCE IN THE 1970S AND 1980S

The possibility of issuing indexed financial instruments was raised on a number of occasions after the Second World War, notably during periods of worsening inflation, which often coincided with times when it proved difficult for the authorities to sell conventional nominal instruments, both non-marketable National Savings and marketable bonds (gilts). The subject first, I believe, arose here in 1950/51. The issue next recurred forcefully in 1974 due to the inflationary climate at the time.

This had several facets. Firstly, the Page Committee appointed to review national savings advocated the introduction of indexed national savings and suggested an outline scheme.[13] Largely because of fears of 'contagion', the government did not make such instruments as widely available as Page had advocated but they did introduce two restricted instruments in 1975. The first of these was an index-linked National Savings Certificate which could be purchased only by retired persons (men over 65 and women over 60); this became known as the 'Granny bond'. The second was an indexed Save As You Earn instrument. Both had ceilings on the amount that could be invested. The sums subsequently invested in such instruments were sizeable at times but only between the fiscal years 1979/80 and 1981/2 did they represent a really major source of government finance, despite periodic relaxations in the age and ceiling restrictions (see Table 6.1).

Besides the particular case for providing an inflation-hedged financial asset for the old age pensioner (OAP), the 1974 upsurge in inflation led to a more general reawakening of interest in indexation. The National Institute of Economic and Social Research devoted much of their November 1974 *National Institute Economic Review* to four papers on various aspects of indexation, and discussed the advantages that could be expected from either a voluntary or a statutory programme of indexation. The arguments for indexation in general, and for encouraging indexed financial instruments to be issued either by the private or public sectors, were taken up and supported in the Press, notably by the influential commentators, Anthony Harris and Samuel Brittan in the *Financial Times*.

Of more immediate relevance to *financial* indexation, the rise in nominal interest rates to over 10 per cent during 1973 had made company treasurers unwilling to float additional conventional debt issues in the UK corporate bond market. This led some innovative characters in the private sector to wonder whether an index-linked issue might be a possible viable alternative source of debt finance and the authorities' reactions were sounded.

The reactions were negative. There were a number of reasons for this. The views of most European official colleagues, expressed in various OECD and EEC Committees, were firmly, and in some cases vehemently, opposed to financial indexation. Current nominal interest rates were then extraordinarily negative in real terms and there were fears that the introduction of an indexed bond with a guaranteed positive real rate, if held to maturity, might somehow (the discussion was a bit confused) drive up interest rates on conventional nominal bonds. There were concerns that the issue of index-linked bonds would require changes in, or put added adverse public pressure on, the non-indexed status of current taxes, such as capital gains tax, which the authorities were not then ready to accept. But above all, following the disastrous 1973 experiment with partial wage

Table 6.1 Net inflows into index-linked National Savings 1975/6 to 1986/7[1] (£ million)

	1975 /76	1976 /77	1977 /78	1978 /79	1979 /80	1980 /81	1981 /82	1982 /83	1983 /84	1984 /85	1985 /86	1986 /87[3]
Net inflow in financial year												
Index-linked NS certificates	246	255	234	268	749	1285	2095	−127	−221	−278	−198	−406
Index-linked SAYE	25	89	88	109	128	130	104	−28	−12	−33	−106	−86
A Total index-linked	271	344	322	377	877	1415	2199	−155	−233	−311	−304	−492
Total net inflow to National Savings												
B(i) as published	500	994	1094	1618	968	2239	4244	3036	3278	3071	2106	3365
B(ii) adjusted for comparability[2]	408	992	1861	1444	1374	2504						
C PSBR	10253	8304	5373	9235	10020	12687	8632	8844	9745	10195	5751	3447
A as percentage of B(ii)	66.4	34.7	17.3	26.1	63.8	56.5	52.1	−5.1	−7.1	−10.1	−14.4	−14.6
A as percentage of C	2.6	4.1	6.0	4.1	8.8	11.2	25.5	−1.8	−2.4	−3.0	−5.3	−14.3

Notes:
1 Main source *Financial Statistics* (1987), table 39.
2 The adjusted figure includes net inflows to the NSB Investment Account throughout (it was treated as an OFI until December 1980).
3 Part estimated.

indexation, the argument that any further steps towards indexation beyond the tightly restricted National Savings instruments might give rise to possibilities of contagion won the day.

Whereas the flurry of excitement and discussion about financial indexation in 1974/75 was largely concerned with the provision of private sector indexed bonds, the next bout of interest in this general topic in autumn 1976, was primarily concerned with the possibility of issuing indexed public-sector gilts. The structure of the London capital market then, with weakly capitalised brokers and (few) jobbers,[14] was such that the authorities felt obliged to maintain a 'tap' system of issues, whereby new issues were made at prices closely in line with market prices on the announcement date. If gilt prices then rose, the new issue might be oversubscribed; if prices fell after the announcement date, there would be few outside buyers and the Bank of England would take the bulk of the issue onto its own books and peddle the issue out again, that is on 'tap', as and when the market showed signs of strengthening. Whatever the advantages of this method, and they were considerable given the structure of the market, it did mean that the authorities found that their debt sales varied between feast and famine. The latter was particularly likely when fears of worsening inflation led to a weak gilts market. Furthermore, in the mid-1970s much greater attention was being paid to the growth of the monetary aggregates. Since debt sales were then, in practice, the authorities' main instrument for restricting monetary growth, a debt sales famine led to faster monetary growth. This could lead, and was accused of so leading in 1976, to the following vicious spiral:

Worsening inflationary fears (from some shock) → debt sales famine → faster monetary growth → worsening inflationary fears → debt sales famine → etc.

The argument for indexation of gilts in 1976 was that they could be sold when conventional debt could not, thereby breaking the spiral. Moreover, the collapse of the exchange rate in 1976 was reviving inflationary fears and commentators were again pressing the merits of indexation. There was now, however, another counter-argument to add to the previous list. If it was the authorities who would be issuing the indexed debt, how would this affect the ability of companies to raise additional funds from capital markets? Companies might be unable or unwilling to follow the authorities' example and raise indexed debt. With the conventional corporate debt market closed, their only other alternative was new equity issues. But might the issue of indexed debt adversely affect equity prices? Equities had proved a poor inflation hedge; with the availability of a better hedge, might not savers, especially the long-term savings institutions, life insurance and pension funds, pour out of equities into indexed gilts?[15] Might the company sector's financing options be adversely affected then by the introduction of indexed gilts?

The possibility of issuing an indexed bond was not, however, the only innovation under consideration for operational use in the gilts market at that time. Two other ideas were floated, a variable interest bond and a convertible, which allowed investors at some future date to opt for a short maturity if inflation and nominal interest rates rose, or a long maturity if the reverse occurred, on terms set out in the prospectus. Both would provide partial protection for investors against unanticipated inflation. It was felt that these might be saleable in conditions when pure nominal conventional bonds were not saleable; moreover, they did not involve or carry with them the more radical implications, or 'spreading' dangers, which many feared from the introduction of indexed-linked gilts. Accordingly, the decision was taken to proceed with these two new forms of gilt, leaving an indexed issue on one side to be reconsidered perhaps if inflationary pressures and monetary control problems worsened.

In the event, the UK economy recovered, the exchange rate strengthened and monetary and inflationary fears eased somewhat in 1977. Although there remained an undercurrent of interest in the question of issuing indexed gilts, the next major bout of official discussion and analysis of the topic did not occur until 1980. Once again the authorities were having difficulty in maintaining monetary control in a regime which now, under the new Conservative government, was placing the utmost emphasis on targeting M3. Periods of bond sale famine or buyers' strikes were even less welcome. It was widely recognised that unfamiliar instruments, such as indexed gilts, would have to be issued by tender auction: there was no existing established market to enable a 'tap' price to be set. Some saw the introduction of tenders of indexed gilts as a means of getting a firmer quantitative grip over the time-path of public sector debt sales.

Moreover, nominal bond yields at all maturities rose in 1979/80 to high levels, though not as high as the year-on-year increase in the RPI which was temporarily inflated by the sharp rise in VAT rates from 8 to 15 per cent in the June 1979 Budget, by the 1979 oil shock, and the collapse of the previous incomes policy restraint on public sector wages. In any case, 10-year bond rates were running at 13.7 per cent at end-June 1980 and the RPI was 21 per cent up on the past year. By then the government had unveiled the Medium Term Financial Strategy (MTFS) in March 1980, intending to reduce inflation determinedly by a steady, gradual reduction in M3. If inflation was to be thus controlled, was not the current high level of medium and long-term interest rates out of line with the government's firm intentions? Would not such borrowing, on conventional terms, prove excessively expensive, and would not the continuation of such borrowing appear to contradict the government's own professed confidence in the reduction of future inflation?

In fact, calculations of the comparative cost of conventional and indexed borrowing did not show such a large advantage for the latter, on the assumption of at least partial success in combating inflation, as might have been superficially expected. Current conventional rates were negative in real terms again. Moreover, the high nominal interest rate was taxable. For investors paying, say, a rate of 40 per cent tax on interest income, the post-tax real rate on conventionals was again markedly negative. Depending on the average tax rate assumed for investors, the inflation rate had to be expected to fall fairly fast to quite low levels to make the predicted cost to the government of issuing indexed bonds cheaper.

With the comparative-cost argument turning out to be less clear-cut than initially expected, much turned on views of how the general public would perceive the step. Would the issue of indexed gilts be received as a sign of contra-inflationary confidence, for example by reducing the benefits from future unanticipated inflation,[16] or might they be viewed as a measure to ease the stress of living with inflation, a prelude to giving up the battle? While presentational conditions were considered important, for example that they should not be issued until the rate of change of the year-on-year figure for the RPI had turned downwards and monetary conditions appeared under better control, the counter-inflationary determination of the government was so patent that the confidence effects could be expected to be beneficial.

Among the authorities' counter-inflationary policy measures were steps aimed to *reduce* the ambit of indexation in other fields, such as government expenditures and possibly public sector pensions.[17] Moreover, the argument that those worried about contagion had expected to hear – that is, the claim that if the rentier's (bond holder's) real income is to be hedged against (unanticipated) inflation, then so should be the income streams of other income recipients, such as wage earners – was hardly raised at all in public commentary and discussion. The key counter-argument about contagion was fading.

Finally, there was a minor and largely cosmetic advantage for the presentation of government finances. The shift from conventional to indexed gilts – assuming an *exactly equal* ex-post cost – reduced recorded interest payments, especially in the earlier years, and these were included in the CGBR and PSBR. This was achieved at the expense of much larger maturities in the later years but, under existing statistical accounting practice, these latter did *not* affect the size of the PSBR. Thus, the switch could cause a quite sizeable cosmetic improvement in the appearance of government finances.

Against these putative benefits, the general argument about contagion, though now weakened, could still be made. Concern about the effect on equity prices and on private sector corporate financing opportunities remained, as it had earlier in 1976. Moreover, in part associated with the question of allowing the private sector to compete on level terms in the issue of indexed bonds, their issue would highlight the embarrassing fact that capital gains tax was being levied on purely inflationary, not real, price rises. There would seem to be some likelihood of indexation spreading into further parts of the tax system.

The major new objection to indexation in 1980 came, however, from the external side. There were reports that OPEC was pressing both for the indexation of oil prices and for the availability of indexed financial instruments in which to invest. Certain OECD countries were opposed, often vehemently, to indexation in general and to OPEC's floated ideas in particular. The United Kingdom might be seen to be breaking ranks. More important, the availability of this new form of financial instrument, an indexed bond issued by a major country with a broad and liquid capital market, was considered possibly attractive to non-residents. At that juncture, however, the sterling exchange rate was already under great upward pressure due to a combination of North Sea oil and tight counter-inflationary policies, and the prospects of a further boost to the rate were unpalatable, perhaps the more so in view of the extreme uncertainty about how large such inflows and the resulting appreciation might be.

In the event, the two concerns relating to the external effect and to the tax implications, were side-stepped by restricting the investors eligible to take up the indexed issue[18] to a limited class of eligible holders, that is UK pension funds and life insurance companies undertaking pension business. Since these counted as 'gross funds' not subject to tax on income or capital gains, there were no consequential tax implications. The first issue was for £1 billion and the demand at the tender was such that it sold at par with a coupon of 2 per cent. Subsequently, real yields on all gilts, including indexed gilts (IGs) rose. The appetite of institutional investors for indexed gilts was less than had been expected and there was diminishing enthusiasm at the subsequent two tenders for such restricted IGs, £1000 million of IG 2006 in July 1981 and £750 million of IG 2011 in January 1982.

So there was a market reason (to encourage a wider demand) for relaxing the eligibility restrictions. More important, by the winter of 1981/82, the sterling exchange rate was sinking back quite fast from its earlier peaks; the world at large had not taken much notice or made much fuss about this experiment; finally, the Chancellor of the Exchequer was preparing to extend indexation in fiscal matters, notably to capital gains tax in his 1982 Budget. So, at a stroke, all the arguments for restriction fell away and it was removed in that Budget.

Indexed gilts were then available for all to buy and no limitations were imposed that would prevent private sector borrowers from following suit. Many of those engaged in the debates up to this point had felt that it was an important step with potentially large unknown implications. The somewhat surprising impression in the subsequent years is, instead, how little change this step has made. The demand for IGs, both by residents and – as far as can be ascertained – by non-residents has been patchy and the issue of IGs has raised approximately £12 billion, out of total gilt issues of £96 billion between March 1980 and March 1987.[19] Perhaps this was due to the fact that, at times when inflation is coming down quite sharply, IGs tend to under-perform conventionals. What might happen to the balance between IGs and conventionals if inflation was to rekindle has yet to be seen. Be that as it may, the issue of IGs had less effect on debt management overall than the changing attitudes towards over-funding and the structural changes to the capital market caused by Big Bang in October 1986.[20]

Moreover, the authorities' lead has been resolutely ignored by the private sector. By summer 1987, no company had attempted an indexed issue, though some had given the subject some thought. Given the availability of a safe indexed asset to hold, one might have expected financial intermediaries to issue indexed liabilities that would still seem to have some fiscal advantages. No steps in this direction have, however, yet appeared. Given the government's lead and the removal of barriers, the remaining reservations that the private sector apparently feel about financial indexation such as the difficulty of choice of appropriate price index, legal complexity, and so on, are quite unclear. The potentially explosive charge has turned into a damp squib.

One final word of warning is perhaps necessary. The existence of indexed debt is often taken to provide a good estimate of longer-term future inflationary expectations, for example by subtracting the calculated real yield on IGs from the yield on conventionals. To start with, the calculation of the real yield on the IG is complicated by the administratively necessary link to a slightly *lagged* RPI change. Next, the structural changes to the eligibility rules 1981/2 make the calculation particularly fraught in the early years. The patchy nature of demand and occasional tenders led to market price movements in the short run that have had little relationship to underlying inflationary expectations. The tax position of IG holders will differ from short to long maturities and, in general, will *not* be the same as that of holders of conventional gilts, with the discrepancy probably greatest at the long end. Such tax considerations mean that the calculated differential will be sensitive to the coupon on the matched-maturity conventional and, of course, matched maturities will imply differing *durations*. Furthermore, inflationary expectations and risk aversion to (unanticipated) inflation are *not* homogeneous. IGs will attract those who are more fearful. A widening of the dispersion – with a constant mean expectation – could encourage demand for IGs. Similarly, a narrowing of the dispersion, for example after an election, could reduce the demand for IGs even without any change in mean expectations. Those attempting to use the IG/conventional yield spread as a proxy for inflation expectations should be aware of its limitations.

Notes

1. Both Huston McCulloch in his discussant's note, 'Beyond the historical gold standard', in C. D. Campbell and W. R. Dougan (eds), *Alternative Monetary Regimes* (Baltimore: Johns Hopkins University Press, 1986) p. 75, and I, in my paper, 'How can non-interest bearing assets co-exist with safe interest-bearing assets?', *British Review of Economic Issues*, vol. 8, no. 19, Autumn 1986, pp. 1–12, have argued that this technical problem could be overcome by offering lottery prizes, based on random drawings of the serial numbers of outstanding notes, so that the *expected* return on currency holding was the same as on other assets.
2. See J. Tobin and W. Buiter, 'Fiscal and monetary policies, capital formation, and economic activity', chapter 11 in J. Tobin, *Essays in Economics* (Cambridge, Mass: MIT Press, 1982).
3. A. Leijonhufvud wrote in 'Inflation and Economic Performance', mimeo, 1981, subsequently published as a 'Kieler Vortrag' pamphlet by the Institut für Weltwirtschaft (year unknown):

> The quick and painless way to end an anticipated inflation is a currency reform that I call the 'blueback' scheme. Since, under the assumed conditions, 'greenback' dollars depreciate in real purchasing power by 15 per cent a year, one could create a new 'blueback' currency and make it, by law, appreciate relative to greenbacks at 15 per cent per year. On the initial date the exchange rate between the two monies is one for one, but from that day onward bluebacks grow constantly in their legal capacity to extinguish debts contracted in greenbacks. One year later, 85 cents blueback will pay off a $1 greenback debt; two years later, it takes about 71 blueback cents; ten years later 19 cents.
>
> If the originally held expectations of constant 15 per cent greenback inflation of indefinite duration were indeed rational, then the blueback reform will ensure perfect price-level stability indefinitely. The scheme has two advantages over disinflation. First, employment is entirely unaffected. It is not necessary to suffer through a recession to get back to constant prices. Second, no one is swindled in the process. The real terms of contracts remain to be fulfilled as originally envisaged. The creditor who after 10 years received 19 cent blue, instead of $1 green, is getting exactly what he expected to get in real purchasing power.
>
> Both of these advantages of the currency reform over disinflation stem, of course, from the fact that nothing is really done about the greenback inflation. The rate of greenback inflation is not reduced at all; it is only made subject to an arithmetical conversion. It is a cheap trick, if you will. But it does not 'evade the real issue'. On the contrary, 'really doing something' about the greenback inflation would be an irrational, destructive policy under the conditions assumed. It is assumed that we start from a quite stable monetary standard which happens to have the somewhat

peculiar property that the money depreciates in real purchasing power at 15 per cent a year. To disinflate is to adopt a policy that is inconsistent with this system of expectations. It breaks the prevailing regime and wreaks havoc, therefore. The Blueback system, in contrast, merely removes the peculiar property of this stable regime.

In the text above, I ignored the inflation tax on real balances and its allocative effects. In the case where greenback money is being taxed at 15 per cent per annum, the blueback scheme introduces a new non-taxed money that will, therefore, immediately displace the old currency. Since the demand for real balances will be larger once money is no longer taxed, a larger nominal supply must be provided in order to avoid deflationary pressure on the blueback price-level and the associated, probable consequences for employment.

4. Originally published in *Weltwirtschaftliches Archiv,* 114 (4), 1978, pp. 810–32; reproduced as chapter 1, in S. Fischer, *Indexing, Inflation and Economic Policy* (Cambridge, Mass: MIT Press) 1986.
5. See B. McCallum, 'On "real" and "sticky-price" theories of the business cycle', *Journal of Money, Credit and Banking*, vol. 18,no. 4, November 1986, pp. 409–10.
6. Thus, Fischer, in *Indexing, Inflation and Economic Policy*, p. 154, suggests that:

> An issue worth further investigation is that of the possible existence of both indexed and non-indexed equilibria. Given that individuals typically want to be hedged, the incentive for an individual to introduce an indexed contract in a non-indexed economy may be small, and since money is used as both unit of account and medium of exchange, there is a bias toward the economy not being indexed. But if indexation is already extensive, the private incentives may be to use indexed contracts. This argument can be seen very clearly in the case of financial intermediaries, who would likely be willing to issue indexed liabilities if they could hold indexed assets. But it applies also to households, who would be more willing to borrow indexed short term if their incomes were indexed.

7. See, for example, S. Fischer, 'On the nonexistence of privately issued index bonds in the US capital market', originally published in *Inflation Theory and Anti-inflation Policy*, ed. E. Lundberg (London: Macmillan, 1977), reproduced as chapter 10 in Fischer, *Indexing, Inflation and Economic Policy*.
8. And the costly experience with the 1973 Rentes Giscard, which were indexed to gold, served to reinforce doubts about the wisdom of indexation.
9. Thus, in the *Evening Standard* 'City comment' of 2 December 1976, it was reported that Professor Simonsen, who had introduced financial indexation to Brazil, had stated that index-linked government stocks should be avoided:

> Professor Simonsen stated unequivocally that he would not recommend any country to embark on indexation if it could possibly avoid it, because it undoubtedly did build inflation more or less permanently into the system. If, however, you had got to the stage where something drastic had to be done, indexation was probably the least harmful choice.

10. This problem could be partially circumvented by the provision of a bond paying inflation compensated interest, that is a real interest rate of x% plus

an add-on for the actual recent rate of inflation. This is quite close to a variable rate instrument, except that in the latter bond the real rate may vary while in the proposed instrument it would be fixed. Such inflation compensating bonds were analysed and considered by both private sector bodies and by the authorities in the United Kingdom in the 1970s and 1980s but were not, in the event, introduced.

11. Originally published in *Stabilisation of the Domestic and International Economy*, Carnegie-Rochester Conference Series on Public Policy, vol. 5 (Amsterdam: North-Holland, 1977) pp. 107–48, reproduced as chapter 5 in Fischer, *Indexing, Inflation and Economic Policy*. Thus, from p. 164 in the latter: 'In summary, indexing shields real output from nominal disturbances by permitting constancy of the real wage in the face of such disturbances; indexing does not permit the stabilising effect on real wages that would otherwise result from price level movements when disturbances are real.
12. Originally published in *Journal of Money, Credit and Banking*, vol. 14, no. 1, February 1982, pp. 1–19, now reproduced as chapter 4 in Fischer, *Indexing, Inflation and Economic Policy*.
13. *Committee to Review National Savings*, Cmnd 5273 (London: HMSO, 1973) especially pp. 190–98.
14. For further details, see Goodhart, 'The structure of the London capital market', in *The Operation and Regulation of Financial Markets*, ed. C. Goodhart, D. Currie and D. Llewellyn (London: Macmillan, 1987).
15. For a theoretical treatment of this issue, see S. Fischer, 'The demand for index bonds', *Journal of Political Economy*, vol. 83, no. 3, June 1975, pp. 509–34, also reproduced as chapter 9 in Fischer, *Indexing, Inflation and Economic Policy*.
16. They were even described as 'sleeping policemen' to deter a future more inflationary government.
17. There was much adverse comment about the favoured (indexed) position of public sector pensions in relationship to unindexed private sector pensions, and it was widely thought that the government sympathised with that criticism and wished to curtail such indexation. They appointed the Scott Committee to consider this question, amongst other things, and its report not only supported the continuation of the indexation of civil servants' pensions but talked of extending it to the private sector. So, in the event, nothing was done.
18. Announced in the Budget of 1981, with simultaneous publication of prospectus, for tender on 27 March.

	Total	*of which index-linked*	*index-linked percentage*
1980–1	16084	346	2
1982–2	10904	2564	24
1982–3	10609	2234	21
1983–4	15674	2222	14
1984–5	15862	1623	10
1985–6	11648	825	7
1986–7	15028	2309	15

19. Cash receipts from issues of British government stocks by the National Loans Fund (£ million): main source, *Financial Statistics*, table 3.6.
20. See C. Goodhart, 'The economics of "Big Bang"', *Midland Bank Review*, Summer 1987, pp. 6–15.

7 Recent Developments in the Money Markets

Ray Shaw

INTRODUCTION

This chapter reviews the changes which have occurred in the UK money markets since 1983, with a particular emphasis on the discount houses and their relationship with the Bank of England and monetary policy. During this period the Bank has revised various aspects of monetary policy and operations in the market, but probably the single most significant event which occurred was the deregulation of the London financial markets on 27 October 1986, known as 'Big Bang'. So far the impact on the money markets has been relatively limited; the future, however, remains uncertain.

This chapter covers two broad areas: a review of the principal changes which have occurred in the role and structure of the discount market; monetary policy and the money market.

BACKGROUND

The changes which have emerged both leading up to and during the 'Big Bang' are likely to have far-reaching effects on the whole of the financial sector of the economy. The changes are much wider than just the securities market, affecting a whole variety of mechanisms for bringing borowers and lenders together through deposit and loan markets, or through markets in money instruments. The developments also affect a range of intermediaries such as discount houses, banks, building societies and stockbrokers and stockjobbers. Particular concerns have been voiced about the protection of investors, and the liquidity and solvency of the institutions taking part. There are arguably even greater concerns as to whether or not the world's capital and money markets can absorb the metamorphosis which is taking place without creating increased economic instability.

CHANGES IN THE ROLE AND STRUCTURE OF THE DISCOUNT MARKET

Money markets and capital markets – concepts

It is not unreasonable at the outset to pose the question, 'Is it possible to distinguish clearly between the money market and the capital market?' If this question had been posed ten or fifteen years ago, the answer would have been a more positive yes than it is today. In 1988, the position appears to be blurred, certainly from an institutional point of view, by the interchange which has taken place between a whole range of financial institutions which have accomplished strategic changes by extending their business activities and markets, and by introducing new monetary instruments which effectively overlap the short- and long-term markets for money.

Simply defined, a money market is a market for prime quality financial assets which are close substitutes for money and which mature in one year or less. Its basic function is identical to a capital market, namely, to maximise the satisfaction of financial asset holders and debt issuers. This function is performed through the exchange of money for new financial claims as well as financial claims already existing in the secondary market.

The capital market, however, is a market for financial assets other than money or near-money substitutes. It is a network of facilities which provides for the transfer of long-term claims and funds. It augments the flow of loanable funds and is a means of readjusting a given stock of financial assets and liabilities.

The arbitrary distinction which is drawn between the two markets is one of maturity, with the line being drawn at one year. The reason for this is that the true distinction between bills (short-term money) and bonds (long-term funds) is one of risk difference and transaction cost. Generally speaking, the transaction cost of refinancing short-term money is less than for long-term money. The two major risks are credit risk and money risk, and money market instruments are usually subject to far less risk than are capital market securities.

Credit risk is the risk that the borrower may be unable to meet commitments when they fall due. This risk is minimal in the money market because transactions are limited to prime quality borrowers over short periods of time. The dangers inherent in money risks in the capital markets have been well illustrated by the fall in world stock market prices in October 1987. Thus credit risk as well as money risk is considerably lower in the money market than the capital market.

This important distinction arises because the money market is more homogeneous than the capital market. The participants in the money market are simultaneously borrowers and lenders in the market – an institutional feature which closely ties together the participants in the various short-term money markets.

In the past the banking sector and dealers in government and other securities have played a significant role in welding the money and capital markets together; now the forces for change noted in the introduction to this chapter have accelerated and substantially increased this process of coalescence. Short-term funds are borrowed to finance the purchase and carrying of long-term assets, and long-term securities ultimately become money market instruments as they approach maturity. The position is examplified by various commercial paper and multi-option facilities such as note issuance facilities (NIFs) and revolving underwriting facilities (RUFs).

Commercial paper in the United Kingdom[1] may be issued for maturities ranging from 7 days to 364 days but typically in practice is seldom issued beyond six months. It is sold by dealers on a best-efforts basis and is not underwritten.

By contrast, multi-option facilities are normally underwritten by a group of banks, usually for a period of five to seven days. Under these facilities the company issues short-term paper and, if funds are not forthcoming at competitive rates, the back-up facility is activated.

Such transactions constitute securitisation of company debt and provide companies, in effect, with a long-term agreement to meet part of their funding needs through short-term paper.

The second part of this chapter, dealing with monetary policy and the money markets, includes further comment and discussion of difficulties which have arisen for the authorities (see section headed 'The Interpretation of the Monetary Aggregates').

Conceptually therefore, as well as practically, it is not possible to make a sharp distinction between money markets and capital markets.

The economic function of the discount market

The discount houses still provide the focus for Bank of England operations in the money market, through which it influences interest rates and provides or removes liquidity from the system.

At present there are eight discount houses who have unique access to the Bank of England as lender-of-last-resort. The principal functions of the discount houses are as follows:

1. to make the call money market in London;
2. to cover the Treasury bill issue;
3. to assist the merchant banks by providing an independent market for the discounting of bills accepted by these banks, and also to discount non-government paper;

4. to assist directly the Bank of England in re-financing the national debt by dealing in short bonds and other gilts nearing maturity;
5. to provide a source of liquid assets for banks;
6. to make the secondary market in sterling and dollar certificates of deposit (CDs);
7. to provide an alternative source of short-term funds for trade and industry;
8. to operate in the financial futures and options markets (in the case of the larger houses).

The banking system places large amounts of money, currently about £1100 million, at call with the market and it receives in return a rate of interest close to that on the underlying instruments in which the discount houses trade. The banks can withdraw their funds if they are short of cash and the houses can replace the funds from another bank with a surplus. If, however, there is an overall shortage, then the discount houses can borrow directly from the Bank of England as lender-of-last-resort. This is a unique facility available only through the discount market.

The clearing banks now seem less vociferous about their desire to deal directly with the Bank. This appears to represent an interesting change of tack by the clearers who traditionally have argued strongly for the abolition of the privileged position of the discount market.

The dominant functions of the discount houses remain their role as intermediators between the Bank of England and the banking system, and providers of short-term capital for industry, the government, local authorities and the banking sector. (These are functions 1, 2, 4, 5, 7 and 8 noted above.)

Despite revisions to the operation of monetary policy since 1983 (discussed in detail in the second part of this chapter), the Bank has not sought to change either the positioning or role of the discount houses in the monetary system.

Private sector influences on the market

Clearly,the discount market performs its intermediary role efficiently and effectively, and it is other private sector developments, in particular increasing levels of competition through new players in the market, which have determined the need to diversify into new sectors of business. Even though these market pressures have been heightened since 'Big Bang', they nevertheless represent no more than an extension of a process which began to emerge in the early 1970s. At that time the discount houses principally dealt in Treasury bills and government stocks, and these accounted for between 60 and 70 per cent of total assets. Reference to Table 7.1 shows that by 1987, approximately only 2.5 per cent of assets

Table 7.1 Selected discount market assets and liabilities 1983–7

(a) Liabilities (£ million)

Dec.	*Total*	*Of which call money* *UK monetary sector*	*Other UK*	*Of which foreign currency*
1983	6667	5838	738	71
1984	7435	6124	1255	383
1985	7564	5786	2468	254
1986	8972	6983	1986	274
1987 (October)	11066	8348	2541	146

(b) Assets (£ million)

Dec.	*Assets*	*Treasury bills*	*Eligible bills*	*Other UK bills*	*Government stock*	*CDs*	*(Of which) (b/soc)*	*Curr CDs*	*Other sterling*
1983	6860	31	3731	207	364	2044	(220)	70	–
1984	8096 + 18%	222	2733	729	401	2702	(522)	302	367
1985	8712 + 7.6%	50	2711	751	291	3279	(550)	148	618
1986	9539 + 9.5%	240	3323	735	23	3370	(348)	124	923
1987	11609 + 21.7%	261	4406	802	35	4452	(747)	38	771

(c) Movements in key assets 1983–7 (percentage of total assets)

	1983	*1984*	*1985*	*1986*	*1987*
Treasury bills	1/2	3	1	2	2
Eligible bills	54	34	31	35	38
Other UK bills	3	8	8	7	7
British government securities	5	4	3	1/4	1/4
CDs – sterling	29	33	38	35	38
currency	1/10	4	4	1	1/3
Other sterling assets	–	4	4	10	7

Sources: *Bank of England Quarterly Bulletin*; CSO *Financial Statistics 1983–88*.

were invested in public sector holdings, the remaining 97.5 per cent falling in the private sector.

This extraordinary shift in asset mix arises principally from the volatility in the interest rate structure over the period (and the consequent difficulty in operating profitably in such an environment) and changes in the government's policy on funding as reflected by the declining PSBR. It also reflects a similar switch away from gilts by the banking sector and the importance of the certificate of deposit as a major vehicle of banking liquidity. CDs accounted for 38 per cent of discount market assets in 1987 and have exceeded 33 per cent since 1983. A parallel growth also occurred in the use of the commercial bill by the corporate sector as a means of raising short-term funds. The counterpart of the latter change is the holding of eligible and other bills by the banks themselves, for liquidity purposes and to gain the benefit of a better yield than would have been obtainable by deposit in the discount market.

There has also been a significant increase in business transacted with building societies. The increases have affected both the asset and liability sides of the balance sheet and account for a large proportion of the houses' growth of some 70 per cent (£6860 million to £11 609 million) in total assets between 1983 and 1987. Building society deposits are also of growing importance in the liability portfolio, and reflect the continuing efforts by the discount market to diversify its funding base.

The eligible bill and other UK bills have accounted for over 40 per cent of total assets since 1983, excepting 1985 when they totalled 39 per cent. Apart from a short period in the 1950s, the commercial bill has historically always been the core business of the houses and it remains a key area of business activity.

Structural and competitive issues

The main structural changes that have taken place arise from the City revolution and certain houses have been taken over by banks: Citibank bought Seccombe Marshall; Prudential Bache bought Clive Discount; Banque Belge bought Quin Cope; Crédit Lyonnais bought Alexanders.

The number of houses reporting to the Bank in 1983 and 1987 are shown in Table 7.2. Since 1983 the number of houses has fallen from ten to eight, and is accounted for by a number of amalgamations. Smith St. Aubyn was merged with King and Shaxon, Gilletts became part of Jessel Toynbee and the latter merged company was subsequently taken over by Alexanders.

Prospective new participants in the market will be faced by the traditional houses' longstanding expertise in trading in government securities and trading in Treasury bills; their infrastructure to manage successfully portfolios of assets and liabilities on the finest of margins; their expertise as

Table 7.2 The London discount houses, 1983 and 1987

December 1983
Alexander Discount plc
Cater Allen Ltd
Clive Discount Company Ltd
Gerrard & National plc
Jessel Toynbee & Gillett plc
King and Shaxon plc
Quin Cope Ltd
Seccombe Marshall & Campion Ltd
Smith St. Aubyn Ltd
Union Discount of London plc
December 1987
Cater Allen plc
CL-Alexanders
Clive Discount Company Ltd
Gerrard & National plc
King & Shaxson plc
Quin Cope Ltd
Seccombe Marshall & Campion plc
Union Discount Company of London plc

Source: Bank of England.

traders in the futures and options markets; the fact that the traditional houses have the confidence and respect of the Bank of England.

It is significant that two houses have been bought by US companies, both of which have considerable experience of trading in securities in New York, including the use of new technology. Other possible US or Japanese entrants to the market would probably bring formidable trading expertise and no doubt would be strongly capitalised.

Although such potential competitors do unquestionably pose a threat to the independent houses for the future, they will have to overcome the possible prejudices of prospective clients who may still prefer to trade with a strongly capitalised independent such as Union Discount or Gerrard & National.

Operations in the gilt-edged market

As has been previously mentioned, the discount market's holding of Treasury bills and government securities now amounts to only 2-3 per cent of total assets. In the past the houses have been major traders in public sector paper and retain considerable expertise in dealing, and there is no doubt that if they once again saw profitable opportunities in government securities they would return in strength to these market segments.

It is interesting to note that only three houses – Cater Allen, Gerrards and Alexanders – have opted to become gilt-edged market-makers (GEMM) in what has become the most troubled and controversial of London's markets.

Even prior to Big Bang, fears were being expressed that the London gilts market was not large enough to support 27 market-makers who had injected some £600 million in capital. Before Big Bang the amount of capital devoted to the gilt-edged market was approximately £75–£80 million and came mainly from two jobbing firms, Wedd Durlacher and Akroyd and Smithers. A year after Big Bang the pundits' worst fears seem to have been realised, and what was once a small and highly profitable cartel has been transformed into a large and fiercely competitive market.

No doubt many 'free marketeers' would argue that the latter situation is the more healthy and will lead to better and more efficient services for the customers. The reality so far is that margins have been minimal whilst investment costs are enormously high. The consequence has been a dramatic fall in gilt market revenue from £100 million during the twelve months prior to Big Bang to about £40 million one year later.[2] The revenue from dealing spreads fell 25 per cent and the losses incurred by the 27 market-makers was nearly £60 million by October 1987. These figures do not include the cost of capital and tax.

Following these market difficulties a number of firms have withdrawn from the market including Lloyds Bank, Royal Bank of Canada, Hill Samuel, Wood Mackenzie and Prudential Bache. Amongst the successful firms is Cater Allen, which has taken a tough, single-minded approach to its gilts operations, as have a number of other smaller players. They have sought only a small market share and have avoided unprofitable business. This tactic has led to their larger competitors complaining to the Bank of England that the minnows of the market are not fulfilling their duties as market-makers, by making consistent two-way prices.[3]

Inevitably, the success of firms such as Cater Allen and Morgan Guaranty has raised a number of important questions for the future operations of the gilt-edged market. The Bank of England offers special privileges to market-makers, including direct access to the Bank when it issues stock, and questions are being asked as to whether or not this and other privileges should continue. Two other related questions are whether the advantages of scale are really effective in the gilt market, and whether the large firms encourage customer loyalty through their ability to offer a more comprehensive service, including consistent dealing and quality market research.

The smaller firms claim that the crucial factor in writing business is price, and that there is a clear limit beyond which it becomes impossible to integrate and act upon the volume of information produced, to take positions and quote finer prices.

The large companies argue that they are the ones to provide an orderly market in which depth, breadth and resilience prevail. Moreover many of the larger firms such as Salomon Brothers, Shearson Lehman and some Japanese securities houses feel that they need a presence in the UK bond market to back up their 24-hour trading operations which serve very large worldwide corporate clients. Their need to dominate the market and make large profits is less pervasive than for others in the market. All of these matters are likely to cause continuing fragility and place even greater stress on those who remain in the market.

MONETARY POLICY AND THE MONEY MARKETS

This section summarises the main features of the monetary control system which was introduced with effect from 20 August 1981[4] and the changes which have subsequently taken place. Particular emphasis is directed towards the impact upon the money markets.

Monetary control

The cash ratio

Institutions in the monetary sector have to hold non-operational, non-interest-bearing deposits with the Bank of England. This cash ratio was set at 0.5 per cent of an institution's eligible liabilities, where these average £10 million or more. It replaced the 1.5 per cent of eligible liabilities held in non-interest-bearing accounts at the Bank of England by the clearing banks. The objective was that the new ratio, combined with the operational balances voluntarily held by the clearing banks, would provide approximately the same aggregate total funds to the Central Bank.

Eligibility

A bank may apply for eligibility at any time. The Bank judges applications by banks wishing their acceptances to become eligible for discount at the Bank.

In return each eligible bank undertook to maintain secured money with members of the London Discount Market Association (LDMA) and secured call money with money brokers and gilt-edged jobbers such that:

1. the total funds so held normally average 6 per cent of that bank's eligible liabilities;

2. the amount held in the form of secured money with members of the LDMA does not normally fall below 4 per cent of eligible liabilities on any day.

Banks were expected to go below the minimum only in exceptional circumstances and to explain their position to the Bank of England. This was known as 'Club Money'.

Interest rates

Minimum lending rate was suspended from 20 August 1981, although the Bank of England reserved the right 'to announce in advance the minimum rate which, for a short period ahead, will apply in lending to the discount houses'. In practice, the market discovers by trial and error at what rate the Bank is prepared to conduct open-market operations in eligible bills with the discount market.

The authorities aim to keep very short-term interest rates within an unpublished target band. To this end, the Bank intervenes in bills in four maturity bands:

Band 1	up to 14 days
Band 2	15–33 days
Band 3	34–63 days
Band 4	64–91 days

The monetary sector

The old banking sector was redefined to include all recognised banks and licensed deposit takers, certain banks in the Channel Islands and Isle of Man which specifically opted to join it, and the Banking Department of the Bank of England.

Changes to the system

There have been only two amendments to this system of monetary control since its inception in 1981.

'Club Money'

In August 1983 the requirement for eligible banks to hold a certain percentage of eligible liabilities in secured money with discount houses, money brokers and gilt-edged jobbers was reduced to 5 per cent on average and 2.5 per cent on any one day. This change was made because rapid growth in banks' eligible liabilities had caused the level of funds held with the discount houses to be higher than intended and this would, if it continued, produce an undue bargaining advantage in favour of the discount houses.

The requirement was abolished altogether in September 1986 as part of the prelude to Big Bang. Banks are not, however, expected to deviate substantially from these levels pending the introduction of a new prudential requirement to hold minimum levels of specified liquid assets. New arrangements are still subject to discussion with the banking sector and the Bank.

'Cash Ratio'

In October 1986 the cash ratio was reduced from 0.5 per cent of eligible liabilities to 0.45 per cent in line with the move to end-calendar-month reporting. This was a technical change designed to ensure that the level of cash ratio deposits did not rise, since end-calendar-month eligible liabilities were historically somewhat higher than end-banking-month eligible liabilities.[5]

It would be unwise to assume from the small number and limited nature of these amendments, however, that the last few years have been uninteresting ones for the money markets. This is not the case at all. There have been several developments in what the Governor of the Bank of England refers to as the 'form' of monetary policy, rather than its 'substance'.[6]

Objectives of monetary policy

The overriding objective of monetary policy was articulated by Gordon Richardson, former Governor of the Bank of England, before the election of the Thatcher government and the introduction of monetary targets:

> Our first order of business must be to restore confidence in the framework of the system. The crucial economic decisions, for example to undertake investment, involve an act of faith in the future. That faith has been undermined by uncertainty – uncertainty about the future value of money, externally and internally.[7]

This was recently reiterated by the present Governor, Sir Robin Leigh-Pemberton, who went on to underline the role of monetary policy in the 1987 Mais Lecture:

> this is the limited, but vital, role which monetary policy can play in contributing to the more effective working of the economy. It is a necessary – though not in itself sufficient – condition for the achievement of . . . a strong and growing economy and higher employment and living standards.[8]

Thus the ultimate objective of monetary policy remains the reduction of inflation. There have, however, been several shifts of emphasis in the way policy has been carried out, that is in the intermediate objectives. These changes have had their impact upon the money markets as this will be evident following the course of policy over the last five years.

The policy shifts can be summarised as follows:

1. The adoption of a pragmatic approach to policy, whereby the authorities take account of economic indicators other than the growth of money and credit in assessing the stance of policy, notably the exchange rate.
2. The move away from overfunding the PSBR in order to offset the expansionary effect on money supply of the rapid growth in bank lending. This was announced officially by the Governor in the Autumn of 1985, but it had been evident for some time before that overfunding was no longer a priority.
3. Finally, the abandonment of an explicit target for broad money supply. M3 (formerly known as sterling M3) was reduced in status from a target to a monitored variable in the Autumn of 1985 and abandoned altogether in the Spring of 1987. The development of monetary targets is summarised in Table 7.3.

Table 7.3 Monetary targets

Target period[1]	*Target aggregates*	*Target growth (%)*	*Outturn (%)*
1983–4	£M3	7–11	9.7
	M1	7–11	11.1
	PSL2	7–11	12.3
1984–5	£M3	6–10	9.5
	M0	4–8	5.5
1985–6	£M3	5–9	4.8
	M0	3–7	3.5
1986–7	£M3	11–15	8.1
	M0	2–6	1.0
1987–8	M0[2]	2–6	9.5

Notes:
1 February to April of following year.
2 M0: gradual reduction in target range to 0–4 per cent by 1990.
Source: Bank of England Quarterly Bulletins (various).

Monetary targets and funding policy

The present system of monetary control was introduced at a time when strict adherence to monetary targets was seen as the key to the ultimate objective of reducing inflation. From the start, however, this policy was hampered by the unexpectedly rapid growth in bank lending, the reasons for which will be examined briefly below. In order to neutralise the impact of this growth on the money supply the authorities engaged in a policy known as overfunding, that is the sale of gilt-edged stock to the UK non-bank private sector in excess of the PSBR. To offset the shortages this created in the money markets the Bank bought eligible bills from the discount houses.

Bank lending proved to be peculiarly intransigent to interest rate changes and overfunding became substantial. As a result, shortages in the money market were unexpectedly large and persistent, and the Bank's purchases of bills became known as the 'Bill Mountain'. This policy was explained by Professor Andrew Bain in terms of a structural imbalance in the financial markets. There was a 'a surplus of long-term funds, matched by a corresponding deficiency of short and medium-term finance' due to the strength of the long-term institutions, the effects of building society competition with the banks for short-term savings, and the effect of inflation which led to a considerable reduction in new issue volume and which caused firms to augment their working capital (of which banks are a prime source).[9]

In the Autumn of 1985 the Chancellor[10] announced the effective suspension of the £M3 target. This had important implications for funding policy. It was decided to do no more than fund the PSBR, taking together the sales of debt to the no-bank private sector and external and foreign currency finance of the public sector.[11]

Table 7.4 traces the development of overfunding in recent years. The switch in policy between 1984/5 and 1985/6 is clearly evident. In 1985/6 the growth in £M3 was a clear reflection of the growth in sterling bank lending and well outside its target range. In the March 1986 Budget £M3 was reinstated as a target variable, but its range was raised to 11–15 per cent from the 5–9 per cent originally set for the previous year. This increase was to allow for the rapid fall in the velocity of circulation which had been observed in recent years. However, by May the growth in £M3 had reached some 19 per cent; the velocity of circulation continued to fall and £M3 remained outside the upper limit of its target range. In March 1987 the only target aggregate to be announced was MO, which has remained within its target and which has exhibited a steady upward trend in velocity.

Table 7.4 Overfunding and the money supply (£ billion)

	1982–3	*1983–4*	*1984–5*	*1985–6*	*1986–7*
PSBR	8.9	9.8	10.2	5.7	3.3
Public sector debt	−8.4	−12.6	−12.6	−3.5	−1.5
Sales to non-bank* private sector:					
External and foreign	−2.3	−1.3	−2.0	−1.8	−1.5
Current finance* of public sector:					
Overfunding*	−1.9	−4.1	−4.5	0.4	0.3
Sterling bank lending	14.4	15.4	18.6	21.4	30.3
External + foreign currency					
transactions of monetary sector	−0.8	−1.3	0.3	−0.7	−0.6
Net non-deposit liabilities	−1.9	−2.3	−2.7	−2.0	−4.7
Change in M3	9.8	7.6	11.8	19.1	25.4

Note:
* increase = −, i.e. a positive sign denotes underfunding.

Source: *Bank of England*, various issues.

The interpretation of the monetary aggregates

This decline in the velocity of broad money has been a feature of all broad money aggregates since 1980, and is in sharp contrast to the rise in velocity throughout the 1970s and, indeed, throughout most of the post-war period.[12] The velocity of broad money has fallen by an average of 4 per cent per annum, with that of £M3 falling by an accelerating rate. This is explained in terms of:

1. The removal of the corset in 1981 which, not unexpectedly, led to a sharp rise in bank activity as banks took advantage of their new freedom.
2. Competition between the banks and building societies on both the asset and liability sides of their business, which has distorted the growth of any one measure of money at the expense of another at various times, in particular £M3 and PSL2. Thus shifts in funds between the banks and the building societies make the interpretation of these measures particularly complex.
3. The behaviour of the various sectors of the economy, which have all enjoyed a simultaneous increase in debt and liquidity.

The personal sector

The entry of banks into the mortgage market and the removal of restrictions on hire purchase provided an added impetus to the growth of consumer credit. At the same time the competition for personal sector deposits between the banks and building societies – evidenced in interest-bearing cheque accounts, and so on – enhanced the attractiveness of liquid assets. The growth in personal sector liquidity since 1980 is regarded by the authorities as being largely attributable to a redistributiion of assets between banks and building societies. Therefore, it does not carry 'the same threatening message about future inflation'.[13]

The corporate sector

Industrial and commercial companies have also increased both debt and liquid assets. They have been particularly affected by the rapid pace of financial innovation in recent years, such as the move to securitisation and the development of new instruments, and interpretation is not only difficult but complicated by changes in the tax treatment of leasing, not to mention major deficiencies in the data. Nevertheless, the official interpretation is to regard the developments as representing 'a different pattern of financing company spending without any necessary implications for company spending itself',[14] prompted not least by the higher returns available on assets and the lower borrowing costs which have resulted from financial innovation and competition.

The non-bank financial sector

This sector has been affected by many of the same developments as the corporate sector.

Given these difficulties in interpreting the behaviour of the monetary aggregates, it is not surprising that monetary targets as such should have been all but abandoned. Indeed, one of the most difficult tasks for the monetarists has been to explain why the fight against inflation has been so successful when the fight to achieve monetary targets has been so evidently unsuccessful – an experience which has not been unique to the United Kingdom.

The Governor of the Bank of England, however, has cautioned against reading too much into the lack of a broad money target. He reminds us that:

> The £M3 rule has never operated in a purely mechanical way . . . Equally the absence of a £M3 target emphatically does not mean that the behaviour of broad money and credit is regarded as of any less importance than before.[14]

Indeed, during 1987 the monetary aggregates were redefined and a new aggregate, M4, was introduced (see Table 7.5), with an unequivocal

Table 7.5 Monetary aggregates: old and new

M0	Wide monetary base: Notes and coin in circulation + bankers' operational deposits at the Bank of England.
M1	Notes and coin in circulation plus private sector sight deposits in sterling.
M2	Non-interest component of M1 plus other retail deposits with banks, plus shares and deposits with building societies and national savings ordinary accounts.
M3	Old £M3. Notes and coin in circulation + private sector sight and time deposits and CDs in sterling.
M3C	Old M3. New M3 + private sector foreign currency deposits.
M4	New M3 + private sector holdings of building society shares, deposits and sterling CDs + building society holdings of bank deposits and bank CDs, and notes and coin.
M5	Old PLS2. M4 plus private sector holdings of money market instruments, certificates of tax deposit and national savings instruments (except certificates, SAYE and other long-term deposits).

statement that there can be no unique definition of broad money. These aggregates will be used in the assessment of monetary conditions. No one aggregate will be given preference since the dividing line between those financial assets included in it, and those excluded from it, would inevitably be invalidated by developments in the financial system.

Influences on interest rates

When the present system was introduced in August 1987, a primary aim was to allow market forces to play a greater part in the determination of interest rates. As Sir Jeremy Morse, Chairman of Lloyds Bank, pointed out, the new system represented a 'return to the original spirit of competition and credit control, which aimed to eliminate inefficient and inequitable controls on banks and to give interest rates a central function in the operation of monetary policy'.[15] In suspending minimum lending rate and maintaining an unpublished target for very short-term interest rates, it was also hoped to reduce some of the political heat generated over interest rate changes.

The key to the control of short-term interest rates is the Bank's ability to create a shortage of liquidity in the money market. It then chooses the rate at which this shortage is alleviated by buying bills from the discount houses, or by adopting a higher profile and publishing the rate at which the Bank has lent to the market at 2.30 p.m., the equivalent of the previous MLR announcement.

While the Bank certainly cannot ignore market forces the policy of overfunding has led to such large purchases of commercial bills that the Bank itself had become the dominant force in the bill market. By the end of 1984 Bank holdings of commercial bills – the so-called 'Bill Mountain' – exceeded £10 billion.

Initially it was understoood that the Bank would intervene primarily in very short-term bills (Band 1), while interest rates in subsequent bands were to reflect, to a progressively greater extent, market forces. It quickly became apparent, however, that the Bank had to deal actively and set interest rates in all four bands in order to alleviate the substantial and unexpected money market shortages.

The extent of the Bank's operations meant that bill rates and other money market rates sometimes moved out of line, allowing arbitrage opportunities. In particular, 'round-tripping' between bills and deposits occurred, whereby it was profitable for short periods for companies to borrow through bill finance and redeposit the proceeds at a higher rate, thus raising both bank lending and bank deposits. It was impossible to discover the extent to which round-tripping was occurring, and the Bank of England took the stance that it did not occur on a large enough scale to account for the growth in bank lending to corporates in 1984.

In addition, the Bank's operations may have made the yield curve steeper than it would otherwise have been, thus reducing rates at the short end by the issuance of substantial amounts of debt. This was, however, justified on the grounds that the more rapid growth in £M3 which would have occurred in the absence of overfunding would have inflationary expectations, thus raising interest rates, so that interest rates at the long end were, in fact, lower than they might otherwise have been. In order to foster a revival in the corporate bond market, and thus to encourage industry to borrow in the capital market rather than almost exclusively from banks, the Bank concentrated its gilt issues at the shorter end of the maturity structure.

These distortionary effects were, as noted above, important considerations in the move away from overfunding and strict adherence to monetary targets. Despite the abandonment of overfunding, there is, as the Governor described it: 'a popular perception that the monetary authorities dictate the general level of interest rates'. The Bank of England is at pains to stress that this influence should not be exaggerated, although it recognises that 'we are able to exert a very considerable influence on it'. It is, however, the case that the Bank always tries to 'work with the grain of the markets', rather than against it.[16]

While the aim of giving market forces a greater role to play in the determination of interest rates was thwarted to a large extent by the policy of overfunding, the objective of reducing the political heat surrounding interest rate changes was partly frustrated by the exchange rate and its increasingly important role in the determination of monetary policy.

Since the current system was introduced the sterling dollar exchange rate has fluctuated between extreme strength and extreme weakness, returning to a position of relative strength. The relative strength of the pound against the dollar largely determined the extent to which it was possible to 'decouple' sterling interest rate trends from those in the United States. January 1985 and January 1986 both saw sterling crises which necessitated large rises in interest rates. Indeed in January 1985 the authorities felt it necessary to reintroduce MLR for a period. Even this was not sufficient to halt the fall in the pound, however, and a further 2 per cent rise in interest rates occurred before the end of the month. In 1986 most, if not all, policy actions were taken in response to pressures on the exchange rate. The *Financial Statement and Budget Report* in March 1987 recorded that 'monetary conditions are assessed in the light of movements in narrow and broad money and the behaviour of other financial indicators, in particular the exchange rate'.

With a more co-ordinated international approach to the stabilisation of the foreign exchange markets, the Bank of England, in concert with other central banks, has intervened to support the dollar. Co-ordinated intervention is, however, only a very short-term measure with the familiar problem that unsterilised intervention is most effective, but the purchase of dollars and sale of sterling by the Bank adds to domestic liquidity and increases the money supply. Sterilising this liquidity through sales of government debt to non-banks may prevent a decline in government bond yield which does nothing to discourage further capital in flows and alleviate pressure on the currency. Since intervention can be only a short-term measure, this throws the burden onto interest rates as being the prime method of dealing with the exchange market pressures which are not perceived as temporary.

Supervisory issues

The way ahead?

Government paper at present amounts to only about 3 per cent of total discount market assets. In contrast, commercial bills holdings account for some 45 per cent of assets. This dominance of the commercial bill has arisen for two main reasons. Since the late 1970s the Bank of England has pursued a policy of overfunding the PSBR in its attempts to control £M3. The overfunding policy forced the Bank to buy short-term assets from the banking sector, but the outstanding Treasury bill issue was too small to meet this requirement. Consequently, the Bank used commercial bill transactions as the principal vehicle of managing money market liquidity and interest rates. There were at the same time restrictions on the commercial paper market which prevented its growth as a major vehicle for non-bank investors. The outcome of these policies has been to concentrate the commercial bill holdings in the banking sector, and the discount market in particular.

Recent policy developments would seem to indicate that the Treasury bill may once again achieve much greater importance in monetary policy thereby reducing the influence of the commercial bill. A return to a focus on the Treasury bill could recur. Firstly the Bank has now abandoned overfunding and targeting £M3, so it would be perfectly feasible to revive the Treasury bill by increasing the weekly issue. Secondly, there are already signs emerging that the Bank is attempting to manage the long-term capital account of the balance of payments as an aim of debt management. It could be useful at times when the exchange rate is under pressure as a result of capital inflows and outflows, to adjust the size of the Treasury bill issue to alleviate some of the distortionary monetary effects of foreign exchange intervention.

GEMMs dealers and discount houses – an anomaly

The foregoing analysis indicates that the Bank has already changed its focus away from overfunding, and it is also clear that the commercial paper market continues to grow. Ultimately, of course, the shift towards the commercial paper market will not depend solely on the cost of borrowing in the bill market, but also on the liquidity of the bill market as determined by Bank monetary policy. A further important influence will be the extent to which the large corporations move into the market. Large corporations will only enter the market in force if they are satisfied that the banks concerned are effective managers of commercial paper borrowing programmes. Given these developments, and the issues debated earlier in this section, the Bank may well come under pressure to allow firms to merge the roles of discount houses and gilt-edged market-maker (GEMM). At present a distinction exists in as much as a discount house may only deal in Treasury bills and GEMMS are allowed to deal only in gilts.

This situation, therefore, has a number of implications for securities market participants:

1. At present there effectively exists double counting of capital requirements in the market where GEMMs constitute part of a larger group.
2. The establishment of the new style financial groupings is important for the Bank's own role. It is not the Bank's responsibility to concern itself with the stock market activities of banks. Nevertheless it has been

recognised that operations in securities have considerable relevance for overall capital requirements of a banking group and for general confidence. The domino effect of the failure of a GEMM could adversely affect its parent, as well as London as a financial centre. (There was the example of the withdrawal of Lloyds Bank from the capital market at a time when it was already under pressure following its LDC debt problems.)

3. The merging of the roles of a discount house and a GEMM would, through netting-out, enable the more efficient use of capital in the market.
4. Money market management could be simplified because a GEMM could obtain finance directly from the Bank by swapping Treasury bills for new stock or through a bill repurchase agreement.
5. Under a merged system it would be sensible to relax the requirement on GEMMs to make markets in all maturities of stock and circumvent some of the criticisms presently voiced by the larger market participants against the smaller niche market operators. Certainly if more sharply focused market segmentation emerged then a more profitable (and liquid) market should develop, thereby achieving what the regulators intend.
6. A further possibility might be for the Bank to extend its money dealings to all banks. If that were the case then the Bank might also begin to use the inter-bank market for its operations, but this seems unlikely given the historical relationships which exist. It would no doubt require very compelling reasons to shift its present focus of monetary control from the discount market. In any case the advantages of this system would be preserved by dealing only with the GEMMs.

CONCLUSION

The period under review since 1981 has witnessed a significant shift in the stance of the Bank of England towards the implementation of monetary policy. The move away from overfunding and monetary targets is already affecting the way the money market functions. The single most important event during this time was undoubtedly the 'Big Bang', and its future influence will be far-reaching.

The bank has a difficult pivotal role to pursue in controlling the banking sector whilst recognising that the banks, in involving themselves in the securities business, are playing new games. There now exists an interlocking system of regulatory and supervisory structures. The interlocking nature of these bodies, coupled with new problems related to the techniques required to deal with a large variety of new instruments in the financial markets and the growing size of off-balance sheet business of the banks, only serve to compound the problem of achieving stable and competitive markets. It may well be that in the future market-related influences are the ones which will prove all-pervading. The present dichotomy between a discount house and a GEMM with banking roots clearly has implications for the future, particularly if the Bank were to adopt a US style system of money management. In such circumstances banking groups not owning a GEMM would be at a disadvantage as they would not enjoy informational and other privileges associated with a direct dealing relationship with the Bank.

Notes

1. M. S. Mendelsohn, 'Sterling CP tries out the market', *The Banker*, July 1986.
2. *Financial Times*, 14 December 1987.
3. Ibid, 14 December 1987
4. For a full version, see *Monetary Control – Provisions*, Bank of England, 5 August 1981.
5. *Cash Ratio Deposits*, notice issued by the Bank of England, 21 August 1986.
6. 'Financial Change and Broad Money', Loughborough University Banking Centre Lecture in Finance, 22 October 1986, reproduced in the *Bank of England Quarterly Bulletin*, December 1986.
7. First Mais Lecture, *Bank of England Quarterly Bulletin*, February 1978.
8. 'Instruments of Monetary Policy', Mais Lecture at City University Business School, 13 May 1987, reproduced in *Bank of England Quarterly Bulletin*, August 1987.
9. 'Bank lending, monetary control and funding policy', Bank of England Panel of Academic Consultants, *Panel Paper* no. 19, July 1982.
10. 'Problems of Monetary Policy and Change in the City', Governor's Mansion House Speech, October 1985, reproduced in *Bank of England Quarterly Bulletin*, December 1985.
11. *Bank of England Quarterly Bulletin*, December 1985, p. 518.
12. 'Measures of broad money', *Bank of England Quarterly Bulletin*, May 1987.
13. See note 6.
14. See note 8.
15. 'Monetary control in the United Kingdom. History, problems and prospects', Nika Tiivola commemorative volume, *Banking and Economic Policy* (Helsinki, 1982).
16. See note 8.

8 Bank Borrowing, Small Firms, and the USM

Roger Buckland and Edward Davis[1]

INTRODUCTION

In this chapter we address the issue of small firms' access to bank finance, in the context of their entry to secondary equity markets and specifically Britain's Unlisted Securities Market (the USM, set up by the Stock Exchange in late 1980). Previous research, such as Bates (1964), Wilson (1979a), or Ray and Hutchinson (1983), indicates that small companies employ more debt, generally in the form of short-term borrowing from trade creditors and the banking sector, in their capital structures. That research suggests that, given the risk associated with small firm lending, banks could be reluctant to lend in the absence of a strong equity capitalisation.

The quotation of a firm's equity presents an important event in which crucial strategic objectives must be set in the context of the firm's relationship with economic agents, comprising not only the firm's shareholders or potential investors, but also the suppliers of debt. In the past, new quotation has been closely concerned with the ability to repay borrowings (Davis *et al.*, 19774; Vaughan *et al.*,1977). The main objective in this chapter is to examine the extent to which firms' financial positions are related to their motivation for entering new equity markets, and to determine whether quotation is followed by significant movement in the financial structure of small firms.

SMALL FIRMS AND FINANCING INSTITUTIONS

Concern with small firms' relationships with financing institutions (and with the banking sector in particular) is of very long standing in Britain. In 1931 the Macmillan Committee identified what it saw as a 'finance gap', which prevented small firms gaining access to the risk capital needed for their independent growth (Macmillan, 1931). This supposed deficiency in the provision of long-term lending to the small business sector was a criterion later adopted by the Radcliffe (1959) and the Bolton (1971) Committees. Essentially, the line of argument runs that small firms are peculiarly reliant upon risk capital at a stage in their development when their ability to offer good tangible asset security, or to provide timely and good quality information, is restricted both commercially and also by the nature of their development. Without risk capital the small firm is inhibited from growing as fast as is possible and is restricted in its access to lower cost commercial debt markets. The 'gap' thus traps the emergent small firms in a high-cost, low-volume finance market which frustrates its growth, leading either to a slower pace of growth in the economy (the macro problem) and/or to the precipitation of merger and takeover by existing, larger enterprises (the micro problem).

Theoretically, this is an example of chronic agency problems between the growing firm and its financing partners. (For a general discussion of the concept of agency, see the work of Jensen and Meckling, 1976.) Where the resources of a small firm's operators or managers become inadequate to finance its continued growth, then outsider-financers must be attracted to commit some part of their wealth to the control of the firm's management. Such a change, from insider-managers to outside-financers, requires a departure from the previous close control of the business and of its information systems. Whereas an insider will be able to acquire timely information about the utilisation of his or her funds, the outsider is distanced in time, in the degree of intervention possible, and in sheer comprehension of the business progress within the firm. There is no reason to believe that any outsider will be prepared to commit resources to managers' control without some *quid pro quo* of information, collateral and security.

Unfortunately for the growing small firm, it is peculiarly unfitted to propose any resolution of these agency problems which it faces. Not only is it relatively expensive for the small firm to provide high-quality, timely information, but its assets are likely to be concentrated in closely held, private knowledge about its markets or its processes of production. Revealing that knowledge in a way which resolves the agency problem between its managers and its potential financers may jeopardise its ability to profit from its own comparative advantage in business. The obvious alternative in attempting to resolve the agency problem is to offer some tangible security to the potential lender: a mortgage on property; a first charge on physical assets; or increased use of hire purchase and leasing facilities. All such devices involve a cost in terms of depriving the owners, or other financers, of the benefits of the security offered by those assets: thus the attempt to face any agency problem with one source of finance may rebound by increasing the perception of risk and the agency problems faced by others.

With this background of the agency problems faced by the growing small firm one can more easily understand the reasons for such businesses' reliance upon clearing bank finance and upon the extensive use of trade credit exposure. A clearing bank, by the nature of its record systems and the oversight of the client firm's cash flow, receipts and payments, possesses timely and pertinent information which reduces the agency problems faced by the bank. At the same time the confidentiality of its relationship with the client ensures that this privileged information is not open to exploitation by actual or potential competitors. Small firms' suppliers and clients will themselves possess relevant information about the commercial value, quality and market prospects of the firm's products; they will have an interest in the continued success and financial health of the firm and will thus also face a different agency problem, less costly to resolve.

British small firms' problems

In 1975, 52.3 per cent of the capital employed by the average small business was represented by current liabilities; bank lending accounted for 11.1 per cent and trade creditors for 34.9 per cent, according to figures from the analysis of the accounts of small companies, in Wilson (1979a, table 3). These figures can be contrasted with those for long-term lending, averaging only 3 per cent of capital employed for the small firm, and for shareholders' interest averaging 29.5 per cent.[2] When compared with the data for 'large' companies (as defined by the Department of Trade and Industry's survey published annually in *Business Monitor MA3*) the scale of the financing 'gap' can be appreciated: 1975 figures are given in Table 8.1.

Table 8.1 Comparative balance sheet structures of small, intermediate and large firms, at end 1975

	Small	*Intermediate*	*Large*
Fixed assets	32.4	32.8	39.7
Current assets	67.6	67.2	60.3
Capital and reserves	47.7	51.3	58.9
of which:			
Shareholders' funds	29.5	36.1	39.1
Long-term funds	3.0	6.6	10.3
Current liabilities	52.3	48.7	41.1
of which:			
Trade creditors	34.9	29.6	25.2
Bank overdrafts	11.1	13.4	9.7

Note: All figures expressed as percentage of total book assets.

Source: Wilson (1979a) table 3.

This table clearly sets out the financing problem of the growing small firm. Fixed assets available as security are relatively low; shareholders' funds are restricted; and financing from banks and trade creditors dominates. The table also establishes the deterioration of this position in the transitional phase, as these 'small firms pass through the growth stage of 'intermediate' sized businesses. Exposure at banks is still higher, on average, for these intermediate-sized firms.

Research on firm's trade credit exposure in the 1970s established that small firms and medium-sized businesses were vulnerable to credit squeezes, with pressure being exerted by larger firms taking credit in such periods (Davis *et al.*, 1974). The accounts analysed for the Wilson Committee's report further confirmed that: 'Alone among the subgroups of small companies, the intermediate manufacturing companies remained net extenders of trade credit throughout the period (of 1972 to 1975) and showed no tendency for this position to improve' (Wilson, 1979a, para. 25). The shortage of suitable security and the vulnerability to creditor pressures make it vital that small growing firms have access to some route or routes out of their financial predicament. The Wilson Committee recognised this in the conclusions of their Interim Report: while concluding that 'none of this necessarily constitutes a bias' against small firms (Wilson, 1979b, para. 2.3), the Committee considered that 'small firms are at a considerable disadvantage in financial markets' (ibid, para. 2.1); and that a series of measures should be taken to improve small firms' access to finance, both from conventional sources and by innovation of novel ones.

New issue markets and small firms

Entry to an organised secondary exchange in the firm's equity is a key event in the continuing growth of the independent business (see Buckland and Davis, 1989, ch. 3). By having the firm's shares traded on a secondary market owners increase the value of their holdings, improve their equity's status as security for lending both now and for the future, and lower the costs of informing a wide and wealthy potential market in finance for the business. Without secondary quotation, on the other hand, shareholders are restricted to those with close relationships with the business, the equity is poor collateral for long-term or institutional borrowing, and consequently the cost of funds is relatively high (see Gupta, 1969). Unless there are good and continuing reasons why the firm can earn profits and provide returns which remain above those required for the risk of its business, then a lack of quotation will contribute to the firm's stagnation and eventual demise in liquidation or takeover.

During the 1970's the numbers of entrants to Britain's secondary equity markets declined very markedly. Both the Stock Exchange and the Wilson Committee identified the main reasons for this substantial decline, which saw entrants drop from 96 in 1973 to a low point of 18 in 1976. The oil shock of 1974 and the collapse in UK share values which followed it were undoubtedly the major factor, but the Wilson Committee also levelled criticism at the Stock Exchange's restrictive attitude towards new entrants: 'they may have also been deterred by the Stock Exchange's listing requirements . . . which put obligations on firms' directors which they may prefer to be without' (Wilson, 1980, para. 759). In their recommendations the Committee wished to see more liberal access to listed status, with more emphasis on the 'unlisted' and less formal markets (ibid, paras 1177–82).

In the later 1970's there was indeed a growth in trading of equities of companies which either could not join or did not, to wish to join the first-tier, Official List market run by the London Stock Exchange. This unlisted market (later to become part of the UK Over-The-Counter, or OTC, market) run by brokers M. J. H. Nightingale (now Granville and Co.) was growing quickly and the numbers of unlisted equities traded under the Stock Exchange's own Rule 163 was also expanding. The response of the Stock Exchange to these pressures was to formalise a second-tier market, to be called the Unlisted Securities Market, or USM, in order to capture the demand for trading in unlisted shares, but with the retention of some degree of the traditional investor protection through regulation of entrants and codification of the information which they would provide to the market.[3] The USM, coinciding with a resurgence of share values post-1979, has seen considerable growth in its first few years of operation, with over 600 entrants up to the end of 1987.

The efficiency and effectiveness of the USM as a market in equities and in quotation has been analysed elsewhere (Buckland and Davis, 1989). Here, we are concerned to judge how its introduction relates to the finance 'gap' faced by the small growing firm: whether entrants are using the USM to resolve their financial dilemmas and whether, by using the USM, they succeed in overcoming the limitations of their small firm status. On the basis of a small sample of entrants from manufacturing industry, Hutchinson *et al.* (1988) have concluded that USM entry is associated with firms' response to financing crises. We shall examine the argument in the light of an analysis of all UK entrants to the USM between its inception in November 1980 and a cut-off date of 31 March 1985.

USM ENTRANTS' BORROWING BEHAVIOUR

The methodology of our research is to analyse in cross-section all entrants to the USM and to use the contemporaneous entrants to the Official List (the first-tier market) as a control. In most instances the function of this control is to contrast the practices, the entrants, and the experiences of USM and Official List markets. Here, the Official List entrants are important in that they capture a sample of relatively large firms, allowing a closer examination of the dimension of smallness in the USM sample. This research design matches that adopted in previous research into the new issue market (Merrett *et al.*, 1967; Davis *et al.*, 1974; Vaughan *et al.*, 1977).

We would not expect to capture any significant numbers of the 'small' firms as defined by the Wilson (1979a) or Bolton (1971) criteria. The entrants to secondary quotation are typically either large (as in the Official List) or 'intermediate' sized businesses. In 1980 prices, 282 out of 324 USM entrants showed total assets of under £7.5 million; 55 of the 117 Official List entrants were of a similar scale. In terms of the smallest firms in these samples, 149 USM entrants had total assets of under £2.5 million, compared with only 12 Official List entrants. Substantial numbers of these entrants might be expected to lie within the categories regarded by Wilson as problematic, therefore. The average gearing of the entrants is presented in Table 8.2.

The anticipated size effects on opening gearing are not very marked, with many entrants showing gearing levels well below or well above the averages. The statistical tests show that size alone does not account for the differences in entrants' gearing ratios, although individual components

Table 8.2 Borrowing of entrants to equities markets, 1980–5

Size-category	*USM Entrants*		*Official List*	
	Debt:TA %	*CA*[a]*:TA* %	*Debt:TA* %	*CA:TA* %
< £2.5 million	57.52	27.35	59.56	29.14
£2.5–7.5 million	52.16	26.66	55.08	29.93
£7.5–15 million	48.63	19.50	51.66	22.58
> £15 million	55.81	21.71	52.35	20.13
All sizes	54.44	26.07	53.89	25.13
F ratio[b]	2.19*	2.24*	0.77	3.38*
K-W statistic[c]	4.96	8.44**	1.80	7.48*

Notes:
a Creditors and accruals.
b Marked * if differences significant at p>0.10; ** if p>0.01.
c The Kruskal-Wallis non-parametric test of differences in means.

Debt here comprises all borrowing by the firm declared in the balance sheet as presented in the issue prospectus. Size is measured by total assets in that balance sheet.

such as creditors and accruals do have the anticipated links. In the USM the correlation coefficient[4] between gearing and total assets is a mere -0.09^{*} at issue, becoming positive (0.18^{**}) only in the following year. In the Official List these coefficients are -0.06 and -0.14^{*} respectively. There is some evidence of a size effect when market values are introduced: if gearing is measured by the debt-equity capitalisation ratio, the USM coefficient becomes 0.40^{**}, the Official List -0.08. Overall, however, the size of the firm at entry is not shown to be very strongly associated with particularly high, or particularly low, gearing ratios.

It is, of course, known from previous studies of new equity issue markets that entrants' financial structures are a common trigger for entry. Both Davis *et al.* (1974) and Vaughan *et al.* (1977) showed that to be true for entrants to the Official List. Small scale studies of the motivation of USM entrants have identified it as a continuing concern (see Bradley-Jones and Hussey, 1985). Entrants to the markets must advertise a prospectus when marketing their company and within the prospectus they will typically give a reason or reasons for their recourse to quotation and issuing. Some 16 per cent of USM entrants during this period gave the repayment of loans as a reason for their actions; 23 per cent stated that they required additional working capital; 23 per cent that funds were needed for fixed capital investment; and fully 33 per cent of USM entrants cited the access to capital markets as their reason for gaining quotation.

In Hutchinson *et al.* (1988), quotation was seen as a remedy for the lack of access to borrowing: USM firms were seen as characterised by 'their high gearing and low liquidity which are indicative of the financial stress of growth' (p. 17). When the full range of entrants is examined, one sees in contrast that, even if a gap or deficiency in financial structure forms the motive for quotation, it is by no means clear that this is simply associated with correction of an over-reliance upon debt financing. Table 8.2 shows that size itself is not a powerful influence on its own; the entrant's industry class is likewise of little relevance, picking out only the group of oils and minerals extraction businesses, with their low gearing and liabilities ratios (see chapter 6 of Buckland and Davis, 1989). It is just as possible, indeed, that the unquoted firm has been prevented from gaining access to debt (and has hence become restrictively undergeared) as that it has been prevented from expanding its equity base. Moreover, the two markets cannot be separated in terms of the average gearing levels or liabilities ratios of entrants: size for size, USM entrants are no more or less likely to have signs of 'financial stress'. Instead, one sees that USM firms embrace a very wide spread of financing positions. There were substantial numbers of entrants to both markets with little borrowing in their balance sheets and many with no long-term institutional lending at all (Buckland and Davis, 1989, table 6.2).

The spread of gearing levels within prospectuses is wide, particularly in the USM, and this can be related to the explicit motivation for entry. Averages disguise considerable variation in individual entrants. Although many small USM entrants utilised quotation to reduce their gearing levels from starting points of 60 per cent or more of total assets at entry, there are equally entrants which increased borrowings subsequent to quotation from much lower levels. Table 8.3 shows how the smallest firms in the USM during this period reacted to their opening gearing levels. The table gives the change in the debt:total-assets ratio from prospectus to twelve months after quotation, split according to the level of that ratio at quotation.

It is clearly evident from Table 8.3 that the smallest USM entrants do make significant changes to their gearing and borrowing positions subsequent to entry.

Table 8.3 Gearing reductions for USM entrants with total assets of £2.5 million and under (1980)

Gearing in prospectus (%)	<35%	35–50%	50–65%	>65%
Average reduction[a] over 12 months (%)	−13.50	4.45	11.01	26.43
	22	29	34	54
	22.70	13.17	13.84	29.74

Note:
a Figures given are mean, number of firms, and standard deviation. F ratio of 17.80 is significant at $p<0.01$.

The pattern of change pictured here for the smallest companies is different from that observed for USM entrants as a whole: there is a significant relationship between the size of the firm and the reduction in borrowing after quotation, but only within USM firms. Correlation coefficients between total assets and gearing change are $+0.21^{**}$ in the USM, -0.06 in the Official List. It would appear that, in the USM, the smaller firms reduce their overall borrowing levels by a greater amount than do larger businesses (see Buckland and Davis 1989, appendix table 4).

Growth of small firms and the USM

The evidence found for the influence of USM entry on the small firm sector is not strong and cannot be interpreted solely in the traditions of the 'finance gap' literature. There is clear evidence that the USM is being used by small firms to unlock rigidities which may have accumulated in their financial structures. The small entrants do indeed appear to be similar in profile to the firms, particularly the 'intermediate' scale firms, sampled by the Wilson Committee's investigations of the 1970s. They have relatively high average gearing ratios and relatively high ratios of current liabilities to total assets. These averages mask considerable variability, however, with some entrants showing debt ratios of 60, 70 or more per cent of book assets, while others have very little borrowing at entry. There is also strong evidence that USM entrants are motivated by the desire to correct imbalances in financial structures, but once again, these may be perceptions of under-borrowing as easily as they may be reflections of overextended debt positions. We have commented elsewhere that, while entrants to equities markets may be moving towards some 'target' borowing in the Marsh (1982) sense, there is little logic apparent in their choice of target, with the debt ratios adopted after entry being inexplicable by any observable measures of the firm's industry or risk class (Buckland and Davis, 1989, ch. 6). The size effect predicted by proponents of the gap closure hypothesis can be observed, but it is not at all strong and is not significant in relation to the variability of behaviour that is observed in practice.

IMPLICATIONS FOR THE SUPPLY OF FINANCIAL SERVICES

Examination of USM entrants, even more than Official List entrants, implies that one is looking at growth small firms at a crucial stage of their independent development. The success of the USM in terms of the large numbers of entrants which have been attracted in its initial years of operation suggests that the Macmillan gap feared by analysts in the late 1970s was present to some extent. The financial characteristics of its smaller entrants further supports this finding, in that they have been, on average, relatively more highly geared and more heavily reliant on finance by current liabilities than larger firms.

The USM entrants also show, however, that while many small growth firms are inhibited by dependence on debt, there are many others where access to debt is itself the objective of entry. While for the former the lack of quoted status and associated dependence on bank borrowing had acted as a constraint, for the latter group debt capacity was itself constrained by the absence of security attaching to unquoted equity.

Banks' attitudes to corporate gearing

It has often been argued that British banks are cautious in corporate lending for reasons other than those of commercial caution and proper prudence. International comparisons of gearing ratios show the United Kingdom (and the United States) to be relatively cautious lenders to the corporate sector, with debt:shareholders'-funds ratios around 50 to 60 per cent, compared with 100 per cent or more in West Germany, Japan, or other OECD competitors (see Wilson, 1980, paras 523–7). Were this to be expressed in terms of market values rather than the book values of balance sheets, the position would appear yet more cautious. The position is clearly one which is related to the traditional resolution of agency problems between bank and borrower. Equity markets are relatively well-developed in both the United Kingdom and the United States, with a consequential sharpening of the division of risk bearing by owner and debt provider; the United Kingdom is characterised by cautious attitudes towards the security demanded by lenders when making term loans.

This latter approach to the resolution of the agency problem is logical, particularly if the lender is not familiar with the business, the markets, or even the commercial culture of the borrower; but it can be especially penal for the growing small firm. As we have seen above, such businesses tend to have lower proportions of tangible assets in the first instance and they are likely to have to offer higher multiples of the lending as security. As the Wilson Committee's investigations discovered, 'The most common complaint . . . was that the level of security demanded by the banks was excessive . . . In about 70 per cent of cases, the banks seemed to insist on at least a 2:1 ratio of assets to borrowing. In some cases the ratio was as high as 6:1' (Wilson, 1979a, II, para. 24). In the context of firms coming to new quotation, the measurement of 'gearing' at book values may be very restrictive. Accounting conventions of prudence, particularly as they affect intangible assets, managerial dynamism and goodwill, can be viewed as especially inhibiting for the growth small firm. Through quotation an alternative, 'economic' valuation of equity is derived, independent of the written down historic cost of net tangible assets and managers may be able to borrow against the security of some part of this market premium of their net assets. We have indeed found that both gearing at quotation and firms' behaviour in altering gearing post-quotation are linked strongly with the market premium accorded to firms' net assets (Buckland and Davis, 1989, ch. 6). This is particularly so for USM entrants, for 'smaller' USM entrants (measured by balance sheet assets), and especially for entrants with fast growth in their recent histories.

Contemporary criticism of institutional attitudes to the corporate sector has become entwined with the criticism of 'short-termism': the view that the UK financial sector as a whole has developed a culture centred upon earnings in the immediate future rather than the economic value of commercial investments. Evidence of short-termism is very hard to find, of course. The corporate sector will always be frustrated by its inability to convince sceptical lenders of management's own views about economic value; the financial sector will always be driven to rely upon objective evidence of value at the expense of contentious and subjective assessments. The Confederation of British Industry itself concludes that the gap is an attitudinal, even educational one, rather than a financial one (CBI, 1987).

Banks' attitude to the corporate client

Apart from the structural reaction of the financial sector in developing and expanding the venture capital institutions, the banking sector has significantly changed the way in which it organises its relationships with corporate clients. Large deposit banks have experienced much greater competitive pressures in this key sector of business in recent years. The influx of overseas banks to London is one facet of this new competitive pressure, but it is represented also by the development in large multinational companies of in-house, centralised corporate treasuries (see Collier and Davis, 1983). This has resulted in the formal assumption by such firms of individual responsibility for many aspects of financial management and control which previously had been the preserve of the company's traditional banker. Thus on the one hand the rise of the modern treasurer reflects changes in financial marketing, leading to the recognition of profits to be made from internal functional specialisation in cash, banking and foreign exchange management. On the other hand, the banks themselves have been driven to respond by the creation of their own corporate banking divisions, designed to accommodate the specialist requirements of more financially sophisticated corporate clients.

This shift in orientation to the large corporate client – the phenomenon of 'relationship banking' – inevitably redirects the corporate banking divisions of the traditional clearing banks towards the culture of the traditional merchant bank. In many cases, indeed, there have been rationalisations, takeovers and mergers which associate the traditional merchant bank sector with the deposit banks and clearers. The involvement of the corporate banking arm of the National Westminster Bank (County NatWest) in the takeover bid by Nestlé for Rowntree Mackintosh in 1988 is simply one example of the growing involvement of the traditional banking sector in corporate activity which was once the preserve of specialised merchant bankers.

The emergence of integrated banking businesses with specialised corporate divisions trickles down to the banks' attitudes towards smaller or emergent corporate clients. Because of these changes in financial markets many banks today are stressing the importance of relationship banking, in which emphasis is placed upon maintaining involvement with principal corporate customers. Such an approach has evidently become the primary focus of banks' strategy, contesting or supplanting the arms-length, security-based attitudes which underlay the era of overdraft facilities and caution towards commercial investment.

The USM and the Third Market

In this trickling-down towards the smaller business – and especially to the growth small firms which will need quoted status if they are to remain independent – the new cultural orientation implied by the deposit banks' specialisation and divisionalisation will need to meet a continuing readiness to minimise entry barriers for firms which seek quotations. The reduction of entry barriers to the USM has been substantial (Buckland and Davis, 1989, ch. 5) and the market has avoided the failure of both entrants and dealers which has characterised the UK Over-The-Counter market. The experience of the OTC in the early 1980s suggests that the degree of investor protection had been set too low and was too lightly policed (Tait, 1986).

The Stock Exchange's Third Market, begun in 1986 as a competitive response to the OTC, is a natural extension of the process begun with the USM. By institutionalising the admission of smaller and less mature businesses, the Stock Exchange differentiates its product, permitting firms to change their status and relationship with financial markets at different stages in their development. The Third Market, however, has had a less propitious beginning than the USM. Despite the impact of deregulation in autumn 1986, which liberalised brokers' ability to become market-makers in their own right and, potentially, deepened the pricing expertise of the exchanges, the Third Market has been severely affected by the reversal of market prices in October 1987. As world prices fell, investors seeking cash liquidated their holdings of small company securities in narrow markets. The USM's fall exceeded that of the Official List,[5] and the Third Market fared even worse, forfeiting all the gains made during its first year of operation.

It remains to be seen whether the junior markets can regain their buoyancy and confirm their function as a liberalising force which enables growth small firms to adjust their relationship with the banking sector more readily and more valuably. The thinness of trading in the USM had become a continuing difficulty even before the 1987 crash (Buckland and Davis, 1989, ch. 8), although volumes and bargains remained strong relative to secondary market experience in many other OECD countries. In the longer term, it is not unreasonable to suppose that smaller companies, with intrinsically greater flexibility than larger firms, should generate greater earnings per share and out-perform the average Official List company. The advantages of investor protection in the Third Market over the OTC market may induce a shift away from the OTC market amongst stronger OTC companies, now that they can preserve the tax advantages of BES status[6] on a recognised stock exchange market.

SUMMARY AND CONCLUSIONS

This research on the entrants to the new USM market between 1980 and 1985 has identified that smaller businesses are using access to quoted status to resolve difficulties which they face in financing their continued independent growth. These difficulties are not solely those of restricted and expensive access to debt capital. Many entrants seek quotation in order to raise their use of debt finance rather than to release an accumulation of expensive debt. The image of a financing gap for the growth small firm is a simplistic one about which the USM entrants' experience informs us. Indeed, the variability of entrants' gearing ratios dominates the size effect which can be observed.

That variability can be ascribed to the difficulties in resolving the agency problems peculiar to growth small firms. The innovations of junior markets in equity quotation have improved and expanded the options open to the independent small firm, and they are complemented by the parallel developments in the organisation and cultural orientation of the major financing institutions. As the clearing banks respond to specialisation by large corporate clients, so they have to innovate and redirect their own products, with closer attention to relationship banking and a more direct involvement in the business of their clients. As this attitude extends to banks' attitudes in resolving the agency problems between themselves and the growth small firm, so the prospects for such firms' continued independent existence improve. That there is still much room for improvement is indicated by the continued necessity of new USM entrants to readjust their fianancial structure on entry to quotation. If alternative bases of raising capital were available from the banking sector, then such firms might not have sought quotation at all, or might have done so at a later stage of their growth and at inevitably lower costs. It is in this market segment, therefore, that notwithstanding the developments by banks of active venture capital and corporate banking subsidiaries, some rethinking of approach may be warranted. Innovations such as the securitisation of corporate credit markets could have their counterpart in the development by the banking system of their own version of an OTC market.

Notes

1. Ted Davis is Lloyds Bank Professor of Business Finance and Roger Buckland is Lecturer in Finance at the Management Centre, Aston University. The research on which this chapter is based was carried out with the assistance of a grant from the Economic and Social Research Council.
2. These 'small' firms have capital employed in 1975 of under £250 000. They are all limited, incorporated businesses filing annual accounts at Companies House. The group of larger 'intermediate' companies referred to later in the chapter lies in the range from £250 000 to £4 million (see Wilson, 1979a, paras 5–19 for more detail).
3. USM entrants contract to abide by the 'General Undertaking', which is a list of regulatory requirements less onerous than those in the 'Listing Agreement' applied to companies on the Official List.
4. All correlation coefficients reported are non-parametric measures, with coefficients' statistical significance reported as a trailing * if p. <0.1, ** if p. >0.01.
5. In 1987 the Datastream USM Index fell 42 per cent from its peak, compared with a fall of 34 per cent for the FTSE 100 share index.
6. The Business Expansion Scheme (BES) offered tax relief for investors who committed equity finance to unquoted businesses for a minimum 5-year period. The USM was excluded from BES benefits, but not the OTC. Third Market participants, however, may qualify for BES status.

References

Bates, J. (1964) *The Financing of Small Business* (London: Sweet & Maxwell) (2nd edn, 1971).

Bolton (1971) *Report of the Committee of Enquiry into Small Firms*, Cmnd 4811 (London: HMSO).

Bradley-Jones, R. and R. Hussey (1985) *The USM Experience: A Survey of Companies' Opinions* (London: Spicer & Pegler).

Buckland, R. and E. W. Davis (1989) *The Unlisted Securities Market* (Oxford: Oxford University Press).

Business Monitor MA3: Company Finance, annually from the Department of Trade and Industry (London: HMSO).

CBI (1987) *Investing in Britain's Future: Report of the CBI City/Industry Task Force* (London: Confederation of British Industry).

Collier, P. and E. W. Davis (1983) *Treasury Management in the UK* (London: Association of Corporate Treasurers).

Collier, P. and E. W. Davis (1985) 'The management of currency transaction risk by UK multinational companies', *Accounting and Business Research*, 15 (60), pp. 327–34.

Davis, E. W, K. A. Yeomans and R. Buckland (1974) *Company Finance and the Capital Market*, Department of Applied Economics Occasional Paper no. 39 (Cambridge: Cambridge University Press).

Gupta, M. K. (1969) 'The effect of size, growth and industry on the financial structure of manufacturing companies', *Journal of Finance*, 24 (3), pp. 517–29.

Hutchinson, P., I. Meric and G. Meric (1988) 'The financial characteristics of small firms which achieve quotation on the UK USM', *Journal of Business Finance and Accounting*, 15 (1), pp. 9–20.

Jensen, M. and W. Meckling (1976) 'Theory of the firm: managerial behavior, agency costs and ownership structure', *Journal of Financial Economics*, October, pp. 305–60.
Macmillan (1931) *Report of the Committee on Finance and Industry*, Cmd 3897 (London: HMSO).
Marsh, P. (1982) 'The choice between equity and debt: an empirical study', *Journal of Finance*, 37 (1), pp. 121–44.
Merrett, A. J., M. Howe and G. D. Newbould (1967) *Equity Issues and the London Capital Market* (London: Longman).
Radcliffe (1959) *Report of the Committee on the Working of the Monetary System*, Cmnd 827 (London: HMSO).
Ray, G. H. and P. J. Hutchinson (1983) *The Financing and Financial Control of Small Business Development* (Aldershot: Gower).
Tait, N. (1986) *Investors Chronicle*, 15 November.
Vaughan, G.D., J. Grinyer and S. Birley (1977) *From Private to Public* (London: Woodhead-Faulkner).
Wilson (1979a) *Committee to Review the Functioning of the Financial Institutions: Research Report no. 3, The Financing of Small Firms* (London: HMSO).
Wilson (1979b) *Committee to Review the Functioning of the Financial Institutions: Interim Report*, Cmnd 7503 (London: HMSO).
Wilson (1980) *Committee to Review the Functioning of the Financial Institutions: Report*, Cmnd 7937 (London: HMSO).

Part IV
International Banking and Finance

The 1960s and 1970s witnessed a marked 're-awakening' of international banking and finance; these were the decades of spectacular growth in the euromarkets. The 1970s have been described as the 'golden age' of international banking. Rapid and fundamental changes in international banking and finance have been characteristic of the 1980s. Securitisation, globalisation and technology developments have figured highly in these developments. Traditional institution-based intermediation has been challenged increasingly by the post-1982 trend towards market-based intermediation. Banks and other financial institutions have been involved in a radical restructuring process to match all of these new challenges.

Chapter 9 examines the theory and empirical evidence of international bank profitability. The theme of Phil Bourke's paper is that our understandig of the functioning of banks and banking systems outside the United States is comparatively underdeveloped. In Chapter 10 an extensive survey is undertaken of the current restructuring of the international financial services industry. Joël Métais argues that economists should devote more attention towards the strategies of firms and the structure of the international financial industry. Chapter 11 examines the role of Swiss banks in international finance: Leo Schuster provides an insight into the structure and strategies of Swiss banking. The following Chapter 12 explores international trade in insurance, and Robert Carter suggests a number of stages that are necessary for trade liberalisation in insurance services.

9 International Bank Profitability: Theory and Evidence

Phil Bourke

INTRODUCTION

A theme of this chapter[1] is that our theoretical understanding of the functioning of banks and banking systems outside the United States is relatively undeveloped. In large measure this is because finance literature has tended to concentrate on the American bank system and to use empirical data which produce results which cannot be applied outside the American environment. For instance, in banking studies it is commonplace to use data drawn from small banks in unit branching states.

In the context of this present work it is appropriate to recall that Professor Jack Revell has been instrumental in encouraging the study of banking on an international basis and those results which I present owe their inspiration to his lead. My objectives are to discuss the implications of the finance literature in so far as they bear on a study of international banks, and to discuss the results of research which I have conducted on large banks in fifteen countries or territories around the world. Issues that are discussed include market structure, regulation and several of the internal determinants of profitability.

FACTORS AFFECTING BANK PROFITABILITY

Factors affecting bank profitability may be divided into those which are internal to the bank and those which are external, and this applies whether the bank in question forms part of a domestic study or an international study, as in this case. Many of the internal determinants reviewed in the literature rely for their estimation on data which are available in limited, local, typically American circumstances but which may not be obtained in an international survey. Examples are funds source management and funds use management (Haslam, 1968). Other variables for which data are available and which are suggested in the literature are capital and liquidity ratios, the loan/deposit ratio (in practice, the reciprocal of the liquidity ratio), loan loss expenses and some overhead expenditures (Short, 1979; Bell and Murphy, 1969; Kwast and Rose, 1982).

External to the bank, several factors have been suggested as affecting profitability, such as regulation (Jordan, 1972; Edwards, 1977; Tucillo, 1973); bank size and economies of scale (Benstock, Hanweck and Humphrey, 1982; Short, 1979); competition (Phillips, 1964; Tschoegl, 1982); concentration (Rhoades, 1977; Schuster, 1984); growth in market (Short, 1979); interest rates as a proxy for capital scarcity (Short, 1979); and government ownership (Short, 1979). Finally, in their exposition of the Galbraith-Caves hypothesis, Edwards and Heggestad (1973) and Heggestad and Mingo (1976) suggest that market power experienced by banking corporations may be translated into risk avoidance by way of a 'low risk' loan portfolio rather than by being reflected in higher profits. They suggest that a lower level of service as measured in a variety of ways is detectable.

The testing of most of the variables described above as being represented in the literature does not present major difficulties. Some aspects of the literature, however, must be reviewed in some detail because of the differing emphases that US domestic studies must have as compared to international studies.

Regulation

Almost all the theoretical literature in the field of regulation, whether of financial intermediaries or otherwise, derives from an examination of the American experience. In part this is because governments in other countries seek to exercise control over markets through ownership of commercial organisations rather than through regulation. Banking, however, is one field where regulation co-exists alongside government ownership and where it could be expected that the theoretical literature emanating from the United States would have a wider applicability. The fact that the US banking regulation literature does not have a ready acceptance abroad must largely be a function of the uniqueness of American banking structures; large numbers of small unit retail banks sometimes serve markets particularly dependent on one or two industries and operate within the same economic system as large money centre branching banks. Because the US banking market taken as a whole is much less concentrated than other national banking markets, US supervisors may very well be less concerned with the possibility of system failure than other national authorities.

It is clear, for instance, that the ability of regulators to prevent the failures of large banks is relatively modest, particularly if we accept the implications of Kane's regulatory dialectic (1977 and 1981) portraying the constant see-sawing between industry and agency. It is also clear that while deregulation has increased the risk inherent in financial markets, if only because change induces risk, there is as yet no evidence of failures springing from the effects of the deregulatory process. In fact the origins of the international debt crisis are embedded in the regulated 1970s. On reflection it would be surprising if regulators had acquired the ability to prevent failure at a given cost, because:

1. There has been little debate on the cost effectiveness of financial institution regulation for any given set of objectives and costs.
2. More importantly, no theory exists to guide regulators in an understanding of the micro-economics of bank operations and particularly in relation to how banks approach the critical risk assessment and portfolio allocation decisions (see below).
3. Equally, theory is only now beginning to develop models to allow regulators to assess the inherent riskiness of banks. This is proceeding on the basis of options pricing theory (OPT) and the use of market discipline (Ronn and Verma, 1986). In particular the use of OPT to set appropriate capital levels may provide useful guidance to regulators and markets.
4. Theory also suggests that, irrespective of other economic costs induced by regulation, the influence of regulation may be malign in that it suppresses the disciplining role of the market and may underwrite the effects of 'herding' (Jain and Gupta, 1987). It is interesting to observe that the major single plank of bank regulatory policy is to increase capital ratios. However, the extent to which capital should be increased is unclear. Whether capital ratios in the order of 5 per cent are any better or worse than the ratios of 40 per cent to 70 per cent prevalent 150 years ago is a matter on which theory is silent, except to the extent that OPT shows considerable promise in formulating worthwhile models in this area. Because the cost of capital is an important part of the costs of intermediation, it is desirable that capital levels are not set too high (from an efficiency perspective) or too low (from the risk management viewpoint).

The current initiative by the world's central banks (led by the United States and United Kingdom) to introduce a regime of risk-adjusted capital, weighted in relation to regulators' perceptions of riskiness of certain assets, must be viewed in the context of our inability to determine optimal crude levels of capital. Capital, as is well known, can be regarded as a 'deductible' in insurance terms so that capital levels and deposit insurance premia are inversely related to each other. It is hard to understand how the authorities can simultaneously adopt the position that risk-related capital levels are desirable and variable rate deposit insurance premia impossible of calculation. Already anecdotal evidence is becoming available of internal bank portfolio allocation decisions being made on the basis of these arbitrary risk weightings, and a further possibility is that these weightings will ultimately be used for monetary control purposes in the same way as liquidity reserves in several countries are thinly disguised taxation or monetary policy tools.

Furthermore, until bank accounting is more firmly pinned to market-related asset values, the credibility of any capital policy must be seriously in doubt. It is important, in this connection, to recognise that securitisation is already providing a mechanism to bring bank accounting closer to reality.

More specifically in relation to the purpose of this chapter there is an implied assumption that within the United States the intensity of regulation is a constant; there may be a presumption that regulation outside the United States varies from country to country. Accordingly, the literature has never adequately examined the consequences of changes in the intensity of regulation. The empirical problems of doing so are, however, daunting since regulation is not readily susceptible of comparative measurement. I considered several approaches and the most promising was a Delphi/Jury of Expert Opinion ranking of the intensitivity of regulation on a limited scale. While it may be possible to locate experts who are familiar enough with regulation in each of the sample countries to provide a comparative ranking for a particular year, it proved impossible to do this in a time series study extending over ten years. (However, I report below the preliminary results of the effects of regulation based on a more limited assessment of regulatory intensity.)

It also has been proposed that the severity of regulation may be examined by constructing a matrix to investigate the presence or otherwise of various restrictions in different countries such as entry barriers, interest rate restrictions, credit ceilings, and so on. However, the direction of any of these individual effects is unclear. For instance contestable market theory and, indeed, regulation theory in general, point to the importance of barriers to entry in enhancing profitability while some of the other regulatory interventions may depress profitability.

The issues of regulation, competitive behaviour and concentration are related because the source of the correlation between profitability and concentration may be a correlation between concentration and regulatory protection on banks, and regulatory protection and profitability. I will return to the question of entry barriers and related issues under the heading of Industry Structure but in the absence of a clear theoretical model, a matrix or tabulation of various regulatory interventions will assist us little in the attempt to measure the differential effects of regulation across countries.

It has also been suggested that differences in the capital ratio could be used as a proxy for regulation on the basis that the market would equalise capital ratios for banks of the magnitude and stature of the banks in this sample. However, this requires that market-derived cost of capital figures be first obtained and excess costs of capital be computed for banks in each country. Aliber (1984, p. 670) suggests the use of Q ratios (Q ratios relate the market value of the firm to its book value) in examining changes in cost of capital for banks in different countries. Goodman (1984), p. 685) questions the conceptual appropriateness of the use of book value as a proxy for replacement cost but, in any case, many of the banks included in this research are not publicly traded, usually because they are state owned and no market capitalisation figures exist.

Of greater immediate relevance are the expense preference theories of Franklin Edwards (1977) who postulated that excess or supernormal profits of regulated industries may be diverted away from net profit into sub-optimal expenditure patterns related to management as opposed to shareholder preferences. There is also the possibility, particularly relevant in countries where the banking industry is unionised, that the super-normal earnings of firms in a regulated industry may be appropriated in the form of payroll expenditure.

Bank behaviour

We know remarkably little about the microeconomics of the large banking firm as typified by the dominant banks in markets outside the United States. For example, in relation to a crucial aspect of bank operations – economies of scale – there appears to be little to guide policy-makers. For instance, Gilligan and Smirlock (1984) find that only small banks enjoy economies of scale, but their analysis is confined to unit banks, and their definition of a 'large' bank is one with total assets in excess of $25 million. They rightly criticise other studies such as that of Benston, Hanweck and Humphrey (1982) for relying on the assumption that bank output is non-joint. In other words, that the cost of producing one output, say a cheque account, is independent of the costs of producing other outputs such as passbook accounts. However, Tschoegl (1983) produces some evidence that large international banks do not benefit from economies of scale.

It is interesting that the literature has failed to address many of the issues which are observed to be unresolved aspects of bank performance. Why, for instance, are German banks willing to take equity stakes in non-financial firms while British banks, in general, are not? Why do banks tend to operate within a narrow risk band and appear to be unwilling to accept greater risk in return for higher margins? How do we explain bank lending behaviour, particularly in relation to LDC lending?

The financial literature is strangely silent on these international issues. Models of bank dynamics (Klein, 1971; Baltensperger, 1980) tend to focus on how a bank arranges its portfolio of assets and liabilities, but not on how it determines the riskiness of individual asset components and, more specifically, not on how it forms perceptions of expected cash flows and associate variances. This, of course, is of particular relevance in the issue of the causes of the LDC debt problem.

Guttentag and Herring (1984) offer some interesting insights on some of these issues. Firstly, they show that the observed bank behaviour of failing to make trade-offs between risk and loan interest returns can be best explained in terms of agency theory. They postulate that higher interest rates decrease expected net cash flows to the borrower which in turn increases the likelihood that the borrower will attempt to capture more upside potential by choosing riskier projects whose downside risk would be carried by the lender. Extrapolating from the Guttentag and Herring hypothesis it is possible to argue that lenders are attempting to lend to projects whose perceived risks are relatively low, otherwise they would, in the absence of agency constraints, prefer to lend to higher risk projects at commensurately higher interest rates. Observational support for this hypothesis is derived by examining the low margins over LIBOR at which 'big ticket' loans are booked. Bourke (1987) also provides data in relation to the provisions for credit losses in 1985 of 116 large banks throughout the world with provisions in general running at substantially less than 2 per cent of gross loans. While provisions for loan losses are notoriously subjective (see Bourke, 1984) they do provide an indication *ex post* of banks' prior expectations of loan losses.

A related issue is the extent to which banks 'herd' or indulge in 'lemming'-like behaviour in relation to their credit assessment procedures (see Lessard, 1983; Jain and Gupta, 1987). Specifically, 'herding' is defined as the explicit policy to take only the credit and portfolio decisions of other banks into account when reaching these decisions. Jain and Gupta test for the presence of such effects among US banks between 1977 and 1982 and find that the evidence in support of herding behaviour is weak, and consistent with lenders using the same models to evaluate country risk. (McDermott, 1986, also produces some evidence in support of this similarity of model proposition.) Their model, however, lacks certain important variables, for example market strength and access to channels of loan distribution, and the issue must still be regarded as open. They do, however, make the important point relevant to the discussion of regulation below, that a pattern of 'herding' presents moral hazard problems for prudential authorities because it is based on the concept of 'strength in numbers' and the expected inability of a lender-of-last-resort to differentiate, when providing assistance, between troubled banks whose difficulties arise from the same cause.

The crucial ingredient which, however, is missing from the herding theory as a means of explaining bank behaviour is that it does not comment on the process by which the leaders of the 'herding' process made their credit decisions which others ultimately followed. For this insight, Guttentag and Herring are important. However, because a regulator's perspective is system-wide in addition to being focused on individual banks, Jain and Gupta's analysis may provide a clearer picture of how a system problem develops.

As noted above, much of the US banking literature is based on studies of small banks, frequently without branches, and has little relevance to our understanding of the operations of large money-centre and, indeed, international banks. The lack of a clear theoretical guide increases the difficulties in correctly formulating appropriate research in an international context. Accordingly, it is difficult to translate either the Guttentag and Herring or the 'herding' theories into workable hypotheses to be applied in the international context excepting so far as the Guttentag and Herring approach may have a bearing on the Galbraith–Caves and Edwards–Heggestad–Mingo hypotheses of risk avoidance (see below).

Industry structure

Studies of market structure for the banking industry within the United States have a long history and most research work has concluded that concentration is positively and moderately related to profitability. Rhoades (1977) provides an extensive review of empirical work in this area. However, more recent work casts doubts on the validity of these findings and, in particular, Gilbert (1984) in a critical review of the literature, suggests that earlier studies were unable to take advantage of the implications of the subsequent development of the contestable market theory (Baumol, Panzar and Willig, 1982) with its emphasis on entry restrictions. He also summarises the evidence in favour of the proposition that the correlation between concentration and profitability may reflect superior efficiency among the larger firms rather than the use of market power – the 'differential efficiency' hypothesis. There is no direct evidence to date on this effect in banking markets but Chappell and Cottle (1984) report an experiment which has a bearing on the design of the present study. They examined the relationship between the average price-cost margin for industrial firms (sales less cost of materials less payroll expenses/sales) and concentration in two settings. Firstly, when efficiency variables (in this case related to efficient plant size) were included they found that the price-cost margin was positively related to concentration for the four largest firms but no significant relationship was found for the smaller firms. Secondly, when efficiency variables were included, concentration is found to have an insignificant relationship to all firm sizes although interestingly the sign is negative. Unfortunately the data required to support a similar study in the international banking sector are not available; however Chappell and Cottle's use of the price-cost margin approximates to my 'value-added' variable (see below). An industrial study by Peltzman (1977) also found a signficant negative correlation between changes in concentration and unit costs for industrial firms. In his conclusion Peltzman notes that his findings are 'consistent with an eclectic view but one in which efficiency effects predominate'.

Smirlock (1985) takes this discussion a little further in the banking context in that he examines the effect of market share and concentration on profitability, and finds that market share rather than concentration has a signficiant and positive impact. Smirlock raises an important caveat about his work. His research is confined to limited branching states (Colorado, Kansas, Missouri, Nebraska, New Mexico, Oklahoma and Wyoming) and the extension of his approach to branching states (and obviously countries) may not be appropriate. I believe that this caveat may be related to differences in the nature of barriers to entry, which are regulatory in limited branching states but commercial and regulatory in other states.

On the other hand Rhoades and Rutz (1981) have shown a significant negative relationship between concentration and firm rank stability (which is itself a proxy for competitive behaviour) for US banking markets. They also found no significant relationship between concentration and market share in these markets.

An interesting study by Hannan and McDowell (1984) relates the rate of diffusion of automated teller machines (ATMs) to several independent variables, including concentration. Having controlled for factors such as wage costs, they found that the rate of diffusion was positively related to concentration. These findings are difficult to interpret in the context of industrial organisation literature, in the sense that ATM diffusion may be regarded as competitive behaviour and accordingly the expected relationship with concentration should be negative. It is likely, however, that the findings are more in keeping with the 'differential efficiency' hypothesis in so far as dominant firms may have attained that position by continually investing in cost-saving equipment.

I have already raised the topic of barriers to entry in relation to the measurement of the effects of regulation and it must also be considered under the heading of market structure as Gilbert (1984) has pointed out. Contestable markets theory holds that the adverse welfare consequences of concentration (if any) may be ameliorated if barriers to entry are not present. Two questions arise. What is the extent of regulatory barriers to entry? Does the existence of concentration in itself constitute an effective barrier, particularly in retail markets?

Looking firstly at the question of the existence of regulatory barriers, paradoxically these barriers when they exist may well be more apparent than real. For instance while many countries in this survey maintained formal entry barriers, particularly in relation to foreign banks, almost all countries had experienced a growth of potential competitors to traditionally organised banks such as building societies in Britain, Ireland and Australia, Trustee Savings Banks in New Zealand, thrifts in the United States, and so on. Additionally, there are very few examples of completely new entrants to banking markets attempting to compete in the retail sector and, in fact, examples are scarce of any form of retail activity transferring successfully across international frontiers in recent years. Tschoegl (1987) provides a comprehensive discussion of the factors affecting foreign direct investment in retail banking. He suggests that regulatory constraints are only one of many factors.

Baer and Mote (1985) present evidence that concentration is higher internationally than in the United States, and within the United States is higher in branching than in non-branching states. They also make the important point that studies of market structure must adequately define the relevant market, which in the banking context includes non-bank financial intermediaries. Their approach to market definition is similar to that adopted in my work.

International evidence in the literature is also scant in relation to the question of whether concentrated markets themselves constitute a barrier to entry. Ball and Tschoegl (1982) suggest that concentrated markets may offer a price umbrella under which new, fringe entrants may shelter (p.417) but offer no empirical evidence.

Spiller and Favaro (1984) present evidence from Uruguay of changes in competitive behaviour among dominant banks when barriers to entry were lowered and local non-bank financial intermediaries were allowed to enter the market.

Rhoades (1983) has found that the market share of international business held by banks from outside the United States is increasing; the share of the international deposit market (as defined by the deposits of the top 100 banks in the world) held by US banks has fallen from 28.97 per cent in 1970 to 13.51 per cent in 1979 and, obviously, the extent to which the Federal Reserve can act as a 'natural' lender-of-last-resort to the US dollar part of this market has also diminished. Aliber (1980) estimated from BIS and IMF sources that dollars accounted for 73 per cent of external deposits denominated in dollars, marks, Swiss and French francs, sterling and guilder. Some interesting research by Poulsen (1986) shows that Japanese banks react to a tightening of credit conditions in Japan by using resources generated by their offices in the United States to lend back into Japan. Dufey and Giddy (1984) have drawn attention to the practical problems caused for regulators when assets and liabilities are located in different legal jurisdictions. Poulsen's research is an indication of the complexity of forces governing the management of international banks and their prudential supervision.

In summary the present state of the literature offers little clear-cut guidance in relation to the role of concentration in bank profitability determination. In some instances lack of data makes the testing of some promising concepts impossible for international markets.

Risk avoidance

The Edwards–Heggestad (1973) and Heggestad–Mingo (1976) variant of the Galbraith–Caves hypothesis (Galbraith, 1967), as noted above, submits that market leaders in concentrated industries take a significant portion of the potential profits latent in their position of market power in the form of avoiding uncertainty. In the case of banking this avoidance of uncertainty largely takes the form of a reduced risk profile on its loan book.

INTERNATIONAL BANK PROFITABILITY – THE EVIDENCE

Having reviewed the literature in this area, some empirical evidence is presented from research which I have conducted in the field of international banking.

The research is based on data drawn from the financial statements of 116 banks each year in the fourteen years from 1972 to 1985 in fifteen countries or territories – Australia, New Zealand, California, Massachusetts, New York, Canada, Ireland, Scotland, England and Wales, Belgium, France, the Netherlands, Denmark, Norway and Spain. The banks included in the sample were every bank in these countries which fell within the top 500 banks in the world in June 1980, ranked by total assets.

As far as possible data were standardised to remove differences in local accounting practices particularly in relation to the treatment of reserves.

Value added measures

As a further step towards dealing with this general problem, I have suggested the concept of 'value added' as part of the solution process. Two variants on this approach are used. In industrial terms, value added is usually taken to mean the difference between selling price and all bought-in inputs excluding labour. In banking terms, value added would be strictly defined as loan interest and other revenue less deposit interest and other non-wage expenses. In the light of international data problems, I believe that the following two measures of value added used are a reasonable proxy.

Firstly, net income before tax + staff expense is used to test the expense preference theory on the basis that this measure of value added largely removes the possibility of either managerially induced expenditure or labour union-negotiated wage demands appropriating excessive proportions of net income, and allows the relationship between concentration and other independent variables and this dependent variable to be estimated.

Secondly, net income before tax + staff expenses + loan losses is a proxy for gross margin which is frequently unavailable on an international basis and allows the determinants of gross profit to be tested. Additionally, by observing the relationships between net income before tax + staff expenses + loan losses and concentration, comment may be made on the possible operation of the Edwards–Heggestad–Mingo effect.

Economies of scale

The results may be divided into three separate studies:

1. an econometric review of the determinants of bank profitability which is presented in summary form (1972–80);
2. preliminary conclusions from a study of the relationship between profitability, staff expenses, regulation and deregulation (1972–85); and
3. more descriptive statistics in relation to bank performance (1972–85).

Determinants of bank profitability

The econometric results all relate to asset (as opposed to capital) based returns and, in general, show capital ratios, liquidity ratios and interest rates as being positively related to profitability. The detailed results are not presented here but may be found in Bourke (1988). The finding in relation to capital ratios is to be expected as, in accounting terms, capital represents a 'free' resource and Revell (1980) had noted an inverse relationship between capital ratios and costs of intermediation. It is also possible to speculate that well capitalised banks enjoy access to cheaper (because less risky) sources of funds, or that the prudence implied by high capital ratios is maintained in the loan portfolio with consequent improvement in profit rates. The results in relation to liquidity ratios are less expected as conventional wisdom holds that liquidity holdings (particularly if imposed by government) represent an expense to banks.

As was expected, staff expenses show an inverse if weak correlation with pre-tax return on assets.

The results in relation to concentration require some consideration. In line with findings in other parts of the literature, concentration is shown to be moderately and positively related to pre-tax return on assets. However, when used in equations having one of the measures of value added as dependent variable, the sign of the relationship changes to an inverse relationship.

It had been postulated that if, for instance, support were to be shown for the expense preference theories, the sign of the relationship would remain positive and the relationship would strengthen in the case of the dependent variable 'net income before tax + staff expenses as ratio of total assets'. The change of the sign of the concentration variable implies that, as concentration increases, staff expenses are squeezed. Support for this contention is found in Heggestad and Mingo (1976) who found that higher levels of concentration were associated with lower levels of service and, presumably, lower staffing costs.

In relation to the dependent variable 'net income before tax + staff expenses + loan losses as ratio of total assets' a similar phenomenon is evident as the sign of the concentration variable changes which carries the implication, in addition to that observed in relation to the 'net income before tax + staff expenses as ratio of total assets'/concentration relationship, that higher levels of concentration are associated with lower loan loss costs. An immediate connection to the Edwards–Heggestad finding may be made – they hypothesised that higher levels of concentration were associated with lower levels of loan portfolio risk. Additionally, a Federal Reserve Board study, cited by Almarin Phillips (1984) found a slight but significant tendency for the rates charged by a bank to decrease as its market share increased. Bearing in mind that the variable 'net income before tax + staff expenses + provision for loan losses as a ratio of total assets' is a reasonably close proxy for gross margin, the present findings are not in contradiction with the results of previous work.

In general the results are in agreement with concentration and bank profitability studies for the domestic US market and support is found for the Edwards–Heggestad hypothesis. No support is found for expense preference expenditure theories.

Effects of regulation and deregulation

Some further work in relation to regulation over the extended period to 1985 has produced the following tentative results: intensity of regulation is associated with higher profitability; deregulation produces no observable effect in relation to profitability; increased staff expenses are associated both with intensity of regulation and with deregulation.

To an extent, these results are in accord with theoretically based expectations (and with observation of certain types of salaries after deregulation) but it should be emphasised that the relationships are weak and subject to further testing.

Some descriptive statistics

The period covered by the study (1972–85) is one of significant economic disruption and upheaval. Oil price increases, recession and volatile interest rates have all presumably affected the performance of financial institutions. In addition, several countries – the United States, Canada, Australia and New Zealand – have experienced deregulatory pressures to a greater or lesser extent.

Tables 9.1, 9.2, 9.3 and 9.4 provide summary information in relation to some critical bank management variables.

Making necessary qualifications for the difficulties associated with working from published financial statements, the picture that emerges from this survey of world banking, particularly since 1979, is that:

1. capital ratios show little sign of improvement even allowing for possible understatement of credit losses (see Kane, 1985, for some US comparisons);
2. profitability in general has improved (this confirms a trend reported in Revell, 1980);
3. there is some evidence that labour productivity has improved in many countries.

Table 9.1 Capital and reserves as percentage of total assets

Capital adequacy

	1972	*1979*	*1985*
Ireland	6.12	5.90	5.64
England & Wales	6.12	5.94	4.26
Scotland	7.80	7.98	7.64
New Zealand	5.57	3.12	4.05
Australia	5.06	6.36	5.27
Canada	5.97	3.33	4.46
Massachusetts	6.29	4.78	5.25
California	4.02	3.61	4.22
New York	4.61	3.61	5.75
Denmark	9.65	7.33	5.83
Netherlands	3.85	3.08	3.50
Norway	5.70	5.02	4.28
Belgium	3.20	3.24	2.28
Spain	6.56	7.17	5.98
France	1.87	2.85	2.18

Table 9.2 Capital and reserves and total borrowings* as percentage of total assets

	1972	*1979*	*1985*
Ireland	8.45	6.78	6.61
England & Wales	7.95	7.34	6.61
Scotland	9.66	8.64	8.17
New Zealand	4.89	3.79	5.57
Australia	21.14	23.77	11.53
Canada	5.90	4.46	6.77
Massachusetts	6.85	8.60	6.79
California	10.46	5.24	5.28
New York	8.27	6.17	5.94
Denmark	7.73	9.78	9.86
Netherlands	12.64	11.01	6.44
Norway	6.00	5.28	5.82
Belgium	3.04	5.49	6.00
Spain	8,88	6.87	6.56
France	6.15	7.27	2.97

Note:
* Total borrowings is used as the best available proxy for subordinated loan stock

Table 9.3 Gross (GP) and net profitability after tax (NPAT) as percentage of total assets

Profitability

	1972		*1979*		*1985*	
	GP	*NP*	*GP*	*NP*	*GP*	*NP*
Ireland	1.27	0.67	3.85	0.91	4.23	0.64
England & Wales	1.34	0.83	2.73	1.08	3.51	0.56
Scotland	2.26	–	3.19	–	2.60	0.51
New Zealand	2.54	0.59	2.38	0.35	3.53	0.92
Australia	0.72	0.39	1.56	0.80	3.48	0.75
Canada	3.22	0.84	1.93	0.45	2.48	0.52
Massachusetts	2.42	0.64	2.82	0.60	3.07	0.67
California	1.94	0.47	2.78	0.67	3.43	0.09
New York	1.95	0.57	2.41	0.59	2.78	0.82
Denmark	4.33	1.10	3.89	0.67	3.64	1.30
Netherlands	1.83	–	2.19	–	2.24	0.33
Norway	2.29	0.31	2.78	0.44	1.94	0.47
Belgium	1.24	0.29	2.35	0.30	1.63	0.24
Spain	1.38	1.14	2.90	0.82	2.69	0.52
France	2.14	0.20	1.65	0.18	2.94	0.07

Table 9.4 Staff expenses as percentage of total assets

Productivity

	1972	*1979*	*1985*
Ireland	2.38	1.06	2.37
England & Wales	1.91	0.64	1.90
Scotland	1.30	1.30	1.30
New Zealand	1.46	1.72	1.46
Australia	–	–	2.02
Canada	1.17	1.14	1.66
Massachusetts	1.65	1.50	1.35
California	1.81	1.32	1.16
New York	1.19	1.25	1.01
Denmark	–	2.07	1.96
Netherlands	1.24	1.36	1.22
Norway	–	1.96	1.38
Belgium	1.62	1.01	–
Spain	1.43	2.07	–
France	2.40	1.61	1.61

This is in contrast to Rhoades and White (1984) who found that productivity in banks from 1972 to 1979 was static, or declining for large branching banks. Admittedly, the most marked change in trend in my data has occurred after 1979.

In summary, a period of rapid market change has been accompanied by higher accounting profits, some productivity increases and static accounts-based capital adequacy.

More detailed information is presented in Tables 9.5 to 9.9. Table 9.5 shows ranking of the performance indicators in Tables 9.6, 9.7 and 9.8 for each of the three averaging periods in those tables.

Table 9.6 shows the 5-year average 1981–5 of the following ratios: NPAT/TA, NPBT/TA, NPBT + Staff Expenses/TA, NPBT-Dividends/TA, NPAT/Capital and Reserves, Capital Reserves/TA, Cash and Bank/TA and Cash and Bank + Investment Securities/TA. (See below for a discussion of the role of these measures.)

Table 9.7 depicts the 5-year average 1976–80 for the same ratios.

Table 9.8 shows the 14-year average 1972–85 for the same ratios.

Table 9.9 is a summary table for 1985 and 1981: it summarises gross margins, staff expenses and net margin, all as percentage of total assets.

Table 9.5 Ranking of performance indicators

(a) 5-year average 1981–5

	NPAT/TA	*NPBT/TA*	*NPBT & Staff Expenses/TA*	*NPBT Div/TA*	*NPAT/ Cap & Res*	*Cap & Res/TA*	*Cash & Bank Inv Sec/TA*
Ireland	7	5	4	5	10	3	7
England & Wales	8	9	6	7	9	6	14
Scotland	10	7	8	6	15	2	12
New Zealand	2	2	3	2	1	10	10
Australia	3	4	2	4	2	7	15
Canada	8	8	11	9	5	11	11
Massachusetts	4	3	1	3	4	4	6
California	11	11	7	12	11	9	13
New York	5	6	10	8	6	5	9
Denmark	1	1	5	1	3	1	2
Netherlands	12	13	13	11	14	13	5
Norway	8	12	14	14	7	12	4
Belgium	13	–	–	–	13	14	1
Spain	6	10	9	9	8	8	8
France	14	14	12	13	12	15	3

(b) 5-year average 1976–80

	NPBT/TA	*NPAT/TA*	*NPBT & Staff Expenses/TA*	*NPBT Div/TA*	*NPAT/ Cap & Res*	*Cap & Res/TA*	*Cash & Bank Inv Sec/TA*
Ireland	1	3	3	3	1	5	4
England & Wales	4	1	9	1	5	6	14
Scotland	2	2	2	2	7	2	15
New Zealand	12	10	5	10	8	11	11
Australia	8	5	14	5	12	4	5
Canada	9	11	12	11	4	12	12
Massachusetts	7	8	6	8	10	7	3
California	5	7	8	7	2	10	8
New York	6	9	10	9	3	9	7
Denmark	13	5	1	5	14	1	6
Netherlands	15	12	11	12	15	13	13
Norway	10	12	3	12	13	8	9
Belgium	14	–	–	–	11	14	1
Spain	13	4	7	4	6	3	10
France	11	14	13	14	9	15	2

Table 9.5 cont.

(c) 14-year average 1972–85

	NPBT/TA	*NPAT/TA*	*NPBT & Staff Expenses/TA*	*NPBT Div/TA*	*NPAT/ Cap & Res*	*Cap & Res/TA*	*Cash & Bank Inv Sec/TA*
Ireland	1	4	5	4	5	4	3
England & Wales	4	8	8	3	7	5	14
Scotland	3	3	4	2	13	2	15
New Zealand	7	5	2	5	2	10	11
Australia	11	6	13	6	8	7	6
Canada	8	2	6	9	1	11	13
Massachusetts	5	7	3	8	9	6	4
California	9	10	7	11	6	12	12
New York	6	9	10	10	3	9	8
Denmark	1	1	1	1	11	1	5
Netherlands	14	10	12	12	15	13	9
Norway	10	12	11	13	12	8	7
Belgium	13	–	–	–	14	14	1
Spain	2	7	9	7	4	3	10
France	12	13	14	14	10	15	2

Table 9.6 5-year average 1981–5

	NPAT/TA	*NPBT/TA*	*NPBT & Staff Expenses/TA*	*NPBT Div/TA*	*NPAT/ Cap & Res*	*Cap & Res/TA*	*Cash & Bank/TA*	*Cash & Bank Inv Sec/TA*
Ireland	0.53	0.95	3.14	0.75	9.27	5.68	21.57	35.10
England & Wales	0.51	0.66	2.69	0.68	10.93	4.65	18.43	21.49
Scotland	0.44	0.88	2.12	0.73	7.42	6.00	17.02	21.98
New Zealand	0.78	1.52	3.17	1.36	20.10	3.85	11.86	28.27
Australia	0.76	1.09	3.33	0.88	16.60	4.63	6.76	21.46
Canada	0.51	0.67	1.81	0.50	13.52	3.83	14.83	23.82
Massachusetts	0.72	1.10	3.87	0.90	13.95	5.14	24.96	35.17
California	0.36	0.52	2.16	0.32	8.88	4.12	16.68	21.89
New York	0.67	0.93	2.03	0.64	13.30	5.12	23.53	33.87
Denmark	0.98	1.62	3.02	1.49	15.80	6.08	22.62	43.48
Netherlands	0.28	0.41	1.65	0.33	8.78	3.18	33.00	37.24
Norway	0.48	0.45	1.37	0.23	13.04	3.73	13.85	37.56
Belgium	0.20	–	–	–	8.75	2.30	34.00	63.59
Spain	0.54	0.65	2.05	0.50	12.54	4.41	25.57	34.63
France	0.17	0.29	1.78	0.28	8.85	1.84	39.54	41.74

Table 9.7 5-year average 1976–80

	NPAT/TA	*NPBT/TA*	*NPBT & Staff Expenses/TA*	*NPBT Div/TA*	*NPAT/ Cap & Res*	*Cap & Res/TA*	*Cash & Bank/TA*	*Cash & Bank Inv Sec/TA*
Ireland	0.97	1.46	2.52	1.46	16.55	5.86	25.70	41.80
England & Wales	0.76	1.55	2.20	1.55	13.03	5.75	22.73	30.47
Scotland	0.89	1.54	2.79	1.54	11.91	7.66	22.43	29.03
New Zealand	0.39	0.84	2.50	0.84	11.10	3.67	12.07	33.05
Australia	0.53	1.01	1.07	1.01	8.95	5.91	12.68	40.31
Canada	0.49	0.79	2.04	0.80	13.88	3.52	21.41	32.91
Massachusetts	0.55	0.89	2.47	0.90	10.40	5.42	30.01	43.15
California	0.58	0.92	2.30	0.93	15.31	3.78	25.21	36.36
New York	0.56	0.85	2.13	0.85	14.50	3.84	29.44	37.81
Denmark	0.38	1.01	3.20	1.01	5.03	7.72	18.78	39.81
Netherlands	0.05	0.65	2.05	0.65	1.62	3.15	25.18	31.55
Norway	0.43	0.65	2.52	0.65	8.77	5.00	7.05	36.26
Belgium	0.25	–	–	–	9.38	2.75	20.48	51.06
Spain	0.85	1.03	2.41	1.03	12.35	6.88	16.24	33.78
France	0.40	0.32	1.73	0.32	10.72	2.26	44.35	47.45

Table 9.8 14-year average 1972–85

	NPAT/TA	*NPBT/TA*	*NPBT & Staff Expenses/TA*	*NPBT Div/TA*	*NPAT/ Cap & Res*	*Cap & Res/TA*	*Cash & Bank/TA*	*Cash & Bank Inv Sec/TA*
Ireland	0.73	1.23	2.39	1.15	12.73	5.72	26.22	41.79
England & Wales	0.65	0.96	2.11	1.16	11.70	5.51	22.92	31.47
Scotland	0.68	1.28	2.41	1.25	9.63	7.12	21.67	28.07
New Zealand	0.56	1.12	2.78	1.07	13.88	4.20	14.19	33.19
Australia	0.31	0.98	1.81	0.91	11.65	5.08	12.06	38.42
Canada	0.55	1.41	2.16	0.82	13.94	3.96	20.50	32.57
Massachusetts	0.62	0.95	2.55	0.87	11.48	5.45	27.64	40.18
California	0.46	0.71	2.14	0.63	12.12	3.86	22.62	32.59
New York	0.60	0.88	2.02	0.78	13.75	4.39	26.62	35.87
Denmark	0.73	1.46	3.33	1.41	10.09	7.55	18.86	39.49
Netherlands	0.12	0.55	1.92	0.52	3.77	3.26	27.50	33.58
Norway	0.44	0.53	2.00	0.46	9.76	4.67	10.46	36.77
Belgium	0.20	–	–	–	8.48	2.59	23.99	53.24
Spain	0.71	0.95	2.06	0.90	13.13	6.06	19.52	33.34
France	0.25	0.31	1.77	0.30	10.45	1.91	41.15	43.69

Table 9.9 Gross margin* staff expenses and net margin as percentage of total assets

		1985			*1985*	
	*Gross margin**	*Staff expenses*	*NPBT*	*Gross margin**	*Staff expenses*	*NPBT*
		as % of TA			*as % of TA*	
Ireland	4.23	2.38	1.10	3.67	2.04	1.20
England & Wales	3.51	1.91	1.01	2.90	1.90	0.78
Scotland	2.60	1.31	0.95	–	–	–
New Zealand	3.53	1.46	1.87	–	–	–
Australia	3.48	2.07	1.25	2.34	1.48	0.76
Canada	2.48	1.66	0.73	1.97	1.45	0.70
Massachusetts	3.07	1.35	1.06	3.02	1.46	1.01
California	3.43	1.16	0.18	2.33	1.31	0.63
New York	2.78	1.01	1.08	2.25	1.32	0.84
Denmark	3.64	1.96	2.46	2.83	2.29	0.75
Netherlands	2.24	1.22	0.47	2.09	1.56	0.46
Norway	1.94	1.38	0.43	1.90	2.02	0.47
Belgium	1.63	0.62	–	1.74	0.70	–
Spain	2.69	1.43	0.66	2.29	1.30	0.60
France	2.94	1.61	0.09	2.42	1.36	0.68

Note:
* Gross margin = NPBT + Staff Expenses + Provision for Loan Losses.

PERFORMANCE MEASURES

In general the performance measures used are self-explanatory but some comment may be appropriate on the following:

NPBT Staff Expenses/TA

As noted above, this ratio was developed to examine two aspects of performance: it is a proxy for gross margin or spread which is frequently unavailable in published accounts; it was also designed to examine the possibility that profitability is diverted from net profit into payroll expenses, a possiblity particularly likely in heavily regulated or unionised countries.

NPBT-Dividends

This ratio attempts to deal with the problem caused by the fact that capital is a 'free' source of funds in the sense that there is no accounting cost attached to its inclusion in the balance sheet. Bourke (1988) shows that capital was the most powerful determinant of profitability unless adjusted for this accounting cost problem. Net profitability may be adjusted in two ways in response.

One way is by imputing a national interest cost to capital and reducing reported income accordingly. This suffers from two disadvantages. Firstly, and theoretically, the appropriate cost to be associated with capital is an equity rather than a debt cost – the cost or rate which shareholders require to maintain their shareholding. Secondly, and practically, in an era of rapidly fluctuating interest rates, there is no immediately evident interest rate which appears appropriate, such as year end, average, or start of year. Aliber (1984, p. 670) suggested the ratio of market value to book value as a required rate of return as noted above.

A second way is by imputing a notional cost of equity to the capital. The cost of equity is notoriously difficult to estimate. It is suggested that a workable alternative is the level of dividends paid by the bank. This at least has the practical advantage of being available through the published financial statements. It is also possible to make the theoretical case that dividends represent the cost that bank managements feel they must incur to maintain shareholder support.

RESULTS

The major changes can be summarised as follows:

1. Australia and New Zealand have both emerged as profitable locations. The continuance of high rates of inflation in both of these countries should, however, be borne in mind, although as noted above, the precise effects of inflation are not clearly understood.
2. Britain and Ireland became markedly less profitable in 1981–5 than in 1976–80, or over the 14-year average during 1972–85.

Table 9.5 provides detail in support of the conclusions above, with most performance indicators moving in line. A closer investigation of NPBT/TA and NPBT + Staff Expenses/TA indicates that some of the changes in ranking may be due to a mismatch between gross margin (NPBT + Staff Expenses/TA) and net margin (NPBT/TA) in so far as growth in staff expenses may have absorbed an increasing proportion of the margin. This effect is most noticeable in the case of Ireland, but growth in staff expenses also appears significant in the case of Australia. Table 9.9 examines the relationship between gross margin (now defined as NPBT + Staff Expenses + Provision for Loan Losses), staff expenses and net margin. The general trend is interesting. Gross margins have increased on a worldwide basis and so, in general, have net margins. Staff expenses have declined substantially in all countries except Australia, Canada, Ireland and England and Wales.

This improvement in staff productivity has been little remarked in the bank professional literature although its consequences are obviously far-reaching in their effects on profitability. Several possible explanations exist. Support for Revell (1980) is provided in so far as his contention was that inflation in the earlier years of the study, working through staff expenses, had an inverse impact on profitability. Another, not necessarily exclusive, hypothesis is that the investment in automation has been rewarded in lower payroll costs, although other aspects of this research (not reported here for reasons of space) do not completely support the suggestion of large increases in automated equipment as measured by the ratio of equipment to total assets.

Other factors in profitability have remained largely unchanged as can be seen under the capital adequacy and liquidity headings.

In summary it appears that the major trends during the period 1981–5 were increasing margins as measured by NPBT + Staff Expenses/TA; decreasing proportionate payroll expenditure as measured by Staff Expenses/TA; leading in most countries to an improvement in net margin.

Note

1. Much of the research on which this essay is based was conducted while the author was a member of the School of Banking and Finance at the University of New South Wales, Sydney. The generous financial assistance of Allied Irish Banks is gratefully acknowledged.

References

Aliber, Robert Z. (1980) 'The integration of the off-shore and domestic banking system', *Journal of Monetary Economics*, 6.
Aliber, Robert Z. (1984) 'International banking – a survey', *Journal of Money, Credit and Banking*, vol. 16, no. 4, November, part 2.
Baer, Herbert and Larry R. Mote (1985) 'The effects of nationwide banking on concentration: evidence from abroad', *Federal Reserve Bank of Chicago Economic Perspectives*, vol. 9, no. 1, January/February.
Ball, Clifford, A. and Adrian Tschoegl (1982) 'The decision to establish a foreign bank branch or subsidiary: an application of binary classification procedures', *Journal of Financial and Qualitative Analysis*, vol. 17, no. 3, September.
Baltensperger, Ernst (1980) 'Alternative approaches to the theory of the banking firm', *Journal of Monetary Economics*, 6.
Baumol, William J., John C. Panzar and Robert D. Willig (1982) *Contestable Markets and the Theory of Industrial Structure* (New York: Harcourt Brace Jovanovich).
Bell, Frederick W. and Neil Murphy (1969) 'Impact of market structure on the price of a commercial banking service', *Review of Economics and Statistics*, May.
Benston, George J., Gerald A. Hanweck and David B. Humphrey (1982) 'Scale economies in banking', *Journal of Money, Credit and Banking*, vol. 14, no. 4, November, part 1.
Bourke, Philip (1984) 'Research note, profitability and Irish banks: an international comparative study', *Irish Journal of Business and Administrative Research*, vol. 6, no. 1, April.
Bourke, Philip (1987) 'The evolution of bank performance indicators', University of New England Research Series, November.
Bourke, Philip (1988) 'The determinants of bank profitability in Europe, North America and Australia', *Journal of Banking and Finance,*, vol. 12, no. 4.
Chappell, William F. and Rex L. Cottle (1984) 'Sources of concentration – related profits', *Southern Economic Journal*, vol. 51, no. 4.
Dufey, Gunter and Ian Giddy (1984) 'Eurocurrency deposit risk', *Journal of Banking and Finance*, 8, pp.567–89.
Edwards, Franklin R. (1977) 'Managerial objectives in regulated industries: expense preference behavior in banking', *Journal of Political Economy*, February.
Edwards, Franklin R. and Arnold A. Heggestad (1973) 'Uncertainty, market structure and performance: the Galbraith–Caves hypothesis and managerial motives in banking', *Quarterly Journal of Economics*, vol. 87, no. 3, August.
Galbraith, J. K. (1967) *The New Industrial State* (Boston: Houghton Mifflin).
Gilbert, Alton R. (1984) 'Bank market structure and competition: a survey', *Journal of Money, Credit and Banking*, vol. 16, no. 4, November, part 2.
Gilligan, Thomas W. and Michael L. Smirlock (1984) 'An empirical study of joint production and scale economies in commercial banking', *Journal of Banking and Finance*, 8.

Goodman, Laurie, S. (1984) 'Comment on international banking: a survey', *Journal of Money, Credit and Banking*, vol. 16, no. 4, November, part 2.
Guttentag, Jack and Richard Herrring (1984) 'Credit rationing and financial disorder', *Journal of Finance*, vol. 34, no. 5, December.
Hannan, Timothy H. and John M. McDowell (1984) 'Market concentration and the diffusion of new technology in the banking industry', *Review of Economics and Statistics*, vol. 66, no. 4.
Haslam, John A. (1968) 'A statistical analysis of the relative profitability of commercial banks', *Journal of Finance*, vol. 34, no. 1, March.
Heggestad, Arnold A. and John J. Mingo (1976) 'Prices, nonprices and concentration in commercial banking', *Journal of Money, Credit and Banking*, vol. 8, no. 1, February.
International Monetary Fund, 'International financial statistics' (Washington DC) monthly.
Jain, Arvind, K. and Satyadev Gupta (1987) 'Some evidence on "herding" behavior of US banks', *Journal of Money, Credit and Banking*, vol. 19, no. 1, February.
Jordan, William A. (1972) 'Producer protection, prior market structure and the effects of government regulation', *Journal of Law and Economics*, 15.
Kane, Edward J. (1977) 'Good intentions and the unintended evil: the case against selective credit allocation', *Journal of Money, Credit and Banking*, vol. 9, no. 1, February, part 1.
Kane, Edward J. (1981) 'Impact of regulation on economic behavior', *Journal of Finance*, vol. 36, no. 2, May.
Kane, Edward J. (1985) *The Gathering Crisis in Federal Deposit Insurance* (Cambridge, Mass.: MIT Press).
Klein, Michael A. (1971) 'A theory of the banking firm', *Journal of Money, Credit and Banking*, vol. 3, no. 2, May, part 1.
Kwast, Myron L. and John T. Rose (1982) 'Pricing, operating efficiency and profitability among large commercial banks', *Journal of Banking and Finance*, 6.
Lessard, Donald (1983) 'North-South: the implications for international banking', *Journal of Banking and Finance*, 7.
McDermott, Neil M. (1986) 'Country risk and banker judgement', Working paper, Department of Finance, University of New South Wales.
Peltzman, S. (1977) 'The gains and losses from industrial concentration', *Journal of Law and Economics*, vol. 10, nop. 2, October.
Phillips, Almarin (1964) 'Competition, confusion and commercial banking', *Journal of Finance*, vol. 19, no. 1, March.
Poulsen, Annette B. (1986) 'Japanese bank regulation and the activities of US offices of Japanese banks', *Journal of Money, Credit and Banking*, vol. 18, no. 3, August.
Revell, J. R. S. (1980) *Costs and Margins in Banking: An International Survey* (Paris: OECD).
Rhoades, Stephen A. (1977) 'Structure and performance studies in banking: a summary and evaluation', *Staff Economic Studies*, no. 92 (Washington DC: Federal Reserve Board).
Rhoades, Stephen A. (1983) 'Concentration of world banking and the role of US banks among the 100 largest, 1956–1980', *Journal ofBanking and Finance*, 7.
Rhoades, Stephen A. and Roger D. Rutz (1981) 'A re-examination and extension of the relationship between concentration and firm rank stability', *Review of Economics and Statistics*, vol. 63, no. 3.
Rhoades, Stephen A. (1983) 'Concentration of world banking and the role of US

in the banking and savings and loan industries 1929–1979', *Journal of Banking and Finance*, 8.
Ronn, Ehud I. and Avinash K. Verma (1986) 'Pricing risk-adjusted deposit insurance: an option-based model', *Journal of Finance*, vol. 41, no. 4, September.
Schuster, Leo (1984) 'Profitability and market share of banks', *Journal of Bank Research*, Spring.
Short, Brock K. (1979) 'The relation between commercial bank profit rates and banking concentration in Canada, Western Europe and Japan', *Journal of Banking and Finance*, 3.
Smirlock, Michael (1985) 'Evidence on the (non) relationship between concentration and profitability in banking', *Journal of Money, Credit and Banking*, vol. 17, no. 1, February.
Spiller, Pablo and Edgardo Favaro (1984) 'The effects of entry regulation on oligopolistic interaction: the Uruguayan banking sector', *Rand Journal of Economics*, vol. 15, no. 2.
Tschoegl, Adrian E. (1982) 'Concentration among international banks – a note', *Journal of Banking and Finance*, 6.
Tschoegl, Adrian E. (1983) 'Size, growth and transnationality among the world's largest banks', *Journal of Business*, vol. 56, no. 2.
Tschoegl, Adrian E. (1987) 'International retail banking as a strategy: an assessment', *Journal of International Business Studies*, Summer.
Tucillo, John (1973) 'Taxation by regulation: the case of financial intermediaries', *Bell Journal of Economics*.

10 Towards a Restructuring of the International Financial Services Industry: Some Preliminary Empirical and Theoretical Insights

Joël Métais

INTRODUCTION

For the past two or three years financial magazines have regularly made their front pages with news of spectacular takeovers, merger talks and strategic moves in the financial sector, especially in commercial and investment banking and in insurance. Such a succession of events clearly tells us that the financial services industry is in the throes of a major worldwide restructuring, which will undoubtedly gather momentum after the October 1987 crash. This movement has been especially strong in the United States with the rapid rise of some 'super regional' banks like Wells Fargo, after it bought out Crocker National, or with the new landscale in Wall Street following the merger of Shearson Lehman and E. F. Hutton. Foreigners also played their role in these transformations, particularly the Japanese banks and insurance companies that took stakes in some of the most prominent investment banks, such as Sumitomo Bank in Goldman Sachs; they also acquired some retail banks, especially in California and infused capital into the ailing Bank of America. In Europe some recent events – like the Société Générale de Belgique affair – point in the same direction.

Until now, economists have been more often concerned with the macrofinancial aspects and consequences of the internationalisation of financial agents and activities than with the strategies of firms and the structure of the industry. This may be ascribed to the fact that, until very recently at least, the growing international capital flows and cross-border lending, the ensuing international debt economy, and the exchange and interest rates volatility, have by far overshadowed the effects of their internationalisation process on the operating conditions and returns of the financial intermediaries involved – except in the case of the less developed countries' lending-related losses which many of them recently incurred. However, interest in this industrial organisation aspect should soon prove more and more compelling for economists and policy-makers, because they surely cannot stay isolated for long from the debate which this international restructuring will undoubtedly raise.

This is a broad research topic, of course, and this chapter will try only to give some preliminary and tentative insights into an acceptable theoretical framework for an interpretation of the current evolution and future prospects of the financial services industry in major industrial countries and in the international field. Arguments will mainly be drawn from the theories of industrial economics and, more especially, from some of its most recent developments, such as the theory of the multiproduct firm and industry, and of contestable markets, which seem particularly relevant for the analysis of financial intermediaries' activity.

The structure of an industry depends primarily on two main factors: the technology currently available to firms and the characteristics of the demand faced by these firms. Moreover, in some industries public regulation also plays a major role. This of course, is of particular relevance for banking and financial services. Whenever changes occur in one or all of these factors, they will alter the competitive environment and the rules of the game, and this will entail transformations in the structure of the industry. The latter will go through an adjustment process characterised, among other things, by the evolution of the relative costs of inputs and prices of outputs; the array and degree of differentiation of goods and services supplied; the eventual entry of new players into the industry or a trend towards higher concentration; and by changes in the optimal size and diversification of the participating firms and the optimal number of players in the field.

During recent years, the financial services industry in many countries has clearly been most concerned with tremendous changes in available technologies, its regulatory framework and, perhaps, above all, in the macroeconomic conditions which influence the evolution of the demand for its products and services. According to the conclusions of industrial economics theory, the transformation of the financial landscape that we are currently witnessing must be considered as the logical outcome of these developments.

This chapter will be concerned essentially with an analysis of the driving forces of this structural 're-shaping' of the financial services industry at the world level and especially in the United States and the European Economic Community. The first section will summarise the main features of the internationalisation process in the financial sector during the past two decades, with particular emphasis on the post-1982 period. It will also raise the hypothesis that for many years the financial services industry has been experiencing some over-capacity, especially in the banking sector. The second section will assess the reasons for such a situation and illustrate some of its consequences, although these will also be examined in the following sections. The third section is concerned with changing features in the demand and supply of financial services and their influence on the structure of the industry through the innovation process. This innovation process is, of course, also closely related to the technological changes which are examined in the fourth section. The fifth section focuses on the current deregulation process, its causes and prospects. The sixth section proposed some reasonable scenarios for the evolution of the international financial sector in the years ahead.

INTERNATIONAL BANKING GROWTH FROM THE 1960S TO DATE: AN APPRAISAL

Whereas the 1970s were largely dominated by financial flows, domestic and international, for most intermediated through the banking sector, the 1980s witnessed a shift towards the channelling of financial resources through markets and their operators such as investment and merchant banks or brokerage houses.

The twenty glorious years of the euromarkets

The 1960s and 70s essentially witnessed the spectacular growth of the eurocurrency markets which started from scratch in the late 1950s to reach the US $1500 billion benchmark at the end of 1980. This success story has already been amply documented, and refined theoretical models have been developed to explain this growth. So, for the sake of the following exposé, only a few remarks will be made here.

During the 1960s only the major money centre banks from the United States expanded significantly in the international field, in particular to capture their share of the eurodollar market based in London and dominated by British houses at that time. They appeared as the driving force of this market, which provided them with the growth opportunities not available in their domestic market due to the restrictions imposed by the MacFadden and Glass-Steagall acts.

During the 1970s US regional, European and, less significantly, Japanese banks entered the market. Although the American commercial banks still dominated the scene, they now had to share the eurocurrencies business with major European rivals, with the Japanese showing a rather modest activity, at least during the first half of the decade. A commonly expressed explanation related this trend to the need to recycle oil funds, which soon resulted in the growing indebtedness of the LDCs. However, this view about the role of recycling surplus oil funds in the growing international involvement and exposure of banks from the main industrial countries tells only part of the story, as was evidenced by the still fast-growing cross-border lending in the years 1977 and 1978, at a time when OPEC surpluses were shrinking. In fact, according to the Bank for International Settlements statistics, OPEC deposits never represented more than 20 per cent of the total supply of the deposits (in stock figures) in the euromarkets. So it is more in accordance with empirical evidence to suggest that during these years deposit banks – for many good reasons such as slower growth, credit ceilings and regulatory tightness at home– became eager to shift their portfolio composition towards more international assets and to strengthen their foreign presence and activities.

Some other major features of these two decades of sustained growth of international banking activities can also be mentioned here. These activities essentially relied on the transformation of short-term deposits into long-term bank loans. Some financial innovations played a major role in enabling such a recycling and risks-consolidation process to proceed smoothly: syndicated, loans, certificates of deposits and floating rate notes are among the best known of these innovations.

Competition among the banks occurred mainly in the unregulated eurocurrencies market where price competition, for example through spreads and fees on the syndicated eurocredits, played an essential regulating role, as evidenced by their steady decline after 1976 under the growing pressure of new entrants.

The domestic banking markets, for their part, remained protected and tightly regulated. Only the British and US markets began to offer some significant opportunities to foreign competitors at the end of the period. So banking – and more generally, financial – activities largely remained organised along domestic structural and regulatory lines. Oligopolistic structures and behaviours; limitations on deposit rates, solvency and liquidity ratios; entry restrictions and, sometimes, separation between types of activities – as in the United States and Japan – were a feature of these markets.

Although returns in the international field often proved lower than in the domestic field, the international profits growth helped to counteract a slowing-down of domestic growth and to maintain an adequate return on equity. Nevertheless, international profitability was eroding at the beginning of the 1980s despite the fact that the loan loss record was still better in international activities than in domestic ones.[1]

The 1980s: the years of the 'Bangs'

Following the second oil shock of 1978–9, the 1980s appeared to start in a vein rather similar to that of the mid-70s. But the growing volatility of exchange and interest rates, following a change in the conduct of American monetary policy in October 1979, soon impacted heavily on the mounting LDC debt, resulting in the Mexican debt crisis of summer 1982. Vanishing financial flows to the LDCs and stringent macroeconomic policies in major industrial countries compelled some major debtors to make dramatic adjustments, but a new international configuration of payments surpluses and deficits soon emerged revealing the Unites States as the major fast-gowing debtor, and Japan and Germany as the major creditors. These macroeconomic factors combined with microeconomic factors, such as the loss by deposit banks of their comparative advantage in the channelling of funds between deficit and surplus units, and the flourishing of financial innovations, resulted in a quite new international financial landscape. Innovations, securitisation, globalisation soon became the three 'buzz words' to depict the new environment.

Financing directly through securities issues (bonds, shares, notes, commercial paper) exceeded international bank loans in terms of annual gross flows. According to Morgan Guaranty Trust Company figures, international bond issues reached US $228 billion in 1986 against US $93 billion for international bank credits. In 1981, at the heyday of eurocurrency bank credits, the latter represented US $133 billion and international bond issues US $53 billion. However, 1987 seems to have witnessed a reversal in the growth trend of the securitisation process since bond issues reached only US $177 billion and eurocurrency bank credits recovered to US $123 billion.

As a consequence, investment and merchant banks, securities dealers and brokers have emerged as major players on the new international financial turf, whereas deposit banks have had to reallocate part of their resources towards these new activities or to retreat into their domestic markets (as some US regional banks did some time ago).

This is not the only shift in the balance of power among financial institutions. US banks have had to give up their leadership as international creditors to their Japanese competitors, who have rapidly assumed this position in a world which has seen the yen strongly appreciating against the dollar since the autumn of 1985.[2] The Japanese currently hold almost 35 per cent of all international bank claims as opposed to the Americans' less than 25 per cent. In London, which is still the major centre for international activities of major lending institutions, American banks saw their share of eurocurrency business fall from 38 per cent to 16 per cent between 1975 and 1985. During the same period the Japanese succeeded in enlarging their market share from 13 per cent to 31 per cent.[3]

During the course of globalisation, borderlines between the supranational euromarkets and the domestic markets have blurred so that international competition between financial institutions is now spreading from the former to the latter in the main industrial countries. Among these countries, however, degrees of openness to outside competition (as measured by the share of domestic loans and deposits markets held by foreign institutions) vary widely, with Belgium and Japan standing as, roughly, the upper and lower benchmarks respectively.[4]

As competition has been getting fiercer everywhere – through prices and a flurry of innovations – profitability, at least in traditional banking business, has now reached critically low levels. At least until the October 1987 financial market crash, securities-related and financial engineering business had recorded more satisfactory returns, although these might have been boosted by the declining trend in interest rates from 1984 to mid-1987. Debt reschedulings, loan losses and increased provisions have impaired the resilience of the banking system. This is especially true in the United States where bank failures peaked to a record level of 184 in 1987.

It is sometimes argued that growing openness and the spreading deregulation of the financial services industry feed this growing competition, which in turn results in reduced profitability. This seems, however, to be a one-sided argument. More precisely, it can be argued that during the past three decades the banking systems of the main industrial countries have progressively built up a financial intermediation over-capacity which has largely fuelled the competition and deregulation processes.

THE OVER-CAPACITY HYPOTHESIS: AN APPRAISAL

Following some fundamental articles in the theory of financial intermediaries such as those by G. J. Benston and W. Smith[5] and, more recently, Jack Revell,[6] a growing number of economists now agree that financial institutions may be viewed as firms, with their comparative advantages, factor endowments, market structure and regulatory constraints determining the size and scope of their activities and their returns. Of course, account must be taken of some peculiarities of these financial institutions, and more especially of banks, which derive from their money-creating power, and of related externalities calling for some degree of public regulation and supervision.

In accordance with this approach, although financial intermediaries generally engage in financial intermediation (in the traditional Gurley and Shaw meaning) as a primary activity, more attention must also now be paid to the fact that many of them also conduct other types of business, although in varying degrees. These types of business consist of insurance and risk management; assets trading; participation in non-financial companies; and other services.[7]

Financial intermediation activity consists in the transformation and consolidation of risks (broadly defined). The amount of intermediation services supplied by financial firms derives from their risk-return optimising behaviour within a given market structure, regulatory and internal organisation constraints, resources and operating costs.

The origin of the hypothesis that for many years there has been some over-supply of financial intermediation services, especially from banks, can be traced back to the late 1970s. Some monetary authorities, such as the Bundesbank, and observers of the international financial scene were worried about what they called 'over recycling' of OPEC surpluses and the ensuing piling-up of debt by the LDCs, whereas fees and spreads on medium-term eurocredits became so slim that they could no longer compensate banks with adequate return for their growing risk exposure. Only recently, however, did this hypothesis receive some theoretical foundations[8] which can be summarised as follows.

Banks are unique among deposit-taking institutions since they can provide risk-averse depositors with implicit insurance services derived from their regulation and supervision by public authorities, coupled with lender-of-last-resort (LLR) facilities, and also from deposit insurance schemes which exist in many countries. *Ceteris paribus* this enables them, in their domestic regulated market, to pay less than other financial institutions for their resources and to earn some extra profits derived from this implicit insurance role. After allowing for provisions for the increase in internal funds required by regulations for supporting a growing volume of business, these profits leave them some room to accept a certain degree of internal *X* inefficiency or to cross-subsidise other activities, such as international ones, which can be expanded beyond the size corresponding to the risk-return optimum solution of a perfectly competitive equilibrium context. This explanation has fruitfully been applied to the eurocurrency activities of banks from the main industrial countries, which have expanded since the 1970s as they have benefited from this implicit internal subsidy reaped in the regulated and protected domestic markets.

This explanation can receive further support and some dynamic dimension when the oligopolistic interdependencies, which are a feature of most of the domestic banking markets, enter the picture. Following the long-established equilibrium among the participants to these markets, international expansion by one or two of them in each country appeared as a breach of this status quo which compelled other competitors to follow suit as a loss-minimising strategy. The international market soon proved overcrowded with too many banks chasing after business.

Of course, the slowing-down of domestic activity and profit growth played its part in this move towards the international sector. Nonetheless, there seems to have been an element of 'overshooting' in international lending during the late 1970s and early 80s which traditional explanations seem unable to cope with, but which is more in accordance with the over-capacity argument.

Finally, this latter argument gains further ground when the economic theory of public regulation enters into the picture. Stated briefly, there seems to be a protective bias in the regulatory framework of financial activity, which is concerned (partly at least) with the emergency support of ailing institutions through lender-of-last-resort facilities; this is what is meant by the implicit insurance aspect of bank activity. More generally, it also means that classes of intermediaries whose activities seem to be at risk of being out-competed by new entrants exploiting financial innovations will be protected, at least for some time, by the authorities through more or less extensive regulation.[9] So, despite the emergence of new suppliers, former participants to the markets may still survive for some time. In domestic markets, which are not especially competitive, this may lead to some over-supply of financial assets and services.

This hypothesis of an over-capacity in the supply of financial assets, which seems to be at the heart of some developments of the last decade and is crucial for a better understanding of future prospects, has not yet been extensively addressed by economists although it raises some important issues. Among these are its influence on the evolution of costs and prices in the banking sector; on the financial innovations process and the latter's role in the competitive struggle; and on the sudden redirecting of strategies by the banks retreating, for example, from LDC lending to rush into securities underwriting and trading activities, which may have played a significant part in the recent instability of the international financial system.

THE INTERNATIONAL FINANCIAL SYSTEM IN THE 1980S: A SUCCESSFUL AND IMAGINATIVE FINANCIAL INNOVATIONS PROCESSING FACTORY!

Ample research work has been devoted to financial innovations during the last few years, from an empirical as well as from a theoretical point of view. This work was, of course, largely inspired by the flow of innovations which flooded the domestic and international financial systems. Although the standard model by Ben-Horim and Silber[10] of market structure and/or regulatory constraints-induced innovations is now widely accepted, and seems to fit reality rather satisfactorily, the complementary explanation by the demand of characteristics (of financial assets) derived from Lancaster's consumption theory[11] has not yet received the full attention it deserves.

Moreover, although some authors like Greenbaum and Haywood,[12] following Schumpeter's theories, have tried to stress the role of innovations in the reshaping of the structure of a financial system by raising the important issue as to whether they are exploited by incumbent firms or by new entrant innovators, further research in this field has remained scant. This is one of the major points which must be explored if we want to obtain some understanding of the new balance of power between deposit banks, investment and merchant banks, and securities houses, as well as examining the inroad of non-financial companies into the financial sector or of the newly enlarged scope of activities of what were formerly very small and specialised institutions. It may prove even more crucial for delineating the shape of the international financial system in the years to come.

As an illustration, we shall consider firstly the influence of the evolution of the demand by borrowers and investors for new characteristics of financial assets and services induced by the international macroeconomic and financial environment since the early 1980s. During recent years this environment has revealed three main characteristics: volatility of exchange and interest rates; a new constellation of deficit and surplus countries; and the deterioration of the quality of banks' assets following the near-defaulting or rescheduling of LDC debt.

The first category of factors induced a strong demand from international and, sometimes, domestic corporations, institutional investors and banks for various hedging devices ranging from interest and exchange futures and options contracts to highly sophisticated 'gadgetry' attached to newly issued financial assets.

The second category is largely responsible for the securitisation explosion around 1985, when the United States to some extent overtook the LDCs as a major deficit country – before leading the group of major net debtors – while the OPEC surpluses vanished to reappear in Japan and West Germany. As the respective portfolio preferences and constraints of the deficit economic unit in the United States and of the surplus economic units in Japan and Germany were quite different from those experienced in the 1970s when OPEC and the LDCs were the major players of the recycling game, financial institutions were confronted with a demand for quite different financial assets and services. Japanese insurance companies, mutual funds and other institutional investors were eager to invest in the small personal savers' funds in high-yield, very liquid and low-risk assets that high-standing, massive sophisticated borrowers such as the US federal government and some blue-chip multinational corporations were alone in offering. Of course other factors, such as new regulatory requirements for commercial banks and the downgrading of their assets which caused them to lose their comparative advantage in the intermediary activity, not to speak of technological progress, were also at work and cannot be disregarded.

To understand how these other factors fit into the picture, we have to rely on the theory of constraint-induced innovations. We then have to consider the influence of the constraints evolving from the transformation of the macroeconomic and financial environment on the one hand and of the regulatory framework constraints on the other. To take only one example, the already depicted shifts which occurred among debtors and creditors respectively – and which induced the trend towards securitisation – deprived deposit banks of a significant share of activity through the well-known process of disintermediation. According to the conclusions of the Ben-Horim–Silber model we could expect them to try to recapture some business through innovatons so as to maintain their previous utility level. They did this through, for example, note issuance facilities (NIFs) and revolving underwriting facilities (RUFs) which are typical 'assetless' banking[13] instruments that enabled banks to reap some earnings from activities in commercial paper and notes markets.

When it appeared that the downgrading of their assets after the 1982 LDC debt crisis had lost them their comparative advantage in the channelling of funds between surplus and deficit non-financial units, which now occurred directly through asset markets, banks tried to restore their competitive edge through innovating devices such as debt-equity swaps in order to remove bad assets from their portfolios.

Among regulatory constraints, the strengthening of capital adequacy ratios requested in some countries, like the United States, in the aftermath of the 1982 debt crisis was a main factor in the rapid rise of off-balance sheet activities by deposit banks through instruments such as NIFs, RUFs, letters of credit, forward rate agreements and, above all, swaps.

The conclusion to be drawn from these few illustrative examples is that most innovations result from a set of converging factors, on the supply as well as on the demand side. Moreover, it must also be stressed that technological advances played a very significant role in the processing and the handling of new techniques and instruments, from the 'manufacturing' of mortgage-backed securities to the elaboration of strategies for options portfolio managers. We examine this point further in the fourth section of this chapter.

Nonetheless, a more critical appraisal of the analysis of financial innovations in the international and domestic fields leads to the conclusion that there remains an important gap in the theoretical understanding of this process and of its consequences. More specifically, except for the 'classical' explanation of the causes of innovations at the financial firm or at the macrofinancial levels on the one hand, and the analysis of the macroeconomic consequences of these innovations for the conduct of monetary policy or on the level of systemic risk for the financial system[14] on the other hand, we know very little about this crucial dimension of the financial processes.

An important problem that needs to be examined expeditiously is, of course, the socially optimal level of financial innovations, because these are not patented. The role of competitive pressures in the innovation process also largely remains unclear. This point is linked to more general questions in relation to the over-capacity issue. More fundamentally, in view of the flourishing of minor innovations, many of which appear quickly but are short-lived, it might prove rewarding to investigate the respective roles of market structures; this is especially so of oligopolistic interdependencies when there is uncertainty about the response of demand. It would also be interesting to investigate the way the monopolistic profits derived from innovations by the innovator can be appropriated and maintained through, for example, reputation effects.[15] Now all of these questions may fruitfully be addressed with the recent tools of industrial economics theory, although via complex mathematical apparatus. We can already mention in this respect some research about the introduction of new futures contracts on exchanges which seems promising.[16]

'HI-TECH' ENTERS THE DEALING ROOMS AND THE BACK OFFICE

We do not intend to discuss here those aspects of the role of new technologies already accurately and amply analysed, in particular by Jack Revell.[17] Let us only recall that, when applied to the financial services industry, they have two main types of effects which are often closely intertwined: firstly, they enable financial institutions and markets to provide customers with new products and services and thereby enlarge the menu of available financial assets; secondly, they facilitate a reduction in operating costs through the improved efficiency of production and delivery processes.

The new technologies, therefore, play a very significant role in the financial innovations process, the pace of change being directly linked to the introduction of new developments in computer software and hardware or in the telecommunications fields. Examples of the profound transformations induced by these new technologies have been well documented.[18] We will therefore limit ourselves to asking some important questions about their consequences on the evolution of the structure of the financial services industry.

The standard literature on industrial organisation theory has long stressed the role of the available technology – its progress and the way it is incorporated into products or operating processes – as an important factor in determining the structure of an industrial sector through such steps as the form of the production and costs functions; the optimal size, degree of diversification and scope of the production; the eventual barriers to entry; and the size and number of firms. Nevertheless, this important issue has not yet been fully addressed by all those concerned with the current rapid transformations which are occurring in the financial sector.

We can only mention here some of the topics to be examined in depth if we want to understand what type of structure might emerge at the international level, and what its consequences for the domestic financial sectors might be. Such an understanding is needed by policy-makers and regulators to help them to update their attitudes and fashion new rules of the game. The main critical points seem to be the following, although this list is, of course, not exhaustive.

Banks and financial institutions are multiproduct firms which have traditionally sold many of their products and services through packages: this has resulted, *ceteris paribus*, in the marked cross-subsidisation of many activities. This has gone hand-in-hand with a poor understanding by bank managers of their operating costs, as auditing procedures were comparatively underdeveloped. Economists, for their part, were also embarrassed by the problem of costs and production functions of the financial firms. Although there have been improvements recently on the auditing front in banks, the theoretical problems addressed by economists still remain difficult to solve as new questions arise or as former ones need to be reconsidered.

In this respect, the economies of scale/economies of scope debate is certainly the most critical. These two properties of a productive process are often difficult to distinguish and exhibit, particularly in empirical tests.[19] This is especially true in the financial services field. Whereas many former studies about economies of scale seemed to imply that these were very small across a broad range of sizes of the financial institutions,[20] bankers themselves now claim more and more frequently that economies of scale and low-cost mass production of financial services are a crucial factor in justifying their strategies of acquisitions and mergers. New technologies in the back office seem to be a driving force in this respect. However it remains unclear whether managers of financial institutions are chasing economies of scale or economies of scope through the achievement of synergy effects in the provision of new products and services.[21] So many new financial products have appeared recently, and have induced such large shifts of activities among the various types of financial institutions and markets, that much additional research is needed to investigate thoroughly this field.

A closely linked problem relates to the bundling/unbundling of financial products and services. It seems that one consequence of the innovations process is to enable, and often to require, a separation of formerly joint products. This applies, for example, to the de-packaging of the various risk elements which were previously part of the same financial asset so that these can be shared across different agents through the sale of 'components' more or less directly linked to the asset, such as futures contracts, options, and so on. More generally, the trend towards securitisation and globalisation, and the growing importance of market mechanisms in the distribution and pricing of financial instruments, points more and more in this direction of de-packaging, and strengthens the pure brokerage side of financial activity which is becoming increasingly 'assetless'. Aside from producing a more acute cost and price consciousness, this evolution has at least two other important consequences for the activity of financial services firms and the structure of the industry.

The former state of vertical integration, particularly between the processing and delivery stages of financial products and services, may have to be reconsidered in the light of the new span of the respective comparative advantages of different types of financial firms, according to their role in the innovation process; the new structure of costs and prices; and the new configuration of eventual economies of scale and/or of scope induced by tehnological progress. Some strategic moves during the period of the UK 'Big Bang' of October 1986 seem to illustrate this proposition as the new regulatory framework, however important, does not appear to tell the whole story. Some recently established links between insurance and banking, as well as the entry of some retail chain stores into the financial sector, may also be ascribed to this new situation. New entrants may appear that can specialise in some 'niche segments' of activity and so may be able to 'pick off' the most lucrative activities. Nevertheless, 'hit-and-run' entry strategies, which some bankers often seem to be worried about are uncertain although there are some presumptions about them. This latter point seems in fact one of the major problems raised by the new conditons of financial activity which can be fruitfully handled by the conceptual and analytical framework of contestable markets theory.[22]

Especially important in this respect is the problem of barriers to entry in relation to the amount of capital required to operate and its degree of irreversibility/reversibility in relation to the attendant sunk costs of exiting. Regulatory barriers to entry traditionally were as important as those linked to capital requirements, with technology and know-how playing a secondary role. However, all this needs now to be reconsidered. Regulatory barriers are 'scrambling' and the processing and delivery of new financial products typical of the securitisation and globalisation moves of recent years do not require the same type of fixed capital as the traditional bank products. Extensive branch networks endowed with large staff and low fixed equipment are being replaced by operating units concentrated in the major money and financial markets using small, highly skilled teams which rely heavily on extensive hardware and telecommunications equipment and sophisticated software. It is noticeable that the costs of this equipment and software, although sometimes still very high, are steadily and rapidly declining. Moreoever, the sunk costs associated with them are certainly smaller than those in traditional banking, at least for some types of activity. Despite devices adopted by innovators to protect themselves, new financial techniques spread very rapidly and extensively.

For example, swap techniques are now successfully handled by so many bankers that innovators have to look for highly sophisticated transactions in order to earn some money. 'Hit and run' strategies are all the more likely now in the context of the over-capacity theory previously examined: financial institutions like banks can derive some extra capital from their traditional and protected activity to enter new lines of business and then leave them very rapidly. Although this point needs more detailed investigation, the massive entry of 'market makers' who left hastily when circumstances turned less favourable, so leading to the collapse of the secondary market during the winter of 1986–7, may be ascribed to such strategies. This seems to imply that the level of competition in some markets for financial services may be high, but this view is opposed by some authors who consider that the prices of financial intermediation services can be changed very quickly by incumbent firms so as to deter entry by new competitors. Where 'hit and run' strategies can be so opposed, this means that the financial services markets are imperfectly contestable.

As a result of such weak conclusions, this is a major topic which should be given a high priority in investigations and discussions if we wish to appraise effectively the consequences of the deregulation process now at work and to elaborate new fundamental principles for a reshaped regulatory framework which, sooner or later, will be inescapable.

ARE WE WITNESSING AN ERA OF COMPETITIVE DEREGULATIONS?

Banking and financial activities have been strictly regulated in most countries since the 1930s. Every regulation entails costs in order to achieve the goal of stability aimed at by financial regulation, so there is an escapable trade-off between the efficiency and the stability of the financial sector. During recent years the former, long-established attitude towards this trade-off seems to have shifted towards a new arbitrage more concerned with greater efficiency in the financial system. This, of course, is amply justified by the need for the system to contribute more effectively to the adjustment and restructuring of the economies in the major industrial countries and in some advanced LDCs.[23] This seems to be one of the major reasons why deregulation is now at work in many financial systems, at least according to the arguments of the authorities and policy-makers.

Although financial deregulation has been widespread for some years now, and has sometimes followed rather radical paths – as in the case of London's 'Big Bang' – economists have had very little to say about it as yet, except for some extensive comparative descriptions. This differs somewhat from what happened in the other sectors concerned with deregulation, such as telecommunications or air transport, which have produced many theoretical and empirical studies.[24] These studies, drawing their arguments from recent developments in industrial economics and advanced microeconomics as well as from the economic theory of political choice and decision, helped to explain why deregulation was needed or inescapable, to appraise its potential consequences and, afterwards, to evaluate its real effects.

In a recent article, Hammond and Knott[25] attempted to assess the major factors leading to deregulation in an industrial sector. They first stress that, notwithstanding long-established opinions about the irreversibility of the regulatory process, which they feel to be misconceptions, regulatory regimes are inherently unstable and so deregulation is likely to occur as soon as various hypotheses are fulfilled. These basically refer to the incentive for firms in a regulated industry to undermine the equilibrium regime set up by the regulation; the impact of technological, economic and legal changes on the relationships among firms and between firms and their customers; the degree of heterogeneity among the regulated firms and their customers; and, the degree of fungibility of the regulated industry's products (which is particularly relevant for financial assets). The instability of the regulatory regime and the opportunities for deregulation to occur grow in direct proportion to the magnitude of the variable considered in these six hypotheses. Finally, the authors add that the likelihood of an extension of an old regulatory regime to new competitors is inversely related to the number of outside firms able to enter a regulated industry.

Although specific analyses for the financial sector are still very rare, its seems reasonable to expect that some theoretical explanations elaborated for other industrial sectors can also be of relevance. This is precisely the conclusion reached by Hammond and Knott. Nevertheless, research along these lines is all the more necessary since deregulation in the financial sector seems to proceed practically in a very pragmatic fashion.[26]

Public regulation of an industrial sector plays an important role in influencing its structure and the optimal size of firms which belong to it through entry restriction limitations on allowed activities, and fixed prices. Greenbaum and Haywood[27] consider that it may greatly influence the degree of diversification and the size of financial firms currently observed. So it is in some way tautological to assert that deregulation of a sector will lead to a restructuring of this sector. The main problem raised by such a prospect in the financial services industry is that such a restructuring may not proceed smoothly, because of negative externalities associated with the eventual failure of some institutions (which is precisely what regulation sets out to preclude). Will deregulation induce, for example, a trend towards higher concentration? It so happens that we already have some limited experience in the field of securities dealing and broking which may provide some clues.

One reason frequently invoked for deregulation is that it strengthens competition through the removal of some barriers to entry and the evolution of prices according to market forces. This was typically asserted in the case of the 'May Day' reform of Wall Street in 1975 and, more recently, for London's 'Big Bang'. After more than ten years, what are the results in Wall Street? Following a transition period when many new small firms entered the securities dealing and broking business, a shake-out occurred which soon resulted in a greater concentration than ever before. This concentration increased after the second reform of Wall Street when the 'bought deal' technique for bond issues was introduced in April 1982: whereas the market share for primary issues of the five leading firms still stood at 23.7 per cent between January 1981 and April 1982, it soon reached 44.9 per cent between May 1982 and September 1984.[28]

The same process already seems at work in London after 'Big Bang' where some major banks quickly pulled out of the market-making business, which soon appeared overcrowded in the light of its prospective returns. It must also be mentioned that these changes are in accordance with those observed, for example, in the air transport sector after its deregulation in 1978 in the United States.

It must be stressed that these higher concentration ratios do not necessarily imply that the customers and the community are ultimately worse off after this apparent failure of deregulation. First of all, the concentration process may have been a way to achieve new economies of scale and scope as a result of the new technologies and the financial innovations. As far as the price of financial services and assets charged to customers is concerned, everything will depend on the degree of contestability of the structure of the newly emerged market. As mentioned earlier, this is, of course, a topic where no firm conclusion has yet emerged.

Another important issue as far as deregulation is concerned is its international geographic extension. Although the respective national authorities often invoke the need to achieve a more efficient financial system for domestic economic purposes, they cannot ignore the international aspects of these moves, which is to strengthen the international competitive edge of their domestic financial operators on foreign and international markets and/or to reinforce the attractiveness of their domestic financial centre: London being the most visible example in this instance. This international spread of deregulation has gained such momentum during recent years that it looks as if the main countries have engaged in a process of competitive deregulation, very much like the competitive exchange rate devaluations of the 1930s. Although we still remain rather poorly equipped to deal with the fundamental theoretical aspects of some initial deregulation moves at the domestic level,[29] we can nevertheless mention one interpretation of this international spread given some years ago by Giddy and Allen.[30]

According to these students, who draw their arguments from the economic theory of political and administrative organisations, regulators are suppliers of regulation services which are demanded by the 'regulatees'. In a closed economy, regulators of the banking and financial sector generally enjoy a monopolistic position – except in some countries, like the United States, where there are currently three main regulatory bodies, although with different intervention areas – so that they can impose the overall level of regulation thought desirable or best suited to their internal organisational goals. In an international world, things look quite different. With the emergence of the eurocurrencies market which, by its nature, has always been an unregulated area, a growing number of banks became able to arbitrage between this unregulated market and their own regulated domestic system. This tendency was reinforced with the relaxation of exchange controls by the main industrial countries. As the international capital market is now becoming more and more integrated with the domestic markets, these operators are now able to arbitrage beween different levels of domestic banking and financial regulations. In other words, the repective domestic regulatory bodies are now competing against each other to retain their 'clients', who can always escape their rules by reallocating their activities in other areas. In this situation the equilibrium level of regulation will be lower than in the closed economy case. In the views of Giddy and Allen, regulations which only intend to protect vested interests of some regulatees will be scrapped as financial institutions' clients grow more and more concerned with regulations which provide confidence through insurance-type facilities and uniform public disclosure standards.[31]

The problem which remained unsolved by Giddy and Allen and which nevertheless appears crucial in the light of current events, concerns the dynamics towards this equilibrium, which appear to be worth examining within the strategic game theory framework. In this respect, the eventual existence of co-operative strategies beween the regulators is critical for the type of solution which will emerge. It is easy to understand how such a proposition appeals in the current situation!

In some respects, the recent propositions – in June 1988 – by the Cooke Committee on capital adequacy uniform requirements for banks from the G-10 countries can be seen as the expression of the emergence of such a co-operative strategy among leading regulators. It is easily understandable that these ratios will significantly level off the playing field for the big international banks, whatever their home country, when they become effective at their 8 per cent of total assets level in 1992.

TOWARDS A MORE RATIONALLY STRUCTURED INTERNATIONAL FINANCIAL SERVICES INDUSTRY?

The history of industry suggests that there are roughly three broad stages in the long-term evolution of the main industrial sectors. Following the infancy stage, with many rather 'atomistic' suppliers, firms generally consolidate through failures, mergers and restructuring at the domestic level. Then comes the internationalisation phase which, through international trade flows and production abroad in host countries, results in a new competitive environment. In some sectors, characterised by mature oligopolies[32] at the domestic level, over-capacity may soon appear in the international market. A second consolidation process is then set in motion with an international oligopoly of mega-firms as a possible outcome. Car manufacturers provide a clear example of such a trend. Banking seems to fit in with this kind of logical-historical-order model.

In the main industrial countries, with the noticeable exception of the United States – which can be ascribed precisely to the peculiarities of regulations such as the MacFadden Act which prohibited (at least until recently) interstate banking – national oligopolies emerged as early as the turn of the century. They were further reinforced after the interwar crises. But, although waves of internationalisation had already occurred in the late nineteenth century and in the interwar period, they always broke up before the emergence of a new organisation of banking activities at the international level. The present internationalisation wave represents the third stage in our model and it has now been going on for two decades without major disruption. One may now wonder if we are on the eve of an international restructuring of the structure which has been prevailing for some decades. So what might be the reasonable scenarii if we hypothesise, for simplicity's sake only, that no other major international financial crisis occurs within the next few years and that the trend towards a more liberal framework for international trade in financial services is maintained? Although there is mounting concern about the drawbacks of free trade in international financial services and free movement of capital, the new round of GATT talks will probably result in further liberalisation. Moreover, the EEC area will become an integrated financial services market in 1992.

From the arguments developed in the preceding sections one conclusion seems to emerge: new concentrations seem inescapable as a way to rationalise the supply of financial services, to cope with the over-capacity problem without bank failures and their potential disruptive side-effects, and to reap the benefits of economies of scale and of scope through new technologies and innovations.

Moreover, after the Cooke Committee propositions in early 1988 to impose uniform capital adequacy ratios on banks throughout the Group of Ten countries, the growth of banking intermediation capacity could be severely impaired. Capital is defined according to a two-tier system; tier one consists of equity plus disclosed reserves and tier two of hidden reserves, general provisions, property revaluation reserves and other capital instruments such as convertible and preferred stock and subordinated debt. Following this definition, the ratio will relate defined capital to total assets weighted by their respective degrees of riskiness. By 1992 capital ratios will have to attain the 8 per cent minimum benchmark. Whereas some banks are already in line with this new standard, many of them have a long way to go in order to comply with it, especially the Japanese and some American banks. Of course, those banks concerned will try to raise equity so as to be able to maintain their current level of activity and their growth rate. Barclays Bank and Citicorp have already done so, the former with a £920 million rights issue in April 1988 and the latter with a US $1.1 billion stock sale in 1987. Another solution will consist in cutting assets growth and restoring profitability to generate higher retained earnings. Japanese banks already seem to be looking at this solution, as is evidenced by their recent change of behaviour in the international arena.

More generally the restructuring of the financial services industry will largely depend on the evolution of the regulatory framework that is already changing in three important areas: the United States, Japan and the EEC.

In the United States, progressive relaxation of the MacFadden Act, combined with the structural difficulties of the thrift institutions sector and of some regional banks, has already led to some spectacular mergers (such as the purchase of the ailing Texas Commerce Bancshares by Chemical Bank of New York), the emergence of the 'super regionals' (like Security Pacific and First National Boston), and of very strong 'regionals' (like PNC Financial Corp. and Sun-Trust Banks). Should restrictions on interstate banking be completely removed, this movement would certainly gather momentum and might lead to some unexpected outcomes since several 'money centre' banks look rather weak after their heavy LDC loans and are now vulnerable to 'raiders', either domestic (such as the 'super regionals') or foreign. For example in Spring 1987 Bank of America and Manufacturers Hanover were rumoured to be potential targets for raiders' appetites. But the major shake-up of the American financial services sector appears still to come. The securities industry is accelerating its restructuring after the October 1987 crash: severe job-cuts already planned at Shearson-Hutton, Merrill Lynch, Kidder Peabody, Salomon Brothers and First Boston currently stand at 8400 – and some mergers, like the recent takeover of the brokerage house E. F. Hutton by the investment bank Shearson Lehman. US investment banks may well be confronted soon with commercial banks encroaching into their territory; the Comptroller of the Currency and the Federal Reserve System clearly favour the repeal of the Glass-Steagall Act, and a bill is currently being discussed in Congress. Despite strong opposition from the Wall Street lobby, the new bill might be enacted in 1989, paving the way for a move towards the emergence of some powerful universal banks in the United States.

A similar move might also occur in Japan where the pressure to abolish Article 65 of the banking law (which provides for the separation of commercial banking and securities business) is growing. Moreover, the Japanese financial system is engaged in a rapid, although still incomplete, move towards deregulation. All this invites Japanese financial institutions, as well as some major foreign ones, to reconsider the potentialities of the Japanese domestic market. This will, of course, have some important consequences in the international field where the Japanese have been so active during recent years.

In the same way, the prospective internal market for financial services in the EEC in 1992 will certainly induce European-orientated strategies for major European and foreign institutions. The deregulatory process that 1992 will impose in some still highly protected countries is likely to reveal new growth opportunities. Some banks have already expressed part of their plans in this respect. For example, in 1986 Deutsche Bank established a strong foothold in the Italian retail banking sector through the acquisition of the Banca d'America e d'Italia and is looking for further targets in Europe.

Another important question relates to the organisational forms likely to emerge as 'pillars' of the new structure of the financial services industry after the changes set in motion in these three dominant economic areas. In view of recent evolutionary changes, particularly those induced by the globalisation process following big or little 'Bangs' around the world, conglomerates might prove to be the successful financial firms of tomorrow.[33] They can be built around commercial banks entering the securities and investment banking business through acquisitions and mergers of existing organisations, or through starting them from scratch. The 'universal bank' of continental Europe have a much shorter way to go than the British clearers, American money centre, or Japanese city banks to achieve this result. But investment banks, merchant banks, securities dealers and brokers are attempting to achieve this end from the opposite direction through trying to capture some deposit-banking activities. Much will depend in this area on the capital funds available. In this latter respect the big four Japanese securities houses do not stand on an equal footing with some second-tier American investment banks and the British merchant banks.

Despite the current enthusiasm for conglomerates it is not at all sure that they are the only or the best solution. Some evidence from the observation of industrial conglomerates which finally disbanded tells us that diseconomies of scope and negative externalities relating to the conglomeration organisation itself also exist. In the financial sector they are linked with risks, types of expertise, and information required in different fields. Differences in management culture between deposit banks and investment banks are also cited. Some of these newly built conglomerates have so far not had very successful experiences.

Apart from these giant financial institutions, what might be the other features of the new financial landscape? Highly specialised small houses will probably exist, some of which may well enter the market with new products and specialise very successfully in lucrative niches. The main danger, nevertheless, stems from an eventual dualism between the mega-banks reaping the benefits of their size and innovation capacity at the international level, and offering sophisticated services to top quality customers on the one side, and smaller, less productive, high cost and unsophisticated institutions directed towards ordinary customers at the domestic level.

CONCLUSIONS

No firm conclusion can be drawn from the preceding analysis, and this was not our aim. Moreover, we have been able only to concentrate on a few facets of the current evolutionary trends in the international financial services industry. We have tried to emphasise the fact there is still much to do in order to reach some better understanding of the current movement, but some analytical tools in the related fields of industrial economics theory are available and can be fruitfully used for this purpose. This research work is urgently required for policy-makers, and regulatory and supervisory authorities need some support from economists to help them form their opinions and retain some control over a transformation process that cannot be allowed to continue indefinitely.

Notes

1. For further details, see Jöel Metais, 'Emergence et développement des multinationales bancaires: aspects théoriques et empiriques', in D. E. Fair and R. Bertrand (eds), *International Lending in a Fragile World Economy* (The Hague: Martinus Nijhoff Publishers, 1983).
2. In 1980, only one Japanese bank ranked among the top ten banks of the world; in 1983, two; in 1985 five; and in 1987, seven (according to *The Banker* annual rankings)!
3. Source: 'International banking in London', *Bank of England Quarterly Bulletin*, vol. 26, no. 3, September 1986, pp. 367–82.
4. For further details, see Jean Bensaid et Joël Boissière, 'L'interpénétration des systèmes bancaires en Europe', *Revue d'Economie Financière*, no. 1, June 1987 (Paris: Presses Universitaires de France) pp. 77–84.
5. G. J. Benston and W. Smith, 'A transaction costs approach to the theory of financial innovation', *Journal of Finance,* May 1976, vol xxxi, no. 2, pp. 215–231.

6. J. Revell, 'Towards a microeconomic theory of financial institutions', *IEF Research Papers in Banking and Finance,* RP 87/10 (Bangor: Institute of European Finance, University College of North Wales) pp. 1–19.
7. J.Revell, ibid, p. 4.
8. Cf. for example, A. Penati and A. Protopapadakis, 'Implicit deposit insurance and bank portfolio choices: a positive theory of international overexposure'. Paper presented at the Annual Conference on Recent Research in International Finance, Centre HEC. ISA, Jouy en Josas, France, June 1986. Roneo.
9. Cf. S.I.Greenbaum and C F. Haywood, 'Secular change in the financial services industry', *Journal of Money, Credit and Banking*, May 1971, pp. 571–92.
10. M. Ben-Horim and W. L. Silber, 'Financial innovation: a linear programming approach', *Journal of Banking and Finance*, no. 1, 1977. For a more general theory of financial innovation, cf. the standard presentation of W. L. Silber, 'Towards a theory of financial innovations', in W. L. Silber (cd.) *Financial Innovation* (Lexington, Mass: Lexington Books, D.C. Heath, 1975).
11. 'A new approach to consumer theory', *Journal of Political Economy,* vol. 74, no. 2, 1966.
12. Greenbaum and Haywood, 'Secular change'.
13. The notion of 'assetless banking' is explored by Ian H. Giddy, in Paolo Savona and George Sutija (eds), *Strategic Planning in International Banking* (London: Macmillan, 1985).
14. This question was addressed in depth in two special studies by the Bank for International Settlements: *Financial Innovation and Monetary Policy* (Akhtar Report), March 1984; and *Recent Innovations in International Banking* (Cross Report), April 1986. It must be stressed that the theoretical analysis of the systemic risk aspect nevertheless still remains very poor.
15. The idea that reputation plays a central role in the ability of innovating financial institutions to reap and maintain, at least for some time, the monopoly profit from their innovations, is expressed in Gunter Dufey and Ian H. Giddy, 'The evolution of instruments and techniques in international financial markets', *SUERF Series*, 35A (SUERF, Tilburg (The Netherlands), 1981).
16. R. W. Anderson and C. J. Harris, 'A model of innovation with application to new financial products', in *Strategic Behaviour and Industrial Competition*, ed. by D. J. Morris *et al.* (Oxford: Clarendon Press, 1986).
17. For example, in his paper, 'Effects of new technology on the operations of financial institutions', Talk to a working group of the Conseil National du Crédit, Paris, 6 November 1985 (unpublished).
18. Extensive reports on this topic already exist, such as the Revell Report, *Costs and Margin in Banking: An International Survey* (Paris: OECD, 1980), and more recently (for example) the report from the French Conseil National du Crédit, *L'incidence des technologies nouvellès sur l'activité des intermediares financiers*, 2 vols (Paris: April 1987).
19. Cf. for example, Elizabeth E. Bailey and Ann F. Friedlaender, 'Market structure and multiproduct industries', *Journal of Economic Literature*, September 1982, pp. 1024–48.
20. For a review of recent empirical research in this field, cf. R. Alton Gilbert, 'Bank market structure and competition: a survey', *Journal of Money, Credit and Banking*, vol. 16, no. 4, part 2, November 1984, pp. 617–59. See also

Philippe J. P. Szymczak, *Essai sur la rentabilité bancaire,* Thèse pour le Doctorat en Science Economique (Université de Paris, Panthéon-Sorbonne, 1988) ch. 1.

21. These issues of economies of scale and scope, and of synergy effects on the efficiency of financial institutions are also discussed at length in 'International banking: a survey', *The Economist*, 26 March 1988.
22. This new paradigm in industrial economics, which among other propositions states that the perfect competition hypothesis is only a special case of the more general situation depicted by contestable markets theory, was introduced by William J. Baumol, John C. Panzar and Robert D. Willig, in *Contestable Markets and the Theory of Industry Structure* (New York: Harcourt Brace Jovanovich, 1982); cf. for a discussion, Michael Spence, 'Contestable markets and the theory of industry structure: a review article', *Journal of Economic Literature*, September 1983, pp. 981–90; and for a survey of its more recent developments, William J. Baumol and Robert D. Willig, 'Contestability: developments since the book', in Morris *et al.*, *Strategic Behaviour and Industrial Competition.*
23. The OECD recently conducted important research to appraise the contribution of a more efficient financial system to macroeconomic adjustment; *cf. Structural Adjustments and Performance of the Economies* (Paris: OECD, 1988).
24. The case of the deregulation of the airlines, trucking and telecommunications industries in the United States has been well documented and analysed by Martha Derthick and Paul J. Quirk, *The Politics of Deregulation* (Washington, DC: Brookings Institution, 1985). For a brief (non-technical) survey on these same areas, cf. Elizabeth E. Bailey, 'Deregulation: causes and consequences', *Science*, vol. 234, 5 December 1986, pp. 1211–16. For a short presentation of theoretical grounds for deregulation, see also David Encaoua,'Règlementation et concurrence: quelques éléments de théorie économique', *Economie et Prévision*, no. 76, 1986, pp. 7–46.
25. Thomas H. Hammond and Jack H. Knott, 'The deregulatory snowball: explaining deregulation in the financial industry', *Journal of Politics*, vol 1, February 1988, pp. 3–30.
26. There is already a rather extensive body of literature about the theoretical foundations of regulation of financial intermediaries. Another article on banking deregulation can also be of interest in this debate: see Jean Dermine, 'Banking deregulation', *Economic Policy,* April 1987, pp. 63–9.
27. Cf. Greenbaum and Haywood, 'Secular change', p. 582.
28. According to the annual survey, 'International banking' of *The Economist*, March 1986.
29. As evidenced from the article of Hammond and Knott,'The deregulatory snowball'.
30. I. H. Giddy and D. L. Allen, 'International competition in bank regulation', *Banca Nazionale del Lavoro Quarterly Review*, September 1979, pp. 311–26.
31. Giddy and Allen, ibid, p. 319.
32. According to the classification proposed by Raymond Vernon in his research works and books on multinational firms.
33. For a discussion of the conglomeration movement in the financial services industry, cf. Edward P. M. Gardener, 'Structural and strategic consequences of financial conglomeration', *Revue de la Banque*, no. 9, 1987, pp. 5–15.

11 The Role of Swiss Banks in International Finance

Leo Schuster

NEW DEVELOPMENTS IN INTERNATIONAL FINANCE

Amongst the latest developments in international finance, such as securitisation, disintermediation and deregulation, attention should first be focused on globalisation. If the international financial markets could already be considered as global, there would be far-reaching consequences for today's financial centres. In fact, although they are international, they do offer comparative advantages within their national context, and that is the reason why they still exist.

A global market is a market where all securities and currencies are dealt in according to international standardised criteria, and where the price depends only on supply and demand. This would require a radical standardisation of the legal, institutional and technical frameworks of the monetary and capital markets of the various countries. To achieve this it would be necessary for the national markets to grow together into a common financial centre. There are indeed many developments taking place that are fundamentally changing financial markets. National and international markets are growing increasingly interdependent, so that the borders between the various financial markets gradually disappear. It is therefore harder to distinguish between the international market and the euromarket, between foreign currency, money, credit and capital markets, and between markets with different currencies. Some leading bankers, although they recognise the trend towards globalisation, tend to believe that a global financial market remains a vision. The reason for this belief is the continuation of innumerable restrictions throughout the world: although many countries have dramatically reduced them, nobody has yet totally abolished them.

It is in this context that the role of the Swiss banks in the international financial market is to be seen. Switzerland is, in its own right, an international financial centre. In other words, the Swiss banks' international financial transactions are very strong in their own country but they are also represented in other major international financial centres, either through their own overseas branches or through joint ventures.

SWITZERLAND AS AN INTERNATIONAL FINANCIAL CENTRE

An international financial centre has to fulfil certain conditions: a strong representation of major banks, exchanges of different kinds, a competent central bank as lender-of-last-resort, and a supervisory board to execute the banking laws.

Switzerland fulfils all these conditions, not only as a result of postwar developments, but because of a long and historical banking tradition. However, the structure of Swiss banking, as far as its foreign business is concerned, presents some peculiarities. Most active abroad are the five major banks, which show a high degree of concentration: their balance sheet total amounts to almost 450 billion SFR 1986, that is more than half the aggregate total of all Swiss banks. Furthermore they represent almost half the profits (2.2 billion out of a total of 4.8 billion SFR), and more than 50 per cent of employees (56 600 out of a total of 111 400 in the 607 reporting institutions). Also active in the field of international business are private banks (although there were only 23 of them in 1985), foreign-controlled banks and branches of foreign banks (totalling 120 institutions in 1985), as well as other financial institutions. These play a role as 'parabanks', that is non-bank financial intermediaries, in as much as they are only subjected to the banking supervisory board to a minor extent.

An international financial centre should have a very high degree of deregulation. Although Switzerland has always been regarded as a very liberal financial centre, it has abolished yet further restrictions as recently as Spring 1986. Since that date regulations relating to the duration and the early repayment of public bonds and of foreign debtor's notes no longer exist. Thus both instruments are now virtually identical as far as duration, denomination and negotiability are concerned. Morever the obligation to notify SFR-placements with foreign banks and monetary authorities was abolished in May 1986.

International financial centres also have characteristics that are related to their location, history, structure, laws, and so on. In this sense Luxembourg has been regarded as one of the financial centres for eurocredits, Hong Kong and Singapore as Asian dollar market centres, and Switzerland as a centre where other countries raise capital and as a portfolio management centre. One therefore should not speak of Zurich as the financial centre, but rather broaden this concept to include the whole country. The reason for this is that transactions in Basle focus on Germany and the Alsace; Geneva on France and the Arab countries; Lugano on Italy; Zurich on Germany, the United States and the rest of the world.

Thanks to its stability and richness of languages, Switzerland enjoys many comparative advantages, amongst them the Swiss franc, internationally acknowledged as a non-inflationary currency. However, Switzerland also has its weaknesses: for example the financial centre of Zurich is badly lacking in internationally experienced bankers. The quantitative aspect of this problem can hardly be solved, but the qualitative aspect could be improved with increased training. In 1987 the 'Swiss Banking School' was founded, a national institution created to match the training facilities in the Anglo-Saxon countries.

Swiss banks are constantly complaining of taxes being higher than in other countries, thereby making them less competitive. However, the sales tax on physical gold transactions was abolished in the third quarter of 1986, and in the process of deregulation withholding tax for interbank deals spanning more than one year has been eliminated. On the bankers' agenda itself there still remains the elimination of stamp tax on securities, something which causes competitive disadvantages especially in comparison with Luxembourg and London.

A further shortcoming, especially for an evaluation of international banking, is the quality of statistics. For example, consolidated balance sheets comprising the banks' domestic and foreign transactions carried out through their subsidiaries still remain unpublished. Statistics are also lacking in the field of security transactions, especially in the portfolio management sector where there is practically no statistical reporting.

A 'STRATEGIC SUCCESS' ANALYSIS OF THE SWISS FINANCIAL CENTRE

Switzerland as a centre of capital market transactions

Switzerland has always been a country which attracted foreign capital. The reasons for this are a lasting economic, social and political stability, as well as institutional arrangements such as the legendary banking secrecy provision and the numbered account system. The traditionally low interest rates, far from being an isolated phenomenon, are of course the result of the abundant liquidity in the banking system.

Because of its small size, not all the capital can be invested in the domestic economy and it has to be re-exported. This is why Switzerland is referred to as a centre where other countries raise capital. The instruments for this export of capital are bonds and notes issued by foreign borrowers on the one hand and the fiduciary transactions on the other.

Bonds and notes issued by foreign borrowers

Figure 11.1 shows that in 1987 there was a capital export through the issue of bonds of almost 17 billion SFR and more than 18 billion SFR through

Figure 11.1 Swiss capital market new issue volume (billion SFR)

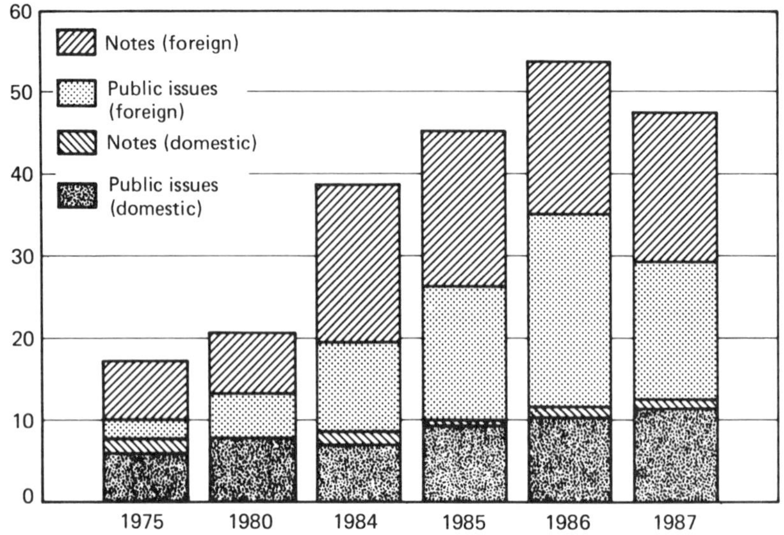

Source: Schweizerischer Bankverein, Obligationen Marktstudie, January 1988, p. 1

Figure 11.2 New international issues 1986

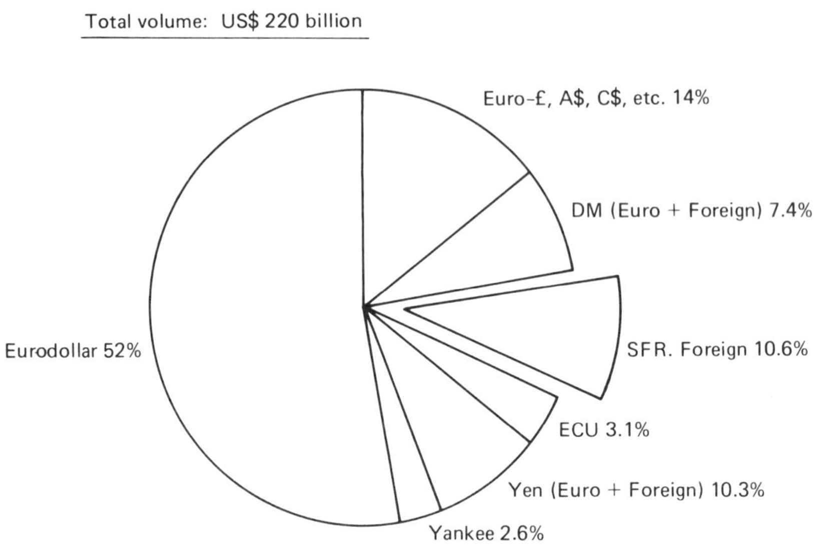

Source: Bank für Internationalen Zeahlungsausgleich (BIZ), 57 Jahresbericht, p. 118

note issues. As far as international issues during the five-year period from 1981 to 1985 are concerned, the Swiss international capital market had a share of 14 per cent. Taking into account the issues in 1986, the share of those in SFR is 10.6 per cent (see Figure 11.2). It should be noted that the Swiss capital market consists of a rather unimportant domestic market and of a much larger foreign sector. The most important foreign country in terms of borrowing has become Japan, with a share of 33 per cent in 1987. A eurocapital market in Swiss francs, however, does not exist since the Swiss National Bank does not allow the issue of SFR foreign bonds abroad.

At the end of 1985 Switzerland's biggest stock exchange in Zurich listed no fewer than 78 SFR bonds, with a market value of 71.2 billion SFR. Table 11.1 shows innovative issues in the Swiss capital market in 1986.

Public bonds are normally issued by syndicates, the largest of which is the syndicate of the major 10 banks. Notes are normally issued by individual banks or by *ad hoc* syndicates.

The Union Bank of Switzerland has the biggest share in the issue of foreign bonds and notes (26 per cent), followed by the Credit Suisse (24 per cent) and the Swiss Bank Corporation (21 per cent).

Fiduciary transactions

Fiduciary transactions are a special phenomenon, indeed a Swiss innovation. They are investments and credits made by a bank in its own name but on account and at the full risk of the customer; in other words the currency, transfer and credit risk has to be incurred by the customer. The customer get the full profit of the deal, and the bank charges a commission. Fiduciary transactions, which are off-balance sheet items, reached 224 billion SFR in 1987 and amounted to more than one-quarter of the consolidated balance sheets of all Swiss banks (see Table 11.2).

The main reason for the existence of fiduciary transactions is the Swiss withholding tax, which at 35 per cent is one of the highest among industrial countries. According to the withholding tax law this tax is only deductible from the profit of domestic investments. Since foreign investments are exempt from withholding tax, most of the capital is invested abroad. As most of the fiduciary money stems from foreign investors, this kind of business further illustrates the function of Switzerland as an investor of foreign funds in other countries. Other advantages of fiduciary investments are the higher degree of secrecy compared with direct investments, and receipt of the normally higher yield of euromarket investments.

Table 11.1 Innovative issues in the Swiss capital market 1986

Month	*Borrower*	*Type of issue*	*Lead-manager*
Jan.	Bank Leu	Warrant bond (gold 200g)	Bank Leu
Mar.	PepsiCo	Foreign interest payment securities (FIPS)	CS
Apr.	Air Canada	Exchange offer: bond issue to bond issue without fixed maturity	SBC
Apr.	Baker Int.	Warrand bond (10-year call-option on US$)	Citicorp
Apr.	Swedish Export Credit	Adjustable long-term puttable securities (ALPS)	Citicorp
May	KLM	Options on sfr.-bond issue	UBS
May	Landis & Gyr	Bond issue without fixed maturity	Landis & Gyr
May	RJR Nabisco	Dual currency bond (interest payment at first in sfr. then in US$)	SBC
Jul.	Montreal Urban Community	Dual currency bond Can.$/sfr.	SBC
Aug.	Philips N.V.	Bull/Bear bond	UBS
Sep.	EchoBay Mines	Warrant bond (gold oz. 6)	CS
Nov.	BZ Bank Zürich	Options on registered shares of Ciba-Geigy	BZ Bank Zürich
Nov.	City of Zürich	Warrant bond (registered shares of Ciba-Geigy)	BZ Bank Zürich
Nov.	SBC	Warrant bond (10 years fixed-interest sfr. bond)	SBC

Source: Ryser, A., Erfindergeist blüht, in Schweizer Bank 1–2/1987, S. 30.

Investment advisory services and portfolio management

Much of the foreign capital flowing into Switzerland is placed with banks for long-term investment. The major banks, the private and the foreign banks, but also financial companies are therefore specialists in investment

Table 11.2 Fiduciary transactions

Year	*Billion SFR*	*Percentage of balance sheet*
1950	0.13	0.5
1960	0.53	0.9
1970	37.92	20.1
1980	120.69	24.7
1981	158.37	28.3
1982	166.43	27.2
1983	182.80	27.8
1984	231.99	32.1
1985	214.97	27.6
1986	224.62	27.8
1987	223.66[1]	26.0[1]

[1] Jan.–Nov. 1987

Source: SNB, Monatsbericht, Jan. 1988, p. 66–7; pp. 82–3.

advisory services and portfolio management. In this sector there are no public statistics, so that one has to rely on estimates. It is generally believed that there are more than 1200 billion SFR deposited in Swiss banks. The bank secrecy provision and the country's stability are the main reasons for foreign investments from all over the world. However, there are major changes expected which are currently worrying Swiss bankers.

First of all, personal savings are decreasing in favour of social savings. A banker once illustrated this by saying that petrodollars will soon be replaced by pension-dollars. As in the United Kingdom these funds are placed with institutional investors such as insurance companies and pension funds and invested by them in capital market instruments. Whereas private investors depend on the secrecy provision, institutional investors are interested in the performance of their investments, independently of where it is to be achieved.

In this context there is a second critical point to be considered. The financial centre of Luxembourg has experienced a considerable decline in its eurocredit business because of increasing securitisation. In order to compensate for this gap it is trying to get a share of the market in portfolio management business. This is a new source of competition for the Swiss banks. Although Switzerland still has considerable competitive advantages, the fact that Luxembourg is entirely liberalising and deregulating its financial markets should be taken as an early warning signal.

A third change in the portfolio management business is the changing relationship between Switzerland and Liechtenstein. The offshore principality has something like a capital-supplier function for Switzerland. An investment coming to Switzerland through Liechtenstein has the benefit of a double and total secrecy. Lately it seems that Liechtenstein's few banks and its many 'parabanks' are trying directly to get a foothold abroad; Swiss banks in their turn seem to be interested in establishing themselves in Liechtenstein. Unfortunately it is no longer possible to see the flow of capital between the two countries. The reason is that, since the currency treaty of 1980 between both countries, Liechtenstein is no longer considered a foreign currency country by Switzerland. The last available statistics, dating back to 1981, show a flow of fiduciary money only into Switzerland amounting to 15 billion SFR. How the traditional co-operation between these two countries will develop is therefore important for Swiss banks.

THE FUTURE CHALLENGES FOR THE SWISS FINANCIAL CENTRE

A British banker once said that in future there would be three crowns awarded to financial centres: one for New York, the second for London and the third for Tokyo. Although this is certainly correct, there will also be room for secondary financial centres. In Europe they will be Germany and Switzerland and, to a minor extent, Paris and Luxembourg.

As London is the most important euromarket centre and played a leading part in the trend towards securitisation, employing the most sophisticated know-how and the highest innovation potential worldwide, Swiss banks have intensified their branch policy in the City of London. It is a well-known fact that the first branch of a Swiss bank was opened there at the end of the last century by the Swiss Bank Corporation in 1898. Today all the important Swiss banks are represented in London, as well as in the Channel Islands; Credit Suisse has taken over the brokerage house Buckmaster & Moore, and the Union Bank of Switzerland has taken over Phillips & Drew. Hitherto, the Swiss Bank Corporation has adopted a different policy, trying to develop its role in the City from its own long-term experience and knowledge. In 1986, the Swiss Bank Corporation International (SBCI) has taken over the London brokerage firm Savory Milln Ltd. But the goal of the three major Swiss banks, as well as of all other foreign banks, was to take advantage of the Big Bang, the most far-reaching deregulation in the history of the City and the security market.

The joint venture of Credit Suisse with First Boston has already had a great success in the euromarket. It ranked first for some time and has now been surpassed by Nomura Securities as far as the amount of issues is concerned, although the number of issues is exactly the same (see Table 11.3).

At this point it seems advisable to analyse briefly the general policies of Swiss banks with regard to co-operation with other financial institutions. Only the Union Bank of Switzerland is currently participating in a multinational partnership (Société Financière Européenne, SFE). Although there are more examples of participation in joint ventures, such as development banks and other special banks, Swiss banks do not seem to enjoy this kind of co-operation very much since they do not want to share the risks taken by the joint venture. They prefer to operate under their own name, which is mostly associated with Switzerland, and avoid sharing the benefits of their operations with others. However, Swiss banks have a different policy as far as takeovers as instruments for the penetration of new markets are concerned. London has already proved this, and Frankfurt is the very latest example. In Frankfurt two of the three Swiss big banks (UBS and CS) have taken over German banks and opened own branches; the third (SBC) has built up its own subsidiary. All three are now playing a decisive role in the new issue business, taking advantage of the deregulated German securities market.

INNOVATION VERSUS TRADITION

Swiss banks are often accused of being too conservative in their domestic and international dealings, thereby missing the benefits from some interesting innovations that have been introduced in recent years. Let me quote an example: in 1976 there were two possibilities for obtaining a US$ credit at a fixed interest rate; in 1981, after the stabilisation of the eurodollar bond market, there were five alternatives; today a debtor has a choice of 56 alternatives.

Amongst the most important innovations are the interest and currency swaps, amounting to more than $350 billion at the end of 1986, of which Switzerland's share is about 1 per cent. Swaps are no longer used only as tools, but there is an increasing tendency to use them as independent instruments – a tendency that is also true for futures and options. The latter are playing such an important role that even the more or less conservative Swiss banks opened a special exchange for futures and options in 1988: SOFFEX, the Swiss Options and Financial Futures Exchange AG. Today there are many changes taking place in Zurich, such as the introduction of permanent quotation for important shares, the increased use of electronics (including back offices), the freely negotiable brokerage fees, and the introduction of a market for options issued by third parties.

Table 11.3 Top 50 bookrunners – all issues (all bookrunners receive full amounts)

Rank 1987	*1986*	*Bank*	*1987 Amount $m*	*1987 No. of issues*	*1987 Share %*	*1986 Amount $m*	*1986 No. of issues*	*1986 Share %*
1	2	Nomura Securities	17885.90	114	13.23	14271.60	128	7.94
2	1	Credit Suisse First Boston	10391.00	114	7.69	20318.60	105	11.30
3	3	Deutsche Bank	7831.23	67	5.79	11860.00	85	6.59
4	10	Nikko Securities	7100.56	52	5.25	5085.18	54	2.83
5	5	Daiwa Securities	6748.00	68	4.99	8829.09	87	4.91
6	12	Yamaichi Securities	6517.17	65	4.82	4323.39	58	2.40
7	6	Morgan Stanley International	4998.39	34	3.70	8522.61	71	4.74
8	4	JP Morgan Securities	4428.23	40	3.28	9771.74	64	5.43
9	7	Salomon Brothers	4386.10	35	3.24	8212.29	54	4.57
10	18	Industrial Bank of Japan	4100.22	37	3.03	2784.49	24	1.55
11	19	SG Warburg	4007.88	36	2.96	2734.39	24	1.52
12	8	Banque Paribas	3588.78	38	2.65	6750.32	67	3.75
13	11	Union Bank of Switzerland	3094.84	26	2.29	4811.71	46	2.68
14	20	Commerzbank	2561.96	27	1.89	2695.37	39	1.50
15	31	Dresdner Bank	2436.47	21	1.80	1577.10	15	0.88
16	16	Swiss Bank Corporation International	2368.51	25	1.75	2877.99	24	1.60
17	14	Goldman Sachs International	2112.25	19	1.56	3654.73	23	2.03
18	28	Baring Brothers	2052.71	17	1.52	1742.51	11	0.97

19	17	Long-Term Credit Bank of Japan	2008.63	16	1.49	2874.18	25	1.60
20	33	Bank of Tokyo	1590.65	14	1.18	1300.64	15	0.72
21	9	Merrill Lynch Capital Markets	1518.40	15	1.12	5845.45	39	3.25
22	45	Hambros Bank	1456.11	37	1.08	541.41	10	0.30
23	–	County Natwest	1406.75	17	1.04	–	–	–
24	24	Westdeutsche Landesbank Girozentrale	1136.95	15	0.84	2108.44	21	1.17
25	13	Shearson Lehman Bros International	1084.60	10	0.80	4112.48	23	2.29
26	29	Morgan Grenfell	1073.46	13	0.79	1734.52	15	0.96
27	26	Crédit Commercial de France	1066.70	12	0.79	1859.53	24	1.03
28	15	Société Générale	1043.20	11	0.77	3090.89	27	1.72
29	42	Citicorp Group	1001.69	15	0.74	697.43	7	0.39
30	43	Kleinwort Benson	999.67	11	0.74	605.67	7	0.34
31	32	Wood Gundy	972.38	14	0.72	1319.27	20	0.73
32	44	Mitsubishi Finance International	870.43	7	0.64	603.82	7	0.34
33	34	Algemene Bank Nederland	860.11	9	0.64	1253.86	14	0.70
34	30	Amsterdam-Rotterdam Bank	843.45	15	0.62	1600.28	21	0.89
35	37	Barclays Bank Group	841.71	5	0.62	824.31	2	0.46

Source: Annual Financing Report, *Euromoney*, March 1988, p. 4.

The market for euronotes such as eurocommercial paper (ECP) and NIFs is rather unimportant in Switzerland. In 1984 there were two issues, amounting to $1.16 billion of which Nestlé alone had a share of $1 billion, whereas in 1985 there was only one NIF issue amounting to $75 million. Syndicated credits are also fairly unimportant, the reason being that major Swiss corporations are directly accepted into the relevant markets because of their excellent rating. Banks are increasingly worried about being circumvented by their own clients.

It is difficult to say whether the strategic attitude of a banker should be conservative, innovative or imitative. What is important in the long run is success, and in this context Swiss banks have a certain advantage over Anglo-Saxon banks; they have always been universal banks, in contrast to American and British banks, which are only now in the process of becoming fully-fledged universal banks.

Selected publications

Bank für Internationalen Zahlungsausgleich (1987) 57, *Jahresbericht* (Basel).

Euromoney Annual Financing Report (1988) March.

Institut für Bankwirtschaft (ed.) (1987) *Internationaler Wandel im Wertschriftengeschäft der Banken*, vol. 1 (St Gallen).

Ryser, A. (1987) 'Erfindergeist blüht: Finanzinnovationen am Schweizer Kapitalmarkt 1986', *Schweizer Bank*, 1–2, pp. 29–31.

Schuster, L. (1988) 'Deregulierung im schweizerischen Bankwesen', *Die Bank*, 2, pp. 75–80.

Schweizerischer Bankverein (1986) 'Der schweizerische Kapitalmarkt', *Ein Leitfaden für den Kapitalanleger* (Basel).

Schweizerischer Bankverein (1988) *Obligationen Marktstudie*, January.

Schweizerische Kreditanstalt (1986) *Das Emissionsgeschäft in Schweizer Franken* (Zürich).

Schweizerische Nationalbank (1986) *Das schweizerische Bankwesen im Jahre 1986*.

Schweizerische Nationalbank (1988) *Monatsbericht*, January.

12 Obstacles to International Trade in Insurance

Robert Carter

THE CHARACTERISTICS OF INSURANCE

Insurance provides a means whereby a person or organisation exposed to possible financial losses arising from the occurrence of uncertain events may, in return for the payment of a premium, transfer that risk to an insurer. It satisfies a demand for financial security, and life insurance is also an important form of long-term personal saving. All private insurances operate by:

1. spreading the risk of loss over time, and between persons and organisations,[1] and, unlike social security schemes,
2. pooling the premiums collected from policyholders to create a fund from which claims can be paid at a later date.

The spreading of risks through insurance can take place at several levels. In the case of the smaller personal and commercial risks a single insurer may agree to provide the whole of the insurance required, any ensuing loss being paid from the funds he holds. Alternatively, if the risk is too large for one insurer to handle, other insurers may participate in the insurance, each taking an agreed share through a 'co-insurance' arrangement, so effectively spreading the risk over a larger body of policyholders. Even wider spreading of a risk may be achieved through 'reinsurance' when an original insurer transfers part of an insurance he has accepted to another insurer, known as a reinsurer, who in turn may pass on part of his liability to other reinsurers by 'retrocession' contracts. So, through the international insurance and reinsurance markets very large risks are spread widely over a large number of insurers, reinsurers and retrocessionaires located throughout the world. The essential difference between co-insurance and reinsurance is that whereas the original insured has a direct claim against each co-insurer for its share of any claim that arises, generally he has no right of recovery against a reinsurer but equally he has no liability to pay the premium(s) for any reinsurance(s) arranged by the original insurer(s).

Reinsurance is arranged not only in respect of individual large risks but also to protect insurers against accumulations of claims arising from events such as earthquakes or other natural or man-made disasters, or against abnormally large accumulations of claims occurring in any one year.

Insurance business falls into two broad categories – life and other long-term insurances, and general or non-life insurances. The cashflow characteristics of all forms of insurance (that is the collection of premiums when policies are issued to pay for claims which may arise during the period of insurance) lead to the accumulation of funds which provide insurers with investment earnings in addition to the premium collected. In the case of non-life insurances, besides the funds held to pay claims which may occur, the delays between the occurrence and settlement of claims (which for liability and some other classes of business can be a year or longer) mean that funds must also be held to cover outstanding claims. Life insurances generate relatively larger funds because the majority of the contracts are for periods of more than one year; most premiums are payable at regular intervals throughout the period of the insurance, and being fixed at a constant level, the premiums initially exceed the amount required to cover the mortality risk in the early years; most contracts include a savings as well as a protection element, thereby generating additional funds. Therefore, insurers accumulate substantial funds to meet the claims payable upon the death or the survival of a life insured until a predetermined date, or during an annuitant's lifetime. Consequently, in many countries life insurers are major institutional investors.

TRADE IN INSURANCE

Insurance is supplied internationally in two ways; through the 'establishment' by insurance companies of overseas branch offices, subsidiaries and associated companies to supply insurances locally; and through 'cross-frontier trade' where an insurer located in one country will supply insurance services across national frontiers to a resident of another country

Marine, aviation and other transport insurances do not fit neatly into these definitions because, for example, in the case of cargo both the location of the goods will change, and the insurance may be assigned to a new owner during the period of insurance, so that what started as a domestic insurance becomes a foreign insurance. Therefore, transport insurances are usually separately classified in trade statistics.

It is difficult to estimate the volume of either type of trade because of the lack of adequate statistics. However, the data that are available indicate that:

1. international trade in non-life insurance is far larger than in life business, with the latter being conducted mainly through local establishements (Table 12.1);

Table 12.1 Numbers of insurance companies by continent

	Life companies		*Non-life companies*		*Composite companies*		*Total*	
	Number	*% of foreign companies*	*Number*	*% of foreign companies*	*Number*	*% of foreign companies*	*Number*	*% of foreign companies*
Europe	687	16.4	3411	27.7	407	7.4	4505	24.1
North America	2278	5.5	3809	4.6	6	33.3	6093	5.0
Latin America	210	62.9	413	41.6	462	2.8	313	10.6
Africa	84	40.5	241	27.8	138	10.1	463	24.8
Asia	119	47.1	633	43.8	158	21.5	910	40.3
Australasia	99	41.4	326	30.4	9	55.6	434	33.3
Total	3477	14.4	8833	24.4	1182	8.3	13177	15.9

Note: The total number of companies for Latin America excludes Puerto Rico and Trinidad so that the countries covered are the same as for Table 12.2.

Source: Swiss Reinsurance Co., *Sigma*, November/December 1985.

2. the restructuring of insurance markets worldwide has been accompanied by a more than proportionate reduction in the numbers of foreign insurance companies established in the domestic insurance markets of many countries, particularly in Africa, Asia and Latin America (Table 12.2);
3. cross-frontier trade in general insurance has been growing as establishment business has declined, though there has been some reversal of the trend for reinsurance as major international reinsurance companies have opened branch offices and formed subsidiaries in North America and Europe;
4. reinsurance supplied by foreign companies has risen relative to the growth of global demand for non-life insurance over the last twenty years. This reflects not only an increase in the barriers to establishment by foreign insurers but also the growth in the size of both individual transportation and industrial risks, and of conurbations, many in areas exposed to natural disasters.

RESTRAINTS ON TRADE

Since the 1950s there has been a progressive liberalisation of trade in goods under the aegis of the General Agreement on Tariffs and Trade (GATT). Simultaneously trade in services generally, and insurance in particular, has become subject to increasing restrictions. The Communist bloc countries totally exclude foreign insurers from their domestic markets and generally only reinsure internationally those risks with a high potential foreign currency cost. The industrialised countries range from the United Kingdom, the Netherlands and the United States which have traditionally pursued liberal trade policies, to countries such as France, Germany, Italy and Japan which place many restrictions on foreign insurers who seek to supply insurance services to their markets. It is however, the developing countries that have been the most active over the last thirty years in raising the barriers to trade. Many have sought to domesticate their insurance industries, wholly or partially excluding foreign direct insurers from their markets, and setting up state reinsurance corporations to reduce imports of reinsurance from the international market.

REASONS FOR PROTECTIONIST POLICIES

A variety of arguments have been advanced in support of protectionist trade policies in relation to services in general and insurance in particular. Strong support has come for many years from the United Nations Conference on Trade and Development (UNCTAD)[2] and from its of-

Table 12.2 Changes in the structure of insurance markets by continent

	1968			*1985*			*Percentage change in numbers 1968–85*	
	Domestic companies Number	*Foreign companies Number*	*% of total*	*Domestic companies Number*	*Foreign companies Number*	*% of total*	*Domestic companies*	*Foreign companies*
Europe	3950	1580	28.6	3419	1086	24.1	−13.4	−31.3
North America	4967	360	6.8	5791	302	5.0	16.6	−16.1
Latin America	749	257	25.5	690	82	10.6	−7.9	−68.1
Africa	229	674	74.6	348	115	24.8	52.0	−82.9
Asia	382	705	64.9	543	367	40.3	42.1	−47.9
Australasia	409	195	32.3	289	145	33.4	−29.3	−25.6
Total	10686	3771	26.1	11080	2097	15.9	−3.7	−44.4

Source: Swiss Reinsurance Co., *Sigma*, July 1983 and November/December, 1985.

ficials.[3] The reasons given can be grouped under the following three headings[4]:

1. Protection of domestic consumers: In all countries insurance industries are subject to government supervision aimed at protecting the interests of policyholders from the failure of insurance companies to provide at a fair price insurance of the type and quality demanded by personal and business consumers, and to meet their contractual obligations. Such supervision includes restrictions on the entry of new companies to national markets.
2. Economic reasons: This includes attempts to avoid wasteful and destructive competition between insurers; build up local insurance industries by protection domestic insurers from foreign competition; promote domestic employment; retain funds generated by insurance operations for investment through local capital markets; and limit the drain on the balance of payments from insurance and reinsurance imports.
3. Socio-political reasons, including not only socialist political ideology but also religious, cultural and national security considerations.

Skipper adds to the list the status quo factor. Not all governments share the presumption that 'in the absence of strong arguments to the contrary, liberalisation [of trade] is desirable from an economic point of view'.[5] Therefore, until they are convinced that their economies will benefit from the lowering of protective barriers, they believe in maintaining the status quo.

TYPES OF OBSTACLES TO TRADE

The obstacles to insurance trade can be grouped into two types:

1. those measures which 'directly restrict' foreign insurers in supplying insurance services either through local establishments or on a cross-frontier basis, or which prevent the residents of a country from buying their insurances from foreign insurers;
2. those measures which 'indirectly' reduce foreign supply of insurance and reinsurance by making it either less advantageous for foreign insurers to supply their services or more costly for local residents to purchase them. Insurance supervisory regulations (such as minimum capitalisation and deposit requirements, and controls on the investment of funds) and the taxation of insurance companies and insurance transactions may deter a foreign insurer from establishing in or trading with a country. However, provided that foreign insurers are subject

only to the same conditions as local companies, they cannot object to them being discriminatory from a trade policy standpoint.

RESTRICTIONS ON ESTABLISHMENT

A study by the Organisation for Economic Co-operation and Development (OECD) concluded that the most serious restrictions were those relating to the establishment in a country of foreign insurers.[6] The ultimate obstacle is complete prohibition which may arise from either the nationalisation of a country's industry or the total exclusion of agencies, branch offices and subsidiaries of foreign insurers from its market. Some forty countries, including all of the socialist states and many other developing countries (for example India, Iraq, Syria and Zambia) fall in the first category; and an increasing number of developing countries, while retaining a competitive market, have excluded foreign insurers (for example, Indonesia, Mexico and Thailand). In other countries, such as Korea and Taiwan, foreign-owned companies are limited in the classes of insurance they are authorised to write.

Indirect restrictions can be grouped under a number of headings:

1. Measures that adversely affect companies' operations, including the amount of control they can exercise over their business, such as:
   — domestication policies that require foreign companies to operate through locally incorporated subsidiaries with a local, sometimes majority, ownership interest and with the management too in the hands of local nationals. (Colombia, Ecuador, Peru and Venezuela, for example, each require all insurers to be locally incorporated and for foreigners to hold no more than a 20 per cent interest.)
   — employment restrictions which prevent foreign companies from using the services of expert expatriate staff.
   — reinsurance regulations which interfere with a company's reinsurance arrangements by requiring it to cede part of its business to a local reinsurer or place restrictions on its ability to reinsure with its parent company.
2. Measures that increase capital or operating costs, or reduce investment earnings, including minimum capital and/or deposit requirements, or restrictions on investments, that discriminate against foreign-owned insurers or reinsurers.
3. Measures that restrict access to the market such as:
   — government procurement policies that restrict the available market for foreign insurers by requiring central and local govern-

ment departments, government contractors and other organisations in which the government has a financial interest, to be placed with a state-owned insurer or wholly locally owned insurance companies.

— exclusion of foreign insurers from trade associations, which may not only exclude them from benefiting from the services provided by an association but also possibly deterring intermediaries from placing business with them. (This criticism has in the past been levelled against the Institute of London Underwriters.)

4. Exchange controls that prevent foreign insurers from remitting profits back to parent companies.
5. Differential tax treatment in the assessment of taxes on income as compared with locally-owned companies.

RESTRICTIONS ON CROSS-FRONTIER TRADE

Cross-frontier trade is subject to an equally wide range of direct and indirect obstacles. Some industrialised nations (for example Italy) and many developing countries prohibit residents from placing abroad with foreign insurers any domestic risks, and others (such as France and the United States) allow such cross-frontier trade only for risks that cannot be placed locally. Most countries require residents to purchase insurances for certain types of risk, notably motor liability and workers' compensation, and normally recognise only insurances issued by locally authorised insurers. Many developing countries likewise require imports, and in some cases exports too, to be insured with local insurers.

Even when cross-frontier insurances are not directly prohibited the same result may be achieved by exchange control restrictions on the remittance abroad of premiums. Although fewer restrictions are applied to local insurers placing their reinsurances abroad with foreign reinsurers, some governments, by obliging local insurers to transfer a part of the risks they have written to a local (usually state-owned) reinsurer, reduce the volume of business available to foreign reinsurers.

The indirect obstacles to cross-frontier trade include:

1. tax rules that penalise residents who insure abroad; for example, by imposing discriminatory taxes either on premiums paid to foreign insurers, or on claims paid by them, or by excluding insurances effected with foreign insurers from tax relief on premiums.

   Reinsurance transactions are similarly subjected to tax distortions. Sometimes additional costs are imposed on the ceding companies, for example by limiting the tax deductibility of premiums paid to foreign reinsurers (as in Malaysia). In other cases it is the foreign reinsurer who is penalised by taxes being withheld from premiums receivable. The United States imposes a federal excise tax on premiums paid abroad, and Australia withholds tax on imputed profits of reinsurances placed with foreign reinsurers.

2. insurance supervisory regulations which penalise companies that place their reinsurances abroad; for example by not allowing them, when calculating their solvency margins, to take credit for liabilities transferred to foreign reinsurers.
3. legislation requiring the deposit of funds locally to cover the value of provisions for unearned premiums and outstanding claims in respect of reinsurances ceded to foreign reinsurers.
4. measures that restrict market access for foreign insurers such as regulations that prohibit non-admitted insurers from advertising, or ban local brokers from either assisting local residents in placing their insurances abroad or from servicing such insurances.

How effective restrictions have been in achieving the objectives enunciated by governments in implementing them, and what other costs and benefits have flowed therefrom, is a matter for debate. Two examples will illustrate this point. Firstly, governments that have sought to cut the balance of payments costs of insurance imports by excluding foreign direct insurers from their domestic insurance markets usually have succeeded only in generating larger, offsetting reinsurance imports as local insurers have been forced to turn to international reinsurers not only to provide the capacity required to underwrite large risks but also to provide the technical expertise required for underwriting specialist classes of insurance and handling claims. Secondly, restrictions on foreign insurers participating in domestic markets have encouraged major commercial buyers of insurance, and in particular the multinationals, to find alternative ways of arranging their global insurance programmes. It has led to 'fronting' arrangements whereby a locally established insurer issues the required policies and then reinsures a large proportion of the risk back to a chosen foreign reinsurer, often the client's own captive insurer (that is, an insurance company established by the parent group primarily to write its own insurances).[7]

MOVES TO LIBERALISE INTERNATIONAL TRADE IN INSURANCE

Steps to reverse the trend of protectionism have taken place at three levels.

At the regional level there have been a number of examples of co-operation between countries to promote trade within the region, though in many instances at the expense of wider international trade. UNCTAD, for example, has encouraged developing countries to form regional reinsurance pools (such as the five Arab reinsurance pools) and regional reinsurance corporations (such as the African Reinsurance Corporation and the Asian Reinsurance Corporation).[8] More significant has been the progress made, albeit slowly, by the governments of the European Community towards the creation of a common market in insurance within the Community.

Secondly, the industrialised countries that are members of the Organisation for Economic Co-operation and Development have from time to time discussed within a special Insurance Committee the question of freedom of insurance transactions and the related payment and capital flow issues. In 1972 a High-level Group on Trade and Related Problems considered in its report the subject of trade in services and recommended that:

> Insurance probably deserves first attention not only because of its economic significance, but also because more than elsewhere progress towards real liberalisation is held up by involved technical arrangements.[9]

The Committee noted that the Rules of the Code of Liberalisation of Current Invisible Operations concerning insurance were incomplete, that member countries had lodged numerous reservations on liberalised operations, and that they were opposed to liberalisation until such time as national insurance supervisory regulations were harmonised. Given that negotiations were under way within the European Community dealing with those same issues, negotiations within the OECD were then largely suspended. However, following the initiative of the US government in raising the question of services during the Tokyo round of negotiations on the General Agreement on Tariffs and Trade (GATT), the OECD reactivated its Insurance Committee. In 1983 it produced a joint report with the Capital Markets and Invisibles Transactions Committee detailing the existing obstacles within member states to establishment and cross-frontier trade in insurance.[10]

Thirdly, discussions have commenced at a multilateral level within the GATT. Although the attempt by the American government to bring trade in services within the GATT negotiating framework was opposed mainly by developing countries, led by Brazil and India, it was agreed at the GATT ministerial meeting in November 1982 that individual countries with an interest in trade in services should be invited to prepare national studies on the barriers to trade in services. Following the submission of several national studies it was agreed at a further ministerial meeting in

September 1986 that a special Group of Negotiations on Services would be set up to look into how GATT principles and procedures should be applied to trade in services with the aim of establishing:

> a multilateral framework of principles and rules for trade in services, including elaboration of such trade under conditions of transparency and progressive liberalisation and as a means of promoting economic growth of all trading partners and the developing countries. Such framework shall respect the policy objectives of national laws and regulations applying to services and shall take account of the work of relevant international organisations.[11]

Whether trade in services will be brought eventually into the GATT negotiating framework and, if so, how it will be achieved, is far from clear at present. Although the various types of services have different characteristics it would be sensible for negotiators to work towards an arrangement that would embrace services rather than dealing with each type of service separately. On the other hand, one of the major difficulties that will have to be overcome in relation to insurance is how establishment issues can be handled within the GATT. Rodney Gray, who was the head of the Canadian delegation at the Tokyo Round, has pointed out that the 'right to deny a foreign entity access to the national territory is an important aspect of sovereignty'.[12] He concluded that most governments probably will be unwilling to accept a 'right of establishment' in treaty terms, though they may be prepared to accept the establishment of locally incorporated subsidiaries of foreign companies.

Clearly if progress is to be made the lead must be taken by the industrialised countries which still generate over 90 per cent of the total world expenditure on insurance (excluding the Communist bloc). In order to assess what are the prospects for a multilateral agreement covering both establishment and cross-frontier insurance trade, the final part of this chapter will examine the case for liberalisation and the difficulties that have been encountered in bringing about a common market in insurance within the European Community.

THE CASE FOR LIBERALISATION OF INSURANCE TRADE

The economic case for international trade rests on the theory of comparative advantage, which demonstrates that countries should specialise in the production of those commodities in which they have a comparative advantage and rely on trade to meet their other needs. By so doing all of the trading partners will benefit from an increase in efficiency and thus higher output, though the benefits need not necessarily be spread evenly either between each of the trading partners or between different social groups. Moreoever, during a period of resource reallocation, some short-term losses may be incurred. However, there is ample research evidence that over the long term countries do benefit from trade, and the theory is well understood by policy-makers and trade negotiators so that both bilateral and multilateral trade negotiations have been able to progress on the basis of sound economic principles.

Although the theory of comparative advantage was developed to explain the benefits to be derived from international specialisation and trade in 'goods', there is no apparent reason why some countries should not likewise enjoy comparative advantages in the production of one or more services, including insurance.[13] Few countries possess all of the attributes required for the successful conduct of insurance business internationally, including good communications, adequate supplies of well-educated and trained labour, access to international banking and other services, favourable exchange control regulations, and so on. Furthermore, examples could be cited to support the claim that consumers, and in particular large industrial buyers of insurance, frequently could benefit by obtaining from foreign insurers lower premiums and/or insurance contracts more suited to their needs than local companies are willing to offer.[14] Also domestic insurance industries may gain from access to the advanced technical know-how and expertise of major foreign insurers and reinsurers.[15]

To date the amount of theoretical and applied research that has been undertaken has been insufficient to prove conclusively that the theory of comparative advantage is as equally valid for services as for goods. In addition, attempts to analyse the role and economic significance of services to both individual countries and within the international economy are confronted by conceptual and data limitation problems. For example, insurance services embrace both 'trade' and 'investment' activities which raise separate issues, and few countries possess detailed information regarding either the volumes of international business conducted by their own domestic insurers, or of insurance services supplied to residents by foreign insurers and reinsurers either through local establishments or across frontiers. Equally, few governments appear to understand fully the extent and net balance of payments effects of insurance services supplied by foreign insurers through local establishments or across frontiers.[16] It is therefore not surprising that adequate accurate data is hard to find other than for a very few countries.[17]

In 1963 the Organisation for Economic Co-operation and Development undertook a survey of insurance supervision in Europe which, among other things, detailed the obstacles to establishment by foreign insurers.[18] However, it was not until the pioneering work of the Trade Policy

Research Centre, the International Chamber of Commerce and a few individuals[19] in the mid-1970s that any serious attempt was made to assess the obstacles to services trade.

So it is that negotiations on trade in services will proceed without the firm theoretical and empirical research underpinning that has marked the negotiations on trade in goods, though to quote one observer: 'The weight of evidence – such as it is – falls on the side of liberalisation.'[20]

THE LESSONS FROM EUROPE

As noted earlier, the most ambitious plans for liberalising insurance trade have been those of the European Community where, according to the provisions of the Treaty of Rome, a common market in insurance should have been achieved by 1969. The twin freedoms of establishment and of 'services' (that is cross-frontier trade) were to be brought about by directives that, amongst other things, would approximate the laws of the member states 'to the extent necessary for the proper functioning of the common market'.

Agreement was quickly reached on reinsurance because throughout the Community reinsurance transactions were already relatively free. Therefore, both freedoms were implemented by a directive issued in 1964, whereby EC reinsurers were subject to insurance supervision only in their country of establishment. Direct insurance, however, has presented far more difficulties, to the extent that almost twenty years after the original deadline, agreement on freeing cross-frontier trade still has not been achieved.

Not least of the problems confronting the negotiators has been the widely differing views of member governments regarding the protection of insurance consumers.

At the one extreme the British government traditionally had been content to regulate only the financial solvency of insurance companies and, although a number of company failures in the 1960s has led to more extensive controls on the entry of companies to the market and the conduct of business, few constraints were imposed on the ways in which well-managed, financially prudent companies ran their businesses. Also the Lloyd's market continued to operate under a system of self-regulation. The situation in other countries was very different. French, German and Italian insurers, for example, enjoyed far less commercial freedom in that premium rates, policy terms, marketing and the investment of funds were all subject to supervisory control. Their governments took the view that the interests of consumers were best served by regulating competition between insurers.

There were differences, too, in the treatment of foreign insurers. Britain, because of its own extensive overseas insurance operations, did not discriminate against foreign companies wishing to establish there and its residents were permitted to insure abroad. Other countries, to varying degrees, protected their domestic markets from foreign competition. For example French, German and Italian residents could not freely place their insurances abroad, so that established insurers also were protected against competition from non-admitted foreign insurers. Therefore, when negotiating on the freedoms for Community insurers the member governments have also had to agree on what rights of access external (that is non-Community) insurers shall have to the markets of member states, and on what terms.

Other obstacles to agreement have been the substantial differences between member states in regards to such matters as insurance contract law; the rights of contracting parties to choose which laws shall govern the contract; the rights of policyholders on the winding-up of an insurance company; and the tax treatment of insurance companies and insurance contracts.

Consequently it was not until 1973 that the Non-Life Establishment Directive was issued providing the right for direct insurers incorporated and authorised to write non-life insurance in one member state to establish branch offices elsewhere within the Community. It took another six years of negotiations and two judgements of the European Court of Justice before an establishment directive was issued for life insurance.

'Freedom of services' has still to be achieved. An attempt to free cross-frontier trade in the direct insurance of large risks (the Co-insurance Directive of 1978) had little practical effect because of the restrictive interpretations of the Directive's provisions by some member states. This led the European Commission in 1985 to instigate proceedings in the European Court of Justice against the governments of Denmark, France, Germany and Ireland. Although the Court's judgement, delivered in 1986, went some way towards promoting freedom of cross-frontier insurance it nevertheless accepted the right of member governments to maintain some restrictions on insurers supplying insurances to residents across national frontiers.

In December 1987 the Council of Ministers agreed to a draft Non-Life Services Directive, which was adopted in June 1988, to free cross-frontier trade in large industrial and commercial risks where the policyholder is above a specified size. Before freedom of services can be achieved for smaller risks additional consumer protection measures will have to be agreed and incorporated in a further Directive. A target date of 1991 was set in the Commission's 1985 White Paper *Completing the Internal Market* for achieving freedom of services for life insurance. However, there were still considerable obstacles to be overcome due to differences in national supervisory regulations and taxation before all governments could agree that the interests of both insurers and policyholders would be adequately protected.[21] Therefore, the first draft directive issued in February 1989 only provides for individuals, acting on their own initiative, to buy life insurances across EC state frontiers.

What the European Community negotiations have demonstrated is that even when there is political agreement on the principle of trade liberalisation many differing interests have to be reconciled before progress towards it can be achieved. The stages towards the creation of a common market in insurance within the Community do, however, provide a pointer to the possible ways forward for trade liberalisation on a wider stage.

STAGES IN TRADE LIBERALISATION

The first obvious candidate for negotiation is trade in reinsurance, particularly since there is a growing demand for insurance protection against increasingly larger risks. There is less need to supervise reinsurance contracts which are arranged between equally knowledgeable parties. The one necessary condition for consumer protection is confidence in the security of the reinsurer which essentially means confidence in the supervision exercised by the reinsurer's country of domicile. Next should come freedom of establishment; not only does it place a smaller balance of payments strain on a host country's economy but it also assists in the process of technology transfer between countries. As for consumer protection and fair competition between insurers, the European solution has been to adopt common authorisation, solvency and reserve localisation regulations, but to allow member states, if they so desire, to regulate other aspects of insurers' operations, any regulations applying equally to both domestic and foreign companies.

Liberalising cross-frontier trade poses the most difficult problems. The insurance buyers with the most to gain from access to the international insurance markets are the large industrial and commercial companies. especially those who themselves trade internationally and for whom there should be less concern with issues of consumer protection. Two key issues are insurer security, and matters of jurisdiction and the enforcement of court awards. As far as the former is concerned, an international agreement on solvency standards for insurers would be a major step forward in solving that problem.

Finally, it is worth reiterating that if the industrialised nations wish to bring about greater freedom of trade in services it is up to them to set the lead.

Notes

1. J. S. Revell, *The British Financial System* (London: Macmillan, 1973) p. 401.
2. United Nations Conference on Trade and Development, *Reinsurance Problems in Developing Countries* (Geneva: UNCTAD Secretariat, 1975); *Third World at the End of the 1970s* (Geneva: UBCTAD Secretariat, 1980).
3. W. R. Malinowski, 'European insurance and the Third World', *Journal of World Trade Law*, August-September 1971; and José Ripoll, 'UNCTAD and insurance', *Journal of World Trade Law*, January-February 1974, and 'Some thoughts of development and insurance', *Best's Review* (Oldwick, New Jersey) February 1976.
4. R.L. Carter and G.M. Dickinson, *Barriers to Trade in Insurance* (London: Trade Policy Research Centre, 1979), ch. 2; and Harold D. Skipper Jr, 'Protectionism in the provision of international insurance services', *Journal of Risk and Insurance*, vol. 54 no. 1, March 1987.
5. Harold D. Skipper Jr, ibid.
6. Organisation for Economic Co-operation and Development, *International Trade in Services: Insurance – Identification and Analysis of Obstacles* (Paris: OECD Secretariat, 1983).
7. United Nations Conference on Trade and Development, *The Impact of Captive Insurance Companies on the Insurance Markets of Developing Countries* (Geneva: UNCTAD Secretariat, 1984).
8. UNCTAD, *Reinsurance Problems in Developing Countries.*
9. Organisation for Economic Co-operation and Development, *Policy Perspectives for International Trade and Economic Relations*, High Level Group on Trade and Related Problems (Paris: OECD Secretariat, 1983).
10. See note 6.
11. *GATT Press Release*, 25 September 1986.
12. Rodney de C. Gray, 'A not so simple plan for negotiating trade in services', draft paper (London: Trade Policy Research Centre, 1985).
13. Paul F. Butler, *Statement to the President's Export Council* (Washington), 10 February 1983; and R. L. Carter and G. M. Dickinson, op cit.
14. Carter and Dickinson, *Barriers to Trade in Insurance.*
15. Harold D. Skipper Jr, 'Entering a foreign country's marketplace', *Journal of the American Society of CLU*, vol. 40, May 1986.
16. G. M. Dickinson, 'International insurance transactions and the balance of payments', *Geneva Papers on Risk and Insurance*, no. 6, October 1977.
17. Britain's balance of payments data for insurance transactions, although good, still suffer from the distortion of the annual estimates of earnings from the underwriting of overseas insurances by the treatment of claims payments and the additions to reserves for the payment of claims in future years.
18. *Supervision of Private Insurance in Europe* (Paris: OECD Secretariat, 1963).
19. Brian Griffiths, *Invisible Barriers to Invisible Trade* (London: Policy Research Centre, 1975); and Ronald Shelp, 'The proliferation of foreign insurance laws: reform or regression', *Law and Policy in International*

Business, no. 8, 1976, and *Beyond Industrialization: Ascendancy of the Global Service Economy* (London: Praeger, 1981).

20. Harold D. Skipper Jr, 'Protectionism in the provision of international insurance services'.
21. R. L. Carter and E. V. Morgan, *Freedom to Offer Life Insurance Across EEC State Boundaries*, report prepared for the European Commission, 1986 (private circulation).

Part V
Managerial and Micro Aspects of Financial Institutions

The future of financial systems and services will shape – and in its turn be shaped by – the strategic decisions of individual financial institutions. These decisions are helping to re-draw the industrial structure map of banking, insurance and related financial institution sectors. Financial institutions have increasingly moved into new lines of business and developed innovative organisational forms. As traditional barriers between historically segmented financial markets have crumbled, financial institutions have increased the range and sophistication of their decisions. This process has greatly complicated the managerial and micro-economic aspects of the financial firm.

Risk lies at the heart of the business – traditional and new – of financial institutions. In Chapter 13 Mervyn Lewis explores the methodological and practical linkages between banking and insurance. Richard Harrington explores the growth of banking ALM (asset and liability management) in Chapter 14. The new financial environment has been characterised *inter alia* by the increasing importance of ALM in banks and other financial institutions. Joël Métais explored the changing industrial structure of international banking in Chapter 9 (Part IV): in Chapter 15 Ted Gardener focuses on the strategic and organisational consequences of so-called 'bank financial conglomerates'. In Chapter 16 Neil Murphy examines some recent survey evidence from the United States on the use of ATMs. This research was designed partly to analyse any possible inconsistency between patterns in self-service banking and financial institutions' plans to exploit more intensively the existing branch office structure.

13 Banking as Insurance

Mervyn Lewis

INTRODUCTION

Almost every aspect of economic life is subject to uncertainty. The uncertainty comes about because people lack information about future 'states' with respect to resources, needs, preferences and technology. In order to cope with this uncertainty, a series of institutions for sharing and shifting risks has evolved. Markets for insurance services come readily to mind. But the financial system as a whole performs a risk-sharing function.

As Jack Revell observed in a recent paper, 'the management and control of risk lie at the heart of intermediation' (Revell, 1987). We are used to thinking in these terms with conventional insurance: the buyer of an insurance contract purchases financial security, and the seller of the contract accepts a risk on the purchaser's behalf. This is so with most financial contracts. Insurance companies protect against loss to 'assets', broadly interpreted, arising from contingencies such as premature death, fire, and burglary. Mutual funds (unit trusts) pool together a large number of company shares or real estate to provide protection against loss should one of these assets fall in value. Banks and depository institutions offer their customers protection against the possibility of being short of funds from other circumstances.

The common thread of the protection and guarantees offered to customers would lead one to expect a common analytical framework. Yet the literature of insurance and banking has developed along separate lines. This chapter seeks to draw some parallels between banking and insurance. Indeed, defining insurance 'in the broadest sense' as a set of risk-shifting arrangements (Arrow, 1971) enables us to view the risk-processing activities of financial intermediaries, in general, and banks in particular, as a form of insurance.

One reason for treating banking as insurance is to draw together the seemingly disparate elements which make up modern-day banking. There is a well-developed theory of retail banking (see Santomero, 1984). But the differences between retail banking and wholesale banking – first identified in the United Kingdom by Revell (1968) – have never been examined conceptually in a satisfactory way. International banking is typically treated tangentially to retail banking. So also is the recent growth in the off-balance sheet business of the banks, referred to variously as 'contingent commitment banking' (Kareken, 1987), 'assetless banking' (Giddy, 1986), or 'invisible banking' (Gardener, 1986). These four types of banking –

retail, wholesale, international and off-balance sheet – form the basis of the following sections.

RETAIL BANKING

Lenders of funds can always accumulate wealth by holding primary securities (such as mortgages, debentures, common stock, and commercial paper) issued by borrowers of funds. In most developed countries, a shrinking proportion do so, preferring instead to hold claims against financial intermediaries, and delegating to them decisions about the allocation of savings to various ends.

The 'modern' theory of banking and financial intermediation emphasises that this delegation is due to information. Financial intermediaries are specialist producers of information services. As such, they help solve the information and incentive problems which arise from lenders' inability to observe the attributes of borrowers and the contingencies under which they operate (Leland and Pyle, 1977). By means of 'delegated monitoring', intermediaries help overcome the inability of lenders subsequently to ascertain and exercise control over the behaviour of borrowers (Diamond, 1984). Since much of the information acquired is proprietary, 'internalisation' within the firm enables the intermediary to select better investments and monitor their performance at lower costs than would be the case if lenders did so themselves (Bernanke and Gertler, 1985).

The 'old' story of financial intermediation also rests on information imperfections. Lenders want intermediaries to help them manage the 'liquidity risks' of financing. While funds are tied up in long-term loans, spending opportunities and consumption needs may present themselves which lead the lender to want to sell off all or part of the funds lent out. At the same time, borrowers may be tardy in repaying loans or may default, while securities may decline in value. Over the time-period relevant for the liquidity needs, these 'asset risks' give rise to a preference amongst lenders for claims which are convertible in fixed nominal values. Borrowers, for their part, want protection against having to repay borrowings prematurely and refinance at unknown terms.

These liquidity needs cannot be provided for by means of conventional insurance contracts, which rely on the insurable risks being known by all parties (no asymmetric information) independently of the actions of the insured (no moral hazard). In this case, the spending opportunities and needs are known only to the lenders themselves, precluding an objective identification of the 'states' in which consumers find themselves, and giving rise to high monitoring costs (Bryant, 1980; Diamond and Dybvig, 1983; Haubrich and King, 1984).

Financial intermediaries provide the desired financial security on both sides of the balance sheet by issuing contracts to borrowers and lenders which differ from those which would be exchanged under direct financing. Differences in these contracts define what is meant by the description that financial intermediaries 'create liquidity'. For example, borrowers from banks are able to obtain funds for longer periods and depositors lend for shorter periods than would occur in the absence of banking. Depositors can make a claim against the bank on demand in the circumstances of being short of cash.

This last example is not unlike the contract of insurance companies. Policyholders are allowed to make a claim should they be burgled or suffer an accident. This analogy can be taken further. We can visualise financial intermediaries purchasing primary securities from borrowers and re-selling them to lenders of funds with an insurance policy added. The insurance premium is covered in the bid-offer spread and service charges.

Risks may be managed by financial intermediaries in a number of ways. They may reduce or diversify risk; they may shift risk, either onto the parties with whom they contract, that is borrowers and lenders, or onto markets; or they may bear risk by issuing guarantees or insurance policies of various kinds. Intermediaries may also use some combination of these strategies.

These distinctions are important to bear in mind when we consider the operation of banks. Compare the operations of banks and mutual funds. In the case of mutual funds, the asset risk of primary securities is pooled, diversified and thus reduced, but the residual, undiversified risk in the total portfolio is passed on fully to unit-holders. Banks' insurance policies are different. Despite holding assets which individually have some risk, banks assure depositors that their funds can be realised at full capital value. Unlike mutual funds, banks hold many claims for which secondary markets do not exist. Despite holding large portfolios of securities which cannot be sold individually, banks offer depositors the option to withdraw or transfer balances on demand or at short notice. On the other side of the balance sheet, borrowers from banks are insured against daily fluctuations in interest rates on their loans despite daily variations in the bank's cost of funds. Banks assure borrowers that loans will not have to be repaid within the period over which the funds are committed. These 'insurance' contracts are much the same in all types of banking.

Banks are able to provide these guarantees by taking advantage of economies of scale in portfolio management arising from the law of large numbers. As such, the economies parallel those which form the basis of conventional insurance. Almost all insurance arrangements are based on the holding of reserves.[1] Individuals could themselves lay up a fund to cover, say, ill-health and car accidents, and many in fact do so. Others prefer to purchase insurance, leaving the insurer, by virtue of the law of large numbers, to pool reserves more economically. So it is with banks.

A bank must be able to convince depositors that, despite having an asset portfolio composed of (at least partly) risky assets, its deposit liabilities can be redeemed at full value. This is achieved by the institution's buffer stock of shareholders' funds which absorb losses due to default on assets or capital losses on unanticipated security sales. Not all loans fail, or for the same reasons, and so long as there exists imperfect correlation in the fate of the different loans and investments, having a large and diversified range of assets allow more risk of default to be pooled and reduced.

Each depositor may hold the option of conversion into cash on demand but has no idea when the need may arise. When large numbers of liquidity options are combined and large numbers of loans are pooled, regularities emerge which enable banks to guarantee the spendability of their assets while making a profit. More promises to pay out cash are issued than cash is held, in the same way that the sums insured under the policies of private information about funding needs, but those needing the insurance identify themselves to banks when making withdrawals.

Our discussion of scale economies in risk-bearing has been couched in terms of the scale of bank portfolios, but the insurance principle is a general one. When diversifying across independent risk of default and of deposit variability, the principle of the law of large numbers is simple: the larger the better. But nothing is said about the organisation used to achieve size: the pooling can be within the firm or across firms. Consider liquidity risk. With interbank markets and other such co-operative arrangements, the pooling occurs *outside* the firm via the market transactions. In the case of a large bank or a branch network, the pooling occurs *within* the firm. A branch network can be thought of as an intra-bank market. What are the relative efficiencies of the two institutional forms?

As an empirical matter, it is the case that retail banking in most developed countries is concentrated, with a small number of large, multi-branch banks dominating the payments mechanism. The exception is the United States. Branching there has been restricted, but that has acted as a spur to the development of interbank arrangements. Have such arrangements in the United States now largely obviated the need for branch banking systems or have the arrangements merely reduced what would otherwise have been high costs of reserve management? Does the longstanding concentration in banking in Europe reflect the existence of historical and institutional factors inhibiting interbank links, or have such links been made unnecessary by the spread of branch banking? As we shall see, the distinction here between inter-bank and intra-bank market arrangments is the same as that which underlies the difference between retail and wholesale banking practices.

WHOLESALE BANKING

We have argued that retail banks are able to underwrite their insurance policies by adopting the classic principles of insurance, based around the holding of reserves, and owe their existence to economies of scale due to the law of large numbers. These stochastic elements cannot be applied so readily in wholesale banking. Whereas retail banks have a large number of little accounts, wholesale banks typically have a small number of big customers. The customers are large, often multinational companies, governments or government enterprises, and the institutions deal in large-valued transactions usually in small volumes. What is 'large' in retail banking, and 'small' in wholesale banking? As far as retail banks in Britain are concerned, the eight London and Scottish clearing banks in 1987 had between them 55 million accounts. By comparison, the merchant bank in London with the largest clientele in 1987 had 147 corporate customers.

If the usual pooling principles are to be applied, banks would have to be very large indeed and there would be marked tendencies to concentration. But small banks clearly do survive both in the international and domestic wholesale markets.

Some writers argue in effect that the same insurance principles do not need to operate because wholesale banks function in a quite different manner from retail banks and issue different contracts; they are not creating liquidity (Niehans and Hewson, 1976; Niehans, 1984). This view seems difficult to sustain. Wholesale banks are creating liquidity by virtue of the insurance policies they write. They provide the majority of depositors with the assurance that deposits can be withdrawn at short notice, despite holding assets of much longer maturity. They give customers the assurance that sums deposited with them can be redeemed at full value, while themselves holding assets which fluctuate in value. They assure borrowers that loans will not have to be repaid within the period over which the funds are committed. Borrowers are insured against interest rates on their loans fluctuating daily, despite variations each day in the bank's cost of funds. These insurance policies are essentially the same as the contracts in retail banking.

Wholesale banks are said to provide for liquidity risks by means of the principle of 'matching'. The idea is that customers' short-term deposits are matched by the banks' holding of short-term assets, so obviating net outflows of funds and the need for liquid reserves. In fact, for British banks maturity mismatching seems to be the rule in wholesale banking.[2] Ninety-three per cent of sterling liabilities to non-bank customers held by non-retail (wholesale) banks as at January 1987 mature in less than six months. Moreover, 61 per cent of liabilities have a maturity of seven days or less (with half of these in sterling business being at call). A third of assets mature in three years or longer. How are loans of five years to be matched with deposits of seven days' maturity? How can the risk of large loan losses be diversified?

Essentially the same problems face insurance companies, where risks are often large relative to the resources of the firms. Natural-disaster insurance, marine insurance for tankers, aeroplane insurance, are examples of such risks. Individual firms are unable to get the full benefits of the 'pooling of risks' from amongst their own policyholders, in the same way that wholesale bankers cannot get sufficient risk diversification from their own balance sheet. In the insurance industry, the solution is for a number of companies to group together to form a pool. Pooling occurs in two main ways. With co-insurance, the insurance is split between one or more companies, while with re-insurance the initial insurer or co-insurer cedes or transfers some part (perhaps even the major part) of the risk to other insurance companies, that is to the re-insurers. They may in turn re-insure part of their risk with other companies, and so on. When a claim is made, the insured is paid out by the underwriter(s), which then make claims against the re-insurers.[3]

Pooling by co-insurance and re-insurance is an institutional response by private markets which has two main purposes. It spreads individual risks that are too big for even the largest insurance companies, and allows small companies to write more concentrated business than their own reserves or capital could safely support.

Wholesale banking is directly analogous. Institutional mechanisms have been established in private banking markets which enable liquidity creation to occur at a global level. These institutional responses involve loan syndication, the interbank market, and the development of balance sheet options. These are summarised in Table 13.1 and discussed below.

Syndicates are a formal subcontracting of lending risks, precisely equivalent to co-insurance and re-insurance arrangements in international insurance markets. In eurocurrency operations participations have become almost an art form. Individual loans run into billions of dollars, and arrangements have become increasingly complex, with lead managers, co-managers, clubs of managers, agent, underwriters and as many as 150 participating banks. The formal documentation, prepared by armies of lawyers, is akin to co-insurance contracts. In domestic wholesale business, less formal arrangements prevail, which are more akin in their flexibility to re-insurance treaties.

Like co-insurance and re-insurance arrangements, participations are an institutional device for spreading around loan business which is too large an individual exposure for single bank to assume. Consider a loan L which is of such a size that no single bank can bear the risk. If n participating banks can be found, the loan can be broken down into n participations l_i, where

Table 13.1 Comparison of banking and insurance

Nature of insurance	*How provided*	*Retail operations*	*Wholesale, international and off-balance sheet*
Insurance institutions			
theft/loss of possessions	cash payout	Pooling of reserves	Reinsurance Co-insurance
damage to assets	guaranteed restitution	Pooling of risks	
Banking institutions			
liquidity	withdrawal at demand	a Maturity laddering	1 Interbank markets
	instant overdrafts	b Cash and liquid assets	2 Funding options
	backup credit lines	c Diversification of deposit base	3 Securitised assets
credit risks	deposits payable at par	a Equity capital holdings	1 Interbank borrowings
	bankers' acceptance	b Diversification of loan book	2 Syndication of loans
	standby letters of credit	c Government deposit insurance	3 Defacto government insurance

$$L = \sum_{i=1}^{n} l_i$$

and each l_i is a certain percentage share of L. Each of the l_i are fully dependent on each other and objectively have the same risk characteristics. But to an individual bank, the idiosyncratic risk is not important. What matters is the subjective risk in terms of the covariance of the participations with other loans in the bank's portfolio, and thus its contribution to the perceived riskiness of the bank's portfolio. With each bank carrying the partial risk l_i, the whole risk can be borne.

Interbank dealings can be looked upon as, in part, an informal means of risk-sharing, enabling the risk of lending to be spread amongst many different institutions. Loan risks are backed not just by the capital of the lending bank, but also indirectly by the capital of the banks which agree to lend to it. This results in a sharing of risks. By granting a loan to a limited company, the debtholder is supplying the shareholders with an option (put) to default as an implied part of the loan transaction. Shareholders can put the firm's assets onto the debtholders by defaulting on the loan. Banks place limits on interbank loans and there is some 'tiering' of interest rates, according to perceived risk. Here again the language of insurance can be used. The margin levied by the lending bank is in effect a premium paid by the borrowing bank for 'insurance' against the default risk shared, the lending bank being at the same time the insurer.

When interbank lines are negotiated, there is also a sharing of potential funding requirements. As with re-insurance treaties, a 'claim' by the customer against the option of withdrawal is met in part by the bank drawing upon its re-insurance 'contracts' with the other banks. In this way, the need for liquidity as such is largely obviated; interbank and related funds markets give banks confidence that funds to meet balance sheet contingencies will be available.

Interbank markets break up the maturity transformation process. In retail banking, maturity transformation is normally undertaken fully by the bank which accepts the deposit. In wholesale banking, funds may be channelled from ultimate lenders to ultimate borrowers through several banks. In the process, what begin as short-term deposits are transformed into loans of several years' maturity. While the bank making the end placement is likely to carry the largest share, each bank is still left with some share of the transformation process (Ellis, 1981; Bergendahl, 1985).

Finally, because of the financing options issued to customers, banks have developed 'options' on their balance sheets in the form of access to bought funds ('liability management') and the ability to sell off assets by converting loans into marketable paper. Liability management policies enable liquidity risk to be shared amongst the banks. Banks which gain excess funds purchase CDs or notes and lend Federal funds to those which are short of funds, and in this way liquid reserves are not needed. Myers (1977), and Mayers and Smith (1982) have observed that future investment strategies of a firm can be viewed as options. In this respect, wholesale banks retain a presence in the wholesale fund markets so as to keep the funding options alive.

By virtue of these collective devices, no one bank is left with a large share of the process by which large, risky and illiquid loans are transformed into short-term guaranteed deposits. Liquidity and lending risks are shared out in the system as a whole.

Thus the insurance principles stand; the difference between retail and wholesale banking is the arrangement for their achievement. With small (retail) insurance, risk-pooling mostly occurs within the firm; for large (wholesale) risks, risk-pooling occurs outside the firm but within the market. Lending and participating banks can be regarded as a combined risk carrier, with the equivalent of co-insurance and re-insurance arrangements creating a unit or pool which is large enough for the law of large numbers to apply.

This is the position in aggregate, viewed in terms of the risks which are being insured. Looked at from the individual firm's viewpoint, the network of inter-firm dealings has the objective of breaking up large risks into shares or participations which are, in the end, individually small enough to be encompassed and pooled with other participations in an individual firm's portfolio.

In the absence of the network, customers would have to spread deposits and loans over a number of banks, arranging 'co-insurance' themselves. Banks carry out this task more coveniently and cheaply; their economic function is to act as efficient organisers of risk-bearing services. Nevertheless, the collective arrangements provided by banks are far from costless. Decision rules must be formulated in syndicates, documentation prepared, and banks have to monitor their inter-bank exposures.

INTERNATIONAL BANKING

Like banks anywhere, international banks collect idle funds on a short-term basis in one location and activate them by lending in other locations, and in other currencies, often for much longer terms. And in terms of the protection and 'insurance' provided to depositors, that deposits can be withdrawn with short notice at full value, and to borrowers, that funding is guaranteed at pre-set costing over the length of the loan, there is common ground between retail, wholesale and international banking.

Viewed as insurers, banks in their international banking operations can be seen to have followed the classic rules of insurance; that is, that large risks can be covered more easily and cheaply when carried by many independent risk-bearers. Funding risks of large deposits have been spread across the two thousand or so banks with a position in the international inter-bank market. Banks' methods of handling the loan risks have involved the equivalent of re-insurance arrangements to distribute the risks as widely as possible around the globe amongst hundreds of participating firms. What must be questioned is the adequacy of the classic principles of insurance for international banking.

The classic principles of insurance require, firstly, that the distribution of losses be observable by all parties to the contract and not be affected by the behaviour of the insureds. That is, there must not be any information asymmetries between the insurers and the insured which give rise to adverse selection and moral hazard. Secondly, the properties of the risks must be such that as the insurance pool increases in number, the variance of losses around the expected value approaches zero. In short, the risks insured must be capable of being diversified within the pool.

In terms of the risk-pooling characteristics, insurers themselves think of risks as falling into one of three categories: those risks which are insurable on a net basis; those uninsurable on a net basis but insurable in gross account; and those uninsurable on a gross basis.[4] The first corresponds to retail banking, comprising risks which can be pooled on a net basis by individual insurers. But larger risks can be accepted by individual insurers thanks to the ability to cede part of them to other insurers and thus create an industry-wide pool. By virtue of re-insurance, an insurance company is able to accept larger risks on a gross basis without having to assume larger risks on net account. This second category obviously corresponds to wholesale banking business. The question is whether some international banking spills over into the third category, and is 'uninsurable' by private markets.

Uninsurable risks are those which cannot be diversified away within the insurance pool. A positive correlation exists between individual losses such that there is a large, undiversifiable background risk common to all participations (Brainard and Dolbear, 1971; Hirschleifer and Riley, 1979; Doherty and Dionne, 1987). Economic depression, unemployment, natural disasters, and war are examples of these 'social risks'; in other words, risks which derive from a change in the state of nature or state of the world. These are directly significant for many portfolios and insurers refuse to underwrite many such risks. Insurance cover provided by means of the 'reserves principle' would require a thick reserve holding by the underwriting companies and co-insurers to cover the large accumulation hazard, large average losses and infrequent loss experience. Once losses were experienced, costs of broking re-insurance would rise while attempts to rebuild reserves by raising premiums would see 'adverse selection' set in; that is the good risks would leave the pool and self-insure.

All of these hazards of insuring social risks may be seen to apply to loans made by banks to developing countries. Problems arose because of a change in the 'state of the world' in the early 1980s, as the worldwide economic decline took hold. The non-oil developing countries were major borrowers, and were most affected by the world recession, oil price movements and rising interest rates, all of which combined to effectively convert banks' interest rate risk into credit risk.

International bankers pioneered the now almost universal arrangements by which interest rate risks are passed on fully to borrowers at roll-over dates. Pricing at the roll-over period is in terms of funding costs (for example LIBOR, CD rates) plus a 'spread' so making it a cost-plus contract such as those employed for military purchases of new technology, when the government compensates the supplier for all costs plus an agreed profit margin. Such an arrangement can be visualised as a fixed-price (that is rate) contract combined with an 'insurance' contract by which the purchaser takes on the insurance function and reimburses the supplier for unexpected costs. In terms of Raviv's (1979) model of optimal insurance, the shifting of costs would be justified if the borrower is less risk-averse than lending banks. For borrowers such as the developing countries with incomes which are negatively correlated with rising interest rates, the appropriateness of the arrangement can be questioned.[5]

What is undeniable is that the nature of the risk to a bank is changed rather than shifted, since loan default risks are increased and, moreover, no longer have independent fates, rebounding onto the banks. Each bank may have held a diversified portfolio of participations, but risk is not in terms of loans, it is in terms of independent fates. With roll-over credits, risk is perhaps best measured by the amount of outstanding debt of countries on floating-rate terms, net of bank claims held by those countries. By 1982, 75 per cent of the net floating-rate syndicated debt was held by four countries alone: Mexico, Brazil, Argentina and South Korea. Syndication is meant to be an anti-accumulation device, to use a term common in insurance, preventing too much of an accumulation of risk in individual portfolios, but there was clearly accumulation in the aggregate loan portfolio; in a sense there was one risk. Adding interdependent participations does not improve the spread of risks in a bank's balance sheet. In insurance terms, it was as though each insurer sought a diversified portfolio of houses insured for earthquake damage, but it just happened that each lay along the San Andreas fault.

Costs of transacting traditional international bank deposit and lending seems likely to have increased in consequence. International banking, like re-insurance, has tended to be carried out under conditions of *uberrimae fidei*, and the many small banks needed for enhanced risk spreading tended, when buying participations, to rely on the country risk assessment of the syndicate lenders and correspondent banks. As perceived credit risk has grown, many banks, US-owned banks in particular, have curtailed the extent of their interbank activity and are monitoring ongoing exposures more carefully. Suppose that there is a cost c in monitoring each interbank exchange. With n participating banks, each checking one other, total costs will be $n(n - 1)c$. At some point, the enhanced risk bearing to be had from drawing in more banks (increasing n) will be offset by the greater monitoring costs.[6] International bank lending during the 1970s was sustained by pulling in on average sixty new banks every year. For the moment, at least, it would seem that the process of international risk diversification by banks has run its course. Indeed, adverse selection may have occurred, with the banks' prime customers moving to the international securities markets – the process of 'securitisation'. Banks have adapted to the changed circumstances, as exemplified by their spread into 'off-balance sheet' activities.

OFF-BALANCE SHEET BANKING

In recent years there has been a growth of four types of arrangements, both formal and informal, which generate contingent claims against a bank, and thus give rise to potential balance sheet or portfolio risk. The first category is loan commitments, which includes overdraft facilities, credit lines, repurchase agreements and note issuance or revolving underwriting facilities. The second category is guarantees, embracing documentary and standby letters of credit, warranties, and indemnities. The third category, swap and hedging instruments, covers foreign exchange and interest rate transactions in terms of forward, futures and options contracts. Finally, there are the investment or merchant banking activities involving acceptances, market-making in secondary markets for securities, and underwriting and placing of new issues.[7]

Such activities, entered into because of the fee income which they produce and the capital requirements they may avoid, illustrate perhaps more closely than traditional bank activities the parallels between banking and insurance. Many of the fees received by banks for such activities can be interpreted as premiums paid by customers for insurance against particular financial risks. At the same time, there are clear parallels between 'off' and 'on' balance sheet activities.

Insurance against liquidity risk can be provided by note issuance facilities and discount commitments, whereby banks agree to accept short-term paper of their customers and are able to manage the resulting liquidity demands via their ability to rediscount the paper in the markets. As regards on-balance sheet loans, we have visualised banks' insurance to borrowers taking the form of standing ready over a number of years to provide substitute deposits, on agreed terms, should lenders be unwilling to continue with their funding. When it comes to note issuance facilities, banks guarantee the continuance of funding over periods as long as ten years by standing ready to buy the notes which cannot be placed at the interest cost specified in the underwriting contract. In both instances, the costs of servicing the insurance policy are recovered from the 'spread' over funding costs and in service charges.

Banks also insure against asset risk through activities such as bill acceptances, standby letters of credit and other financial guarantees. In these cases, banks 'guarantee' payment of a customer's liability to a holder of its debt should the customer default. Fees charged reflect the benefits of the lower interest rate required by the market on the customer's paper once a bank guarantee is attached. Although the initial incidence of the fee is on the bank's customer (the borrower), the ultimate effect of the lower yield is equivalent to the holder of risky (higher yielding) paper paying a premium to the bank, in terms of forgone interest, for insurance against default. This is precisely equivalent to a depositor accepting an insurance policy from a bank in lieu of uninsured income from primary securities.

These parallels between 'on' and 'off' balance sheet activities have not been lost on regulators, who are raising capital requirements against off-balance sheet exposures. These exposures do not always feature in present capital adequacy requirements because they are contingent claims, for example in the form of overdraft facilities, stand-by credit lines and forward commitments, exercisable at the customers' volition, and do not make their appearance on the balance sheet until the agreement is called upon.

Such commitments made by banks can be viewed as options, as indeed can conventional insurance. A put option enables the purchaser to hedge or 'insure' against the risk of a fall in the price of an asset, while the writer of the put is betting that the price will not decline. Fire insurance, in these terms, is akin to a gamble in which the insurer is betting, for a price and with statistically based odds, that the house will not burn down. Banks can likewise be treated as firms issuing options contracts of various kinds. Deposit withdrawability is a put option held by depositors. Overdraft facilities are a put option, exercise of which gives rise to a call option enabling prepayment of the overdraft. Revolving credit lines, loan commitments, mortgage loans can all be viewed as put options whereby borrowers-to-be can sell their securities to the banks at predetermined interest rates or risk premia.[8]

Commitment accounting might be a useful way of thinking about issues of bank risk management. It has the advantage of eliminating the somewhat artificial distinction between on and off-balance sheet business, by focusing upon the options rather than their realisation. On this conception, we would be thinking in terms of options balance sheets, listing options granted and options held. In principle at least, option pricing formulae could be used to establish appropriate pricing arrangements, as is done with the new explicit options contracts relating to currency dealings. But given the methods currently used for pricing options, the limited marketability of many assets held by banks creates problems in practice. This limited marketability of bank assets is important in defining the special characteristics of 'banking insurance'.

SPECIAL NATURE OF BANKING INSURANCE

Viewing banking as insurance has enabled us to integrate and provide a conceptual framework for comparing retail, wholesale, international and off-balance sheet banking. We conclude by considering the implications for society of this type of insurance.

Banks' liquidity insurance has a special characteristic in that confidence, as well as the natural hazards of life, governs the firms' exposure. Standard forms of insurance rely on randomness, so that losses converge to the expected value with zero variance as the insurance pool grows larger. Similarly, pooling of deposit withdrawals can work only if one depositor's decision to withdraw deposits is largely independent of the decision made by others. That is the case only so long as depositors are fully confident that their cash needs will be met. The history of banking is littered with illustrations of a loss of confidence spreading like a contagion, and demonstrates also that such events cannot be predicted with accuracy. Depositors, seeking to beat the run, exaggerate current liquidity needs in order to secure future requirements.[9] Once a run begins, the bank may be unable to make good the promise to repay deposits at face value.

Bank runs also impose costs on borrowers, for banks provide insurance-type services to borrowers. In the case of loans, we have visualised banks as accepting liquid deposits from lenders of funds and offering them to borrowers with an insurance policy added. The policy, in effect, is a guarantee to stand ready over a number of years to provide substitute deposits, on agreed terms, should lenders be unwilling to continue with their funding. When, instead, premature repayment is demanded, the borrowers may not be able to obtain alternative funds on the same terms, and perhaps not at all, from other institutions.

Communal arrangements have been introduced in most countries to prevent these costs and these are themselves a guarantee or form of reinsurance (explicit in the case of deposit insurance). This reinsurance also has a special feature, since the main aim is to prevent the event rather than to recompense people after its occurrence. These arrangements suffer from a common fault of insurance, that of moral hazard, since the insured's willingness to take risks may increase. The attempted solutions in this case are also those common to insurers: limited coverage (upper limits on payouts), monitoring and imposing bounds upon the insured's behaviour (prudential regulation); and co-insurance (reserve and capital requirements). These are summarised in Table 13.2.

The situation is more complicated in the fields of wholesale and international banking than in retail banking because no formal re-insurance treaties exist with the deposit protection agencies, and risks and liquidity demands are shared up by private markets. Yet, as in retail banking, wholesale banking depends crucially on confidence; confidence that the bank is able to command resources from the wholesale funding markets which permit liquidity creation to occur. In principle, banks lending interbank and customers buying bank debt should assess the riskiness of a borrowing banks' balance sheet and levy an insurance premium in the form of an interest rate risk margin which is appropriate. But there is a growing appreciation that money markets do not price over a continuum and instead ration funds, reacting discontinuously to risk (Grunewald and Pollock, 1985). Once some perceived risk threshold is passed, funds simply dry up and cannot be had at any price. Either a bank is thought to be sound and can borrow at the market rate, or it cannot borrow at all. Certainly, recent bank runs have originated in wholesale markets, and have snowballed rapidly. Under pressure of events, central

Table 13.2 Insurance solutions to 'moral hazard' in government deposit insurance schemes

Method	*Insurance equivalent*	*Banking analogue*
1. Limiting coverage	Insured bearing part of a claim loss	Upper limits on payout Depositor bearing part of loss
2. Co-insurance	Sharing risk with another party (or insurer)	Higher capital equity requirements Subordinated debt
3. Risk reduction activities	Installation of fire protection equipment Safety equipment for workers	Restrictions on activities of banks Limitations on bank holding companies Regulatory interference
4. Premiums related to risk	No-claim discounts for safe drivers Higher health insurance for smokers	Proposals for insurance premiums related to riskiness of banks

banks have provided *de facto* insurance of wholesale depositors. Wholesale business is effectively 'free-riding' upon retail deposit insurance, as is international and off-balance sheet banking.

Some look to reforms of the 're-insurance' arrangements by the substitution of risk-based for flat insurance premiums, but central banks and deposit insurance agencies face difficulties, as do insurers generally, in devising formulae which are free of potential abuse. In the meantime, they have sought additional co-insurance in the form of a thicker layering of capital reserves, a move which gains support from option pricing theory. Merton (1977) and Sharpe (1978) have likened deposit insurance to a put option issued by the deposit protection agencies against the value of the assets of the bank. Since the value of the option increases with leverage, the idea is to alter capital requirements so as to reduce the value of the put in line with the on and off-balance sheet risks of banks.

Others argue that banks go too far in their guarantees and 'insurance', and see a solution to the problem of bank safety in terms of fundamental reforms to the nature of banks and banking contracts. Bank runs occur because deposits are repaid on a 'first-come, first-served, fixed-price' basis, so that any concern that a bank cannot maintain a fixed price for deposits in the face of declining asset values makes it sensible for depositors to withdraw balances immediately. This incentive would diminish if instead banks, like mutual funds, priced all deposits in line with the current market value of assets.[10] This is one aspect of the 'new monetary economics' literature.

In evaluating the idea of mutual fund banking, we must return to our earlier comparison of banks and mutual funds. The proposal ignores both the limited marketability of the primary securities held as assets by banks and the strong desire of depositors to hold claims which give full nominal guarantees. This is really where we came in, for these are the conditions which provide the rationale for banks to become 'insurers'!

Notes

The author thanks P. Bull and his colleagues at the Financial Statistics Division of the Bank of England for their valuable comments. Helpful comments were also made by R. K. Ashton, R. L. Carter, K. T. Davis, S. R. Diacon, C. A. E. Goodhart and participants at a number of seminars, where an early version of the paper was read.

1. 'Insurance is a fund accumulated to meet uncertain losses' (Willett, 1901, quoted in Marshall, 1974).
2. See Lewis and Davis (1987) ch. 4.
3. See Carter (1979).
4. Berliner (1982, 1985).
5. See Arvan and Brueckner (1985). Some writers argue that banks are more efficient bearers and processors of risk than their customers (Kaufman, 1983; Hess, 1984). Others argue that flexi-rate loans 'provide a rough protection to both debtors and creditors' (Tobin, 1984).
6. Monitoring costs in re-insurance markets are analysed in Borch (1985).
7. A fuller discussion is contained in Lewis (1988).
8. A number of papers have used options analysis to examine loan underwriting facilities provided by banks in the form of revolving credit lines (Hawkins, 1982), loan commitments (Bartler and Rendleman, 1979; Thakor, Hong and Greenbaum, 1981), mortgage loans (Das, 1985). Option pricing formulae have also been applied, with mixed results, to the pricing of re-insurance on an excess of loss and quota share basis (Chang, Cheung and Krinsky, 1985).
9. 'The demand deposit contract . . . has an undesirable equilibrium (a bank run) in which all depositors panic and withdraw immediately' (Diamond and Dybvig, 1983).
10. Mutual fund banking is examined in Goodhart (1989), Lewis (1985) and O'Driscoll (1985).

References

Arrow, K. J. (1971) *Essays in the Theory of Risk-Bearing* (Chicago: Markham Publishing Co.).

Arvan, L. and J. K. Brueckner (1985) 'Efficient contracts in credit markets subject to interest rate risk', BEBR Faculty Working Paper, no. 1136, University of Illinois at Urbana-Champaign.
Bartler, B. J. and R. J. Rendleman (1979) 'Fee based pricing of fixed-rate bank loan commitments', *Financial Management*, Spring, pp. 13–20.
Bergendahl, G. (1985) 'The euromarket and OPEC oil revenues: a study of banking intermediation' (Oxford Institute for Energy Studies, University of Oxford).
Berliner, B. (1982) *Limits of Insurability of Risks* (New Jersey: Prentice-Hall).
Berliner, B. (1985) 'Large risks and limits of insurability', *Geneva Papers on Risk and Insurance*, vol. 10, no. 37, October, pp. 313–29.
Bernanke, B. and M. Gertler (1985) 'Banking and general equilibrium', National Bureau of Economic Research Working Paper 1647.
Borch, K. (1985) 'A theory of insurance premiums', *Geneva Papers on Risk and Insurance*, vol. 10, no. 36, pp. 192–208.
Brainard, W. and F. T. Dolbcar (1971) 'Social risk and financial markets', *American Economic Review*, May, pp.360–70.
Bryant, J. (1980) 'A model of reserves, bank runs and deposit insurance', *Journal of Banking and Finance*, vol. 4, pp. 335–44.
Carter, R. L. (1979) *Reinsurance* (Brentford, Essex: Kluwer Publishing).
Chang, S. K., C. S.Cheung and I. Krinsky (1985) *On the Derivation of Reinsurance Premiums* (Hamilton, Ontario, Canada: McMaster University) (mimeo).
Das, S. (1985) 'Option theoretic approaches to loan pricing', *Bulletin of Money, Banking and Finance*, 1984–5, no. 4, Macquarie University, New South Wales, Australia.
Diamond, D. (1984) 'Financial intermediation and delegated monitoring', *Review of Economic Studies*, July, vol. 51, pp. 393–414.
Diamond, D. W. and P. H. Dybvig (1983) 'Bank runs, deposit insurance and liquidity', *Journal of Political Economy*, vol. 91, no. 3, pp. 401–19.
Doherty, N. A. and G. Dionne (1987) 'Insurance with undiversifiable risk', Université de Montréal Working Paper 8710.
Ellis (1981) 'Eurobanks and the interbank market', *Bank of England Quarterly Bulletin*, September.
Gardener, E. P. M. (1986) 'Securitisation and the banking firm', IEF Research Paper in Banking and Finance RP 86/15 (Bangor: Institute of European Finance, University College of North Wales).
Giddy, I.H. (1986) 'Assetless banking', in P. Savona and G. Sutija, *Strategic Planning in International Banking* (London: Macmillan).
Goodhart, C. A. E. (1989) *Money Information and Uncertainty*, 2nd edn (London: Macmillan).
Grunewald, A. E. and A. J. Pollock (1985) 'Money managers and bank liquidity', *Conference on Bank Structure and Competition*, Federal Reserve Bank of Chicago.
Haubrich, J. G. and R. G. King (1984) 'Banking and insurance', National Bureau of Economic Research Working Paper 1312.
Hawkins, G. D. (1982) 'An analysis of revolving credits', *Journal of Financial Economics*, vol. 10, pp. 59–81.
Hess, A. C. (1984) 'Variable rate mortgages: confusion of means and ends', *Financial Analysis Journal*, January/February, pp. 67–70.
Hirschleifer, J. and J. G. Riley (1979) 'The analytics of uncertainty and information – an expository survey', *Journal of Economic Literature*, December, pp. 1375–421.

Kareken, J. H. (1987) 'The emergence and regulation of contingent commitment banking', *Journal of Banking and Finance*, vol. 11, no. 3, pp.359–78.
Kaufman, H. (1983) 'Financial institutions in ferment', *Challenge*, May/June, pp. 20–25.
Leland, H. E. and D. H. Pyle (1977) 'Information asymmetries, financial structure and financial intermediation', *Journal of Finance*, 32, pp. 371–87.
Lewis, M. K. (1985) 'Money and the control of inflation in the UK', *Midland Bank Review*, Summer.
Lewis, M. K. (1988) 'Off-balance sheet activity and its regulation', chapter 9 in *The Management of Bank Assets and Liabilities*, (ed.) J. S. G. Wilson for Euromoney Publications, London.
Lewis, M. K. and K. T. Davis (1987) *Domestic and International Banking* (Oxford: Philip Allan; and Cambridge, Mass: MIT Press).
Marshall, J. M. (1974) 'Insurance theory: reserves versus mutuality', *Economic Inquiry*, vol. 12, no. 4, December, pp. 476–92.
Mayers, D. and C. W. Smith (1982) 'Towards a positive theory of insurance', Salomon Brothers Center for the Study of Financial Institutions, Monograph Series in Finance and Economics, no. 1.
Merton, R. C. (1977) 'An analytic derivation of the cost of deposit insurance and loan guarantees: an application of modern option pricing theory', *Journal of Banking and Finance*, June, pp. 3–11.
Myers, S. D. 'The determinants of corporate borrowing', *Journal of Financial Economics*, 4, pp. 147–75.
Niehans, J. (1984) *International Monetary Economics* (Oxford: Philip Allan).
Niehans, J. and J. Hewson (1976) 'The eurodollar market and monetary theory', *Journal of Money, Credit and Banking*, vol. 8, no. 1, pp. 1–27.
O'Driscoll, G. P. (1985) 'Money in a deregulated financial system', *Economic Review*, Federal Reserve Bank of Dallas.
Raviv, A. (1979) 'The design of an optimal insurance policy', *American Economic Review*, 69, March, pp. 84–96.
Revell, J. R. S. (1968) 'Changes in British banking: the growth of a secondary banking system', Hill Samuel Occasional Paper no. 3 (London). Reprinted in H. G. Johnson (ed.), *Readings in British Monetary Economics* (Oxford: Clarendon Press, 1972).
Revell, F. R. S. (1987) 'Towards a microeconomic theory of financial institutions', IEF Research Paper in Banking and Finance RP 87/10 (Bangor: Institute of European Finance, University College of North Wales).
Santomero, A. M. (1984) 'Modelling the banking firm: a survey', *Journal of Money, Credit and Banking*, November, pp. 576–602.
Sharpe, W. F. (1978) 'Bank capital adequacy, deposit insurance and security values', *Journal of Financial and Quantitative Analysis*, November, pp. 701–18.
Thakor, A., H. Hong and S.I. Greenbaum (1981) 'Bank loan commitments and interest rate volatility', *Journal of Banking and Finance*, 5, pp. 497–510.
Tobin, J. (1984) 'On the efficiency of the financial system', *Lloyds Bank Review*, July, 153, pp. 1–15.
Willett, A. H. (1901) 'The economic theory of risk and insurance', *Studies in History, Economics and Public Law* (New York), vol. 14, no. 2.

14 The Growth of Asset and Liability Management

Richard Harrington

INTRODUCTION

Asset and liability management is not an easy concept to describe, still less to define. After all, is it not something inherent in banking that banks should manage their assets and liabilities and have they not always done so? Of course, the answers to these questions must lie in the affirmative, but the important point is that the ways in which banks manage assets and liabilities vary over time. Modern methods of asset and liability management have been developed to cope with a complicated banking world, and one in which banks have found themselves dealing in an ever-widening range of assets and liabilities expressed in many currencies and frequently booked in many different locations. In the face of this complication, it has become necessary to be more systematic: old ratios and rules-of-thumb are no longer adequate; banks have had to rethink asset and liability management and to devise new techniques and new measures.

In earlier times, a few well-established ratios and a measure of specialisation had largely sufficed. Those banks with deposits subject to cheque had learned, over many years, what amounts of cash and liquid assets were necessary in order to be able to meet all foreseeable demands from customers. And banks that relied for their funds largely on sight deposits or similar short-term liabilities tended to concentrate on short-term lending. Banks that financed themselves from savings deposits – nominally at zero or short notice but, in practice, only subject to infrequent withdrawals – were able to provide mortgages and other forms of long-term lending.

But during the 1960s and 1970s, a number of things began to change. Domestically, in a number of countries traditional demarcations between different types of institution began to break down. What had hitherto been separate markets began to merge and different types of bank found themselves competing with each other for a wider class of business. Internationally, traditional barriers of distance were being rapidly eroded by changes in technology affecting transport, computing and telecommunications. These changes facilitated a growth of international banking on a scale not seen before. London and other European cities, as well as locations in the Far East and the Caribbean, became centres for taking deposits and making loans in US dollars. Dealings in other non-resident monies followed.

The growth of these new international markets had a number of consequences. Firstly, it meant that many banks were now dealing regularly in two or more currencies. Secondly, the new markets had neither externally imposed reserve ratios nor interest rate controls and, since they were composed of banks of diverse origins and traditions, it was improbable that the many tacit agreements, conventions and other restraints on competition, common in domestic banking, would occur in the international arena: the new markets were highly competitive ones. Thirdly, the need for representation by banks in the new markets led to a dramatic rise in foreign branches and hence to a certain interpenetration by banks of each other's domestic markets. New banks brought new ideas, helped to expand the range of assets and thus added their own impetus to the forces making for greater competition in domestic banking.

The number of new banks in the emerging international banking centres led to the development of active interbank markets. These were created, in emulation of the American federal-funds market, as a response to a need for a means of short-term liquidity in a situation where pressures of competition made banks unwilling to hold large amounts of cash or low-yielding reserve assets in the traditional manner. The development of parallel markets in wholesale funds, where not officially prevented, followed naturally as corporate treasurers with large sums to deposit were reluctant to accept rates of interest much below those granted to other banks. Other short-term markets, such as those in certificates of deposit, followed in a number of the larger financial centres. These markets rapidly came to play a crucial role in bank asset and liability management.

LIQUIDITY FROM THE LIABILITIES SIDE

It is common to describe the initial phase of development as liability management. This is misleading; it involved balance sheet management, that is both assets and liabilities, from the start, but it was liability management that was the novelty and which therefore attracted attention.

An active short-term liability management was possible in that the new money markets enabled banks to bid for funds as and when needed. This ability was not automatic and was only there for banks of repute that maintained their creditworthiness in the eyes of their peers.[1] For such banks, it was possible to raise new short-term funds quickly and at little administrative cost, albeit subject to limits. This new ability represented a change of considerable importance. It freed banks, in the short term at least, from dependence on the steady but usually slow increase in deposits garnered through retail networks. It also changed notions of liquidity.

Liquidity is not an easy notion to define,[2] but for most purposes it can be thought of as having funds available when needed. Traditionally, banks met their liquidity needs by holding cash either in tills or on deposit with other banks, and/or short-term assets, such as Treasury bills and accepted commercial bills, which could be sold, discounted or pledged in return for cash, either in financial markets or at the central bank. One could measure bank liquidity, in a rough and ready way, by looking at the amount of a bank's liquid assets and relating this to total deposits. This ratio, the traditional liquid assets ratio, was widely used.

But an alternative to selling an asset issued by somebody else is to sell an asset issued by yourself: an alternative to selling a Treasury bill (issued by the government) is to sell a three-month deposit (issued by the bank itself). The existence of markets regularly trading bank liabilities made such an alternative a real possibility. Banks could therefore get liquidity from the liabilities side. As long as a bank maintained its good standing and had not already borrowed to the limit of what others were prepared to lend, it could obtain funds, when required, by issuing its own liabilities. It was not necessary to conform to any established *asset* ratio in order to be liquid.

During the 1960s, this regular borrowing of short-term funds by banks in organised markets was a novelty in the few centres in which it was practised. In most developed countries it was to expand during the 1970s and early 1980s. For those banks with access to such organised markets, it was clearly a great advantage to be able to raise new funds at virtually zero notice, as and when desired. But it was not an unmitigated advantage and the liabilities incurred in short-term financial markets were different from those to which banks had been accustomed. Usage of the new markets required careful management: it was this that was termed liability management.

Hitherto the bulk of liabilities of most banks, whilst nominally at sight or at short notice, were, in the aggregate, highly durable. Management involved estimating probable maximum outflows and holding cash and liquid assets accordingly. But the liabilities derived from short-term markets were almost wholly at fixed term, both in theory and in practice. At the end of the term, they had to be renewed explicitly or repaid. Renewal, at the discretion of the lender, might or might not be possible; this would often not be known in advance.

What each bank did know was what funds would be maturing and when. Given this, and in so far as it was possible to estimate future demands for loans, it was possible to estimate future funding needs. It was good practice to seek to arrange these in certain ways. Firstly, it was desirable to spread funding over time so as to avoid sudden or large calls on the market at any one time; secondly, it was desirable to spread borrowing as widely as possible across different markets. There was always the risk that the funds sought from any one market, at any one time, would not be available, or would only be available at high cost. The more diversified its funding, both in time and across markets, the less vulnerable was a bank to such local problems.

But if the new forms of market borrowing required careful management, the older asset management did not cease to be important; and the two were inevitably linked.

MATCHING AND MISMATCHING

The ability to sell items from the asset side of the balance sheet did not cease to be valuable just because it was now also possible to create new liabilities at short notice. Furthermore, in the nature of things, assets mature and when they do they provide cash inflows: short-term assets are inevitably a source of liquidity. What mattered to banks, and still matters, is total liquidity and this depends both on liabilities and on assets, and also on the relationship between the two.

Banks continued to manage short-term assets. They were a source of liquidity directly and they also served as evidence of prudent behaviour to outsiders, notably potential suppliers of funds. But the relationship between assets and liabilities is also crucial. To the extent that these could be matched, banks could all but do away with any problem of liquidity. In the limit, a bank could have one-month liabilities matched by one-month assets, three-month liabilities matched by three-month assets, and so on. In the absence of default or of delayed settlement, the bank would have no risk of illiquidity.

Interbank markets, since their creation, have always played a crucial role in liquidity management because here banks can both borrow and lend; and banks can, within limits, use these markets to structure assets and liabilities in ways that they wish. But perfect matching is not normally seen as desirable as it would yield low returns and it would be, in any case, usually impossible. Clients have many varied and individual needs and preferences that banks will normally try to meet, and this will produce a diverse pattern of assets that cannot be precisely matched or hedged in markets dealing in standard contracts, that is rounded amounts for certain specified periods of time. Some maturity mismatching is unavoidable but, in addition, some will be chosen. It was in managing this area of choice, deciding where to seek matched assets and liabilities, where to accept a mismatched position, that modern asset and liability management began.

Assets and liabilities have other dimensions as well as maturity: a crucial one is currency. By the late 1960s, bankers in London and in other centres such as Luxembourg, Paris, Zurich and elsewhere were regularly taking deposits and making loans in foreign currencies, chiefly the US dollar. Thus they had also to think in terms of currency matching and mismatching. Here, virtually complete matching was possible for those banks which sought it. This could be arranged by running separate currency books: for instance, a sterling book with sterling assets financed by sterling liabilities and a dollar book with dollar assets financed by dollar liabilities. And a large and growing foreign exchange market allowed for easy exchange between US dollars and other monies. Many banks took the prudent position and sought complete matching apart from short-term trading positions; but a number were happy to accept mismatched currency positions; a situation that was to be the cause of some large losses following the advent of floating exchange rates in the early 1970s.

Matching and mismatching of assets and liabilities were first documented by Jack Revell in his paper 'Changes in British banking: the growth of a secondary banking system' published in 1968. In this he described the new practices which had, by then, become current among many of the London banks. The following extract explained succinctly these banks' approach to matching assets and liabilities.

> The controlling of the maturity and currency structure of a banker's balance sheet is known as 'matching'. It is, of course, an age-old principle of banking, but it is only in the last few years that it has come into play in British banking with the advent of large deposits and advances, fixed for definite periods and expressed in a number of different currencies. A completely matched balance sheet is one in which for every deposit of a certain amount and in a certain currency maturing on a certain day there is an asset of the same amount and in the same currency maturing on the same day. It has been likened to a Christmas tree, on which branches opposite each other are of equal size. Providing nobody defaults, it is a self-liquidating balance sheet. In practice few secondary bankers have a completely matched position. Because of the narrow margins in this kind of banking, there is very little profit in just 'putting business through', and most secondary bankers aim to increase their profits by having assets somewhat longer than deposits because yields rise with maturity. Nearly all secondary bankers also take a view on future interest rates and exchange rates, although some do so far more than others.

The degree of maturity matching and mismatching at any one bank can, in principle, be shown by drawing up a maturity profile. This divides the balance sheet into a number of categories, and allocates all assets and all liabilities into the appropriate category. Table 14.1 shows a hypothetical maturity profile. From this table it can be seen that the bank in question would have had liabilities considerably in excess of assets for all periods up to three months; liabilities somewhat in excess of assets for maturities

Table 14.1 Hypothetical maturity profile (£ '000)

Term to maturity	*Less than 8 days*	*8 days to less than 1 month*	*1 month to less than 3 months*	*3 months to less than 6 months*	*6 months to less than 1 year*	*1 year to less than 3 years*	*Over 3 years*	*Total*
Liabilities	4055	2891	3490	1964	845	417	1051	14713
Assets	2897	1982	2347	1710	907	1057	3813	14713
Net position as percentage of total assets	−7.9	−6.2	−7.8	−1.7	+0.4	+4.3	+18.8	

between three and six months; and then assets greater than liabilities for all subsequent periods.

This table is by way of an example. Those in use within banks have to be more detailed, with a finer classification of maturities for short-term assets and liabilities. In practice, there are a number of problems that arise in drawing up a realistic maturity profile. Not all liabilities have a fixed maturity. Sight deposits and some savings deposits mature at the discretion of the depositor, and it is a question of judgement as to what average maturity should be allocated to these; in the aggregate, such deposits are usually a durable and predictable source of funds. On the assets side, many assets are widely traded with a current market value and hence can be easily sold before maturity.

A maturity profile that is carefully compiled and kept fully up-to-date will provide valuable information on bank liquidity. It will not be a complete indicator of such liquidity but such indicators do not exist. Liquidity is too complex a subject to be defined by any one simple formula. During the 1970s and 1980s, many banks started to compile maturity profiles on a regular basis and these are now widely used. Supervisory authorities regularly require them as part of their examination of bank liquidity.[3]

Other measures of liquidity can be derived and a number of ratios have been developed, but there is no need to go into these here.[4] But it should be recalled that traditional measures of asset liquidity, that is measures based on the amount of available short-term assets, remain important. In the United Kingdom, concern for the maintenance of adequate liquid assets has been underlined by recent Bank of England proposals for formal supervisory requirements relating to banks' stock of liquid assets.[5]

INTEREST RATE RISK

Given that many bank assets and liabilities are at variable rates of interest, it is not the case that any matching of maturities need indicate a matched interest-rate position. Nor is it the case that mismatched maturities need indicate mismatched interest rates. The two things have to be considered separately.

Mismatched interest-rate positions can cause large losses. This has always been the case and banks have traditionally had assets and liabilities differently sensitive to changes in market rates of interest (and officially determined rates of interest) with the result that such changes have always had an impact on bank profits. How this impact was felt depended critically on how banks priced their loans. In the United Kingdom, Ireland, Australia and in some Scandinavian countries, loans were usually at flexible rates of interest and were expressed as a margin above a reference rate, usually the central bank discount rate. When the reference rate rose, so did rates of interest on bank loans and on interest-bearing deposits; but, since loans constituted a larger proportion of the balance sheet than did interest-bearing deposits, there was a net gain to the banks. This was the so-called endowment effect of which the Prices and Incomes Board made so much.[6] Among other developed countries, it was usual for loans to be at fixed rates of interest, and whilst some deposits were also at fixed rates of interest such deposits were, on average, at shorter term than were loans. So when there was a general rise in rates of interest, rates received on bank assets rose more slowly than rates paid on bank liabilities, with the result that profit margins declined.

But these changes in profit margins were largely cyclical and they were well known. Many banks regularly 'played the interest rate cycle' by raising fixed-rate lending at times when they expected rates of interest to fall. During the 1950s and 1960s, changes in the general level of rates of interest were mostly small and the ensuing variations in profits were not such that they could not be coped with, especially by banks which still retained hidden reserves and smoothed published profits over the cycle.

Active trading in short-term markets brought new and different interest rate risks; risks that were made all the more serious by the greater volatility of rates of interest during the 1970s and early 1980s. In the short-term markets, banks deal, for the most part, in fixed-term, fixed-rate assets. Margins are narrow and, with a mismatched interest-rate position, it requires only a small shift in rates to bring about losses. A bank with short-term assets of average maturity of two months and short-term liabilities of average maturity of one month would stand to lose heavily if rates of interest were to rise.

Interest rate risk from transactions in wholesale markets was there from the beginning, but when such trading was small, obviously the risks were small. As such trading grew relative to total business, so the risks became more important and, of course, the traditional interest rate risks associated with retail banking continued to exist. A bank with a badly structured balance sheet could see margins narrow, or could actually lose money, in both wholesale and retail markets.

With the greater volatility of rates of interest during the 1970s, the potential losses from a mismatched interest rate position became larger, but many banks continued to believe in a predictable interest rate cycle and continued to take mismatched positions in the expectation of adding to profits. In October 1979 a change of policy by the US Federal Reserve Board in favour of closer control of monetary aggregates, led to a period of unprecedented instability of interest rates when many countries saw short-term rates reach record high levels. During 1979 rates of interest had been widely perceived as being high, but in the autumn of that year they rose rather than fell. In 1980 the US Federal funds rate rose to 19 per cent in May, fell to 9 per cent in July and then rose again to 20 per cent by January of the following year. Other countries followed the American roller-coaster. Bankers were unprepared for the sudden move to such high interest rates, and those who had positioned themselves to profit from falling rates inevitably made large losses. Those institutions which were structurally mismatched with large amounts of fixed-rate lending, such as American savings and loan associations, also made large losses.

This experience brought home, both to banks and to official supervisors, the dangers inherent in a badly mismatched interest-rate position. One can go further than this and say that it brought about a heightened concern for asset and liability management in general. The number of books and articles published on the subject grew,[7] and official supervision over banking was increased almost everywhere. A number of supervisors elaborated new requirements for interest rate risk management.

Interest rate risk can be shown in a similar way to liquidity risk by drawing up an interest rate ladder showing assets and liabilities according to time remaining before repricing. In the case of fixed-rate instruments, this time corresponds to term to maturity; in the case of variable-rate instruments, it corresponds to the term to the next re-setting of the interest rate. From such an interest rate ladder, if sufficiently detailed, a bank can see where are its interest gaps and how large these are, and can then go on to calculate how much it stands to gain or lose from any given change in market rates of interest. Table 14.2 shows a hypothetical interest rate ladder.

Table 14.2 Hypothetical interest rate ladder (£ '000)

Time to repricing	*Liabilities*	*Assets*	*Interest gap*	*Cumulative interest gap*
Less than 8 days	1100	900	−200	−200
8 days to less than 1 month	1650	1400	−250	−450
1 month to less than 3 months	800	550	−250	−700
3 months to less than 6 months	300	550	+250	−450
6 months to less than 1 year	150	200	+50	−400
1 year to less than 3 years	300	550	+250	−150
Greater than 3 years	900	1050	+150	0

This table shows a bank that has a mismatched interest rate position with liabilities, on average, repriced before assets. The amount by which repriced liabilities exceed repriced assets is shown in column 4 (for each period) and column 5 (cumulatively). These two columns show the extent of the bank's vulnerability to upward movements in the rate of interest.

For instance, if market rates rose by 1 per cent, then after one week the bank would be paying the new higher rates on liabilities that were £200 million in excess of the assets on which it was receiving the new higher rates. After one month, the bank would be paying the higher rates on liabilities that were £450 million in excess of the assets on which it was receiving the higher rates, and so on.

In practice, an interest rate ladder would need to have finer classifications than are shown here. Large banks operating in money markets need to know their short-term interest exposures on a daily basis. As with the compilation of maturity profiles, there are a number of practical problems in establishing a realistic interest rate ladder and judgement is necessary. Not all assets have clear repricing dates; a number will be redeemable at short notice at the option of bank clients. Also some assets may not be unambiguously at fixed or flexible rates of interest, but may be at flexible rates over some ranges of rates of interest and at fixed rates outside these ranges.

There are a number of other methods of showing interest rate risk but all, inevitably, are derived, in one way or another, from comparisons of repricing dates of assets and liabilities. A discussion of different techniques can be found in a number of recently published sources.[8]

SECURITISATION AND OFF-BALANCE SHEET BUSINESS

If the shock of the unprecedented gyrations in rates of interest in the period 1979–81 gave banks cause to reconsider their balance sheet management and to take the whole subject more seriously, there were more shocks to come which could only reinforce this attitude. In August 1982, Mexico announced that it could not meet its payments obligations to the international banking community. In rapid succession a number of other countries followed suit. This began what became known as the international debt crisis and provoked a lengthy series of negotiations and debt reschedulings which have continued until the present day.

The first, and most dramatic, effect of the crisis was that it raised the serious prospect of the failure of many large banks. If debts were repudiated outright and interest unpaid on a large scale, then a number of banks would quickly become technically insolvent and could expect a run-off of deposits leading to actual insolvency. This doomsday scenario did not happen. With only a few exceptions, debts were rescheduled and interest was paid, but the situation remained very difficult. Apart from the obviously worsened credit risk, there were a number of consequences for asset and liability management. What had been short and medium-term assets were overnight turned into long-term and virtually frozen assets, maturity mismatching had been greatly increased, and bank liquidity reduced.

Banks reacted in a number of ways. In response to the sharp deterioration in asset quality, banks sought to increase provisions for bad and doubtful debts, and to increase equity funds and other long-term liabilities. Balance sheet growth as an objective was downgraded and the emphasis switched rapidly to one of improving profitability. Large sums were put to reserves and new rights issues were made. This served a dual purpose: enhanced capital adequacy made it less likely that future losses would call into question the solvency of the bank; and this in turn meant that the creditworthiness of the bank was raised in the eyes of depositors. Adequate long-term liabilities enabled banks to continue to attract short-term liabilities and hence sustained this form of liquidity.

In response to the specific problem of excessive maturity mismatching, banks sought to increase asset liquidity in other parts of their book by means of securitisation, that is to say by switching some lending from the traditional non-marketable loans which were held until the borrower repaid them, to lending against marketable assets which could be sold to a third party at the option of the bank. This was part of a general trend towards the greater use of securities and securitised assets which had occurred for a number of reasons and in a number of ways.[9] Banks increased their lending by means of the purchase of floating-rate notes and they also helped to develop the market in note issuance facilities wherein borrowers can obtain medium- and long-term funds against the issue of renewable short-term notes. The notes are predominantly of three or six months' duration, so bank lending against the issue of such notes could be seen as creating short-term liquid assets. Although a number of banks did underwrite future issues of notes and in this way they incurred contingent liabilities.

During 1983 and 1984 underwritten notes became a popular form of finance with large companies and this enabled a number of banks to earn fee income by underwriting, namely by giving guarantees to take up notes which could not be sold on future dates at or above agreed minimum price levels. Earning income without expanding the balance sheet was seen as highly desirable by many banks but it did create contingent and off-balance sheet liabilities. Once these became significant, they could not be ignored in asset and liability management. Nor could they be ignored by supervisory agencies: the Bank of England brought the underwriting of note issuance facilities within its rules for capital adequacy in April 1985 and a number of other central banks followed.[10] This made this form of bank guarantee of funds more expensive for the banks and appears to have hastened a trend that was already evident towards the growth of issues of non-underwritten notes in the form of eurocommercial paper. Such paper was not supported by formal bank guarantees but it was common for issuers to have informal standby or back-up facilities from banks.

A further means of securitisation was the introduction of trading of sub-participations in syndicated loans. This began informally after the outbreak of the international debt crisis and grew in importance. By 1984 many new loan contracts were being written with a clause specifically permitting the transfer of participations.[11]

These developments are examples of the importance of balance sheet management in modern banking. Faced with a sudden and, in many cases, large loss of liquidity in part of their asset portfolio, banks sought to compensate for this by increasing the liquidity of other assets, as well as taking action to preserve their ability to generate liquidity by issuing new liabilities. This was all done against a background of ever greater complexity. During the 1970s an important objective of most banks had been balance sheet growth and, whilst it would obviously be wrong to imply that banks were not then concerned with profitability, it was nonetheless true that many banks were very concerned with league tables of size and with their own position in them, and tended to assume that growth in profits followed growth in size. With hindsight, it is clear that the pricing of much bank lending during this period did not adequately reflect the risks involved, and in the end this had its inevitable impact on profits in the form of loss provisions and debt write-offs.

Consequently, banks were faced in the 1980s with the need to improve risk management and to price risk more realistically while, at the same time, trying to raise profits as a necessary condition for improving capital adequacy. But fierce competition meant that more realistic pricing would not always be easy and, if banks became too cautious about risk, margins, and hence profits, would be low. The management of assets and liabilities had to trade off continually the need to earn profits and the need to contain risk. Again, not a new problem in itself but one made more acute by the circumstances of the time.

One seemingly attractive response to these constraints was to look for ways of earning income and/or reducing risks by providing services or undertaking transactions which did not involve adding assets and liabilities to the balance sheet. One such service, already mentioned above, was the provision of guarantees to companies raising funds by means of note issuance facilities. Risks could be reduced in a number of circumstances by transactions in financial futures or traded options, neither of which appear on balance sheets. Financial futures enable banks to take long or short positions with respect to a range of currencies and financial assets and so can be used for hedging, off-setting or modifying on or off-balance sheet risks. In the process, the links between liquidity risk and interest rate risk are further reduced. Transactions in options are an alternative means of hedging a wide range of risks and are, of course, a specific hedge for options granted by banks to their clients.

The scope for hedging has enabled banks to undertake new activities, both on and off-balance sheet, whilst keeping risks to a minimum. Interest rate guarantees, forward rate agreements and unmatched swap transactions are examples of new forms of business which can be offered without incurring more than a modest risk, due to the ability of banks to offset most of the risks involved by trading in spot markets (on-balance sheet) and/or futures and options markets (off-balance sheet).

Banks differ in their use of organised markets in futures and options. For many, off-balance sheet business remains small and systematic use of these markets is not considered necessary. In North America there is evidence that bank use of markets in both futures and options increased significantly during the early 1980s, including use by foreign-owned banks.[12] In Europe a number of banks do regularly use such markets but, in most cases, usage does not appear to be on a large scale.

But even where usage is slight, having access to markets remains important. This applies to all financial markets, both spot and forward. The greater the range of markets to which a bank has access, the greater the range of facilities it can offer, as a matter of routine, to its clients. The more confident a bank is that it can quickly and easily adjust its own assets and liabilities as desired, the more scope it can give to its clients to initiate transactions without giving prior notice.

Off-balance sheet business has to be integrated fully with on-balance sheet business for purposes of asset and liability management. Definite commitments to provide funds in the future should be included in all analyses of liquidity. Where commitments are to provide funds in specific circumstances, a realistic assessment should be made of the maximum amount of funds that the bank can reasonably be expected to have to provide. Similarly, all existing off-balance sheet business, whether arising from guarantees to clients or from transactions in markets, should be included in analyses of interest rate risk. Finally, the currency composition of all off-balance sheet assets and liabilities should be monitored and included in assessments of currency risk.

The essential thing for any bank is to be able to know and to influence its overall position. The risks involved in one type of business may add to the risks of other types of business, or they may offset them. No one type of business, no one transaction, can be judged by itself. What matters is how it fits into the existing pattern of business: whether it worsens liquidity or does not; whether it adds to existing interest exposures or does not. All assets, all liabilities, all commitments have to be included in the assessment.

CONCLUSION

Formal asset and liability management can be seen as a response to complexity. The growing number and variety of bank assets and liabilities at a time of rapid economic and financial change necessitated new methods of control. Most banks, apart from very small local ones, are now dependent for funds on wholesale markets: a poorly managed liquidity position can leave a bank with unduly large needs for funds which can be met only with difficulty or at high cost. Such difficulties will usually be known and, if serious or repeated, will react adversely on the bank's standing in financial markets and hence on its future ability to raise funds. Wholesale markets are highly competitive, administrative costs are low, and margins are narrow. Interest rates can move sharply, so a badly managed interest rate position can quickly produce loss. Any significant currency mismatching also entails the risk of sudden loss.

But no bank can avoid risk entirely and no bank can expect to be always right in its predictions of flows of funds, of interest rates, or of currency movements. The objective is not to avoid risk but to manage it and, whilst sustaining long-term profitability, to keep potential short-term losses to levels the bank can afford. No bank can hope to do this, in the modern world, without a policy of active asset and liability management.

Notes

1. Although, in some cases, standards of creditworthiness were somewhat low, as is evidenced by the UK secondary banking crisis of the early 1970s. On this, see Reid (1982).
2. For a detailed academic treatment of the subject, see Hicks (1962). For more recent discussions of bank liquidity, see Stigum and Branch (1983) and Harrington (1987).
3. See, for example, Bank of England (1982).
4. Some discussion of different measures of liquidity is given in Stigum and Branch (1983), and in Harrington (1987).
5. See Bank of England (1988) and Quinn (1988).
6. See Natioal Board for Prices and Incomes (1967).
7. In addition to works already mentioned, one can cite Swift (1981), Binder and Lindquist (1982), Glavin (1982), and Schierenbeck and Wielens (1984).
8. See, for example, Gardener (1985), Stigum and Branch (1983) and Harrington (1987).
9. For a discussion of securitisation and why it became important, see Bank for International Settlements (1986).
10. See Bank of England (1985).
11. For a discussion of early trading in sub-participations, see Sandler (1984).
12. For an official study of trading in futures and options in the USA, see Board of Governors of the Federal Reserve System *et al.* (1984).

References

Bank for International Settlements (1986) *Recent Innovations in International Banking*, The Cross Report (Basle).
Bank of England (1982) 'The measurement of liquidity', *Quarterly Bulletin*, September.
Bank of England (1985) 'Off balance sheet risks', *Quarterly Bulletin*, June.
Bank of England (1988) *Proposals for a Stock of High Quality Liquidity*, consultation paper issued March.
Binder, B. F. and T. W. F. Lindquist (1982) *Asset/Liability and Funds Management at United States Commercial Banks* (Bank Administration Institute, Rolling Meadows, Illinois).
Board of Governors of the Federal Reserve System, Commodity Futures Trading Commission, Securities and Exchange Commission (1984) *A Study of the Effects on the Economy of Trading in Futures and Options*.
Gardener, E. P. M. (1985) 'Interest rate risk management is here to stay', *The Banker*, February.
Glavin, W. M. (1982) *Asset/Liability Management: A Handbook for Commercial Banks* (Bank Administration Institute, Rolling Meadows, Illinois).
Harrington, R. L. (1987) *Asset and Liability Management by Banks* (Paris: OECD).
Hicks, J. R. (1962) 'Liquidity', *Economic Journal*, December.
National Board for Prices and Incomes (1967) *Bank Charges*, Cmnd 3292 (London: HMSO).
Quinn, B. (1988) 'The management of liquidity', *Bank of England Quarterly Bulletin*, May.
Reid, M. I. (1982) *The Secondary Banking Crisis 1973–1975: Its Causes and Course* (London: Macmillan).
Revell, J. R.S. (1968) *Changes in British Banking: The Growth of a Secondary Banking System*, Hill Samuel Occasional Papers (London).
Sandler, L. (1984) 'The great debate over LDC loan swapping', *Institutional Investor*, May.
Schierenbeck, H. and H. Wielens (1984) *Bilanzstrukturmanagement in Kreditinstituten* (Frankfurt: Fritz Knapp Verlag).
Stigum, M. L. and R. O. Branch (1983) *Managing Bank Assets and Liabilities* (Homewood, Illinois: Dow Jones Irwin).
Swift, E. W. (1981) 'Asset/liability management: history and technique', *NABW Journal*, May/June.

15 Financial Conglomeration: A New Challenge for Banking

Edward P. M. Gardener

BACKGROUND

The new financial conglomerates in London pose important challenges for the future of financial systems and services. The emphasis in this chapter will be on the broad industrial organisation and related strategic aspects of these challenges. A primary objective is to explore important strategic dimensions that are apparently neglected in the contemporary microeconomics of banking. This examination raises a number of questions on the roles, theoretical and practical, of organisational design in competitive banking strategies. The line-up of financial conglomerates on Big Bang day in London illustrated not only their importance in the new, fast-developing industrial structure of banking, but also the extraordinary variety of the different kinds of groupings. The Stock Market crash of 1987 has tested severely the resilience of these new groupings.

THE FINANCIAL CONGLOMERATE PHENOMENON

(a) Defining a financial conglomerate

A financial conglomerate, or bank financial conglomerate, is an all-purpose financial group, a kind of multipurpose bank. It provides a wide range of financial services and is organisationally constructed as a collection of managerially separate financial service units under common ownership. Under this definition a financial conglomerate is similar to the Continental form of universal bank that has evolved in countries like West Germany and Switzerland. An important kind of financial conglomerate that developed rapidly in London during the 1980s is characterised by diversification and the provision of conventional banking business as well as investment and merchant banking activities, like underwriting and dealing. The strong organisational drive into securities business and capital market products[1] has characterised London's financial conglomerate movement.

'Pure conglomeration' in industrial economics occurs where a firm produces products that are apparently unrelated in production or demand. This kind of diversification is differentiated from the concentric (or related) diversification that often characterises horizontal or vertical diversification. Like many industrial companies, however, modern banking groups do not fit neatly into these rather tight definitions. An important feature of banking financial conglomerates is their underlying strategic attempt to achieve a high degree of complementarity between the different services provided through the various parts of the organisation: Maycock (1986, p. 2) emphasises this point. This complementarity objective also reflects a desire to provide everything the client may need: 'one-stop financial shopping'.

Some bankers in London have objected to the organisational label 'conglomerate' or 'financial conglomerate'. They argue that movement into capital market activities is strategically congruent with their other financial service activities. Not only are their capital market activities directed towards the integrated provision of a range of related products, but they are also seen as part of a wider strategic orientation. Capital market products, for example, are viewed as important for various other sectors of bank corporate borrower. Privatisation moves have also increased the emphasis on getting personal customers involved in share transactions, thereby stressing the growing importance of securities business to retail banking.

Despite these views the label 'financial conglomerate' has become a part of financial terminology and folklore. This is one reason for using the term. The other justification is also pragmatic. Early experiences in London have already confirmed that bringing together two different corporate cultures, like commercial banking and securities origination and trading, is not easy. These experiences suggest that London's financial conglomerates are not immune from some of the most important distinguishing features of so-called pure conglomerates in the industrial economics literature. These features include the bringing together of two dissimilar production functions under one corporate umbrella.

The frenetic conglomerate activity in London since 1983 has important implications for the industrial structure of banking. For the past five years or so London has been involved in its greatest ever financial upheaval. The crash of 1987 has taken some of the froth out of London's overheated markets, but financial change continues at a high rate. Much of this change will be linked to the experiences of the new financial conglomerates and those older ones that have adopted more aggressive strategies in their cpaital market business.

Table 15.1 summarises the 'marriages' of UK clearing banks and merchant banks that took place in the Big Bang environment. These data exemplify the wide range of merchant and investment banking activities conducted by the new groups. Big Bang in London helped to spawn the

Table 15.1 Clearing banks and UK merchant banks after Big Bang

Banks/group	*Stock exchange capitalisation (£ million)*	*Main purchases or partners in London*	A	B	C	D	E	F	G	H	I	J	K	L	M	N	O	P	Q	R	S	T	U	V	W	X	Y	Z
UK clearing banks																												
Barclays	3570	de Zoete & Bevan (s)	X	X	X	X	X	X	X	X		X	X	X	X	X	X			X	X	X	X		X		X	X
		Wedd Durlacher Mordaunt (j)																										
	2236	Barclays Merchant Bank (m)																										
Lloyds		Black Horse Agencies (e)			X	X	X	X	X	X		X	X	X	X	X	X			X	X	X	X	X	X	X	X	X
	1291	Lloyds Merchant Bank (m)																										
Midland		Samuel Montagu (m)	X	X	X	X	X	X	X	X		X	X	X	X	X	X		X			X	X		X			
	3737	W. Greenwell (s)																										
National Westminster		Fielding, Newson-Smith (s)	X	X	X	X	X	X	X	X		X	X	X	X	X	X	X	X	X	X	X	X		X		X	X
		County Bank (m)																										
		Bisgood Bishop (j)																										
UK merchant banks																												
Barings	---	Wilson & Watford (j)		X	X	X	X	X	X	X		X			X	X	X			X	X	X	X		X	X		
Hambros	381	Strauss Turnbull (s)	X	X		X	X	X		X		X	X	X	X	X	X				X	X	X	X	X	X	X	X
		Mann & Co (e)																										
		Bairstow Eves (s)																										
Hill Samuel	332	Wood Mackenzie (s)	X	X	X	X	X	X	X	X		X	X	X	X	X	X			X	X	X	X		X	X	X	X
Kleinwort Benson	479	Grieveson Grant (s)	X	X	X	X	X	X		X	X	X	X	X	X	X	X		X	X	X	X	X		X		X	
		Charlesworth & Co (j)																										
Mercantile House	233	Laing & Cruickshank (s)	X	X	X	X				X	X	X	X		X	X	X	X			X	X	X		X			
		Alexanders Discount (d)																								X		

Morgan Grenfell	664	Pember & Boyle (s)	X	X	X	X	X	X	X	X	X	X			X	X	X						X	X				X	
		Pinchin Denny (j)																		X							X		
N. M. Rothschild	– – –	Smith Bros (j)	X	X		X		X	X	X		X	X		X	X	X		X			X	X	X			X	X	
Schroders	160	Helbert Wagg, Anderson, Bryce Villiers (s)	X	X		X	X	X	X		X	X	X	X	X	X	X		X			X	X	X		X		X	X
S. G. Warburg (Mercury International)	399	Akroyd & Smithers (j) Rowe & Pitman (s) Mullens (s)	X	X	X	X	X	X	X	X	X	X			X	X	X					X	X	X				X	

Key:

A UK equities market making
B International equities market making
C Gilts primary dealing
D Futures, options and swaps
E Eurobond market making
F Eurobond underwriting
G Eurocommercial paper
H US treasuries market making
I Equity issues
J Retail stockbroking
K Retail banking
L Wholesale banking
M
N Foreign exchange
O Mergers and acquisitions
P Commodities
Q Bullion
R Consumer finance
S Unit trusts
T Fund management
U Private client investment
V Estate agents
W Mortgages (sterling)
X Commercial property
Y Venture capital
Z Insurance

Notes:
(c) commercial bank
(d) discount house
(e) estate agent
(j) jobber
(m) merchant bank
(s) stockbroker

Source: Gardener and Molyneux (1988, table 2.3).

rapid formation of new kinds of 'superbank' or 'megabank'. These financial groups often span commercial banking, stockbroking activities and traditional merchant banking. Some large US banks (like Chase Manhattan and Citibank) and the major continental European universal banks (like Deutsche Bank and Swiss Bank Corporation) also typify the important new trend in London's internationally-orientated financial markets.

(b) Conglomerate versus specialists

The accelerated formation of larger intercontinental and inter-institutional groupings of institutions has stimulated many important questions. To some extent the financial conglomerate 'model' in London is a European one. In this respect the specialist investment banks and securities houses 'model' may be regarded comparatively as a US/Japanese one, although there is now a strong drive to eliminate regulatory barriers separating banking and securities business. One important question that bears on the future industrial structure of banking is what 'model' (if any) will dominate in deregulated capital markets? The 'specialist model' has many positive attributes: a long track record, developed expertise and a long cultural experience with investment banking activities and products. These specialists have been partly a product of regulatory history, but this is often the pattern in banking and financial systems. Once established, these organisational forms acquire a life and momentum of their own.

But there seems to be a marked trend in all capital markets towards financial conglomerates – multipurpose banks driven by commercial and investment banking. These groupings possess apparent operational advantages over more specialist firms. They have, for example, a steady stream of core retail deposits, capital strength, a developed international network, a good track record in financial innovations, large and diverse balance sheets and expertise in credit and risk management. Other advantages include attractive diversification potentials in combining stock exchange and investment business and a developed ability to handle a large, diversified portfolio of business.

Nevertheless, some bankers argue that bigger is not necessarily better: this thesis is supported by the apparent lack of correlation between size and profitability. Inapproriate diversification by a bank may also add costs without the corresponding incremental revenue; diseconomies of scale may be experienced. Diversity does not necessarily imply greater strength.[2]

Many of the large conglomerate institutions, however, remain heavily committed to the preservation of their global strategic position in deregulated capital markets.

(c) Strategic issues and challenges

Several of the new conglomerate groupings in London have extensive financial expertise, enormous distribution powers and high capitalisation. These resources should allow them to benefit from the shift in credit flows away from institution-based intermediation[3] towards so-called market-based intermediation that is associated with the modern securitisation trend (see Gardener and Revell, 1988). The massive investments in London of these new superbanks indicate their view of London as the apex of global money and securities markets.

The Japanese (unlike some of their US and European competitors) have generally adopted the strategy up to now (1988) of not building up their London operations through the purchase of existing UK institutions. Nevertheless, the sheer size of the big Japanese houses represents a major strategic challenge. Another major strategic challenge to the new conglomerates has been the high start-up financial costs of new capital market activities in London and abroad.

A key challenge has been the organisational and managerial problems of integrating different corporate cultures and styles. Hardly a bank in London has escaped problems in this area. Bringing together traders and bankers involves a marked class of corporate styles. US banking experience has found that it can take up to ten years to marry successfully these disparate corporate groups.

Staff costs and human talent are important issues. Alongside high staff costs many banks have experienced difficulties in attracting and retaining key talent and keeping teams together. From the beginnings of the present phase of conglomerate formation in London, the problems of securing and maintaining high-level capital markets teams have figured highly in conglomerate strategies.

The large increase in stock market turnover after Big Bang severely pressured the front and back office capabilities of all market participants: back-office capabilities were generally found to be inadequate compared to the front-office. In the aftermath of the crash banks are able to reassess these capabilities. 'Chinese wall' problems and cases of alleged insider dealing have been well-publicised problems for some operators. Increasing demands on capital are also likely with the new (December 1987) convergence agreement on capital adequacy – see Committee on Bank Regulations and Supervisory Practices (1987). New regulatory measures being developed between the Bank of England and the TSA (The Securities Association) could affect significantly the strategies and organisational structures of banks in London.

CONGLOMERATION AS COMPETITIVE STRATEGY

(a) Competitive strategy in banking

Financial conglomeration strategies in London are part of the competitive response by banks and other institutions to changing environmental conditions. These institutions have also helped to mould the financial environment through their own aggressive innovations. The emergence of so-called globalised capital markets has added new dimensions to bank competitive strategies. Intensifying competition produced an environment where strategic positioning by banks may have dominated other business and financial considerations.[4]

The contemporary theory of the banking firm does not appear to handle satisfactorily these strategic aspects of banking behaviour. The finance literature also appears to neglect the strategic processes by which practical decisions are formulated and through which they are translated into action plans. In this general connection Porter – in a foreword to Ballarín (1986) – observes:

> Research in economics tends to view firms as faceless responders to outside forces. Growing out of the research in business strategy, however, is a competing view that firms are unique entities that can influence to varying degrees their environment as well as set themselves apart from rivals. Reality is a mixture of the two.

Porter's work (1980, 1985) on industrial organisation analysis has its roots in industrial economics: his concern is predominantly with strategy development and its formation under different competitive conditions.

Conglomeration is a phenomenon that may be analysed as an important element of banking strategy. Micro-level strategy is a component of banking industrial economics studies, but the latter are still at a comparatively early stage of development. In a survey of the largely US banking S–C–P (structure–conduct–performance) research, for example, Gilbert (1984) and others were critical of much of the recent empirical work. Limited empirical evidence was found for the existence of scale economies in banking: see also Revell (1987). The kind of specific issues associated with the modern conglomerate movement have been comparatively neglected in this literature. In some important respects the study of the industrial structure of banking and the related economics is still at the same stage as the early (non-banking) industrial studies.

These early industrial studies were characterised by detailed analyses of specific industries; this methodology was distinguished by careful historical analysis and a close study of industrial structure.[5] Revell (1987) has been one of the prominent European banking academics who has developed this same kind of approach since the late 1960s, independently of Porter and his students. In this respect he states (1987, p. 1):

> Beyond these hypotheses[6] lies a belief that banking is like other industries in having an economic structure that transcends national boundaries, and that there is a branch of applied economics that can be called the industrial economics of banking. This point would not be worth making were it not for the fact that many academic economists, particularly in recent years, have tended to treat banking as a subordinate part of monetary theory, in which banks are merely the transmission mechanism for monetary policy.

It is clear that Revell's approach has many methodological similarities to the work of Porter and his students in the banking arena, like Ballarín (1986).

Ballarín (1986) adopts the methodological framework of Porter by combining a careful historical analysis of US banking, a study of industry structure and close attention to the strategic choices faced by individual firms. Porter, in his forward to Ballarín (1986), p. 1) sees the approach as 'an example of a new breed of studies of competition'. This general framework is a useful model on which to hang much of the following analysis. The basic Porter model is outlined in Figure 15.1.

Figure 15.1 Framework for industry analysis

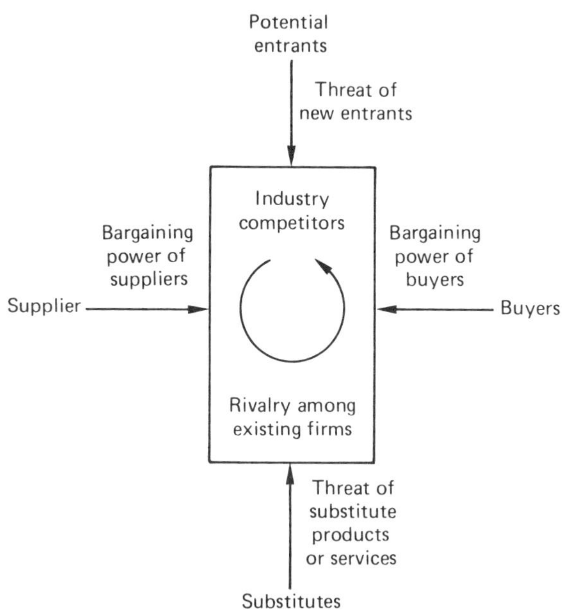

Source: Adapted from Ballarín (1986, figure 2.1, p. 24).

The model can be used to analyse the structural elements of an industry under the following headings:

— barriers to entry faced by potential competitors
— degree of rivalry existing among companies that are already competeting in the industry
— bargaining (negotiating) power of suppliers
— bargaining power of buyers
— risk that substitute products may emerge

Porter analysis of the kind depicted in Figure 15.1 was applied to the US banking industry by Ballarín: the integrating analytical concept was 'value chain analysis'.[7] This Porter model is an important and well-tested framework for analysing competition and competitive strategies within an industry. For present purposes it provides a useful general framework for helping to explore financial conglomeration as a part of banking competitive strategy.

(b) Competition in the investment banking industry: a summarised review

The financial services industry has been characterised by the dismantling of many traditional barriers to entry (see May, 1987), but a number of significant barriers to entry still exist in deregulated capital markets. New ones related to organisational ability to innovate appeared in the period up to the stock market crash. Aspiring global operators were driven by a desire (and perceived need) to provide a wide and integrated set of financial services. Size and resources are obvious strategic *desiderata* in this context.

Prominent barriers to entry in London have included capital requirements and access to distribution channels (see also Courtadon, 1985). Conglomeration has been a vehicle to re-capitalise important parts of the industry and to widen or consolidate institutions' distribution channels. Capital adequacy is important in key areas like pricing, underwriting and handling transactions of the 'bought deal' kind. Banks must have the resources to carry stock for often long periods of time. Current supervisory re-regulation and the convergence movement in capital adequacy are important challenges to London's investment banks. Government relations, including reciprocity, have also been significant in key segments of London's securities business, like the gilts market.[8]

Rivalry is intense amongst existing firms in the industry compared to earlier periods when cartelisation was more apparent. One indicator is the attention devoted to various league tables, like the regular *Euromoney* poll of top capital market performers. Another indicator is the reduction in commissions that has taken place since 1980. Rivalry has been amplified by changing environmental conditions and high rates of financial innovation. Significant overcapacity in the main capital market sectors in London, intense competition and slackening demand in the wake of the stock market crash have already led to a number of well-publicised exits and losses.

Securitisation trends have increased the bargaining power of the 'suppliers' and 'buyers' in London. The top end of the bank corporate market, for example, has tended to move increasingly towards capital market products, thereby bypassing the traditional bank credit intermediation. In the wake of the 1982 debt crisis, many traditional bank wholesale depositors moved into the bond market. 'In-house' corporate banks in some companies[9] are increasingly bypassing banks for many traditional and new financial services. Substitutes for traditional banking products have appeared with increasing frequency.

A generalised macroeconomic shift in emphasis towards the services sector in some important countries and the movement towards the so-called post-industrialised society have re-emphasised the role of banks as information-processing networks. Information will be an increasingly important strategic resource in the new revolution associated with the so-called post-industrialised society. In the fast-changing and complex environment, the motivating factors for financial conglomerate strategies need to be explored. Many elements of the Porter framework come into play when we attempt to analyse the theory and motives of financial conglomerate activity.

A fundamental 'motive force' that has shaped financial conglomerate strategies has been technology. It has been a distinguishing characteristic of the most important modern financial innovations. Indeed many contemporary financial instruments and financial engineering packages would not be possible without modern technology. Conglomerate strategies are invariably shaped by technological demands – capital is needed to fund new technological investments by banks and managerial expertise is needed to exploit opportunities that technology opens up. Information technology (IT) developments have been important factors in modern investment banking: access to information and the ability to process it accurately are fundamental determinants of successful strategies in key areas like securities trading.

(c) Theory and motives for financial conglomeration

A basic characteristic of financial conglomerates is diversification. This is a part of the process through which the market form of organisation has been slowly replaced by the corporate organisation of production, the rise of so-called 'managerial capitalism'. The Coase (1937) theory is that multiproduct firms will tend to replace single product firms whenever production in the former[10] can be conducted at a lower cost than production in single firms.[11] Alchian and Demsetz (1972) emphasise the role of diversification in collecting information on different combinations of inputs. Many other views exist on the general motives for company diversification, but explaining mergers, especially conglomerate mergers, has been problematic within the general theory of the firm. The empirical evidence is not conclusive, but it tends to cast doubt on academic preferences for profit maximisation and maximisation of shareholders' wealth hypotheses. In a comprehensive survey of empirical work in the industrial field, Mueller (1977, p. 344) found:

> But the empirical literature, upon which this survey focuses, draws a surprisingly consistent picture. Whatever the stated or unstated goals of managers are, the mergers they have consummated have on average not generated extra profits for the acquiring firms, have not resulted in increased economic efficiency.

A number of hypotheses have been advanced to explain industrial conglomerates.

Mueller (1969) proposed a 'growth maximisation hypothesis', where managers seek, as at least one of their objectives, to maximise the growth in physical size of the firm rather than the stockholder welfare or profits. In a critique of Mueller, Logue and Neart (1970) suggest that 'resource allocation synergy' may be a realistic motive for conglomerate mergers: a firm foreseeing major changes has an incentive to merge with a firm producing an unrelated product in order to prevent the demise of its existing product. Melicher and Rush (1973) suggest that conglomerate diversification may be a good way of achieving 'defensive diversification'. Singh's (1975) empirical work on UK mergers also supports the view that increasing relative size may be a better survival strategy than increasing related profitability.

Mueller (1977, p. 317) identified two broad groups of theories of conglomerate mergers, which he called neoclassical and managerial. The neoclassical theories imply some form of financial economy, like taxes, leverage or bankruptcy costs; the managerial group of theories suggest that the separation of ownership and control allows managers to pursue goals other than stockholder welfare maximisation. A number of researchers have argued that mergers are a managerial response to uncertainty. In this respect Amihud, Dodd and Weinstein (1986) recently advocated a 'managerial risk-reduction hypothesis'.[12]

The conglomerate phenomenon has generated a great deal of academic heat, but not too much practical light. Many of the hypotheses advanced in the industrial economics literature, however, would seem to be potentially relevant to financial conglomerate activity in London. The defensive diversification and resource allocation hypotheses, for example, appear useful descriptions of some of the alleged motives that helped to encourage financial conglomerate activity in London.

But there is an important apparent difference between the financial conglomerates. Many industrial conglomerates have been the product of attempts to combine in one organisation quite different elements. Many of these acquisitions lacked industrial logic: they made only to 'strip assets'. In financial conglomerate marriages there is a stronger kind of 'common thread' that may have different organisational consequences. This common thread is the supply of financial and closely related services.

The major parts of a financial conglomerate are concerned with various aspects of financial services provision. This commonality implies that synergy – the celebrated '2 + 2 = 5' effect – may be a more important motivating factor in financial compared to industrial conglomerates. Many financial conglomerate managers in London emphasise that the synergy resulting from a conglomerate marriage gives them an organisation cohesiveness that is typically lacking in their industrial counterparts. This is an area where Porter analysis and recent developments in banking S–C–P work have drawn closer together.

(d) Does synergy exist?

Synergy figures highly in various parts of the business literature. Despite the pleas of many leading students of business management, synergy is often analysed in a loose and ill-strucutured way, typified in those approaches that ask the question 'What business are we in . . .?' This approach is likely to produce over-simplified and sometimes meaningless responses. Ansoff (1965, ch. 5) emphasises the need to estimate benefits where possible in terms of incremental revenue or cost savings.

Various kinds of synergy are hypothesised in the business literature, including economies of scale in production and investment. Synergy may also be present in distribution and sales, especially where products are related and sold through the same distribution channels. Other areas where synergy may exist include purchasing, management, research and development and corporate relations. Synergy and risk are closely related. Market synergy[13] and technological synergy,[14] for example, may both[15] increase a firm's risk. A well-known empirical study in the business literature by Kitching (1967) found that finance functions had the highest synergy payoff, followed by marketing.

If synergy exists, the value of the combined firm V_{AB} exceeds the value of the respective individual firms brought together so that:

$$V_{AB} > V_A + V_B \tag{1}$$

If

$$V = \sum_{t=1} D_t \, (1 + K_e)^{-t} \tag{2}$$

where D is the firm's expected dividend share and K_e is the respective cost of capital, and

$$D = f(E) \tag{3}$$

where E is the firm's earnings stream, then

$$V = f(E,\ K_e) \tag{4}$$

If conglomerate marriages are to yield value, E must increase and/or K_e decrease.

The scholarly literature on finance has usually assumed no synergy. The following condition is taken to hold:

$$V_{AB} = V_A + V_B \tag{5}$$

Finance scholars have assumed that the VAP (value additivity principle) obtains when income streams are merged;[16] this general approach follows the famous Modigliani-Miller (MM) theorems. Tests for synergy in the finance literature have defined it in terms of the properties of the underlying distribution of rates of return to stocks of merged firms. In this view synergy exists when the investor cannot obtain these same distributions through informal combination. Using this approach Haugen and Langetieg (1975), for example, found no evidence of synergy.

But the VAP conditions are very restrictive, and the empirical finance work on synergy has also been limited. In the formal business literature the potential achievement of operating economies of scale has been cited as a strong motivating force for mergers. Another apparent motivating factor has been the increased importance during recent decades of general management functions, like planning and control, and those functions that are centralised at top management levels, like financial and legal. As a result the costs have apparently reduced for managing large and diversified organisations. We may label these as managerial, organisational and administrative economies and these economies are often very difficult to quantify.[17]

Financial conglomeration is linked in part to a broader phenomenon in financial systems, concentration. In most important financial institution sectors a strong merger movement has been under way for some time. Sectors have become increasingly dominated by a smaller number of larger institutions.[18] This is also the trend in deregulated capital markets if US experiences are any guide. In 1979, for example, the top ten securities firms on Wall Street claimed 45.8 per cent of all industry capital and 48.7 per cent of all revenues; by 1984 these had risen to 54.7 per cent and 57.0 per cent respectively.[19]

Synergy appears in the Porter framework in the concept of 'value added'. 'Value chain analysis' is used to provide possible clues on the viability of a financial conglomerate strategy for an institution. The technique is used to focus on the value increments available from combining different activities. Value chain analysis applies the learning curve principle to activities rather than individual products: attention is focused on each of the cost activities. Ballarín (1986) argues that value chain analysis and its focus on shared costs may be a useful approach for stimulating renewed attention towards synergy in banking. Synergy is achieved in this framework by structuring activities in such a way that pre-eminence may be obtained in some shared activities without having a leadership position in some of the individual products.

Recent empirical work in banking has explored the existence of economies of scope; these arise from the simultaneous production of a mix of goods and services. If $C(x_1, x_2)$ represents the cost of a bank producing x_1 and x_2, and $C(x_1)$ and $C(x_2)$ depict, respectively, the costs of producing x_1 and x_2 separately, economies of scope exist if:

$$C(x_1, x_2) < C(x_1) + C(x_2)$$

Intuitive reasoning and the arguments of many market participants imply that this kind of synergy may exist (or be perceived to exist) for many financial conglomerates in London. Recent empirical studies have found some evidence for economies of scope in US commercial banks, but this is still a very new field of research.[20] The new industrial structure of banking, with its increasing emphasis on information dissemination as a major characteristic of strategic success, may require a new approach to synergy. Shared information networks and complementary information processing expertise may become fruitful avenues for research that aims to identify and quantify synergy.

Post-1987 experiences in London have vindicated for some merchant banks the viability of so-called 'cluster strategies'. These involve focusing on groupings of services, customers, or geographical areas. Although global status may be needed to operate effectively in areas like international bonds and swaps – capital-intensive markets for banks – medium-sized institutions may be able to select other suitable investment banking product groupings and be competitive. This may be the route for medium-sized investment banks to prosper in the post-1987 financial environment. The emerging evidence suggests that these banks have to play to their strengths in developing successful cluster strategies. Synergies are being played down as a 'strategic driver' for banks in post-crash London.

Whether synergy does exist between certain banking activities or between the latter and other banking activities is an empirical question. The long-term viability and resilience of 'cluster strategies' also remains an open question. For many key investment banking activities, however, information is a key resource: recognition of this fact should help to shape bank strategy. Feldman and Stephenson (1988, p. 16) argue that the market overcapacity associated with Big Bang also suggests that many firms did not recognise fundamental barriers to competing in the over-the-counter (OTC) markets.[21] They point out:

> These barriers make becoming a successful large-volume player difficult; they render many niche strategies indefensible long term; and they make becoming a medium-sized player virtually impossible.

In OTC markets conventional wisdom about economies of scale and synergy may be of limited use. The important strategic requirement is to control access to information on supply and demand. It is information and not market share that drives profits in securities trading.

(e) Bank financial conglomerates: selected experiences

For the moment synergy remains an elusive concept to evaluate. Against this background it will be useful to explore a small sample of bank conglomerate strategies. We will focus on three apparent 'success stories' in financial conglomerate strategies[22] in order to draw out some general points: these are the strategies of Deutsche Bank, Merrill Lynch and the UK TSB (Trustee Savings Bank). Each exemplifies a different kind of conglomerate strategy.

West Germany's Deutsche Bank is a good practical example of a financial conglomerate. It combines the functions of issuing and distributing paper, market-maker in securities and investment management. A strong domestic savings rate in West Germany and a comprehensive branch network support a global and complex organisational structure. A relatively benign regulatory framework has been conducive to universal banking in West Germany. Deutsche Bank is now expanding its European presence and transforming itself into a broadly based financial services empire. Merrill Lynch moved into banking through its innovatory and highly successful CMA (cash management account). The US regulatory environment, especially Regulation Q, was an important factor in this move. The British TSB, on the other hand, is a good example of a domestic financial conglomerate, a traditional specialist in the retail financial services sector. A substantial part of its profit base comes from non-banking activity, especially unit-linked assurance. TSB may be looking to Europe for expansion and it has initiated a strong drive into corporate banking; its recent acquisition of Hill Samuel gives it a substantial merchant banking capability. Nevertheless, TSB is now in an important and demanding stage of its life-cycle, and further structural reorganisation is likely before the organisation settles into the next phase of its development.

In these three examples the regulatory environment has been important. Until recently takeovers played a minor role in the conglomerate strategies of these three banks. Both in the United States and in the restructuring of London's securities trading in the run-up to Big Bang, there has been a high volume of bank mergers. Eight of the top ten banks in *The Banker*'s 1987 real-assets-growth top 50, and five of the next ten, were involved in acquisitions and mergers.[23] These include Kleinwort (ranked 21), Morgan Grenfell (ranked 7) and S. G. Warburg (ranked 13).

The UK clearing banks, the Big Four, have followed different conglomerate strategies in their investment banking. 1987, the year of the first complete set of results after Big Bang, was not a good year for the clearing banks: investment banking losses and Third World debt provisions made a big impact on their results. In 1987 UK profit strategies were increasingly influenced by a heavy dependence on retail banking profits.[24] Table 15.1 summarised the marriages between the UK clearing and merchant banks in order to develop their investment banking capabilities.

Barclays (via Barclays de Zoete Wedd Ltd (BZW)) and NatWest (through County Bank) both set out to develop global capabilities in investment banking by purchasing other firms in the new London environment. County NatWest recorded high losses in 1987, but investment banking remains a vital part of the group's strategy. Despite losses of £19 million in November 1987, Barclays BZW ended the year with a loss of only £11 million. Midland and Lloyds have adopted different strategies. Midland – through Samuel Montagu – adopted a strategy that lies somewhere between the business purchases, global commitment and aspirations of NatWest and Barclays, and the Lloyds' approach. Lloyds has tended to be distinguished from the other main clearing banks in the City revolution by attempting to grow its investment banking expertise 'in-house'. The well-publicised exits by Midland and Lloyds[25] from selected market-making activities imply a lesser commitment to full-scale investment banking activities compared to NatWest and Barclays.

The UK merchant banks[26] have generally embarked on comparatively risky strategies in order to build up their investment banking capabilities. The general feeling among those banks who compete in market-making and securities trading is that a critical mass of talent and resources is needed: size is important in this respect. There also seems to be a consensus that organic growth does not seem to be so successful as buying in proven expertise.[27] The banks have had to cope with massive start-up costs in London and other financial centres, high salary bills, staff problems and increasing supervisory demands on capital. It is still early days to assess the comparative success of these different conglomerate strategies.

The UK and European financial conglomerates in London face an awesome challenge from the established US investment banks and Japanese houses. Table 15.2 gives a rough profile of changes in concentration within the primary eurobond market since 1975. The number of firms with over 5 per cent of issues has moved roughly in line with the concentration ratio; the number with over 1 per cent has tended to increase over time. There has been a corresponding marked change in the nationality of the top five lead managers. German and Swiss institutions have remained in the top five, but the US dominance (from around 1981) has been broken by the spectacular rise of the Japanese. Nevertheless, European financial conglomerates in London are rated highly for their professional skills.

Table 15.2 Selected indicators of primary eurobond concentration

	5-firm proportion	*Herfindahl Index*[1]	*Numbers equivalent*	*Number over 5%*	*Number over 1%*	*Nationality of top 5 lead managers*
1975	40	0.052	19	8	21	G, US, B, G, S
1980	34	0.039	26	4	29	S, G, UK, US, F
1985	37	0.048	21	6	29	S, US, US, US, G
1987	36	0.043	22	5	22	JP, S, G, JP, JP

Note:
1 Based on shares of the top 20 firms.

Key:
G Germany
S Switzerland
JP Japan
US United States
B Belgium
F France

Source: Davis (1988, table 11, p. 10).

Table 15.3 summarises a recent *Euromoney* poll of the borrowers' view of the most professional overall in international capital markets. Both Deutsche Bank and Union Bank of Switzerland are ranked in the top ten. In this same survey Banque Paribas was ranked number four (with Merrill Lynch) as the most innovative firm in the eurobond market in terms of new instruments and pricing. Swiss Bank Corporation was ranked number four as the most professional arranger of euronotes and related instruments. Deutsche Bank was ranked number three and Union Bank of Switzerland was number ten in the rankings of banks as the most professional arrangers of eurobonds. NatWest was ranked number ten in the rankings of most professional banks in the eurocommercial paper market.[28]

Table 15.3 The borrowers' view of the most professional overall in the international capital markets

Rank	*Bank*	*Vote (%)*
1	Morgan Guaranty	18.2
2	Credit Suisse First Boston	16.2
3	Citicorp	11.0
4	Morgan Stanley	6.4
5	S. G. Warburg	4.2
6	Merrill Lynch	3.5
7	Swiss Bank Corp.	3.5
8	Deutsche Bank	3.4
9	Union Bank of Switzerland	2.7
10	Chase Manhattan	2.0

Source: Lee (1987, p. 188).

These European financial conglomerates are now making their presence felt in the very top echelons of global investment banking. It is also important to note the regular appearance of Nomura Securities in these same rankings. Many of the major Japanese (especially) and European financial conglomerates have the strategic advantage of a very large captive client base, which gives them extensive placing power. Rankings, results and market opinions help to build up a general picture of the competitive structure of deregulated capital markets and the associated strategic pressures on banks. We may use this background to explore specifically the role of conglomeration in the context of financial innovation and organisational design. This leads us to some fundamental issues and questions for the future.

(f) Conglomeration, financial innovation and organisational design

Financial conglomeration in London has been an organisational response to deregulation, intensifying competition and general financial innovation. At one level it represents a general movement of bank organisational designs towards more market-orientated institutions and strategies. The emergence of market-driven organisational designs in major banks is a phenomenon of the 1970s and 1980s. In retail banking, for example, the concept of strategic marketing control is developing rapidly:[29] this concept emphasises the increasing role of market demands in shaping organisational and business strategies. It reflects organisational strategies designed to anticipate and react to future demands.

The organisational design of a bank refers to the development of its organisational structure in order to perform two fundamental tasks – specialisation and co-ordination. The structuring of these two tasks is synonymous with bank organisational design. Organisational design in banking is concerned operationally with sub-dividing tasks into different departments or divisions (specialisation) and then managing (co-ordinating) this portfolio in such a way that the organisation's strategic objectives are achieved.

The emergence of a higher market (and marketing) orientation in bank organisational designs is a process that accords with wider financial developments. The Rybczynski (1985) model posits that countries like the United States and United Kingdom are now in the 'strongly market orientated' phase of their development. Finance theory depicts these developments as a more general, deregulation-induced movement towards 'complete' financial markets; a complete financial market obtains when the financial system is capable of meeting all possible demands on it. At a theoretical level a full set of Arrow-Debreu markets exists. In practice we may describe contemporary financial markets in London as 'reasonably complete'.

These market and related technological developments are a clear threat to traditional banking strategies and the historically 'accepted' role of banks in financial systems. Price (1987, p. 13) suggests that those banks who do not recognise these developmets and respond accordingly 'will go the way of buggy-whip makers'. Financial innovation is a fundamental motive force in the trend towards financial conglomeration strategies in bank organisational design. Organisational design strategies provide for responsive and appropriate interchanges with the external environment in order that a bank may pursue and achieve set objectives.

This view of bank organisational design as an 'interchange system' with the external environment is operationally useful. Any external environmental innovation, such as securitisation, or internal innovation, for example the development of a new product or the adoption of a new management 'style', may render obsolete the existing organisational design for banks. There is some evidence that states of organisational crisis may help to provoke innovation: deliberate or controlled organisational tensions may be a vehicle for innovation stimulation.[30] But uncontrolled or inappropriate organisational change may be a recipe for disaster.[31]

US experiences imply that it is the 'medium-sized' institutions who may be most vulnerable in deregulated capital markets. Deregulated capital markets typically become dominated by a small number of very large institutions. Only these have the vast resources and skills needed to compete on a broad front in global capital markets. At the other end of the size spectrum in the United States, new investment banking boutiques have been taking on the big names of the banking world.[32] Very small institutions can offer the speed, flexibility and personal service that a bigger organisation finds increasingly difficult to provide. Nevertheless, US experiences may not necessarily be a good guide for the developing global markets in which modern investment banks compete.

Although it is early days to assess the comparative success of different financial conglomerate strategies and whether conglomerates will increasingly dominate in deregulated capital markets, some empirical evidence is emerging. In the wake of the 1987 stock market crash, for example, the advantages of the widely diversified business mix that typifies financial conglomerates appear to be emphasised. Comparatively good profit performance in retail banking, for example, has helped the London clearing banks to cushion the investment banking losses that 'bunched' in 1987. Nevertheless, the emergence of a kind of revisionist thinking on the strategic appropriateness of so-called 'cluster strategies' in post-crash London suggests that the medium-sized and smaller 'niche institutions' can prosper in deregulated capital markets. As we saw earlier, this has been the experience of more specialist bank financial conglomerates, like those within the UK merchant bank sector.

But there are still several problems to overcome. Marrying the two different corporate cultures of banking and trading is likely to cause continuing problems. The high salaries of investment compared to commercial bankers has been a source of friction in many organisations. Deciding on the appropriate 'strategic mix' of products to provide will be crucial if 'value added' is to be achieved through the conglomerate route. The dangers of cross-infestation, 'Chinese Walls' and the supervisory challenges presented by the large financial conglomerates are other contemporary problems.

The biggest single challenge to the future of the large financial conglomerates is likely to be the managerial problems that they pose. At one level financial conglomerates are an alternative to organic growth or making contracts in the marketplace. In practice a financial conglomerate typically combines elements of all three of these strategies – merger and acquisition, organic growth and making external contracts in the market. As financial conglomerates expand into new territories and consolidate existing ones, the problems of managing them are likely to become more acute,[33] especially for those organisations that have recently adopted the conglomerate route. A fundamental question is whether the new financial conglomerates will ultimately be manageable and responsive enough to market demands. Will the quality of management and advances in banking strategic management match the decision-making needs of the new organisations?

The new 'superbanks' that are forming pose important macoeconomic issues. Moral hazard problems may arise if global capital markets are eventually dominated by a few large institutions. These new superbanks may pose significant barriers to entry that curtail the contestability of markets. Global power structures in banking and finance could emerge where strategies like mutual forbearance and reciprocal dealing become the norm. The economic consequences of this scenario are not clear, but they imply a possible decline in the allocative efficiency of financial markets.

Modern banking organisations are essentially information-processing firms. The ubiquitous nature of information- processing and related technology developments impose a constraint on the apparent monopoly potential of banks in global finance markets. This is evidenced by the emergence of new competitors[34] – banks, non-banks and non-financial firms – in traditional banking and finance markets. New forms of competition have appeared. Networking and sharing arrangements make these markets more contestable; deregulation[35] consolidates this potential. These developments may counteract some of the apparent negative potentials of the financial conglomerate trend.

THE FUTURE

Financial conglomerates have long been an important part of developed financial systems. The present movement towards combining traditional banking and securities business is likely to consolidate the importance of this organisational form. The stock market 'crash' of 1987[36] has slowed the growth of securitisation, but this reduction in activity is not likely to endure so long as governments remain committed to structural deregulation. Contemporary deregulation is likely to stimulate new kinds of financial conglomerates encompassing investment banking that do not have traditional commercial banking as a core activity. Managing these new organisational forms into the next evolutionary stage of banking will dominate banking strategies for some time.

Regulators and supervisors also have to adapt their methods to reflect the international diversified character of the business mix of this new breed of 'superbank'. The European Commission's internal market proposals for 1992 may stimulate a new impetus to the financial conglomerate movement in Europe. It is likely to help precipitate a new emphasis on inter-country and inter-continental links in financial conglomerate strategies. Lower segments of the corporate banking market[37] and retail banking are likely to be more prominent in the next cycle of the financial conglomerate movement. No serious student of banking and finance can ignore the implications of these developments for the future of financial systems and services.

Notes

1. London's Big Bang was, of course, an important stimulating factor. Other (related) important environmental trends included securitisation, the rise of market-based intermediation, and globalisation.
2. The Chief Executive of Lloyds Bank – see Hewitt (1988, p. 27) – has emphasised these operational points. Feldman and Stephenson's research (1988) supports the general view that size does not necessarily guarantee success in investment banking.
3. This is Gurley and Shaw financial intermediation, or indirect finance.
4. This concern was expressed in the BIS (1986) report – the so-called Cross Report – on innovations in international banking. Empirical evidence that banks in London are possibly making sub-optimal risk/return evaluations – related to their corresponding business mix – in respect of capital adequacy was provided by Hislop (1987).
5. This kind of methodology for studying financial systems is sometimes labelled the 'Continental approach'. It is distinguished from the so-called 'US approach' that focuses on the role of regulation (especially taxation) in shaping financial flows and associated developments.
6. The hypotheses that Revell (1987, p. 1) was referring to were:
    1. that all banking systems have gone through a process of concentration, which is not yet complete in most cases;
    2. that the factors causing mergers between banks are not constant but differ according to the stage of development of a banking system.
7. This involves breaking down the 'value chain' of a business into its component parts and studying them in detail. In the Porter model the value chain links the 'value added' by each activity undertaken by the firm. Attention is focused particularly on the existence of shared costs: see Ballarín (1986, p. 33).
8. This is evidenced by the need to obtain GEMM (gilt-edged market-maker) status from the Bank of England. In a more general vein, reciprocity between countries is also important. London's new 1986 Financial Services Act, for example, includes 'reciprocity clauses'.
9. This reflects the rise in sophistication and strategic profile of corporate treasury divisions in some large companies, like BP and Volvo.

10. Where input allocation between divisions is decided by managerial discretion.
11. Where the allocation of inputs between products is determined by factor markets.
12. An interesting aspect of this hypothesis is that it did not require a market failure scenario, unlike many other so-called managerial theories.
13. Selling products to the same market segments in order to meet the similar needs of customers.
14. Linked technologies, for example, may both be made redundant by technological advances.
15. Either singly or in combination – market synergy and technological synergy may be closely related.
16. Value is conserved.
17. Kitching (1967), for example, excluded organisational efficiencies from his empirical survey because of the difficulties in quantifying them.
18. Deregulation and the erosion of traditional barriers between financial institution sectors and between financial markets have also made it much more difficult, both methodologically and practically, to measure concentration.
19. See Auletta (1986, p. 232).
20. See Mester (1987).
21. This applies to OTC markets in general, whether they be government and corporate bonds, UK gilts, commercial paper, euroequities, etc.
22. See Gardener (1987).
23. See Jones (1987).
24. See Molyneux (1987).
25. See Hewitt (1988).
26. The UK merchant banks may be regarded legitimately as financial conglomerates, although their business mix generally contains much less traditional and retail banking activities than a clearing bank.
27. See *The Banker* (1987, p. 21).
28. Midland Bank was another European bank that appeared in the top rankings: it was ranked number five for banks presenting their offer telexes most concisely.
29. See Clarke *et al.* (1988).
30. See Mottura (1986, p. 110).
31. The fall of the House of Lehman – chronicled by Auletta (1986) – is one dramatic banking case that is relevant in the context of this chapter. It illustrated the practical organisational problems of bringing together banking and trading groups.
32. See Thackray (1986) and Feldman and Stephenson (1988).
33. Since the early 1970s banks have been deploying major resources towards improving managerial quality and strategic management capabilities (see Dalbey, 1986; Channon, 1986; and Clark *et al.*, 1988).
34. Johnson (1988, p. 4) makes the point that 'from an innovation point of view at least, the differences between financial and non-financial firms are not that important'. For present purposes this also reflects the changing industrial structure of banking that is evidenced in liberalisation trends and the entry of new competitors into traditional banking markets.
35. Structural deregulation policies have been concerned with 'levelling playing fields'. Supervisory re-regulation, on the other hand, may operate to reduce the economic benefits sought by structural deregulation initiatives, like London's celebrated Big Bang. Restrictive supervisory entry and exit conditions, for example, could restrict the contestability of markets.

36. A more specific examination – building on this chapter – of bank financial conglomerate strategies after the crash was undertaken by Gardener (1988).
37. These comprise middle and small business segments, including venture capital.

References

Alchian, A. A. and H. Demsetz (1972) 'Production, information costs and economic organisation', *American Economic Review*, December pp. 777–95.

Amihud, Yakov, Peter Dodd and Mark Weinstein (1986) 'Conglomerate mergers, managerial motives and stockholder wealth', *Journal of Banking and Finance*, 10, pp. 401–10.

Ansoff, H. Igor (1965) *Corporate Strategy* (New York: McGraw-Hill).

Auletta, Ken (1986) *Greed and Glory on Wall Street: The Fall of the House of Lehman* (Harmondsworth, UK: Penguin).

Ballarín, Eduard (1986) *Commercial Banks and the Financial Revolution* (Cambridge, Massachusetts: Ballinger Publishing Company).

Bank for International Settlements (BIS) (1986) *Recent Innovations in International Banking* (Basle: BIS).

Banker, The (1987) 'The tough class of '87', June, pp. 20–30.

Channon, Derek F. (1986) *Bank Strategic Management and Marketing* (Chichester: John Wiley).

Clarke, Paul D., Edward P. M. Gardener, Paul Feeney and Phil Molyneux (1988) 'The genesis of strategic marketing control in British retail banking', *The International Journal of Bank Marketing*, vol. 6, no. 2, pp. 5–19.

Coase, R. H. (1937) 'The nature of the firm', *Economica*, 4, pp. 386–405.

Committee on Bank Regulations and Supervisory Practices (1987) *Proposals for International Convergence of Capital Measurement and Capital Standards* (Basle: Bank for International Settlements).

Courtadon, Carol L. (1985) 'The competitive structure of the eurobond underwriting industry', Salomon Brothers Monograph Series in Finance and Economics, no. 1 (New York: Graduate School of Business Administration, New York University).

Dalbey, Homer (1986) 'Planning on both sides of the Atlantic', *The Bankers Magazine*, March/April, pp. 33-46.

Davis, E. P. (1988) 'Industrial structure and dynamics of the primary eurobond market', mimeographed paper read to the School of Accounting, Banking and Economics (SABE) seminar at the University College of North Wales, Bangor on 31 May 1988 and forthcoming as a Bank of England Discussion Paper.

Feldman, Lyn and Jack Stephenson (1988) 'Stay small or get huge – lessons from securities trading', *Harvard Business Review*, May-June, pp. 115–23.

Gardener, E. P. M. (1987) 'Structural and strategic consequences of financial conglomeration', *Revue de la Banque*, no. 9, November, pp. 5–16, and (in Italian) in *Banca Impresa Societa*, no. 1, April 1988, pp. 3–27.

Gardener, E. P. M. (1988) 'A strategic perspective of banking financial conglomerates in London after the crash', Institute of European Finance Research Papers in Banking and Finance, RP 88/22.

Gardener, E. P. M. and P. Molyneux (1988) *Structure and Regulation of UK Financial Markets*, IEF Research Monograph in Banking and Finance no. 6 (Bangor: Institute of European Finance, University College of North Wales).

Gardener, E. P. M. and J. R. S. Revell (1988) *Securitisation: History, Forms and Risks*, Institute of European Finance Research Monograph in Banking and

Finance no. 5 (Bangor: Institute of European Finance, University College of North Wales).
Gilbert, R. Alan (1984) 'Bank market structure and competition', *Journal of Money, Credit and Banking*, vol. 16, no. 4, November, pp. 617–60.
Haugen, R. A. and T. C. Langetieg (1975) 'An empirical test for synergism in merger', *Journal of Finance*, vol. 30, no. 4, September, pp. 1003–4.
Hewitt, Garth (1988) 'Brian Pitman – guiding the dark horse', *Banking World*, April, p. 24.
Hislop, Angus (1987) 'Making sense of capital adequacy', *The Banker*, vol. 37, no. 2, February, pp. 32–3.
Johnson, Leslie T. (1988) 'The theory of financial innovations: a new approach', IEF Research Paper in Banking and Finance no. RP 88/11 (Bangor: Institute of European Finance).
Jones, Colin (1987) 'Mergers make their mark', *The Banker*, July, p. 163.
Kitching, J. (1967) 'Why do mergers miscarry?', *Harvard Business Review*, November/December, pp. 84–105.
Lee, Peter (1987) 'The Euromoney poll', *Euromoney*, September, pp. 188–202.
Logue, D. A. and P. A. Naert (1970) 'A theory of conglomerate mergers: comment and extension', *Quarterly Journal of Economics*, November, pp. 663–7.
May, Thornton (1987) 'When barriers are irrelevant or undefended: non-banks cash in', *Business Horizons*, July/August, pp. 51–5.
Maycock, James (1986) *Financial Conglomerates: The New Phenomenon* (Aldershot, UK: Gower).
Melicher, R. W. and D. F. Rush (1973) 'The performance of conglomerate firms: recent risk and return experience', *Journal of Finance*, May, pp. 381–8.
Mester, L.J. (1987) 'Efficient production of financial services: scale and scope economies', *Business Review*, Federal Reserve Bank of Philadelphia, January/February, pp. 15–25.
Molyneux, P. (1987) 'Credit where it's due', *International Correspondent Banker*, December, pp. 11–12.
Mottura, Paolo (1986) 'Organisational aspects of financial innovation', *Economia Aziendale*, vol. 5, no. 2, pp. 109–21.
Mueller, D. C. (1969) 'A theory of conglomerate mergers', *Quarterly Journal of Economics*, vol. 83, November, pp. 643–59.
Mueller, D. C. (1977) 'The effects of conglomerate mergers', *Journal of Banking and Finance*, 1, pp. 315–47.
Porter, Michael E. (1980) *Competitive Strategy: Techniques for Analysing Industries and Competitors* (New York: The Free Press).
Porter, Michael E. (1985) *Competitive Advantage: Creating and Sustaining Creative Performance* (New York: The Free Press).
Price, Kent (1987) 'Should bankers be in banking?', *Banking World*, February, pp. 12–13.
Revell, J. R. S. (1987) *Mergers and the Role of Large Banks*, IEF Research Monograph in Banking and Finance no. 2 (Bangor: Institute of European Finance, University College of North Wales).
Rybczynski, T. (1985) 'Financial systems, risk and public policy', *The Royal Bank of Scotland Review*, December, pp. 35–45.
Singh, A. (1975) 'Take-overs, economic natural selection, and the theory of the firm: evidence from the post-war United Kingdom experience', *The Economic Journal*, 85, September, pp. 497–515.
Thackray, John (1986) 'The catchy rhythm of the one-man bank', *Euromoney*, May, pp. 27–46.

16 One-Stop Financial Service Delivery Opportunities in a World of Automated Self-Service Banking: Some Evidence from the United States

Neil Murphy

INTRODUCTION

In recent years, there has been a trend toward expansion of powers (product offerings) for banks in the United States. Indeed, the distinction between previously segmented commercial banks and savings institutions (savings and loan associations, savings banks, and credit unions) has largely disappeared, especially for household customers. Moreover, banks (including all of the previously segmented depository financial institutions) have been acquiring powers, such as securities brokerage, and expanding their menu of retail financial services. The trend is clearly towards further liberalisation, with expanded insurance powers being the next likely target.

One motivation for this expansion is more intensive use of the delivery system established by banks largely in an environment of regulated deposit interest ceilings, which was known as Regulation Q. Since banks were precluded from paying market-determined rates to attract deposit dollars, they substituted non-price methods, or 'implicit interest'. One such method was to provide convenience in the form of many branch offices. This large number of branch offices was a costly endeavour involving the expenditure of resources on the buildings, the personnel to staff the offices, and the equipment necessary to deliver the services. Once the deregulation of deposit interest ceilings occurred, the banking industry was faced with the problem of simultaneously paying higher interest to depositors and maintaining a costly delivery system designed for a different environment. Essentially, banks now pay both explicit and implicit interest.

One way of reducing the cost of the delivery system is to use it more intensively. The branch system can sell a greater number of services with a less than commensurate increase in costs because of the fixed-cost nature of much of the expense of maintaining the delivery system. Hence, the banks have achieved the ability to offer securities brokerage services to their retail customers through their branch system and are actively seeking expanded insurance powers for similar reasons.

However, there is a counter trend in motion. For the last decade and a half, American banks have been actively installing self-service banking machines (automated teller machines, or ATMs) for the purpose of reducing the cost of transactions. About 40 000 such machines have been deployed. Moreover, banks have joined together in networks to expand the usefulness of having an access card. A customer with a card issued by his or her bank may transact business with that bank through any ATM deployed by a bank participating in the network. There are both regional and national networks existent in the United States.

Somewhat of a paradox therefore exists in US banking. On the one hand, banks want customer traffic into the branch office to conduct business – normal 'banking' business as well as other transactions such as securities transactions and insurance business. On the other hand, banks are encouraging people to conduct business away from the branch office by the aggressive deployment of ATMs, so that customers may transact business at many off-premises locations. Does it make sense to invest in new service offerings, partially for the purpose of spreading the cost of 'brick and mortar' over more product lines, while simultaneously encouraging customers to conduct banking business off-premises through ATMs?

The purpose of this chapter is to review some evidence on the use of branch facilities, ATMs, and the desire on the part of customers to patronise one-stop financial service providers. The results are based on a telephone survey of approximately 1500 households in the United States taken in the Spring of 1985.

WHO USES ATMs?

The expanding use of ATMs may have important practical effects; ATM use may be related to customer characteristics that are desirable from the perspective of marketing more services. That is, the very customers who are the best prospects for other services may be those who avoid the branch due to the availability of ATMs. Over 60 per cent of those households which dealt with a financial institution that offered access to an ATM had an ATM card. This excludes households with no banking relationship and those whose bank did not offer such a service. When compared to the entire sample, including those without ATM access, the percentage is 40 per cent. Moreover, those who do have ATM cards do not always use them. When all is compared, the proportion of active users is approximately 27 per cent of the total population.

The usage patterns by households with ATM cards is shown in Tables 16.1 to 16.4. In Table 16.1, the usage pattern is compared to household total income. Frequent users are defined as those who use the ATM once a week or more. Frequent use is related to household income, with almost 45 per cent of those in the $50 000-and-above income category being frequent users compared with approximately 27 per cent in the $10 000–$15 000 category. Those who never used the ATM were concentrated in the lower income categories. Almost 37 per cent of those in the under-$10 000 category never used their ATM cards, while only 20 per cent of those in the highest income category never did. Thus, the most frequent users tend to be those in the highest income categories – presumably the very people who are most likely to be prospects for other financial service offerings.

Table 16.1 Frequency of use of ATMs and household income (per cent of households with ATM cards in each income category using ATM as indicated)

Annual income category	*Weekly*	*2–3 per month*	*Once per month*	*Less than once per month*	*Never*
Under $10 000	35	15	7	7	37
$10–15 000	27	26	10	11	26
$15–20 000	34	14	16	22	15
$20–30 000	36	16	16	14	18
$30–50 000	41	19	6	12	21
$50 000 and above	45	15	7	12	20

Note: Percentages may not sum across to 100 due to rounding.

Table 16.2 shows the age distribution of frequency of use. The youngest category is that in which the head of household is less than 30 years of age. Frequency of use is highest in this category, at almost 48 per cent, compared with only 12 per cent of those in the 60 years of age or older category. Less than 9 per cent of the youngest category never use their ATM cards, while over 50 per cent of the oldest category with ATM cards had never used them.

In Table 16.3, frequency of use is compared to education of the head of household. Those with less than a high-school diploma were much less likely (11 per cent) to be frequent users than those who were college graduates (43 per cent). Moreover those who never used the ATM card

Table 16.2 Frequency of use of ATMs and age of head of household (per cent of households with ATM cards in each age category using ATM as indicated)

Age category	*Weekly*	*2–3 per month*	*Once per month*	*Less than once per month*	*Never*
Under 30	48	18	13	12	9
30–44	38	17	11	3	8
45–59	27	13	8	19	34
60 and over	12	13	7	15	52

Note: Percentages may not sum across to 100 due to rounding.

Table 16.3 Frequency of use of ATMs and education of head of household (per cent of households with ATM cards in each education category using ATM as indicated)

Education category	*Weekly*	*2–3 per month*	*Once per month*	*Less than once per month*	*Never*
Less than high school	11	18	9	16	45
High school diploma	28	15	12	16	29
Some college	42	17	9	12	20
College graduate	43	16	11	11	20

Note: Percentages may not sum across to 100 due to rounding.

they possessed were more likely to be in the less-than-high-school category (45 per cent) than those non-users in the college-graduate category (20 per cent).

Finally, in Table 16.4, the degree to which the household's country is urban or rural is related to the frequency of usage of ATMs. Frequency of use is highest in the most urban areas (42 per cent) and lowest in rural/suburban counties (19 per cent). For those who had the ATM card and never used it, the proportion of households is highest in the rural areas and lowest in the urban counties. In summary, frequency of use of ATMs is highest among upper income, highly educated, young, urban households. These households are those that are most likely to be prospective purchasers of financial services.

Table 16.4 Frequency of use of ATMs and location of household (per cent of households with ATM cards in each location category using ATM as indicated)

Location category (county)	*Weekly*	*2–3 per month*	*Once per month*	*Less than once per month*	*Never*
Mostly urban	42	17	9	13	18
Urban/Suburban	39	15	11	13	22
Suburban/Rural	19	18	13	14	36
Rural	19	8	14	11	47

Note: Percentages may not sum across to 100 due to rounding.

WHO GOES INSIDE THE OFFICE?

Because there are alternatives to actually entering the bank office, households were asked whether they entered the bank when they conducted their bank business. This was broken down into the following categories:

1. Every time
2. Most of the time
3. About half the time
4. Less than half the time
5. Hardly ever
6. Never

Tables 16.5 to 16.7 compare the frequency of going inside the bank with income, age and education. In Table 16.5, it can be seen that there is a pattern for those who go inside the bank office every time they go to the bank. Those with incomes of less than \$10 000 are almost twice as likely to go inside the bank as those in the \$50 000-and-above category (31 per cent of those in the lowest income category compared with 16 per cent of the highest income category). The pattern is reversed in the group of households that actually go into the bank less than half the time. The table shows that the higher income category household is more likely to go inside the bank less than half the time than is the low income household. Thus, the most likely households to generate the traffic inside the bank office are the lower income households.

In Table 16.6, the age distribution of the frequency of going inside the bank office is shown. Examining those who go inside every time reveals a

Table 16.5 Frequency of going inside the bank office and household income (per cent of households in each income category going inside the bank office as indicated)

Income category	*Every time*	*Most of the time*	*Half the time*	*Less than half the time*	*Hardly ever*	*Never*
Under $10 000	31	15	16	7	19	12
$10–15 000	28	15	18	5	27	7
$15–20 000	27	21	19	14	15	4
$20–30 000	17	17	21	17	23	5
$30–50 000	12	20	21	16	28	4
over $50 000	16	20	23	16	20	5

Note: Percentages may not sum across to 100 due to rounding.

Table 16.6 Frequency of going inside the bank office and age of head of household (per cent of households in each age category going inside the bank office as indicated)

Age category	*Every time*	*Most of the time*	*Half the time*	*Less than half the time*	*Hardly ever*	*Never*
Under 30	17	18	19	15	24	6
30–44	15	16	21	18	26	4
45–59	21	21	21	7	22	7
60 and over	40	21	13	6	13	7

Note: Percentages may not sum across to 100 due to rounding.

Table 16.7 Frequency of going inside the bank office and education of household (per cent of households in each education category going inside the bank office as indicated)

Education category	*Every time*	*Most of the time*	*Half the time*	*Less than half the time*	*Hardly ever*	*Never*
Less than high school	32	15	19	6	16	13
High school graduate	25	18	17	12	21	7
Some college	19	19	19	16	24	4
College graduate	16	21	20	15	25	3

Note: Percentages may not sum across to 100 due to rounding.

definite age pattern. Those in the 60 years of age or older category are more than twice as likely to go inside the bank every time (40 per cent) compared with the youngest (under 30 years of age) category (17 per cent). For those who go inside the bank 'hardly ever', the pattern is reversed. The youngest age category is almost twice as likely to 'hardly ever' go inside the bank (24 per cent) compared with the oldest category (13 per cent). Table 16.7 compares the frequency of households going inside the bank office with educational categories. Once again there is a definite pattern. Those in the category of less-than-high-school education are almost twice as likely to go inside every time than those in the college-graduate category. For those households who 'hardly ever' go inside the bank, the opposite pattern occurs. Those in the college-graduate category are one and a half times as likely to 'hardly ever' go inside the bank (25 per cent compared to 16 per cent).

Of course, not all bank business can be transacted at an ATM or a drive-up window. The transaction may be complex; it may require a decision on the part of an officer, as regards, for example, a loan; it may involve a large number of items; or it may have other characteristics that preclude the use of outside facilities. For that reason, households that indicated that they do go inside the bank were asked whether or not the business transacted could have been done at the drive-in window or at an ATM. There is only one demographic variable that is related to the likelihood of a household indicating that they could have transacted the same business outside the bank. In Table 16.8 the relationship between transacting business that could be transferred outside is related to household income. Households in the lowest income category have the highest likelihood of doing business that could be transferred while the households

Table 16.8 Percentage of transactions inside the bank office that could have been shifted to ATM or drive-in window (percentage of households in each income category who could have shifted transaction to ATM or drive-in window)

Income category	*Transaction shiftable*
Under $10 000	72
$10–15 000	62
$15–20 000	64
$20–30 000	63
$30–50 000	64
over $50 000	55

in the highest income category were least likely to do so (72 per cent versus 55 per cent).

In summary, there is a finding that those who go inside the bank office rather than use an ATM or drive-in window follow a pattern; they tend to have lower incomes, are older and are in the lower educational categories. Thus, as expected, there is a contrast with those who use ATMs. The ATM user is likely to be the best prospect for more financial services but is least likely to be found inside the bank office.

WHO WANTS ONE-STOP FINANCIAL SERVICE INSTITUTIONS?

Households were asked whether or not they would prefer doing their financial business with either one institution that had a broad range of services or with separate institutions. This will allow a comparison among the demographic characteristics of those who desire such arrangements compared with those who have already established a pattern of use of the bank office and the self-service facilities outside the office.

The preference for a one-stop financial institution is related to household income in Table 16.9. The three-way classification of preferences shows a mild relationship between income and a preference for a one-stop financial institution. However, the relationship is negative; that is, the preference peaks at almost 34 per cent in the \$10 000 to \$15 000 income categories and falls to 28 per cent in the \$50 000 and above category. However, the preference for separate facilities shows a strong relationship to income. The preference for separation is strongest in the highest income category, 43 per cent, compared with only 16 per cent in the lowest income category. When educational categories are compared with preference for a one-stop financial institution, a similar pattern emerges, as is shown in Table 16.10. Preference for separate financial institutions is strongest in

Table 16.9 Preference for one-stop financial institutions and household income (percentage of households with preference for one-stop financial institutions (or separate or no preference) in each income category)

Income category	*One-stop*	*Separate*	*No difference*
Under \$10 000	29	16	55
\$10–15 000	34	23	43
\$15–20 000	30	27	43
\$20–30 000	32	26	42
\$30–50 000	29	38	33
Over \$50 000	28	43	29

Table 16.10 Preference for one-stop financial institutions and educational category of head of household (percentage of households with preference for one-stop financial institutions (or separate or no preference) in each education category)

Education category	*One-stop*	*Separate*	*No difference*
Less than high school	30	13	57
High school graduate	30	25	45
Some college	30	33	37
College graduate	25	43	32

the college-graduate category, 43 per cent, compared with only 13 per cent in the less-than-high-school category. In summary, the stated preference for separate financial institutions compared with one-stop financial institutions has a pattern that is related to income and education. The desire to maintain separate financial relationships seems strongest among those who are most likely candidates for the use of more and diversified financial services. When households were asked which type of financial institutions they would prefer if they were looking for a one-stop financial institution, the results indicated the following institutional preference pattern:

Banks (including savings institutions)	47.3
Insurance companies	1.6
Brokerage firms	4.0
Credit unions	9.8
Retail stores	0.2
No difference or don't know	37.1

Thus, banks have the best chance of getting such business *if people are interested*. The biggest non-bank financial institution with any allegiance is the credit union which has bank characteristics, the most important of which is a Federally insured deposit account.

Finally, households were asked whether the availability of financial planning services would be considered important in choosing a one-stop financial institution. As the availability of financial instruments and services proliferates and they become more complex, many households may feel the need for expert advice in making the best choice. In the case of a one-stop financial institution, all the services would be available, and, if financial planning were available, the household could be guided in making the best choice, given its needs and risk preferences. Almost 63 per cent of the households indicated that the availability of financial planning was either very or somewhat important to them in the choice of such a financial institution. There were no major demographic patterns except that of age. Households headed by younger individuals were much more likely to consider financial planning as being important to them.

SUMMARY AND CONCLUSIONS

This chapter has analysed the behaviour of a sample of US households with respect to their use of ATMs, their use of the inside of bank offices, and their preference for a one-stop financial institution. The reason for analysing such behaviour is to determine any possible inconsistency between patterns in self-service banking and plans to utilise the existing branch office structure more intensively.

The results indicate that the demographic patterns for revealed preference (use of ATMs and office traffic) and for potential preference for one-stop financial service institutions raise questions about the success of strategies based upon more intensive use of the branch. Customers who are most likely to be candidates for more financial services consistently prefer dealing directly with ATMs rather than coming into the bank. When such customers do come inside, it is more likely to be because the transaction could not be handled at an ATM. Moreover, high-income, high-education customers showed a marked preference for conducting their financial business with several suppliers rather than a one-stop financial institution.

This does not necessarily mean that banks cannot or should not diversify their financial service offerings. However, it seems doubtful whether such new service offerings should be predicted on more intensive use of the existing brick and mortar delivery system. To the extent that households prefer one financial institution to another, banking seems to dominate. Moreover, the availability of financial planning to assist households in the choice of financial services appears to be something that can be helpful in implementing a movement to a broader-based menu.

Part VI
Regulation

Preceding chapters have already emphasised repeatedly the importance of regulation in the contemporary financial environment. Regulation will undoubtedly remain an important 'motive force' of change for the future of financial systems and services. The contemporary commitment of governments to structural deregulation – the 'opening up' of institutions and markets to greater competitive freedoms – is unprecedented in modern economic history. A concurrent trend has been the reregulation and convergence of supervisory regulations. These trends have generated a host of complex policy and research questions. The number of contributors to this volume who opted for regulation (or a related topic covered in earlier sections) attests to the perceived importance of this area for the future of financial systems and services.

The October 1987 stock market crash has raised important questions on the future of financial regulation. Richard Dale – in the opening Chapter 17 of this section – examines the lessons for regulators from the global collapse of equity prices during October 1987. The international convergence of capital adequacy systems has been a major regulatory issue throughout the 1980s. In Chapter 18 Peter Cooke provides a detailed analysis of the convergence process from the perspective of a regulator intimately involved in the process. Chapter 19, contributed by Hyman Minsky and Claudia Campbell, explores the problems involved in reforming the present US crisis in deposit insurance. Minsky's financial instability hypothesis is used to help explore formally the processes that lead to 'fragility' in financial systems.

The final three essays in this section of the volume focus on Italian experiences with regulation. In Chapter 20 Marco Onado explores the general lessons for deregulation from Italian experiences. One lesson from Chapter 20 is the enduring problem of incorporating economic normative principles into the legal regulatory framework. Francesco Cesarini, in Chapter 21, examines the prudential regulation of large loans in the Italian banking system. He examines Italian data on large loan exposures and compares Italian regulation in this field with that of the EEC Recommendation of 22 December 1986. The final chapter of the volume is concerned again with capital adequacy, a topic that has tended to dominate Part VI and, indeed, it has been one thread throughout the whole of this volume. Cesare Bisoni analyses capital adequacy developments in the Italian banking system. Capital adequacy is clearly going to be especially important for the future of financial systems and services throughout the 1990s.

Chapter 22 is a fitting conclusion to a volume devoted to a UK academic who was virtually alone during the early 1970s in emphasising the growing importance of capital adequacy and supervision. Chapter 1 discussed Jack Revell's contribution in this respect. This kind of contribution is typical of an academic who has distinguished himself by his emphasis and 'feel' for the industrial structure, business and practical policy issues within financial systems. Revell's approach is a reminder of the need to recognise practical market features and constraints in research that is concerned with applied policy issues. Imputing the real world and the development of associated policies to improve it can be a dangerous activity.

17 Stock Market Instability and Financial Regulation

Richard Dale

INTRODUCTION

The global collapse of equity prices during October 1987 has prompted a major review of the regulation of financial markets worldwide.[1] Some have argued that financial deregulation has been carried too far and that what we are witnessing are the destabilising consequences of an excessively permissive regulatory regime. Others take the opposite view and warn that the introduction of new and more stringent regulatory constraints in the aftermath of the crash could further undermine confidence while also imposing needless additional costs on market participants. The eventual outcome of the debate is far from clear but it seems probable that the major deregulation trends will persist despite the events of October 1987 and that any policy changes that may emerge from the present regulatory review will focus on a few specific concerns. The purpose of this chapter is to reassess the longer-term prospects for deregulation/regulation in the light of the recent financial upheaval.

DEREGULATION

So far as deregulation is concerned there are a number of areas where the dismantling of controls is likely to proceed unchecked.

First, there is the broad question of competitive pricing of financial services. Just as the 'Big Bang' abolition of fixed Stock Exchange commissions in London was a response to global market pressures, so other financial centres are having to bow to market forces by phasing out price-fixing arrangements. Last October the Tokyo Stock Exchange cut its brokerage commissions by an average of nearly 10 per cent and this is just one of several steps aimed at bringing Japan's commission rates more closely into line with rates charged elsewhere. The big Swiss banks have been reducing their fixed underwriting commissions on Swiss franc foreign bond issues, a move which may be viewed as the beginning of the end of this particular cartel. Another example of the shift to competitive pricing is the phasing-out of interest rate controls in Japan, although this still has some way to go. More generally, the globalisation of wholesale financial markets is making it increasingly difficult to sustain cartel or officially administered pricing arrangements, since users of financial services are induced to take their business elsewhere.

However, it is worth noting that current moves towards harmonising capital adequacy standards for multinational banks may put a 'floor' on the pricing of certain banking services by requiring a minimum capital backing for different categories of financial activity.[2] Therefore, less may be heard in future of the alleged 'dumping' of euromarket loans by Japanese or other national banking groups.

Secondly, international competitive pressures will also continue to have a liberating influence on other, non-price, aspects of domestic capital markets. For instance, the Japanese Ministry of Finance is seeking, through 'shelf-registration' and other means, to simplify issuing procedures in the domestic (Samurai) bond market, so as to attract more business away from the euroyen bond market. Similarly, the US Securities and Exchange Commission, backed by the US Treasury, is reviewing its registration and disclosure requirements for foreign issuers with a view to bringing back to the United States some of the new issues business that has been driven offshore. In the words of the Assistant US Treasury Secretary for Economic Policy, Michael Darby, 'the globalisation of financial markets and the ensuing increased competition underscores the need to re-evaluate restrictions on financial institutions in the United States if we are to preserve our comparative advantage'.[3] More generally, national authorities are responding to the challenge of the euromarkets by adopting a more flexible approach to the regulation of domestic capital markets.[4]

A third area where the trend towards liberalisation is likely to be maintained concerns the authorisation of innovative financial instruments and techniques. Again, competition between financial centres ensures that innovations accepted in one major country are soon adopted elsewhere. In 1985 the Bundesbank, somewhat reluctantly, felt obliged to approve the introduction in West Germany of floating rate, zero coupon and dual currency bonds linked to currency and interest rate swaps. Today the Japanese authorities are having to devise appropriate market mechanisms for dealing in financial futures. Several countries, including the United Kingdom and Japan, have recently authorised domestic commercial paper. The stock market collapse has not shifted the presumption that regulators should follow the market in matters of financial innovation and that official intervention should, where necessary, take the form of safeguards such as additional capital requirements rather than outright prohibition.[5]

That is not to say, however, that the financial markets may not themselves take a more cautious view of financial innovation. The crisis in the market for perpetual floating rate notes that erupted in 1986/7, together with the collapse and temporary shutdown of the US stock index futures market in October, may encourage market participants to exercise greater restraint in their use of new financial instruments and strategies.

Fourth, there are no signs that the cross-border movement of financial institutions will be inhibited, let alone reversed, by recent events. On the contrary, since October 1987 we have seen the addition of sixteen foreign firms to membership of the Tokyo Stock Exchange; the approval by the Bank of England of applications by Nikko Securities and Yamaichi Securities to operate banking units in the United Kingdom; and the decision by the Federal Reserve Bank of New York to allow a subsidiary of Nikko Securities to become a primary dealer in US Government Securities. Such reciprocity deals involving Japanese financial institutions are likely to continue. At the same time the relatively 'closed' capital markets of West Germany and Switzerland are now attracting an increasing number of institutions from outside due, among other things, to the relaxation of restrictions on foreign banks acting as lead managers of foreign bond issues. All the indications are that the interpenetration of national financial markets by foreign institutions will continue as part of the deregulation trend.

A fifth aspect of deregulation, which is unlikely to be halted by the stock market crash, is that of financial diversification and the breaking-down of traditional distinctions between categories of financial institution. For instance, in Japan the Ministry of Finance is considering proposals for abolishing the rigid distinction between ordinary commercial banks and long-term credit banks, and also between commercial banks and trust banks. In the United States and United Kingdom there is every reason to believe that the distinction between commercial banks on the one hand and building societies/savings and loan institutions on the other will continue to diminish. And banks will continue to expand their activities in securities markets – for instance, the placement of commercial paper – even in those countries where there are formal legal barriers between banking and securities business. Moreover, the EEC Commission's proposal for a Second Banking Co-ordination Directive, released in January 1988, will in effect impose the universal banking model throughout the Community. This is because under the Commission's proposal the list of banking activities subject to mutual recognition includes own account trading in securities, securities broking, underwriting and distribution of services as well as portfolio management and advice.[6]

Nevertheless, the equity market crash does have important implications for the relationship between banking and securities business – a matter considered in some detail below.

Finally, as far as deregulation is concerned, there are likely to be further moves to reduce the tax burden on certain categories of financial activities – yet another aspect of the rivalry between financial centres. In recent years we have seen the establishment of reserve-free international banking zones in the United States, Japan and lesser financial centres; the removal by several countries, including the United States and West Germany, of withholding tax on interest received by non-residents from domestic bonds (although West Germany is now proposing a modest withholding tax to apply to *all* forms of interest income); and reductions in stamp duty payable on various security transactions in the United Kingdom and Switzerland. There are growing competitive pressures to abolish the remaining half per cent stamp duty in the United Kingdom, to abolish or reduce Swiss withholding tax on bank deposits and to eliminate West Germany's securities transfer tax as well as Switzerland's stamp duty in respect of eurobond and other international securities transactions. Against this background, further moves towards fiscal deregulation of financial markets can be expected.

REGULATION

Having identified those aspects of financial deregulation which are unlikely to be seriously affected by the stock market crash, it is necessary to consider the regulatory issues raised by recent financial market upheavals. These can be considered under three broad headings: the problem of volatility; the potential for contagious disorders overflowing from securities markets into the banking sector; and the need for a common regulatory framework for the global market in bank lending and securities trading–the co-ordination issue.

VOLATILITY

In looking at the question of price volatility in securities markets it is worth recalling what happened in the United States on Monday 19 October 1987. In morning trading the Dow Jones Industrial Average first fell over 200 points, then climbed almost 100 points, before dropping by a further 400 points by the close of trading. The closing value represented a loss of 508 points or 22 per cent from Friday's close, and a 36 per cent decline from August's peak. The day's absolute price decline in the Dow Jones Industrial Average was four times the record set the previous Friday; and the percentage decline was twice the previous record, which had been set on 29 October 1929. The *average* daily price movement from 16 to 30 October inclusive was 121 points, more than the previous single day record, and there were twelve 100-point and twenty-one 50-point intra-day price shifts.[7] Of course, there were correspondingly large price movements during this period on stock exchanges worldwide.

The first question to be asked is whether this was a one-off aberration or must it be assumed that the securities markets have become more volatile? The answer is not clear. The Brady Commission concluded that the US stock market, up to 19 October, had shown no increase in volatility relative to the early 1970s and 1940s, and was considerably less volatile than during the 1930s.[8] On the other hand, the SEC Report cited evidence that intra-day, as opposed to inter-day, volatility had been rising prior to October 1987. In any event, stock market volatility, on whatever measurement may be used, has remained high since then and it is far from obvious that historically normal patterns of trading will shortly be resumed.

The second question to be considered, then, is whether increased volatility really matters? The answer to this must be yes. Highly volatile markets increase market-making risks, reduce investor confidence, increase the cost of capital and, in the extreme, may, as on 19-20 October, 'raise the spectre of a full-scale financial system breakdown' (p. 69 of the Brady Report).

If price volatility is potentially damaging can regulators take steps that would dampen price swings? This is where the controversy over the events of October 1987 intensifies. In the United States, the Brady, NYSE, and SEC Reports, all conclude that the failure of market mechanisms – and in particular the disconnection of the stock index futures market from the market in underlying stocks – contributed to the equity market collapse in October. However, the CME Report inclines to the view that the direction of causation was the other way round – in other words, that it was the unprecedented wave of selling that led to the fragmentation of the markets.[9] The London Stock Exchange Report also exonerates the UK market structure from any contributory role during the collapse of the UK equity market.

The critical assessment of the first three US studies mentioned above is founded on two basic propositions. The first is that the US stock market has been destabilised by excessive speculative activity centring on the futures and options exchanges. For instance, the NYSE Report (p. 30) states that cash settlement in these markets, and the leverage which cash settlement makes possible, invites speculative activity which in turn, through arbitrage, forces 'the stock exchanges to embrace a philosophy of short-term trading heretofore antithetical to their investment philosophy'. This is a remarkable conclusion because modern financial markets are structured on the assumption that speculation is, by and large, stabilising – that is to say, successful speculators who correctly anticipate price movements help to move prices quickly to equilibrium levels, whereas unsuccessful speculators are driven out of business. While failing to address the matter directly the three US studies challenge this assumption by implication and propose increased margins on futures trading as a means of increasing the cost of dealing, thereby curbing speculative activity. The CME Report, however, disputes both the analysis and the policy prescription.[10]

The second proposition, on which the first three US studies are agreed, is that 'hedging', as well as speculative activity, conducted through futures markets, may be destabilising. In particular, the possibility of hedging investment positions through futures markets, using portfolio insurance programmes, may, it is argued, encourage institutional investors to retain a higher percentage of equity in their portfolios than might, in view of market fundamentals, seem prudent. According to this view, the illusory belief that massive investment positions could be liquidated suddenly through the future markets, induced fund managers to try to ride the bull market to its apex, thereby sustaining the market's rise and aggravating the subsequent decline.[11] Both the SEC and the NYSE Reports recommend physical, rather than cash, settlement of index futures as a means of discouraging large futures positions, while the Brady Report advocates the introduction of 'circuit breakers' (that is temporary suspensions of trading triggered by, for instance, daily price limits). Circuit breakers have a number of possible functions[12] but they have been proposed in the US context as a way of demonstrating that markets have limited absorptive capacity, thereby preventing portfolio insurers and others from deluding themselves that they can off-load their investment risks at any time. In other words, circuit breaker mechanisms would replace the illusion of liquidity with the manifest fact of illiquidity.

Of course, it might reasonably be argued that if speculation through the futures markets is destabilising and hedging through the futures markets is also destabilising, as the authors of these US studies evidently believe, then the whole rationale of stock index futures is in doubt. The regulatory implications might then be rather more drastic than the authors are prepared to contemplate.

However, there is a more fundamental objection to the US studies' conclusion. Quite simply, if their analysis is correct and institutional investors have indeed been unaware of the limited absorptive capacity of the futures market, then there will presumably be a self-correcting adjustment in market behaviour. As the CME Report (p. 56) states, 'now that this flaw has been widely exposed, we expect that excessive use of this strategy will no longer be a problem'.[13] In short, it is redundant and potentially damaging to impose new regulatory constraints on markets with a view to discouraging behaviour that, because lessons have been learned, is unlikely to recur – at least on anything like the scale that prevailed before October 1987.

To the extent that flawed investment strategies contributed to the October collapse there is some reason to believe that market volatility will decline of its own accord. Nevertheless it may be that we have to learn to live with greater price fluctuations than in the past. And the reason is very simple. Students of animal behaviour tell us that the propensity of a herd to stampede increases with the size of the herd and the proximity of animals to one another.[14] With the globilisation of financial markets the herd has indeed increased while modern communications technology, including video screen information services, has brought market players closer together. Perhaps, therefore, we should not be surprised that stock markets around the world have become more prone to sudden panics. But if it is the case that we must accept greater price volatility than in the past, it may be necessary to insulate the financial system from the shock waves transmitted by the periodic stock market upheavals. That is the next regulatory issue to be considered.

THE 'SEPARATION ISSUE'

The increased volatility in stock markets and the high risks involved in underwriting and market-making in these conditions raise important questions about the relationship between banks and securities markets, and the potential for destabilisation of the banking sector. After all, if banks' balance sheets are exposed to large swings in security prices this could increase the incidence of bank failures while also prompting depositors to withdraw funds from institutions believed to have suffered heavy losses on their securities portfolios. Such a possibility could oblige central banks to become lenders-of-last-resort not only to the banking sector but also to the securities markets.

It should be said at the outset that national banking systems do not appear to have been adversely affected by the events of October 1987. On the contrary, to the extent that there were credit problems, they arose, in the United States, from banks curbing their lending to other non-bank institutions rather than vice versa.[15] Yet the relative calm with which banks were able to ride the storm may have been due in part to the absence of any major failure among securities firms – an outcome which cannot be guaranteed in any future market break.

In looking at this problem it is necessary to distinguish between those countries, notably the United States and Japan, which retain laws separating commercial from investment banking, from those such as West Germany and Switzerland which have a long tradition of universal banking, and a third group led by the United Kingdom and Canada which have recently experienced a 'Big Bang' fusion of securities and banking business. However, given the limitations of space, the discussion here will be confined to the United States and United Kingdom.

Turning first to the United States, there have been suggestions that the stock market crash of 1987 will strengthen the hand of those who wish to retain provisions of the 1933 Glass-Steagall Act, which prevents banks from underwriting or taking positions in corporate securities. However, in November 1987 Senators William Proxmire and Jake Garn introduced a Bill which would repeal key sections of the Glass-Steagall Act and permit bank holding companies (but *not* banks themselves) to engage in securities underwriting and other securities activities through separately capitalised securities affiliates.[16] This proposal appears to have the support of the US Administration and has been endorsed, with some qualifications, by the three Federal bank regulatory agencies – the Federal Reserve Board, the Comptroller of the Currency, and the Federal Deposit Insurance Corporation.

The detailed provisions of the Proxmire-Garn Bill are designed to ensure that any losses incurred by a securities affiliate do not infect its sister bank. In order to achieve this objective certain restrictive terms of the Glass-Steagall Act are in effect 'internalised' – that is to say, the separation of commercial from investment banking is maintained through restrictions on banks' dealings with their securities affiliates. Specifically, a bank would not be permitted to lend to its securities affiliates; it could not make loans or guarantees to a company in order to enhance the marketability of the company's securities underwritten by the bank's securities affiliate; it could not make loans to a person for the purpose of purchasing securities underwritten by the bank's securities affiliate; and it could not make loans to a company for the purpose of paying the principal or interest on securities underwritten by its securities affiliate. Furthermore, the securities affiliate could not sell securities to the bank or its trust accounts during the underwriting period or for thirty days thereafter; there could be no director or officer interlocks between a bank and its securities affiliate; and, crucially, the securities affiliate would have to disclose publicly that its obligations were in no way backed by its affiliate bank or insured by the FDIC.

The purpose of these restrictions is to ensure, as far as possible, that banks are financially insulated from the risks incurred by their securities affiliates and that the lender-of-last-resort function need not be extended beyond the banking sector to securities firms. At the same time, securities affiliates of banks would be regulated by the SEC as separate entities, and the assets and liabilities of such affiliates would *not* be consolidated with the bank holding company for purposes of regulation by the Federal Reserve Board. In other words, the principle of separation embodied in the Glass-Steagall Act would continue to be reflected in the operational, financial and regulatory independence of banks and their related securities firms. Arguably, therefore, the Proxmire-Garn Bill would, if implemented, protect the banking system from the risks associated with recent stock market volatility.

Turning now to the United Kingdom, the present position in the aftermath of 'Big Bang' is very different from that either prevailing in the

United States or proposed under the Proxmire-Garn Bill. UK banks are able to engage in all manner of securities activities without any holding company structure. These activities may be located in separately capitalised subsidiaries or affiliates, or they may be conducted by the bank itself. Furthermore, where securities business *is* routed through a separate group company there are no protective 'walls' established between the bank and its related securities firm. Indeed, in such cases, the Bank of England has stated that, on a discretionary basis, it will allow a bank to undertake a group funding role – that is, the bank is free to lend short-term to other financial companies, including securities firms, within the group, thereby exposing itself directly to the risks that may be incurred by such firms.[17] Therefore under present UK regulations there is a direct and unbroken umbilical cord linking banks and securities markets which could, in volatile market conditions, affect the stability of the banking system (although it must again be emphasised that there has been no sign of that to date). Three regulatory consequences flow from this state of affairs.

Firstly, the consolidated group capital of UK financial conglomerates must be strong enough to minimise the risk of destabilisation of banking activities conducted within the conglomerate. The difficulty here, however, is that stringent capital requirements might place conglomerates at a competitive disadvantage *vis-à-vis* specialised financial institutions.

More broadly it is difficult, if not impossible, within an *integrated* financial conglomerate, to apply the principle of 'functional' as distinct from 'institutional' regulation. In the interests of competitive equality it may be desirable to regulate the securities activities of banks as if they were conducted through independent companies (the functional approach) – and not to impose regulatory penalties on such business simply because it happens to be conducted within a banking group (the institutional approach). Otherwise, conglomerates may be deprived of the economic benefits of diversification. However, the principle of functional regulation, which in the United States is incorporated into the Proxmire-Garn Bill, cannot be fully adhered to in the United Kingdom, given that the securities and other non-bank activities of a banking conglomerate may impact the bank itself.[18]

Secondly, since the various operating entities within a UK financial conglomerate must be viewed as financially interdependent, it makes little sense to subject the diverse activities of these groups to separate regulatory standards, still less to separate regulatory agencies – at least so far as prudential regulation is concerned. In other words, the financial standing of securities and banking firms can only be assessed in terms of the whole group to which they belong, and under these circumstances it is unfortunate that Parliament has split the statutory responsibility for regulating combined investment/banking businesses between the Securities and Investments Board and the Bank of England.[19]

Thirdly, because under present UK regulatory arrangements banks and their related securities firms must be viewed as financially interdependent, it follows that the lender-of-last-resort cannot realistically be confined to the banking sector – whatever may be said publicly on the subject. In this context it is worth recalling the following remarks made by the Governor of the Bank of England in September 1986 immediately prior to 'Big Bang':

> What would be the consequences of the failure of an undercapitalised investment house? Contracts would be reneged upon; stock could be dumped on the market; and these developments alone might well threaten the viability of other intermediaries. Then there will be firms that are part of conglomerate groups; their difficulties could well spill over into other markets. It is unlikely, given the very large sums involved and the position of the banks in the payments system, that the commercial banks could remain wholly immune. Banks may be vulnerable because they have built up large exposures to securities businesses (whether or not associates). Those with subsidiaries engaged in securities business will also feel a practical obligation (based on market expectations) to their securities subsidiaries far in excess of the amounts of facilities granted. Such considerations may mean that a bank within a financial conglomerate may be particularly exposed to contagion and a loss of confidence.[20]

If, in the aftermath of 'Big Bang', banks could be destabilised by development in the securities markets in the way described, it would appear that the UK authorities may, under certain circumstances, have little option but to extend the lender-of-last-resort role to securities houses that are parts of banking conglomerates – albeit the support might be provided by using the bank as a conduit. In any event, there is a clear difference between the United States and United Kingdom in this area: the United States is evidently determined to segregate risks in the banking and securities markets, and to limit official financial assistance to depository institutions, while the United Kingdom has promoted the financial interdependence of banks and securities firms to the point where the scope of the lender-of-last-resort role may have to be enlarged.

INTERNATIONAL REGULATORY CO-ORDINATION

imp 1+2

The third and final regulatory issue raised by the crash of 1987 is that of international regulatory co-ordination. Recent events have demonstrated only too clearly how financial disorders can spread from one national stock market to another. It is not merely that stock market panics are subject to cross-border contagion; institutions with foreign affiliates can be threatened by disturbances in overseas markets; as was seen with the BP shares issue, underwriting risks may jeopardise securities firms outside the country where the issue is arranged; and the prospective failure of one segment of a national financial market, such as the Hong Kong Futures Exchange, can spread losses and shock waves worldwide. Just as the Herstatt Crisis of 1974 taught us that major shocks to the international banking system cannot be localised, so the events of 1987 have underlined the interdependence of national securities markets.

In considering the appropriate regulatory response to the globalisation of securities market risks it is useful to review the approach of bank supervisory authorities to international regulatory co-ordination and to contrast the absence of parallel co-ordination in securities markets.

In crude terms, it is convenient to divide the international co-ordination of bank regulation into three phases.

Phase one of the co-ordinating process was the first Basle Concordat of 1975. This was very largely concerned with the allocation of regulatory responsibilities between financial centres in respect of foreign branches and subsidiaries with a view to ensuring that all banks were supervised by someone. No such accord covers the regulation of securities firms which may be able to escape supervision by using certain offshore centres.

Phase two was the revised (1983) Basle Concordat which began to address the problem of applying common regulatory standards. In this context each national supervisory authority is urged to satisfy itself that its banks' foreign operations are being conducted in jurisdictions with sound supervisory practices and that foreign banks to which it is host are subject to adequate supervision in their home jurisdictions. The implication is that national authorities should be prepared, *in extremis*, to exclude foreign banks from jurisdictions with inadequate supervisory standards and to prevent their own banks locating overseas offices in poorly supervised centres. Again, there is no parallel initiative governing national securities markets where regulatory standards are transparently uneven. This is particularly true of futures and options exchanges which have been proliferating in competition with one another without any regard for regulatory co-ordination.[21]

Phase three of the co-ordination of bank regulation began in January 1987 with the Anglo-American accord on capital adequacy measurement, which then became the basis for the proposed multilateral accord on capital adequacy standards published in December 1987 by the Cooke Committee. The significance of this last initiative is that it represents a shift towards regulatory harmonisation in the interests of competitive equality as well as safety and soundness. Indeed the accord may be viewed as a response to the banking industry's concerns about unfair regulatory disparities in the area of capital adequacy requirements. Although there is no equivalent accord governing securities firms it is interesting to note that the same competitive pressures which are forcing international banking into a common regulatory mould are also making themselves felt in securities markets. For instance, in the supervision of London's wholesale money markets the Bank of England's capital adequacy requirements are explicitly based on those of the SEC, with a view to ensuring competitive equality between US and UK-based firms.[22] Nevertheless we are still a very long way from achieving the degree of co-ordination between national securities markets regulators that already exists between bank regulators.[23]

If we were to look well ahead we might envisage a fourth and final phase of bank regulatory co-ordination that would also be applicable in due course to securities markets. That would involve the establishment of a supra-national regulatory body which would not merely impose common rules of behaviour in major financial markets but would also be responsible for supervising the worldwide banking and securities activities of financial institutions.[24] Clearly, such arrangements are not yet on the agenda and it would take further major upheavals to put them there.

Yet what has been made abundantly plain by recent events is that the fragmentation of regulatory responsibilities both geographically, between national authorities, and functionally, between bank, securities market and futures exchange regulators, is becoming outdated in a global financial marketplace in which securities and banking markets are becoming increasingly integrated. Failure to recognise this fact and to re-act swiftly could leave the international financial system dangerously exposed when the next storm blows up. Regulators could then find that they have been merely 'weaving nets to catch the wind'.[25]

Notes

1. The following studies on the 1987 stock market crash are referred to (directly or indirectly) in the text: *Report of the Presidential Task Force on Market Mechanisms,* January 1988 (The Brady Report); *An Overview of Program Trading and its Impact on Current Market Practices,* New York Stock Exchange, December 1987 (The NYSE Report); *Preliminary Report of the Committee of Inquiry Appointed by the Chicago Mercantile Exchange,* December 1987 (The CME Report); *Preliminary Observations on the October 1987 Crash,* US General Accounting Office, January 1988 (The GAO Report); *The October 1987 Market Break,* US Securities and Exchange Commission, February 1988 (The SEC Report); *Final Report on Stock Index Futures and Cash Market Activity During October 1987,* US Commodity Futures Trading Commission, January 1988 (The CFTC Report).
2. See 'Proposals for International Convergence of Capital Measurement and Capital Standards', Committee on Banking Regulation and Supervisory Practices, Bank for International Settlements, December 1987.

3. Statement before the Sub-Committee on Telecommunications and Finance, Committee on Energy and Commerce, US House of Representatives, 5 August 1987.
4. This competition between domestic and euro business is evident in money markets as well as in capital markets. For instance, from 1 May 1986 the Bundesbank lowered the minimum reserve requirements on West German banks' domestic deposit liabilities, the stated purpose being 'to reduce the cost disadvantages in domestic bank lending, arising from the minimum reserve requirement, *vis-à-vis* the euromarkets'.
5. However, the President of the Federal Reserve Bank of New York, Gerald Corrigan, has suggested that unduly risky activities and transactions should be subject to outright prohibition or what he terms 'prior restraint'. See Gerald Corrigan, 'Coping with Globally Integrated Financial Markets', *Federal Reserve Bank of New York Quarterly Review*, Winter 1987, p. 5.
6. Under Article 16 of the Commission's proposal, a bank from one EEC country branching into another EEC country will automatically be permitted to engage in these securities activities if allowed to do so in its home jurisdiction (subject to position risk requirements that may be imposed by the host regulatory authority).
7. See statement by David Ruder, SEC Chairman, before the Senate Committee on Banking, Housing and Urban Affairs, 4 November 1987.
8. The Brady Commission cites the following comparative data on volatility:

Volatility trends and interantional comparisons (average of 60 day annualised volatilities, in percent

	Germany	*Jaoan*	*United States*
1987 (pre-october)	24.4	17.4	17.8
1986	19.3	17.0	15.5
1985	12.6	12.2	14.3
1984	14.7	14.5	18.8
1983	11.8	17.4	17.0
1982	15.1	20.8	19.1
1981	18.3	16.8	21.4
1980	7.8	18.7	18.1
1979	7.6	14.1	19.1
1978	7.8	12.8	18.2
1977	13.0	11.5	24.6
1976	9.9	13.8	20.1
1975	14.5	19.1	43.0
1974	18.9	26.4	33.6
1973	19.1	15.7	14.3
Average (1973–87)	14.5	17.4	21.2
October 1987	58.1	73.0	56.9

9. The CME Report also states (p. 37) that 'it is far from clear that any market system could successfully absorb selling of that magnitude over a time interval as short as an ordinary seven-hour trading day'.

10. The CME Report (p. 44) states that net selling on 19 and 20 October was concentrated among institutional investors and that individual speculative accounts were net buyers on both days. The Report also argues (p. 45) that the only proper function of futures margins is to act as a performance bond.
11. The SEC Report (pp. 3-14 to 3-15) also argues that portfolio insurance destabilises the stock market because it acts as *undisclosed* selling pressure. In contrast to a put option, which it resembles, portfolio insurance sends no direct bearish message to the market: instead investors become aware that there is an increasingly large commitment to sell futures and/or stocks whenever the market moves downwards.
12. According to the Brady Report (p. 65) circuit breakers limit credit risks by providing a 'time-out' to settle up; and also inhibit panic by allowing time for 'value traders' to cushion violent market movements.
13. In contrast, the SEC Report, while recognising that the market will 'self-correct' to some degree, states (p. 3-17) that 'we cannot confidently conclude that the impact of futures trading will be reduced substantially because of lessons learned during the October market break'. It is interesting to note, however, that since October 1987 a number of US securities firms have announced that they are restricting programme trading.
14. I am indebted to Mr Alistair Lawrence, of the East of Scotland College of Agriculture, for evidence on this point relating to the behaviour of Scottish Blackface ewes.
15. The SEC Report (pp. 5-24 to 5-30) notes that some broker-dealers experienced problems obtaining credit during the week of 19 October, to the point where the Federal Reserve Bank of New York felt obliged to encourage certain City banks to support the securities industry.
16. The Bill, entitled the 'Financial Modernisation Act of 1987' would repeal Sections 20 and 32 of the Glass-Steagall Act (restricting affiliations between banks and securities firms), while retaining Section 21 which prohibits banks from directly underwriting corporate and other securities, and also prohibits securities firms from accepting deposits.
17. Under the Bank of England's policy on large exposures, where it is considered appropriate for a bank to undertake a group treasury role, exposures of a maturity up to one year to group non-bank financial companies, will be allowed up to levels agreed on a case-by-case basis. See 'Large Exposures Undertaken by Institutions Authorised under the Banking Act 1987', Bank of England Notice, September 1987.
18. John Townend, Head of the Bank of England's Wholesale Markets Supervision Division, has acknowledged that under the present UK dual regulatory regime banks do not enjoy regulatory parity with securities businesses: 'Seeing that standards at present differ, apparently to their disadvantage, banks are prompted to ask why they should be penalised in this way.' See 'Supervision of the Wholesale Money Market', *Bank of England Quarterly Bulletin*, February 1988, p. 73.
19. The Bank of England and the Securities and Investments Board have tried to develop a 'lead regulator' concept designed to avoid overlapping regulation of financial conglomerates. However, because the SIB's statutory responsibilities cannot be delegated to the Bank nor the Bank's responsibilities delegated to the SIB, this attempt to streamline regulatory procedures has run into serious difficulties. See 'Memorandum of Understanding between the Bank of England and the Securities and Investments Board on the Financial Supervision of Banks', October 1987. In this context Sir Nicholas

Goodison, Chairman of the International Stock Exchance, has suggested that central banks should be the prime regulators of securities markets: 'It is my view, given the heavy investment of banks in securities markets and the risks which this brings to the world financial system, that central banks must and will become the prime financial regulators.' See Speech at the City University Symposium on Industry and Finance, 10 February 1988.

20. Speech to the Group of 30 Symposium on Equity Markets, London, 15 September 1986.
21. On the need for regulatory co-ordination generally, see Richard Dale, 'How Safe is the Banking System?', Hume Occasional Paper, no. 4, 1986.
22. See 'The Regulation of the Wholesale Markets in Sterling, Foreign Exchange and Bullion', Bank of England Regulatory Paper, July 1987, p. 6.
23. In a speech to the Overseas Bankers Club, on 1 February 1988, the Governor of the Bank of England commented as follows on the lessons of the October crash:

    It also means that we will need to look further at how best to develop contact between securities and bank regulators. While I would not wish to devalue the importance of bilateral contact in this matter, there is an obvious question about whether a multilateral panel, similar to the Cooke Committee, might not be necessary in the light of the events of last October.

24. Henry Kaufman, former Chief Economist of Salomon Brothers Inc., has called for the creation of an international regulatory body to establish unified rules of behaviour in major financial markets. See 'Kaufman Seeks Creation of World Markets Body', *Wall Street Journal*, 15 December 1987.
25. The author would like to thank the Royal Bank of Scotland for permission to re-publish this article which originally appeared in the *Royal Bank of Scotland Review*, June 1988. Research for the study was funded by a grant from the Economic and Social Research Council.

18 International Convergence of Capital Adequacy Measurement and Standards

Peter Cooke

This chapter sets out to describe the processes by which major banking nations have, since the early 1980s, edged towards an understanding on a common approach to capital measurement and an international capital standard. These efforts culminated in the publication, in July 1988, of a report by the Committee on Banking Regulations and Supervisory Practices of the Group of Ten major industrialised countries ('The Basle Supervisors' Committee')[1] which sets out an agreed common aproach to capital adequacy measurement and standards for international banks.

The present chapter does not set out to explain in detail the different national positions which had to be reconciled in order to reach consensus and only scratches the surface of a number of difficult issues. But it does outline the main steps in the debate which eventually led to this international agreement. I am grateful to Mr Christopher Thompson, Secretary of the Basle Supervisors' Committee for most of the period covered, for his help in the preparation of this chapter.

INTRODUCTION

It is a commonplace today that the world's major banking and financial institutions are operating in an increasingly integrated global market place. It is a world, however, in which those institutions' activities are governed by a multiplicity of different national legal frameworks and regulatory requirements. Co-operation and a degree of co-ordination therefore has to be the way forward for the foreseeable future in managing all these potentially conflicting rules and relationships. However, in one particularly important area of financial regulation – that of bank capital, its measurement and its adequacy – the process has gone further and convergence is the word which has come to be used to describe the approach. The fruits of this convergence process are the July 1988 report of the Basle Supervisors'

Committee[2] which contains a detailed framework of recommendations, agreed between all Group of Ten countries, for the measurement of banks' capital adequacy and the establishment of minimum standards, to be achieved by the end of 1992, for banks operating internationally. The press release issued by the Governors at the time referred to two important objectives underlying the agreement. These were the need to 'strengthen the stability of the international banking system' and to 'remove an important source of competitive inequality for banks arising from differences in national supervisory requirements'. It cannot, of course, be claimed that the agreement now being implemented at the national level means that all differences have been eliminated and that all the hummocks on the playing field have been flattened. Convergence is relative, not absolute. Indeed the agreement can be the stronger for this built-in flexibility. But it is important that any divergences should not compromise the basic coherence and credibility of the package. It should also be emphasised that competitive equality cannot be achieved simply by agreeing on a common set of prudential rules; other factors, notably monetary policy arrangements and fiscal treatment, can and do have a significant impact on competition. Nevertheless, convergence on capital rules is of major importance in equalising competitive conditions.

The process which led to the approval of the final July 1988 report by the G10 Governors has been a long one but it is an interesting case study of the workings of international supervisory co-operation. This chapter sets out to describe how agreement was achieved among the major countries. Even this agreement, however, is only a staging post – albeit an important one – in a continuing process. The Committee's agreed paper is thus rather the end of the beginning than the beginning of the end on this subject, and is likely to be one aspect of a more general convergence of supervisory rules and standards internationally in the years ahead. Markets will change; innovation will continue; historic perceptions of risk will be modified by experience. Convergence of supervisory practices will undoubtedly be pursued for as long as the globalisation of markets continues to be a reality (and there is little sign at present of that trend reversing itself). The Basle Committee's capital convergence report may be reasonably regarded, therefore, as a significant milestone in the establishment of a common supervisory response to the existence of a single, highly competitive, international banking market. Countries have agreed to reflect this common approach in their national systems in order to help achieve a stronger banking system and a more level playing field internationally.

The playing field, of course, embraces more countries than the Group of Ten comprises and the approach to convergence of capital adequacy measurement and standards that was inherent in the recommendations emanating from Basle would prove acceptable to a wider community.

To this end the final report (and the earlier consultative version of the document) was sent to central banks and supervisory authorities worldwide seeking their views and many have endorsed it and are implementing its provisions.

THE ROLE OF CAPITAL

To appreciate the importance of the objectives of this international accord, it is necessary to understand the central role of capital adequacy measurement in national systems of banking supervision and to examine its significance for the way in which international banks conduct their business.

Capital adequacy lies at the heart of supervision and all G10 supervisory authorities require their banks to hold adequate capital against the risks of potential losses arising from their business operations. This is normally measured as the ratio of capital to some quantum of balance sheet and off-balance sheet engagements as variously defined. 'Adequacy' is expressed as a minimum numerical ratio which the banks are expected to maintain. The technical obstacles to international agreement arose from the fact that each of the twelve countries which are members of the Basle Supervisors Committee had its own definition of capital, its own method of relating capital to the scale of the business, and its own quantitative guideline or required standard for the resulting ratio. These national differences reflected long-established banking, accounting and supervisory practices in the countries concerned.

The issues to be resolved were thus essentially technical matters of measurement and definition. At the same time, the fact that supervisory controls on capital adequacy have a strong influence on the quantity and nature of the business that individual banks and banking systems may conduct carries far-reaching implications for the competitive standing of banks in different countries. Thus the bringing together of different national positions to a result that was both sound in prudential terms and fair in application required lengthy and painstaking discussions, and a willingness to search for compromise and common ground on the part of all concerned.

Against the background of a highly competitive international banking market, disparities in national regulations as regards both the way in which capital adequacy is measured and the amount of capital which banks are required to hold, can have several harmful consequences. First, and most directly, for a given balance sheet, banks subject to high capital standards will be less able to undertake new business compared with their peers subject to less demanding standards. For each unit of capital held by banks in different countries, national rules allow some banking systems to take on two or three times as much lending as others. Secondly, for a given return on capital, banks with lower capital requirements are able to accept substantially lower margins on their lending than their more restricted competitors. This tends to lead, through competitive pressures, to a distortion of prudent risk/reward relationships affecting the banking industry as a whole. Thirdly, where conventional good-quality business fails to provide an adequate return, because of this unequal competition, some banks will be induced to take on riskier, higher-margin lending, or look for devices and loopholes to arrange their business in ways which fall outside the supervisors' measure of capital adequacy. Fourthly, the combination of these pressures can make it difficult for individual national supervisors and individual banks to maintain, let alone raise, prudential standards. Instead all the pressures will tend towards 'competition in regulatory laxity' as a former Chairman of the Federal Reserve Board, Arthur Burns, once described it.

Thus the prudential arguments for convergence towards internationally observed high standards of capital adequacy tend to coincide with arguments for competitive equality in the impact of regulation. It can, of course, be said, and with some justification, that from the standpoint of pure market theory the market itself will, over the longer term, pass its own verdict on weak and inadequately capitalised banks and will reward strong banks for their prudence, unaided by the efforts of supervisors. The reality, however, in banking markets, is of periodic episodes of financial instability which, if left to work themselves out, would cause indiscriminate damage to a widening circle of banks and their depositors as confidence breaks down. Such episodes have in their time been one of the main reasons why all major countries have introduced formal arrangements for banking supervision as an external arbiter of prudent standards. Indeed it was the international manifestation of such problems in the early 1970s associated with the collapse of the Herstatt Bank and the Franklin National Bank, which led to the creation of the Basle Supervisors Committee and its meeting for the first time early in 1975.

EARLY WORK ON CAPITAL CONVERGENCE

The first fruit of the Basle Committee's work was to agree a framework for allocating supervisory responsibility, particularly in respect of solvency and liquidity, for the large networks of foreign branches, subsidiaries and joint ventures which had sprung up in the 1960s and early 1970s. That code of practice, which became known as the Basle Concordat[3], placed primary responsibility for the supervision of international banks' solvency on the supervisory authority where the parent bank's head office and place of incorporation was located. This early focus on the importance of solvency in the supervisory processes led, in subsequent years, to the Committee discussing ways of measuring and setting standards of capital adequacy.

By the late 1970s, virtually all the G10 countries had reviewed or refined their own national approaches for monitoring banks' capital adequacy. The systems employed reflected national circumstances and experience; each had its own distinct characteristics, notably as to those elements of the balance sheet which were admitted within the definition of capital. As to the method of relating capital to the size of the business, the Committee was roughly divided into two camps. Most of the European countries – France, Germany, Switzerland, Belgium, the Netherlands, Sweden and the United Kingdom – favoured an approach which weighted assets according to degree of risk as providing the best measure of the adequacy of a bank's capital. However, Italy and Luxembourg, as well as Canada, Japan and the United States, still used systems based on a gearing ratio approach which related capital funds to the unweighted total of the balance sheet. These differences of approach made it impossible to make meaningful cross-country comparisons of capital adequacy. Moreover, at that time, there was little consensus in the Committee about the value of such comparisons, even if some common, mutually acceptable measure could be devised.

Alongside a range of different national views on how to measure capital adequacy, there was, nevertheless, by the early 1980s a growing unease on the part of most members of the Committee that standards of capital adequacy in banks operating internationally were being progressively, and prospectively dangerously, eroded. The evidence for this in the capital ratios of individual banks was not always clear-cut and it was difficult to generalise by comparing one year with another, but over a longer time-span the evidence of deterioration was unmistakable. This unease was fuelled particularly by the pace at which banks were expanding their international lending and growing doubts began to emerge about the quality of much of the lending to non-industrialised countries which by then had assumed a sizeable proportion of many banks' total assets. At the beginning of the 1980s the Committee began systematically to monitor the capital ratios of the leading international banks in member countries.

In the absence of a common system of measurement, this initial monitoring was based on the varied national systems, but at least it offered some possibility of identifying trends in the capital position of banks in individual countries and served to heighten general supervisory awareness of the problem. Reflecting their concerns, the Committee presented a report to the Central Bank Governors in the spring of 1982 seeking their endorsement of a collective stand to take action to halt the deterioration in the levels of capital in the light of the continued rapid growth in international lending.

In the second half of 1982 the growth of international lending was brought to a sudden halt by the moratorium declared by Mexico and the subsequent inability of other major debtors to service their engagements. The shock to the international banking system, and the demonstration of its fragility in the face of massive exposure to debtor countries, moved the debate on capital adequacy into a different gear. Containment of the problem demanded not merely prevention of erosion of capital but a concerted and sustained effort to strengthen banks' balance sheets. The strategy of burden-sharing, case-by-case treatment, new money packages and support from international agencies was designed to allow all the parties time to work to overcome their problems and, not least, to buy time for the banks to organise their defences.

At the same time, although much international lending had lost its attraction, competition among banks for high-quality corporate business remained intense and profit margins continued to be squeezed. With supervisors pressing for substantial increases in capital, complaints from banks and other parties were increasingly voiced against unfair competition owing to inconsistencies in regulatory standards of capital adequacy.

Against such a background, the need for action to raise capital standards for international banks and achieve greater consistency in supervisory requirements became increasingly accepted. It was also clear that successful action would require not only internationally co-ordinated efforts on the part of supervisors but also high-level commitment from central banks and other supervisory agencies to ensure progress. Early in 1984, Paul Volcker, the Chairman of the Federal Reserve Board, suggested to his fellow Governors that efforts should be made to devise a means of reconciling different systems of measuring capital adequacy through a test of 'functional equivalence' of the various approaches followed in individual G10 countries.

Aside from the general case for common international ground rules, a number of countries had a problem which they needed to resolve arising from this diversity. In the United States, for example, the Federal regulations governing takeovers of US banks require that the acquiring bank should be soundly capitalised according to US standards. In the early 1980s a number of US banks were acquired by foreign banks and the application of the regulation to the capital position of foreign banks presented some difficulty. The US authorities, therefore, needed a means of judging whether the capital standards observed by foreign banks were equivalent to their own national requirements.

In furtherance of the Volcker proposal, as Chairman of the Supervisors' Committee, I was given a personal mandate by the Governors in March 1984 to develop recommendations for:

1. assessing the comparability of different measures of capital adequacy,

2. attaining over time comparable and adequate minimum international capital standards.

The fact that, unusually, the mandate was a personal mandate to the Committee's Chairman was not intended to diminish the involvement and responsibility of the Committee as a whole, but it did reflect the Governors' awareness of the technical difficulties involved and the delicate task of finding a generally acceptable basis for reconciling the differing supervisory approaches to capital adequacy existing in G10 countries.

During the following months wide-ranging discussions were held with central banks and supervisory authorities in G10 countries to seek views on how best to address the first part of the mandate with the object of developing a generally acceptable common method of measurement and comparison. These discussions also extended to those engaged in parallel work in the European Community.

THE EUROPEAN COMMUNITY DIMENSION

Since the late 1970s, work had also been in train in Brussels to develop and test capital adequacy ratios for banks and other credit institutions established in the Community. These ratios were an important element of the Commission's programme which aimed at the eventual establishment of a uniform, legally-binding capital adequacy regime throughout the Community, within the overall programme of achieving a common market in financial services. The Commission's early efforts were directed towards the testing of ratios employing both a risk-weighting formula and the more traditional gearing approach. The tests used both a narrow definition of capital based on shareholders' funds and a wider definition to include also subordinated debt instruments. This work was pursued with the advice and assistance of the Banking Advisory Committee of the European Community, which had been established in 1978 as a high-level committee of bank supervisors and government officials in member countries, and of the EC Contact Group which was an informal grouping of supervisors established to facilitate exchanges of information and discussion of supervisory techniques among regulatory bodies and which had first met as long ago as 1972. These EC systems of measurement were applied to samples of banks in member countries, and a series of 'observation ratios' obtained. However, there were considerable differences of view among the member countries about the conceptual validity of the bases of measurement and, in the early 1980s, there appeared to be little prospect of any technical or political consensus emerging in the short term that would transform the observation ratios into a model for formalised Community-wide regulation of capital adequacy.

The close parallels between the objectives of the Brussels exercise and the Governors' mandate, together with the fact that seven of the twelve members of the Basle Committee were also members of the European Community, presented a dilemma as to how best to advance the work in Basle. Although the work was being pursued in parallel there were some important differences. Among the five non-EC members in Basle were two of the most important banking countries in the world, the United States and Japan, and they could not be expected automatically to adopt an approach developed for application within the Community. Work in Basle was essentially directed at exhorting national authorities towards a common approach, while that in Brussels was designed ultimately to be legally binding on all members; Basle concentrated on banks which were internationally active, Brussels was concerned with rules to cover all credit institutions. But at the same time there were good practical reasons for trying to ensure that the two exercises were based as far as possible on similar analyses and, very importantly, on similar data to ease prospective reporting burdens on banks. From the Community's point of view, maximum consistency between the two approaches would mean there was less danger of the Community regime coming into conflict with the systems in non-Community countries, thus avoiding setting the EC bloc at odds with the rest of the world on matters which everyone recognised should, for good practical reasons, be dealt with in the same way in what was one single global marketplace.

It was eventually decided that the best chance of success for the Committee lay in it formulating its own proposals for convergence, while seeking to ensure close compatibility with the work in Brussels, so as to avoid creating difficulties for the seven countries represented in both centres. As was to become clear during the long negotiations in the Committee, in order to meet their separate objectives both Basle and Brussels in some measure had to relate to each other, and real progress was only possible in an atmosphere of mutual understanding and co-operation.

THE TIERED FRAMEWORK

The outcome of the round of bilateral consultations between the Chairman and the countries represented on the Committee during the spring and summer of 1984 made it clear that there would be no early breakthrough towards a single generally accepted method of measuring capital adequacy. In particular, divisions of opinion on a definition of the capital elements to be included in the measure were too great for any acceptable compromise to be quickly reached. On the other hand, there did appear to be a greater potential measure of agreement on a formula for relating capital to the overall business. A clear majority of members, virtually all the European countries, favoured a risk-weighting measure, a concept with which they were familiar in most of their own national systems as well as through the Brussels exercise where it had become the generally preferred approach.

With the aim of overcoming rather deep-rooted different views on the appropriate elements to be included in the capital base for any common measure, a 'tiered approach' instead of a single measure was developed with the objective of providing a common framework into which different countries' systems could be fitted. Under this approach, admitted elements of capital were to be categorised roughly in descending order of quality and different readings of capital adequacy could be derived according to narrower or wider definitions of the capital base. The idea was that this framework would allow all countries to slot into the system and produce illustrative figures which could be read alongside those for other countries. This would allow some comparative readings of national capital adequacy standards to be drawn and a more comprehensive assessment of the relative capital position of banks from different countries to be made.

Table 18.1 Elements of capital in the original tiered frameword (1983)

Tier	*Elements of capital*	*Countries which did not recognise these elements as being within capital in their own accounting or supervisory systems*
1	Issued and fully-paid ordinary shares Non-redeemable preference shares Share premium Retained profit and general reserves	None
2	plus Undisclosed reserves	Belgium, Canada, France, Germany, Italy, Japan, Luxembourg, Sweden, United States
3	plus Asset revaluation reserves	Canada, Germany, Sweden, Switzerland, United, States
4	plus General provisions	Germany
5	plus Subordinated debt (up to a maximum of 50% of items 1 to 4	Germany, Italy, Japan

Note: Subsequent to the development of the original tiered framework, a new tier 'hybrid capital instruments' was introduced between 4 and 5 to accommodate the new capital instruments which were developed in the market during 1984 and after.

Table 18.1 shows how this tiered framework was initially constructed, with each successive tier incorporating an additional category of capital. The table also lists the countries which did not allow particular elements to be included in the capital base in their own accounting or supervisory systems.

The proposed measure thus incorporated five different tiered definitions of capital which could be built up, ranging from the most restrictive (Tier 1) to the most liberal (Tiers 1–5 inclusive). As just mentioned, the original intention was that each successive element of capital should be placed in descending order of quality particularly in relation to its ability to absorb losses in an ongoing business. However, while there was general agreement in the Committee that Tier 1 (ordinary shareholders' funds) was of the highest quality and that Tier 5 (subordinated debt) was of the lowest quality, there was no consensus on the relative merits and importance of other elements.

The initial tests were run with a denominator arrived at through a risk-weighting approach. Under the risk-weighting system five different weighting factors were proposed ranging from 0 per cent for cash to 100 per cent for commercial lending. The basic framework was similar to that which had been used in the Brussels exercise but there were some important differences, as Table 18.2 illustrates. These differences were to become the subject of protracted technical argument.

The most important difference between the Brussels scheme and the evolving Basle framework was in the approach to cross-border exposures. Brussels made a distinction between claims on the public sector and banks of industrialised countries on the one hand, and similar claims on non-industrialised countries on the other. This was justified as a method, albeit crude, of capturing country transfer risk. The approach originally proposed in Basle by contrast, made no country distinctions other than to allocate a low weight to claims on the domestic government. Despite the absence of credit risk in respect of domestic public sector claims, a small (5 per cent) weight was considered justifiable in view of the investment risk on fixed interest securities issued by governments. The early Basle proposals did not ignore the country risk aspect but suggested it should be reflected through memorandum items which would indicate the proportion of a bank's business in the form of claims on non-industrialised countries and allow qualitative judgements on the portfolio overall.

TESTING THE TIERED FRAMEWORK

The Committee began to test this new framework by applying it to a representative sample of international banks from each of the twelve member countries. The purpose of this first test-run was mainly technical;

Table 18.2 Comparative weights for calculating capital ratios in Basle and Brussels (%) (1984–5)

Category of asset	*Weights suggested for Basle framework*	*Weights used in EC observation ratio exercise*
1 Cash and balance at central bank	0	0
2 Claims on domestic government and government agencies' loans, securities and government guaranteed loans (including contingent claims)	5	0 (Zone A) 100 (Zone B)
3 Loans to banks, CDs and other bank-issued securities (including claims and holdings of bank acceptances)	25	20 (Zone A) 100 (Zone B)
4 Continengent claims other than those which substitute for credits (excluding contingent claims on banks and on domestic government)	50	50
5 Commercial lending (domestic and overseas) and credit-substitute contingent items	100	100
6 Cross-border lending to public sector	100	100 (Zone B only)
7 Fixed assets	100	100
8 Other securities, unless deducted from capital	100	100
Memorandum items		
Unguaranteed cross-border claims as a percentage of total balance sheet assets:		
(a) in respect of non-industrialised countries		
(b) in respect of industrialised countries		

Notes: Zone A countries comprised all EC countries, Australia, Austria, Canada, Finland, Iceland, Japan, New Zealand, Norway, Sweden, Switzerland and the United States.

Zone B comprised all other countries.

Categories of asset refer to Basle framework; EC categorisation is not always strictly comparable.

it was to identify problems in obtaining consistent data and to discover any significant gaps in the system of measurement. The testing confirmed the value of the framework in offering insights into the way in which different countries' banking systems relied on the various elements of capital. Five principal areas of difficulty, however, began to emerge. These difficulties, were on the surface, technical issues relating to measurement but they also reflected the increasing awareness of the implications of the exercise for the relative competitive positions of the various national banking systems.

The first issue concerned provisioning against country risk. By the beginning of 1985 wide variations in provisioning policies by banks in different countries was becoming evident. In a number of European countries, notably France, Germany and Switzerland, banks were making substantial provisions against their claims on the major debtor countries, assisted by an accommodating stance on the part of the fiscal authorities; elsewhere much less progress had been made or, indeed, was deemed to be necessary. There are, of course, close links between capital adequacy and provisioning adequacy and, put simply, the argument advanced by some members was that some of their banks' capital had been put into provisioning and was not reflected in the framework of measurement. In the absence of a more consistent pattern of provisioning, some felt that notional adjustments should be made to the capital ratios to take account of the disparities in provisioning. The Committee responded by introducing, alongside the capital calculations, new memorandum items showing provisions made against the fifteen major debtor countries and the outstanding exposure to those countries.

A second issue related to the large hidden values in Japanese banks' balance sheets deriving from their long-term holdings of equity investments in other commercial companies valued at historic cost. The issue here was whether such non-accounted hidden resources, a 'latent' form of revaluation reserve, could be regarded as a legitimate element of capital. The proven capacity of Japanese banks to use these reserves to offset losses argued in favour of their inclusion in the framework, but doubts were expressed about their value and, in particular, about their susceptibility to sharp movements in stock market valuations or forced sale. The Committee eventually concluded that they could, in some way, be included in the framework of measurement, but the precise formula (admitting these reserves only with a discount of 55 per cent on current market values) was only agreed at the final stage of the debate.

A third problem arose following the development, principally in the United Kingdom and the United States, of capital instruments which combined certain characteristics of equity with those of debt. The UK perpetual debt instruments and similarly the US perpetual preferred stock fell into this category but there were similar innovations in other countries. The essential issue was whether such hybrid capital instruments should be included alongside shareholder equity in the framework or alongside subordinated debt. The Committee decided to create a new intermediate tier to incorporate these instruments (see the footnote to Table 18.1).

A fourth and more fundamental area of difficulty derived from the proliferation of a range of new categories of off-balance sheet business, particularly various forms of underwriting commitment (note issuance facilities and revolving underwriting facilities – NIFs and RUFs) and interest and exchange rate related products (options, swaps, futures, and so on). The basic framework of measurement, somewhat simplisticly, had included traditional off-balance sheet engagements with either a 50 or 100 per cent weight, but supervisors generally were concerned that many of the new innovations were not yet captured in their reporting systems and thus were not included in measures of capital adequacy. The Committee therefore established a sub-group to prepare a detailed study of off-balance sheet risk[4] as a basis for developing a set of proposals for capital weightings to be applied across the whole range of different types of off-balance sheet engagement, both traditional and new. The results of this sub-group's work were subsequently incorporated into the capital framework so that this kind of business would be more comprehensively captured.

Finally, the increasing elaboration and complexity of the framework was beginning to hamper clear interpretation and assessment of the results. Originally it had been intended that five ratios should be calculated deriving from the five different tiered definitions of capital, but the addition of an extra tier of capital in the numerator and the introduction (at the request of those countries which had yet to be convinced of the value of the risk-weighted approach) of an alternative series of ratios based on a gearing measure as a denominator, now meant that twelve separate ratios had to be calculated and assessed. Some banks and banking systems might show up well on one measure but badly on another. The problem, therefore, became one of trying to synthesise the results to obtain an overall assessment.

THE BEGINNING OF CONSENSUS

During the course of 1985 the Committee collected a second, more comprehensive set of data on international banks' capital positions as at the end of 1984 and began to work on a further report with recommendations for attaining comparable and adequate minimum international capital standards – the second part of the original mandate from the Governors. An important development considerably assisted this process, namely that the risk-weighting approach, well established in most European member countries of the G10, began to gain greater acceptance in the non-European countries.

The US regulatory authorities, who had flirted with a similar approach many years earlier, were increasingly coming round to the view that competitive pressures in the market were leading to perverse supervisory readings of the real capital adequacy of a bank when using a gearing measure. It provided an incentive to expand off-balance sheet activity, which was not captured in the measure, and to focus on higher risk assets at the expense of low-risk, liquid assets within the balance sheet. At the beginning of 1986, therefore, the US authorities issued proposals for introducing a risk-weighting measure of capital adequacy into their own system and invited comment from their banks. The Canadians, too, were moving to a risk-weighting approach, and around this time the Japanese authorities also issued their proposals for a risk-weighting measure, although this was to be applied only to their banks' international business.

As a consequence of these moves, the Committee's next report to Governors in February 1986 was able to record progress towards a developing consensus in member countries on the technique of measuring capital adequacy. More importantly, it also carried the debate forward from questions merely concerned with measurement to the ultimate goals of the exercise, in that it analysed disparities in the capital position of banks from different countries, noting in particular that many of the world's largest banks in terms of total assets would not be ranked so prominently on the basis of their published capital. Also, using unpublished data supplied by member countries to calculate the series of ratios under the full tiered framework of measurement, it showed that substantial disparities existed in the prevailing levels of capitalisation (relative to risk assets) of international banks, grouped by country. It was clear that capital adequacy standards set, or expected, by the authorities in G10 countries for banks operating internationally varied considerably.

This report focused for the first time on the goal of convergence towards adequate minimum standards. It also recommended that supervisory encouragement of convergence should focus particular attention on the risk-weighted measure and that particular emphasis should be given to the capital position defined restrictively to include only shareholder equity and disclosed reserves in Tier 1. The arguments for this emphasis on Tier 1, presented in the report and accepted by members of the Committee, were that this element of capital was of the highest quality compared with the various other elements of capital; that it was the only element of capital common to all banking systems and recognised as capital by all members of the Committee; and that, unlike other elements, it was an important factor in the determination of profit margins and the ability to compete. It was also felt that this emphasis reinforced the Committee's long-standing concern to see not only the level but also the quality of international banks' capital improved.

This conclusion, and the fact that the Committee as a whole was willing to endorse it, was an important breakthrough. It also involved an approach to assessing capital which contained elements which were foreign to most countries' systems and, in consequence, reflected the willingness of members to contemplate changes to their own systems in the interests of the prize of a greater degree of real convergence.

Finally, the report also struck new ground in offering for the first time, by way of a sighting shot, a tentative figure of what a minimum numerical standard of capital adequacy might be, based on the analysis of the prevailing ratios of the world's better capitalised banks. This helped to maintain the momentum of the exercise and to look forward toward some more ambitious longer-term objectives.

The Fourth International Conference of Banking Supervisors hosted by the central bank of the Netherlands in Amsterdam in October 1986 provided an opportunity to present the fruits of this developing consensus within the Committee to a wider supervisory audience. The conference was attended by supervisors from some eighty countries and capital adequacy was a major theme. A report, presented to the meeting by the Dutch hosts, urged acceptance of the risk asset basis of measurement used in Basle and concentration on increasing the highest quality elements of capital. The recommendations carried in the report received general support from participants. An important reference in the Press communiqué issued at the end of the conference stated that 'it was also the clear sense of the meeting that supervisors should press ahead to secure agreement on comparable minimum standards of capital adequacy for international banks'.

THE US/UK BILATERAL PROPOSALS

During 1986, there was thus a growing measure of agreement among members of the Committee on a basis of measurement and on a rough order of magnitude for an eventual common standard. However, while a model for convergence was beginning to take shape, a clear sense of how to transform theory into practice was still missing. The system of measurement provided a valuable basis for individual supervisors to make comparisons and set their own standards but it remained no more than a confidential observation framework. Some kind of breakthrough at the political rather than the technical level was needed. Brussels, too, had its observation framework which for some years had been pursued on the basis that it carried no formal commitment from member countries to normative ratios in the longer term. Everyone recognised, however, that it was, in reality, a stepping-stone to a legally based system of measurement covering all credit institutions in the Community, which would in due course lead to the adoption of a common standard capital ratio to be met by all such institutions.

The task of the EC Commission in achieving its ultimate objectives was thus more difficult in many ways than that of the Committee in Basle. Basle could only propose (with the agreement of the Governors); it was up to national authorities to dispose, but only if they wished to do so. This suggested that, while maintaining close co-operation between the parallel efforts in Brussels and in Basle, it was perhaps sensible to consider the work in Basle as the first, and perhaps the looser, step forward and that this more broad-brush accord would in fact prove easier to reach than the more definitive package which was the ultimate objective in Brussels. But even if it was less difficult in Basle, it was still far from easy. It required a push, and it was becoming clear that nothing less than a collective commitment on the part of the Central Bank Governors would suffice.

The stimulus, when it came, grew out of a development which was not only unexpected but at first sight appeared, to some at least, to be potentially counter-productive to the multilateral objectives. Throughout the exercise two of its strongest proponents had been the Bank of England and the US Federal Reserve Board. The US Federal Reserve's own proposals for applying a risk-weighted basis of measurement to US banks, issued at the beginning of 1986, had been a critical move in opening the way to convergence in the Committee as a whole, as it contained many of the main elements of the approach followed in Basle. But it also displayed features very similar to the system in the United Kingdom, most importantly in respect of the definition of capital elements. The US authorities were anxious to move forward their proposals in the face of opposition on a number of points from their banks. At the same time, both the United States and the United Kingdom were concerned to build into their domestic systems as quickly as possible some effective means of capturing the new innovative techniques and instruments in financial markets in the capital adequacy regime.

It soon became apparent, in the course of exchanges on these issues between officials from the two countries, that, with a limited number of modifications, the systems in the two countries could be adapted and extended to provide a common test of capital adequacy and a common standard applicable to banks in both countries. At the end of 1986 the two central banks announced publicly their proposals for common regulations with a view to applying a common definition of capital adequacy and system of measurement to their two banking systems, and they issued parallel consultative papers for comment.

In many ways this move provided the breakthrough that the exercise needed. Instead of slow and uncertain convergence through observation of confidential data and private discussion among supervisors, convergence, for these two countries at least, was to be achieved by the public promulgation of near-identical regulations backed by the Governors of the two central banks involved. At the same time, this initiative also carried some risk of upsetting the slowly emerging multilateral consensus. Although the US and UK authorities emphasised that they hoped their proposals would form the basis for a wide multilateral accord, some G10 members were concerned that the two countries concerned, having settled on a formula satisfactory to themselves, would not be prepared to renegotiate it to take account of the position of other countries. For example, it was noted that the definition of primary capital in the US/UK proposals included general loan-loss provisions and perpetual debt capital issues, elements which were important to the banking systems of those countries but were not recognised in all other G10 countries. In a European Community context, there was also concern at the impact of the bilateral proposals on the progress of the work in Brussels.

In the event, however, the outcome of the US/UK initiative was to give a renewed impetus to the work in Basle. All G10 members recognised the overriding value of a multilateral accord to deal with a global problem, the importance of bringing Japan into the centre of the debate (which had up till then mainly been engaged in a European setting or on a North Atlantic axis), and the importance of sustaining the work of the Basle Committee as the focal point for international co-operative efforts in supervisory matters.

MULTILATERAL AGREEMENT

At its first meeting in 1987, the Committee concentrated attention on how it should set about securing an early multilateral agreement and set itself a timetable, later endorsed by the Governors, of achieving this by the end of the year. However, while the US/UK agreement provided a model for international convergence and a spur to achieving agreement within the Committee, in a number of important respects the formula proposed by the UK and US authorities was not one which was likely to be acceptable to other members without several important adjustments, particularly on the definition of capital. Aspects of the measurement system proposed also presented problems to a number of countries in the light of their current arrangements.

The challenge to the Committee was to come up with a formula that would provide an acceptable compromise between the different views of the members. This challenge was all the more difficult since, following the US/UK proposals, the presumption was that the end result would be a common system of measurement and a target standard capable of being implemented through national regulation rather than merely through an observation framework. This shift of focus in Basle towards efforts to find a basis of agreement on a common regulatory structure for capital adequacy incorporated within national systems also brought it rather closer in its approach than previously to the work being undertaken in Brussels by the European Commission; it underlined the need to achieve, as far as possible, mutually compatible results in the two forums. To this end, as the momentum in Basle gathered pace, it was felt that it would be eminently sensible, indeed necessary, that representatives of the European Commission should be kept abreast of the evolving debate in Basle. They were accordingly invited to attend the sessions of the Committee addressing the capital issue as observers and this proved to be helpful to the work in both centres.

At the same time it was recognised that, reflecting the scale of Japanese banks' involvement in international markets, a successful outcome to efforts to secure multilateral agreement also hinged importantly on the full-hearted support of the Japanese authorities for the exercise. Following the publication of their bilateral proposals, the US and UK authorities had clearly signalled the importance they attached to bringing Japan – one of the three major international market-places – into any multilateral scheme. To this end, high-level exchanges took place about the importance of the objectives and acceptance of the goal of convergence. The Japanese authorities had played a constructive role throughout the earlier phase of discussions on the development of a framework of measurement but, like other countries, they were initially, and not unnaturally, somewhat cautious in accepting a commitment to the now more ambitious aim of setting common minimum standards to be achieved through consistent national regulations, not least because it involved significant modification to their existing national system. In the course of 1987, however, the Japanese authorities were able to give their firm backing to the exercise and this made a material contribution to its successful conclusion.

With strong encouragement from the Governors to reach a positive conclusion to what had become, unusually for the Committee, more in the nature of international negotiations than discussions with a view to finding common ground, the Committee held a series of meetings during 1987 with capital convergence as the objective.

Three main elements had to be resolved: the system of measurement, and in particular the weights to be applied to different assets and off-balance sheet obligations; the definition of capital; and the minimum standard of capital adequacy to be recommended for general application.

As far as the first element was concerned, the weights to be applied were generally not too contentious but involved painstaking consideration of a number of detailed features of the framework, notably the off-balance-sheet items. All countries recognised that a certain broad-brush character to the judgements on appropriate relative weightings was essential to achieve an international accord. Also it was acknowledged that the different special features in national markets made it inevitable that some variations at the margin should be permitted, certainly initially, to reflect established national arrangements. Two particular aspects deserve mention, however.

An important difficulty arose over the degree to which the weightings should reflect the different degrees of cross-border risk which were felt to exist between the public sector debt of the stronger and the weaker economies. The debate on this subject ebbed and flowed between those who felt that the appropriate distinction should be between claims on domestic public sector and all cross-border claims, and others who felt that there should be some categorisation, reflected in the weightings, between less risky and more risky cross-border claims. The debate was complicated by the knowledge that, before too long, there was likely to be a Community instrument requiring all EC member countries to treat each other's central government debt in the same way as domestic government debt, thereby creating an EC 'club' in terms of the weighting structure proposed. The consultative document of December 1987 set out the pros and cons of the two arguments but came down on balance in favour of the first course (the domestic/all-foreign split), while recognising that it would have to be reviewed as European legislation progressed. The views of the commercial banks were particularly invited on this matter.

Another aspect of importance was the treatment of the many new innovative off-balance sheet instruments and techniques. It was clear to everyone that any capital adequacy system had to capture these risks in some way. It was also clear that there was very little historic experience on the basis of which to judge the relative risks of different transactions. Furthermore, the weights chosen were to be set, in a fairly complex section of the paper, in relation only to the credit or counterparty risk arising from the transaction. Other kinds of risk, such as interest rate risk and foreign exchange risk, were not captured in this framework. This aspect, it was recognised, was one which needed to be studied and refined further in the future.

The second main element of the framework to be resolved was the definition of the capital base. This was a more contentious area. One particular complication arose from the wide diversity of reaction by banks in G10 countries to the international debt problem, in particular with respect to the provisioning levels they established against claims on the heavily indebted countries. At the beginning of 1987, US, UK and Japanese banks had generally made only very modest provisions against their exposures to the major indebted countries, whereas banks in most continental European countries were holding provisions amounting on average to around 30 per cent of their exposure.

These varied policies were brought closer together, in part at least, during 1987 as a result of the decisions by the major US money centre banks, followed later by the major UK banks, to make substantial, and substantially increased, provisions against these exposures. But imbalances still existed and in a few countries provisioning levels remained very low. Also, the different methods used – particularly the US banks' treatment of their general loan loss reserves as part of capital compared with other countries' creation of specific or earmarked provisions against third world debt *outside* their capital base – raised even more acutely the difficulties of establishing clearly, in all countries on a consistent basis, the appropriate boundary between provisions which could be accepted within the capital base and those which should be excluded, and indeed the appropriate borderline between reserves and general provisions.

Another problem remained, in relation to equality of competition, of how, bearing in mind differences in national approach, the relative real strength of banks could be reflected by taking some account of both their capital and their provisions against a major area of risk. Some countries were minded to exclude all provisions which could not be genuinely demonstrated as being wholly unearmarked against particular assets. Others, particularly in circumstances where banks had made substantial provisions but where capital ratios traditionally were low, favoured an approach that would take account of all provisions in order to arrive at a fair basis of comparison internationally for measures of capital adequacy. In different countries, the fiscal treatment of provisions exercised an important influence. This area is one in which further work will be necessary, as the Committee's final paper makes clear.

There were also other unresolved problems. As referred to earlier, the Japanese authorities, whose banks also tended to hold relatively low capital on the basis of published balance sheets, were concerned to ensure that hidden values on investments in securities which, in their view, were readily available to meet losses, were incorporated into the measure. Several other countries felt that term subordinated debt and revaluation reserves, which were recognised within their own systems, should be accorded some weight within an international measure. On the other hand, the German authorities maintained their long-standing opposition to any widening of the definition of capital beyond pure shareholders' equity, on the grounds that to accept supplementary and, in their view, less reliable forms of capital would lower standards and undermine the main prudential objective of the exercise – to improve the overall level and quality of capital in international banks.

The third element, the minimum standard, also provoked a good deal of discussion with most member countries agreeing that it was necessary to promote a particular ratio as a basis for consultations with national banking systems. One or two members, however, felt that the testing used to arrive at this provisional figure was not soundly enough based to justify its promulgation until after the framework had been fully exposed to and discussed with commercial banks. The figure of 8 per cent was eventually incorporated in the consultative document, although two countries indicated they would not be held to it in their discussions with their banks. 8 per cent was settled upon because there was a broad consensus in member countries that it reflected levels of capital currently maintained by the better capitalised banks and that it was a reasonable target level for all banks to attain in the course of the transitional period to end 1992.

Discussions on the capital base earlier in 1987 had centred around a formula that was somewhat similar to the US/UK approach in that it admitted equity, undisclosed reserves and general loan-loss provisions as a primary element, but allowed other elements (such as revaluation reserves, latent hidden values, perpetual debt, and subordinated debt) to count towards total capital, subject to an overall limit of 50 per cent of the primary elements. This formula found some support among members of the Committee but provoked serious reservations at both extremes of the national positions from others.

Against this background, a new formula was proposed at the June 1987 meeting of the Committee. This formula reverted to an earlier emphasis in the Committee's thinking by recognising shareholders' equity (core capital) as the primary element in the definition of capital but allowed all other admitted elements of capital (supplementary capital) up to a limit of 100 per cent of core capital, with a separate sub-limit within supplementary capital for term subordinated debt of 50 per cent of core capital. Importantly, countries were not required to include within their national definition all the admitted elements; they were free to fill the supplementary capital element from as many or as few of the non-core elements as they wished, or if they preferred, with additional amounts of core capital above the minimum set. So discretion for individual countries to maintain higher quality standards of capital for their banks if they wished was allowed for in the framework.

This basic split of the capital elements, combining purity with pragmatism, received general support from members as a fair compromise between different national positions. The agreement achieved on this, perhaps the most critical component of the framework, was later embodied in the consultative document. After intensive debate at further meetings throughout the autumn, compromises were also found on a number of the other issues where national differences were significant. At the end of a year of hard talking and extended discussions, the report was issued as a consultative document to G10 banking associations in December 1987. The risk weightings proposed in this document are set out in Table 18.3.

Table 18.3 Proposed risk weights in the Basle Committee's Consultative Paper, December 1987

0%	(a)	Cash
	(b)	Balances at, and claims on, domestic central bank
	(c)	Loans to domestic central governments
	(d)	Securities issued by domestic central governments[1]
	(e)	Loans and other assets fully collateralised by cash or domestic central government securities[1] or fully guaranteed by domestic central governments
0 or 20%	(a)	Claims on IBRD and regional development banks (at national discretion) (EEC countries would treat EEC institutions consistently)
20%	(a)	Claims on domestic and foreign banks with an original maturity of under 1 year
	(b)	Claims on domestic banks with an original maturity of 1 year and over and loans guaranteed by domestic banks
	(c)	Claims on foreign central governments in local currency financed by local currency liabilities
	(d)	Cash items in process of collection
0, 20 or 50%	(a)	Claims on the domestic public sector, excluding central government (at national discretion) and loans guaranteed by such institutions
50%	(a)	Loans to owner-occupiers for residential house purchase fully secured by mortgage
100%	(a)	Claims on the private sector
	(b)	Cross-border claims on foreign banks with an original maturity of 1 year and over
	(c)	Claims on foreign central governments (unless 20 per cent – see above)
	(d)	Claims on commercial companies owned by the public sector
	(e)	Premises, plant and equipment and other fixed assets
	(f)	Real estate and other investments (including non-consolidated investment participations in other companies)
	(g)	Capital instruments issued by other banks (unless deducted from capital)
	(h)	All other assets

Note:

1 Some member countries intended to apply weights to securities issued by their domestic central government to take account of investment risk. These weights would, for example, be 10 per cent of all securities, or 10 per cent for those maturing in under one year and 20 per cent for those maturing at one year or over.

CONCLUSION

The consultative period ran until June 1988 and comments were sought and received from banking associations in G10 countries, supervisory authorities outside G10 countries and other interested parties. The response of banks generally was to welcome the purpose and the general form of the convergence proposals and to encourage their application at the national level in a common form to the maximum degree possible. A number of non-G10 supervisory authorities also expressed support for the proposals and indicated their intention to use the framework as the basis for modifications to their existing national systems. Alongside this background of broad support, a number of comments were also received from individual banks and banking associations suggesting possible modifications to the framework. The Committee reviewed all the representations received and after further discussions several amendments which carried general support among supervisors and banks in G10 countries were incorporated into the final report. At the same time, there were a range of comments which the Committee did not find it possible to accommodate, particularly relating to the definition of capital, as to do so would have weakened the emphasis on high-quality core capital or altered the competitive neutrality already embodied in the framework (which would have risked undermining its general acceptability to supervisors and banks in all countries).

The central features of the Committee's report were reaffirmed. The Committee concluded that it did not wish to modify the basic definition of capital in the consultative paper. It also confirmed the minimum ratio of 8 per cent to be achieved by end-1992. Moreover, while the German authorities maintained their view that they would prefer the definition of capital to be confined to core capital alone, all members of the Committee were able to accept the document in its final form.

Some modifications to the framework set out in the discussion document were also agreed, mainly involving the risk weights applied to different categories of asset or contingent liability. The most important change was to reintroduce a very broadly based and somewhat arbitrary distinction between countries to incorporate within the framework some differentiation between different degrees of transfer risk. This distinction was in the view of all the banking associations in G10 countries a necessary feature if the framework as a whole were to have credibility. To reflect this distinction, the Committee agreed to introduce reduced risk weights to central government and certain other categories of obligor in OECD countries.[5] Claims on all other central governments will also bear a nil or low weight, provided that these claims are denominated in local currency and backed by funding in that currency.

Two other material changes were also agreed. In response to representations from the development banks, it was agreed that claims on the five main multilateral development banks (IBRD, IADB, AsDB, AfDB, EIB) should be standardised at a weight of 20 per cent. Also the concessionary weight of 50 per cent for residential house mortgages, agreed at a fairly late stage of discussion on the consultative paper, was extended from loans to owner-occupiers to include loans to certain other parties fully secured by mortgage on residential property, thus including housing available for rent as well as owner occupation. The weightings finally agreed are set out in Table 18.4

The final agreement, which was presented to and endorsed by all G10 Governors, was issued in July 1988. It represented the culmination of more than four years' hard work by all member countries at over thirty or so meetings of the full Committee and of various sub-groups.

The great significance of the final document is that it was unanimously approved, notwithstanding one or two national caveats on the detail of the proposals. Undoubtedly, there are elements of the agreement which can be built upon and the framework improved and refined over time. All G10 countries are now in the process of deciding on the detailed application of the framework within their national systems. At the time of writing, a number of countries outside the G10 have already indicated their intention of adopting the Basle framework in their national arrangements. At the Fifth International Conference of Banking Supervisors held in Tokyo in October 1988, at which some ninety countries participated, the press release agreed at the end of the meeting said:

> The opportunity was taken to review the framework for convergence of international banks capital adequacy measurement and standards . . . Conference participants welcomed the work which had been done by the Basle Committee and acknowledged the agreement to be a significant contribution to the strengthening of the stability of the international banking system and to removing an important source of competitive inequality. The Conference felt it was important that the present agreement should now be put into effect and its implementation observed in practice, although, reflecting the discussion in the Conference, it was recognised that there were several aspects of the framework which might appropriately be reviewed before the end of the transitional period in December 1992. A number of non-G10 representatives indicated that their countries had published or were developing a revised regime for their own banks, based closely on the Basle framework, thus helping to build a standard which could have world-wide application.

To get so far may certainly be considered an achievement, but it may, with some justification, be said that it is no more than is necessary in

Table 18.4 Agreed risk weights in the Basle Committee's Final Report, July 1988

0%	(a)	Cash[1]
	(b)	Claims on central governments and central banks denominated in national currency and funded in that currency
	(c)	Other claims on OECD[2] central governments[3] and central banks
	(d)	Claims collateralised by cash or OECD central-government securities[3] or guaranteed by OECD central governments[4]
0, 10, 20 or 50% (at national discretion)	(a)	Claims on domestic public-sector entities, excluding central government, and loans guaranteed[4] by such entities
20%	(a)	Claims on multilateral development banks (IBRD, IADB, AsDB, AfDB, EIB)[5] and claims guaranteed by, or collateralised by securities issued by such banks[4]
	(b)	Claims on banks incorporated in the OECD and loans guaranteed[4] by OECD incorporated banks
	(c)	Claims on banks incorporated in countries outside the OECD with a residual maturity of up to 1 year and loans with a residual maturity of up to 1 year guaranteed by banks incorporated in countries outside the OECD
	(d)	Claims on non-domestic OECD public-sector entities, excluding central government, and loans guaranteed[4] by such entities
	(e)	Cash items in process of collection
50%	(a)	Loans fully secured by mortgage on residential property that is or will be occupied by the borrower or that is rented
100%	(a)	Claims on the private sector
	(b)	Claims on banks incorporated outside the OECD with a residual maturity of over one year
	(c)	Claims on central governments outside the OECD (unless denominated in national currency and funded in that currency – see above)
	(d)	Claims on commercial companies owned by the public sector
	(e)	Premises, plant and equipment and other fixed assets
	(f)	Real estate and other investments (including non-consolidated investment participations in other
	(g)	companies)
	(h)	All other assets

Notes:

1 Includes (at national discretion) gold bullion held in own vaults or on an allocated basis to the extent backed by bullion liabilities.

2 'OECD' comprises countries which are full members of the OECD or which

have concluded special lending arrangements with the IMF associated with the Fund's General Arrangements to Borrow.

3 Some member countries intend to apply weights to securuties issued by OECD central governments to take account of investment risk. These weights would, for example, be 10 per cent for all securities or 10 per cent for those maturing in up to one year and 20 per cent for those maturing in one year or over.

4 Commercial loans partially guaranteed by these bodies will attract equivalent low weights on that part of the loan which is fully covered. Similarly, loans partially collateralised by cash or securities issued by OECD central governments and multilateral development banks will attract low weights on that part of the loan which is fully covered.

5 Claims on other multilateral development banks in which G10 countries are shareholding members may, at national discretion, also attract a 20 per cent weight.

---

today's global market-place. That so much has been accomplished is a measure of the wish, indeed the perceived best interest, of all the countries involved to arrive at a positive result. In Basle, ultimately, it is only possible to achieve what those involved want to achieve.

The Basle Committee's report, even in its definitive form, is not the final word on this subject. New risks, new judgements on the risks and new forms of business will appear and will need to be addressed. The document itself signals several areas in which further work needs to be undertaken over the next few years. It is, however, a significant step forward in the effective co-ordination of national banking regulatory arrangements, reflecting and responding to the internationalisation of financial markets, and one which hopefully will be built upon in the years ahead.

Notes

1. The Committee comprises representatives of the central banks and supervisory authorities of Belgium, Canada, France, Germany, Italy, Japan, Netherlands, Sweden, Switzerland, United Kingdom, United States and Luxembourg.
2. 'International Convergence of Capital Measurement and Capital Standards', July 1988. Copies of this document are available from the Secretariat of the Basle Supervisory Committee at the Bank for International Settlements, Basle, Switzerland.
3. 'Principles for the supervision of banks' foreign establishments'. This document, originally issued in 1975, was subsequently substantially revised in 1983. Copies are available from the BIS.
4. 'The management of banks' off-balance sheet exposures: a supervisory perspective'. This paper was prepared for commercial banks and was widely circulated early in 1986. Copies are available from the BIS.
5. The categorisation 'OECD countries' comprises countries which are full members of the OECD or which have concluded special lending arrangements with the IMF associated with the Fund's General Arrangements to Borrow.

19 Getting Off the Back of a Tiger: The Deposit Insurance Crisis in the United States

Claudia Campbell and Hyman Minsky

INTRODUCTION

Crises in financial markets and widespread failures of financial institutions are marked characteristics of the 1980s. These phenomena may be more prevalent in the United States than in the other financially important centres. As a result, the seemingly irresistible drive to deregulate the financial services industries that dominated policy in the United States since the 1970s has been replaced by a search for an appropriate structure of intervention and regulation to maintain the orderly functioning of financial institutions and markets.

Rising financial institution failures have caused the near collapse of US federal deposit insurance, a premium-funded insurance programme set up by Congress in 1934 to protect small deposits at bank and thrift institutions.[1] As a result of the crisis, Congress has been forced to intervene to maintain public confidence in this 55-year-old institution, once thought to be the cornerstone of the stability of the US banking system and the economy in the postwar era.[2]

The crisis of deposit insurance is that the funds accumulated from member premiums are insufficient to offset the negative net worth of a rising number of insolvent institutions.[3] The manner in which this crisis is ultimately resolved is likely to affect the mix of institutions and markets engaged in the financing of various segments of the economy, as well as the availability of interest-earning, default-free, liquid assets. In a significant sense the future of mass depository institutions is at stake.[4]

The current breakdown of deposit insurance is not a new phenomenon. State deposit guaranty systems, as far back as the Michigan bank note guaranty system in 1842 and as recent as the Ohio and Maryland state funds in 1986, have succumbed to insolvency. The illiquidity and insolvency of deposit insurers at the federal level, however, add a new, and serious, dimension to the problem, for federal deposit insurance carries the full faith and credit of the federal government. Much depends upon how this guarantee is fulfilled.

The dilemma confronting economic policymakers is how to resolve the deposit insurance crisis without initiating adverse macroeconomic repercussions; that is, how to get off the back of a tiger without being eaten by the tiger. If 'deposit insurance' is allowed to default, which means that the government guarantee is repudiated, a market solution for insolvency and illiquidity will take place. The resulting liquidation of the assets of negative net worth institutions and the flight to quality by depositors are likely to cause a reduction of investment and thus initiate a major recession or even a depression. If the guarantee is honoured, the refinancing of the deposit insurance corporations will expand federal government debt and more than likely lead to a rise in bank reserves. This infusion of debt and high-powered money into the economy will produce a further depreciation of the dollar and may well set the stage for a burst of inflation.

Congress and the current Administration continue to assert the full faith guarantee of insured deposits even as they resist funding either the liquidation or the merger of member institutions with negative net worth. Policymakers seem to be placing their bets on a Micawber solution, in other words that 'something will turn up'. This passive, government response also reflects the credence gained during the Reagan era of the theory that a government that intervenes least, intervenes best. The identification of the problem and the proposed solutions in this chapter rest on a different view, that financially complex economies require interventions to contain endogenous instabilities.

PRIORS AND POLICY

Every analyst and commentator approaches issues of government regulation of financial institutions and the need for intervention in financial markets with priors that reflect views about the fundamental characteristics of capitalist economies with sophisticated and ever-evolving financial structures. These priors may be rational and conscious, which hopefully is the case for economists (although prejudice often intrudes), or emotional and subliminal, which is undoubtedly true of many in politics and the press.

In the United States over recent years economic policy has been overtly dominated by the theoretical tradition of Adam Smith. This tradition holds that if each worker, consumer, businessman or financier follows his own self-interest he is guided, as if by an invisible hand, to advance the good of society. In the language of modern economics this becomes the proposition that 'A competitive equilibrium is a Pareto optimum'.

As a result of this dominance, government regulation of finance is often approached from the Smithian perspective, even though the invisible hand proposition has never been shown to be valid for financially complex economies. Only under very restrictive conditions, which are at great variance with what is true of the real world, has the existence of a competitive equilibrium been proven. Moreover, neither the uniqueness nor the stability of a competitive equilibrium has been demonstrated.[5] Economic theory offers no support for non-interventionist policy regimes and unregulated finance in systems as complex as the modern economy.

It is not unusual, however, for policy arguments to be advanced which assumed that decentralised and unregulated markets in a complex, financially sophisticated economy produce a stable and optimal growth trajectory.[6] With such priors, if the economy exhibits an unstable growth trajectory, the blame for the deviation is imputed to the system of regulation and intervention which, in a strict Smithian view, is always mischievous.

OUR PRIORS

Our priors are not Smithian; they are post-Keynesian. In post-Keynesian theory the endogenously determined processes of capitalist economies become incoherent as a result of their own dynamics. Post-Keynesian theory is consistent with the well-established, mathematical proposition that complex non-linear systems are likely to exhibit incoherence from time to time.[7] By imposing constraints, reasonably coherent behaviour can be generated out of non-linear systems whose internal dynamics lead to a breakdown of the system.[8] Analytically, constraints can be interpreted as interventions that stop the endogenous dynamics and start them up again with 'new' initial conditions. Deposit insurance is just such an intervention that can be interpreted as thwarting the endogenous thrusts to incoherence.

In general, economic regulation and intervention can lead to reasonably coherent behaviour for an economy which, if left alone, would degenerate into incoherence.[9] By aborting or containing incoherence, apt regulation can be constructive.

But apt regulation to prevent or contain incoherence needs to be designed. It cannot rest upon mere mathematical knowledge about the characteristics of complex non-linear equation systems nor upon historical data about episodes of economic instability and crisis. Apt intervention depends upon knowledge; that is, a theory combined with a command of the 'facts' of what makes a particular economy at a particular time susceptible to episodes of incoherence. This requires a model of how finance, production and household behaviour relate and interact.

The Financial Instability Hypothesis version of post-Keynesian theory is just such a model. Profit-seeking agents who finance holdings of capital assets, invest in real resources and manage money are essential actors in the economy. They are also the catalysts who transform a stable growth trajectory into one that is likely to explode or collapse. In post-Keynesian theory, normal developments in capitalist economies include crises and business cycles as well as the transformation of initially robust financial structures into fragile structures, such as has occurred in the past forty years.

The Financial Instability Hypothesis also explains why regulatory structures eventually become obsolete or perverse. The normal profit-seeking activities of agents lead to innovation in order to create new sources of profits; innovations can be in products, processes or finance. The search for profits also drives agents to avoid, evade and adapt to the structure of regulation and intervention put in place to constrain incoherence. In time this undermines the effectiveness of a regime of intervention that 'stabilises the unstable system'. Therefore, if regulation is to remain effective, it must be reassessed frequently and made consistent with evolving market and financial structures.[10]

Because of its explicit consideration of how the financial structure of an economy becomes hospitable to instability, the post-Keynesian perspective throws light on the current problems of deposit insurance in the United States. These problems are the result of competition for profits that has transformed an initially robust financial structure into a fragile system and in so doing made obsolete the structure of deposit insurance established fifty years ago. In particular, as the financial system evolved, payouts from deposit insurance reserves have become systemic and frequent rather than isolated and intermittent. When one institutional insolvency breeds multiple offspring, insurance reserves that would be adequate for individual insolvencies are quickly exhausted.[11]

THE TRANSFORMATION OF FINANCE

To summarise our priors, apt regulations and intervention can contain the intermittent thrusts to incoherence inherent in the normal functioning of decentralised markets in financially sophisticated economies. Any regulatory structure imposed on such an economy, however, will eventually break down and become ineffective as agents learn how to evade, avoid and adapt to regulation and intervention. What is an apt structure at one time is likely to become inept at a later date.

Any regulatory structure imposes out-of-pocket costs, forgone opportunities and rigidities upon organisations that operate in a dynamic, evolutionary and innovative economy. All too often regulations become frozen in stone and vested interests grow up that benefit from, and therefore seek to perpetuate, the existing regulatory regime. Furthermore, regulators and interveners are often taken over by the regulated, which makes change and adaptation difficult.

Eventually markets are either ill-served by regulation or prices in the market become such that it pays to evade or avoid the regulation. By creating new institutions and novel instruments, profit-seeking agents exploit the opportunities offered by price differentials. Because of the universal validity of the proposition that there is nothing new under the sun, the novel feature is often the return of previously outlawed practices under new guises.[12] A good example is the survival of state banking in the United States in the face of the monopoly of currency issue granted to the National Banks during the Civil War.[13]

THE MAKING OF BANK RUNS

The image of runs was set in the 1930s. As in the popular film, *It's A Wonderful Life*, depositors in imperfect queues clamoured to exchange their deposits for currency. Such runs, and the fear of runs, forced the sale of assets for cash (in what banking jargon calls 'the making of position by the sale of position') and led to banks hoarding cash. The underlying cause of runs is losses on assets; the emergence of non-performing assets. As making position by selling assets lowers the price of assets, a cascade of unrealised paper losses takes place. These paper losses spread the 'run' from bank to bank.

Bank hoarding of cash means that loans are cut back or restricted. This leads primarily to a decline in bank financing of investment and, sometimes, of consumption. The decline in bank-financed spending causes a decline in profits and wages. With aggregate profits down, an increment of borrowers cannot fulfil their payment commitments; non-performing assets increase. Thus runs spread, and unless intervention aborts the process, a collapse of the system becomes imminent.

The Financial Instability Hypothesis and runs

The Financial Instability Hypothesis explains bank runs. When there is reason to believe that the cash flows to a bank or other deposit institution will fall short of what is needed to fulfil responsibilities and induce depositors to roll-over maturing instruments, runs occur.

For a modern financial economy to operate well, cash flows from production must validate prior debt commitments. In a layered system, an intermediary remains viable if the cash flows from financial assets are sufficient to validate liabilities. This cash flow from 'contract' fulfilment may be supplemented by negotiating the sale or the pledging of assets. A break in the chain of cash flows initiates a financing crisis.

Systemic bank runs create such breakdowns. The rapid withdrawal of deposits forces banks to try to get cash by selling assets on the market. Such forced sales reduce asset prices, making it harder for initially unaffected institutions to meet payment commitments to depositors. As a result, market values of portfolios of institutions holding the same types of assets decline even as their 'book values' remain unchanged. If the need to sell assets to make position is not contained by lender-of-last-resort refinancing, then runs lead to a decline of bank intermediation. Banks stop lending and hoard cash.[14]

Systemic bank runs or any type of collapse or suspension of cash flows will force central bank intervention to avert a crisis. This is an important implication of the Financial Instability Hypothesis. Federal deposit insurance, by preventing the losses to covered deposits, has acted as a non-discretionary lender-of-last-resort. However, deposit insurance makes the insured institution dependent on the government's guarantee.[15] Net worth can be eroded and become negative, making the institution insolvent, without inducing runs as long as depositors are confident that they are protected by insurance.[16]

Modern runs, in a regime of deposit insurance, do not take the form of queues of depositors clamouring for currency; modern runs involve a refinancing crisis initiated by uninsured depositors.[17] The collapse of the Continental Illinois Bank in 1984 was brought about when banks throughout the world withdrew their multi-million dollar, uninsured deposits. The deposits at Continental Illinois were the 'reserve' deposits for eurodollar banking. The Federal Reserve refinanced Continental Illinois to contain the run of these deposits.[18]

The second phase of the Continental Illinois intervention took place when the Federal Deposit Insurance Corporation purchased the assets that Continental Bank had pledge for loans from the Federal Reserve Banks and infused sufficient cash in the bank to validate all deposits, both insured and uninsured. In this process, the deposit insurance guarantee was extended beyond the Congressionally mandated limit of $100 000. This expansion of insurance coverage took place without any concomitant increase in premiums or provision of additional funds to the insuring agencies. The use of accumulated reserves to protect other than the well-defined, contractually limited, insured deposits set a precedent that is a major factor in the 1987 crisis in deposit insurance.[19]

The emergence of insolvency without runs

The sharp and protracted rise in interest rates in the late 1970s and early 1980s had an adverse effect on the net worth of thrift and other deposit institutions. In as much as the rise in interest rates reflected a shift in government policy, the use of deposit insurance reserves to contain and offset this development may well have been unwarranted.[20] In particular, the mutual savings banks and the savings and loan associations were locked into assets that reflected long-standing government policies. With changes in these policies, the thrift institutions were unable to adjust rapidly enough to avoid a serious erosion of their equity.

Net fund income in thrift institutions

The income of financial intermediaries is derived from managing a fund and receiving fees for services. Fund income arises from the excess of earnings on assets over the costs of liabilities. The costs of liabilities consist of interest paid and services supplied to depositors, either free or at a fee that is well below the cost of supplying the services. An example of such services is the 'free' chequing accounts that banks offered depositors in the era of deposit rate ceilings and zero interest demand deposits.

Fee income consists of service charges of various kinds including, in American practices, various fees that are assessed when mortgages are originated. As there has been an active secondary market in mortgages since the Second World War, financial intermediaries need not hold the mortgages they originate. Some fee income arises from sales of mortgages in the secondary markets. The originating institution often collects additional fees for servicing the mortgages they sell.[21]

On entering the high interest rate period, income-earning assets of the savings and loan associations and the mutual savings banks in the United States consisted mainly of long-term fixed interest, fully amortized mortgages with initial terms to maturity between 20 and 30 years. Therefore net fund income of these mortgage-holding institutions was sensitive to fluctuations in the cost of liabilities, that is, the interest paid on ordinary deposits as well as on retail (small denomination) and wholesale (large denomination of $100 000 or more) certificates of deposit.

A decline in net fund income can sharply erode the equity base of the institution. For example, if the pattern of interest rates and other costs leads to a negative fund income that is 1 per cent of assets, then a thrift with 6 per cent equity can lose 16 per cent of its equity in one year even though it possesses a sophisticated ability to manage assets.

Thus the viability of the savings and loan associations and the mutual savings banks depended upon maintaining a stable, low interest rate environment or guaranteeing low financing costs. This was accomplished for most of the postwar period by imposing interest rate ceilings on various insured liabilities and a monetary policy regime that sustained low and slowly changing interest rates.

Competition from money market funds

Money market funds started in the early 1970s and became quite large in the late 1970s as interest rates rose. Money market funds were able to pay significantly higher rates than the deposit institutions. The result was funding problems and disintermediation at mortgage-holding institutions.

Modest changes in regulations in the 1970s enabled the thrifts to respond better to the outflow of deposits into money market mutual funds when rates rose, even as this raised their deposit costs. However, no legislation was passed until 1980 and 1982 to ease the asset restrictions that prevented thrift institutions from diversifying and shortening their asset maturities.[22] While deposits became more interest-sensitive, the income-earning assets of the thrifts remained predominantly in the form of long-term, fixed-rate mortgages.

The Volcker fight against inflation, which de-emphasised interest rate stability and substantially increased deposit costs, would have had only minor negative effects on the net fund income of thrift institutions and the reserves of the deposit insuring agency if thrift institution portfolios had consisted mainly of floating-rate mortgages. For floating-rate mortgages to be the rule in 1979, however, the shift from fixed-rate mortgages would have had to begin in 1969 or so! As it was, the equity of the thrifts was significantly eroded by the extended period of high funding rates that occurred after 1979.

The role of deposit insurance in deposit institution failures

The Smithian interpretation holds that manager incompetence, regulation and exploitation of deposit insurance are to be blamed for the rising rate of deposit institution insolvencies.[23] In this view deposit insurance creates conditions under which managers will increase risk exposure. This higher risk implies higher expected insolvency rates and the depletion of deposit insurance fund balances. To remain actuarially sound, the deposit insurers must raise premiums. The remedy that has been proposed is some form of co-insurance or risk-related insurance premiums.

Throughout the postwar era deposit insurance confronted cases of fraud or gross incompetence. Indeed, this was what it was set up to do. But deposit insurance, no matter how its premiums or payoffs are structured, is viable only when fraud or incompetence is at issue; deposit insurance is unable to cover bankruptcies brought about by policy regimes that include fixed-rate long-term mortgages, market term funding, and protracted periods of high and variable market rates in which net fund income remains negative.

If periods of rising and quickly changing interest rates, such as ruled after 1979, are to be consistent with the payment of market rates to depositors and a free flow of mortgage funds, then the long-term, fixed-rate, fully-amortized mortgage has to be abandoned. In truth, that is what happened in the early 1980s. Floating-rate and short-term mortgages, which require refinancing after four or five years, came into widespread use. The substitution of floating-rate for fixed-rate mortgages in the portfolios of institutions that specialise in mortgage financing is necessary for them to remain viable in an unprotected environment.

THE RESCUE OF THE THRIFT INSTITUTIONS AND THE FSLIC

The emergence of systemic thrift institution insolvency that occurred after 1979 was not costless even though runs were avoided. The thrift institution failures depleted the reserves and threatened the solvency of the Federal Savings and Loan Insurance Corporation (FSLIC). The problem confronting the deposit insuring agencies and the Congress in 1987 was not the prevention of a deposit insurance panic; this had been accomplished by federal deposit insurance. At issue was who would bear the cost of the containment of this crisis and whether this cost could be minimised?

Three major pieces of bank legislation – the Deposit Institutions Deregulation and Monetary Control Act of 1980 (DIDMCA), the Garn-St. Germain Depository Institutions Act of 1982 (Garn-St. Germain), and the Competitive Equality Banking Act of 1987 (CEBA) – attempted to address the plight of the thrifts and the FSLIC.

The DIDMCA eliminated deposit rate ceilings by 1986 and allowed savings and loan associations to issue interest-paying chequable deposits, expand consumer loans, issue credit cards and offer trust services.[24] But these reforms were not enough to halt the erosion of the equity of the mortgage-holding institutions. By 1982 many were insolvent on a mark-to-market (present value) basis, even as their equity, as conventionally measured by historic asset values, was diminishing.

In 1981 the FSLIC insurance fund used for resolving thrift failures was being quickly depleted, threatening the public's confidence in thrift institutions.[25] In March of 1982, Congress passed a Joint Resolution asserting that the full faith and credit of the US government stood behind federal deposit insurance liabilities.[26] Much of what has transpired since then can be interpreted as efforts by Congress to avoid fully funding this Joint Resolution.

Garn-St. Germain, passed in October of 1982, was directed at both saving the thrift industry and speeding up the deregulation of the deposit institutions.[27] The act gave federal insurers greater discretion in resolving institution failures. The FSLIC was permitted to arrange both interstate mergers of thrifts and acquisitions by non-financial corporations of insolvent thrifts. Furthermore, in order to enhance the net worth of failing institutions, the FSLIC was allowed to exchange promissory notes for 'net worth' certificates issued by the thrifts. These certificates were treated as capital on the books of thrift institutions, even though they were no more than an accounting gimmick which inflated the net worth of the thrifts. At the same time, markets and instruments previously restricted to banks were opened up to thrifts. Specifically, thrift institutions could invest up to 55 per cent of their assets in certain types of commercial loans.[28] Many of the thrifts lacked the experience and the staff to operate profitably in these markets.

Garn-St. Germain gave the FSLIC greater scope to avoid liquidating thrifts with negative net worth. However, keeping equity-impaired institutions operating encouraged 'go for broke' strategies by managers and owners.[29] Gerald Hanwick argues that very risky investments with high expected returns, if successful, may have been the only chance for problem thrifts teetering on the edge of insolvency or already insolvent, to become viable again.[30] In thrifts with negative net worth and in reconstructed thrifts, which were created by large infusions of FSLIC equity, owners and managers had virtually nothing to lose and a lot to gain from adopting high risk investment strategies. Such strategies had large potential payoffs if all went well, even though the expected return was negative. Deposit insurers had an incentive to condone the risky strategies of the thrifts, for success would obviate the need to expend insurance funds. When these risky 'bets' paid off as 'expected', a further deterioration of the net worth of the deposit institutions occurred, which increased the unfunded liability of the FSLIC.

Congress, like the thrifts and the deposit insurers, gambled. Its members bet that interest rates would come down and revive the thrifts, so that there would be no need to fund the full faith and credit guarantee of insured deposits as promised in the 1982 Joint Resolution. Congress has lost this gamble. When inflation and nominal interest rates did decline between 1982 and 1984, systemic declines in oil, farmland and real estate prices and incomes in regions dependent upon oil and agriculture took place. This led to widespread loan defaults. As a result, the cash flows that supported the payment commitments of many deposit institutions were devastated. Thrift institution losses because of interest rate movements were augmented by an explosion of non-performing assets. Many thrifts that survived the assault on their net worth by interest rate volatility succumbed when loan defaults exploded.

The combination of negative fund income (owing to interest rate volatility) and non-performing assets took its toll on the US savings and loan associations. By 1986, 347 out of 540 savings and loan associations that reported losses were insolvent.[31] In 1987, 10 per cent of the thrifts were insolvent and one-third experienced losses. Deflation in oil prices and real estate subjected regional thrifts to greater losses. Sixty per cent of the failed institutions were in Texas.[32]

By early 1987, the FSLIC was unable to fund either a payoff of depositors or purchase and assumption packages for insolvent thrifts.[33] With the assets of the FSLIC depleted, the 1982 Congressional Joint Resolution guaranteeing insured deposits was the only thing that prevented a massive run by thrift industry depositors and a major financial crisis. In August of 1987, after much higgling and haggling over dollar amounts, Congress passed a modest plan to rescue the FSLIC. With the Competitive Equality Banking Act of 1987 (CEBA), Congress attempted to shore up public confidence in the deposit institutions. Title IX of this package confirmed the full faith and credit guarantee of 'all insured deposits'.

The Competitive Equality Banking Act of 1987

As the third legislative intervention to protect the thrift institutions in the 1980s, the CEBA was a response to the inability of the FSLIC to fulfil its insurance obligation. In Title III of CEBA, Congress created the Financing Corporation whose purpose is to finance deposit insurance operations of the FSLIC.[34]

The structure of financing in this act is complex. The Federal Home Loan Bank Board is to invest funds in the Financing Corporation. These funds will purchase zero-coupon, long-term, Treasury securities. Upon maturity these securities will finance the repayment of principal on $10.8 billion in debt securities that the Financing Corporation is to sell to the public. The proceeds of the $10.8 billion sale of bonds are to be transferred to the FSLIC, which will use the funds to either liquidate and pay off or to merge failed firms. Interest on the Financing Corporation liabilities is to be paid from assessments on surviving insured thrifts.[35]

While the Treasury securities assure the principal, the bill provides no government guarantee of the interest payments on the Financing Corporation bonds. This means that bondholders face a possible default on interest payments by the Financing Corporation. This default risk will be reflected in the interest rates on the bonds.[36] It is likely that concerns about the rising budget deficit and the desire to provide a 'market' solution led to the refinancing method chosen by Congress for the rescue package. But it also reflects the evasion by Congress of its full faith and credit responsibility.

In Title III of the CEBA Congress evaded the responsibility it accepted in Title IX. The Congress is obligated under Title IX of CEBA to fund insured deposit payoffs if the FSLIC is unable to do so. Instead, the costs of keeping the FSLIC in business are being forced upon both insolvent and profitable thrifts at a time when they must compete directly with other financial institutions for assets and liabilities.

The CEBA placed a one-year moratorium on the right of institutions to withdraw from the FSLIC. In addition, when institutions do withdraw they must pay an exit tax. But profitable thrifts will have an incentive to build up their equity so they can leave the FSLIC and buy insurance from the financially more robust FDIC. If this happens, the interest obligation of the Financing Corporation will increasingly be borne by the less viable thrifts who remain in the FSLIC. If assessments are increased to make up for lost members, the competitive position of remaining thrifts will continue to be weakened. The funding base for the bonds of the Financing Corporation is likely to be eroded.

The Congressional rescue package forces the FSLIC to resolve institution failures with insufficient reserves. As a result, FSLIC decisions will continue to be weighted heavily by short-run cost considerations, which tends to make financing the purchase and assumption of failed institutions cheaper than liquidating institutions and paying off insured depositors. Consequently, many of the problem and reconstructed institutions, safe under the FSLIC umbrella, will continue to take excessive risks in attempts to survive. The negative expected value of this risk exposure will increase the unfunded liability of the FSLIC. In the long run, the costs to the US Treasury will be higher and the damage to the thrift industry greater than if Congress had promptly accepted its full faith and credit responsibility and provided the funds necessary to liquidate insolvent thrifts.

CONCLUSION

Federal deposit insurance always carried an implicit commitment of 'the full faith and credit' of the government that insured deposits will not depreciate in their nominal value. In the 1987 partial refunding of the Federal Savings and Loan Insurance Corporation this guarantee was made explicit. However, neither the Congress nor the Administration has supplied the funds to offset the negative net worth of depository institutions: they wish to avoid the larger deficit and the addition to overt government debt required to finance either closing failed thrifts or making them financially viable. The opportunistic legislation that has been passed offers only transitory relief. The shortage of funding prevents the deposit insurers from taking actions necessary for a long-solution.

Had the thrifts been free of asset restrictions, interest rate ceilings, and deposit insurance protection, perhaps they would have been less vulnerable to interest rate fluctuations or to the systemic declines in oil, real estate and farm prices. However, the history of unregulated and uninsured banks and thrifts does not confirm this conjecture; epidemics of financial institution failures during unregulated eras are well documented.[37]

The fundamental lesson from experience is that neither deposit institutions nor the deposit insuring agencies can weather system-wide and contagious losses. Moreover, intervention, such as deposit insurance, is effective only if it reflects the understanding that systemic failures are normal outcomes of dynamic, financially complex economies. The effects of systemic failure on the economy can be minimised by providing default-free assets. Deposit insurance converts assets of small net worth households that would have been subject to default risk into default-free assets. By protecting small depositors against fraud and poor management, the insurance of deposits has its place as a regularisation of one facet of central bank responsibility.

The appropriate response of deposit insurers to both idiosyncratic and systemic failures is to liquidate failed organisations and pay off insured depositors. However, premium-funded deposit insurance reserves cannot act as a substitute for lender-of-last-resort interventions nor can they insulate deposit institutions from major shifts in government policy. In an economy where systemic instability occurs, the viability of deposit insurance is always contingent upon the full faith and credit obligation of the state. Full faith and credit responsibility means that, if necessary, deposit insurance payouts will be funded by general revenues.

In a post-Keynesian perspective the gains from deposit insurance and other interventions are the greater stability and growth of the economy. Post-Keynesian theory imputes the greater overall success of the economy in the forty years since the Second World War, as compared with other similar periods in our economic history, to the impact of big government and regulation in stabilising the economy. Because the benefits of financial stabilisation are generalised, the use of general revenues to fund the contingent government liability of deposit insurance is justified.[38]

So, how does the economy get off the back of a tiger without being eaten by the tiger? The answer is 'with knowledge, understanding, and care'.

Notes

1. In the United States, there are different legal entities that insure deposits nationwide: the Federal Deposit Insurance Corporation (FDIC) insures deposits in banks and the Federal Savings and Loan Insurance Corporation (FSLIC) insures deposits in thrift institutions. The immediate crisis in 1987 that required federal government refinancing is in the FSLIC. An FDIC crisis has not yet emerged. We will use the term 'deposit insurance' when discussing theory. The specific evidence will be drawn from the separate agencies.

2. Milton Friedman and Anna J. Schwartz, in *A Monetary History of the United States 1867–1960* (Princeton: Princeton University Press, 1963) state:

> As we have seen in earlier chapters, banking panics have occurred only during severe contractions and have greatly intensified such contractions, if indeed they have not been the primary factor converting what would otherwise have been mild contractions into severe ones. That is why we regard federal deposit insurance as so important a change in our banking structure and as contributing so greatly to monetary stability – in practice far more than the establishment of the Federal Reserve System. (pp. 440–41)

3. The deposit insurance corporations can resolve deposit institution insolvency in several ways:

    1. They can close the failed institution and pay off insured depositors. With the proceeds that are left from the liquidation of the assets of the institution, insurance reserves are reimbursed, and uninsured depositors and other creditors are partially paid off.
    2. They can help arrange a merger with a viable institution. Mergers often require financial assistance from the deposit insurer to offset the failed institution's negative net worth.
    3. When no buyers can be found and the payoff of depositors cannot be financed, the deposit insurer may take over the failed institution and install new management in an effort to revive it.

4. Although the international stock market crash of 19–20 October 1987 did not directly and immediately have an impact upon the institutions with insured deposits, it did adversely affect the fortunes of market-oriented intermediaries, the investment banking firms and the organisations, such as mutual funds, whose assets are mainly market instruments.
5. See Kenneth Arrow and Frank H. Hahn, *General Competitive Analysis* (San Francisco: Holden-Day, Inc., 1971); and Bruno Ingrai and Giorgio Israel, 'General economic equilibrium theory: a history of ineffectual paradigmatic shifts', *Fundamenta Scientiae*, vol. 6, no. 1, pp. 1–45, and vol. 6, no. 2, pp. 89–125 (1985).
6. The most sophisticated of such arguments comes from Rational Expectations theory. See Robert E. Lucas, Jr, 'Expectations and the neutrality of money', *Journal of Economic Theory*, 4, April 1972, pp. 103–24, reprinted in Robert E. Lucas Jr, *Studies in Business Cycle Theory* (Cambridge, Mass: MIT Press, 1981).
7. Coherence refers to the variables in a system being connected logically or naturally, as by a common principle. General economic equilibrium is an extreme form of coherence. For a mathematical development of the concept of coherence, see Richard L. Day, 'Irregular growth cycles', *American Economic Review*, 1982. Also see Arrow and Hahn, *General Competitive Analysis*, chapter 12.
8. J. M. Blatt, 'On the econometric approach to business-cycle analysis', *Oxford Economic Papers*, 1978.
9. See Hyman P. Minsky, 'Monetary systems and accelerator models', *American Economic Review*, December 1957, pp. 859–83.
10. Hyman P. Minsky, *Stabilizing an Unstable Economy* (New Haven: Yale University Press, 1986), and Paul Davidson, *Money and the Real World* (New York: Wiley, 1972), are two statements of post-Keynesian theory that emphasise monetary relations.

11. See Claudia Campbell and Hyman P. Minsky, 'How to get off the back of a tiger or, Do initial conditions constrain deposit insurance reform?', *Conference on Bank Structure and competition: Proceedings* (Federal Reserve Bank of Chicago, 1987) pp. 253–67.
12. As Henry Simons noted:

> Banking is a pervasive phenomenon, not something to be dealt with merely by legislation directed at what we call banks. The experience with the control of note issue is likely to be repeated in the future: many expedients for controlling similar practices may prove ineffective and disappointing because of the reappearance of prohibited practices in new and unprohibited forms. It seems impossible to predict what forms the evasion might take or to see how particular prohibitions might be made more than nominally effective.

Henry Simons, 'Rules versus authorities in monetary policy', *Journal of Political Economy*, 1936, reprinted in Henry Simons, *Economic Policy for a Free Society* (Chicago: University of Chicago Press, 1948) p. 172.

13. The development of money market funds in response to the rising interest rates of the 1970s shows the pervasiveness of banking, discussed by Simons in 'Rules versus authorities', for money market funds are nothing more than banks with limited service functions.
14. For example, the collapse of stock prices on 19–20 October 1987 was accompanied by a decline in bank lending to block traders. *Wall Street Journal*, 20 November 1987, p. 1.
15. Deposit insurance has been a substitute for deposit institution capital. This was noted by Peltzman in 1970 and is obvious in 1988. See Sam Peltzman, 'Capital investment in commercial banking and its relationship to portfolio regulation', *Journal of Political Economy*, 78, January/February 1970.
16. As an example, the 'lifeline letter' from the Federal Home Loan Bank Board is all that is preventing a cutoff of funds from Wall Street lenders to the insolvent Financial Corporation of America, the largest thrift institution in the United States whose net worth is currently negative. See David B. Hilder, 'Financial Corp. is anxious over Bank Board', *Wall Street Journal*, 29 January 1988.
17. Revell argues for the insurance of all deposits, including interbank deposits, where the goal of deposit insurance is to reduce risk in the financial system. See Jack Revell, *Solvency and Regulation of banks: Theoretical and Practical Implications* (University of Wales Press, 1975) p. 109.
18. According to Irvine H. Sprague, who was Chairman of the FDIC at the time, another reason for refinancing Continental Illinois was concern for the liquidity of over 2000, and the solvency of between 50 and 100, correspondent banks with deposits in Continental Illinois. Irvine H. Sprague, *Bailout: An Insider's Account of Bank Failures and Rescues* (New York: Basic Books, Inc., 1986) p. 155.
19. In the Franklin National case of 1974–5, the bankrupt bank was kept alive by the Federal Reserve Bank of New York until almost all its large denominated certificates of deposit were run off. When it was finally declared insolvent, Franklin National's funding consisted of insured deposits and loans from the Federal Reserve Bank. It may have been a mistake not to have made the Fed take losses on its loans to Franklin National.
20. Revell argues that because monetary policy and prudential regulation are not independent, these functions should be consolidated under one agency, preferably the central bank. This would force the central bank to consider

the effects of changes in monetary policy on the liquidity and solvency of banks. See Revell, *Solvency and Regulation of Banks*, p. 127.

21. Securitisation of mortgages by savings and loan institutions has enhanced their fee income.
22. Koehn finds that asset restrictions severely affect the profitability of thrift institutions. See Michael F. Koehn, *Bankruptcy Risk in Financial Depository Intermediaries* (Lexington, Mass: D.C. Heath and Co., 1979).
23. See, for example, Edward J. Kane, *The Gathering Crisis in Federal Deposit Insurance* (Cambridge, Mass: MIT Press, 1985); and George J. Benston and George G. Kaufman, 'Risk insolvency regulation of depository institutions: past policies and current options', *Staff Memorandum* (Federal Reserve Bank of Chicago, 1988).
24. Kerry Cooper and Donald R. Fraser, *Banking Deregulation and the New Competition in Financial Services* (Cambridge, Mass: Ballinger Publishing Co., 1986) p. 116.
25. Ibid, p. 160.
26. Edward J. Kane, 'No room for weak links in the chain of deposit insurance reform', *Journal of Financial Services Research*, 1, 1987, pp. 77–111.
27. Cooper and Fraser, *Banking Deregulation*, p. 127.
28. Other changes included an increase in consumer lending limits from 20 to 30 per cent of assets and permission to invest in state and local government revenue bonds. Cooper and Fraser, ibid.
29. See Kane, 'No room for weak links'.
30. Gerald A. Hanwick, 'A model of S&L failure and "go-for-broke" management behaviour' (unpublished manuscript: George Mason University, September 1987).
31. Anna J. Schwartz, 'The lender-of-last-resort and the Federal safety net', *Journal of Financial Services Research*, 1, 1987, pp. 1–17.
32. Bill Kester, 'S&L problem is far from being solved', *St. Louis Post Dispatch*, 9 December 1987.
33. According to Kester, ibid, the FSLIC needs an estimated $25–$45 billion to liquidate properly or merge insolvent thrift institutions. In 1987, the resources of the FSLIC were a negative $6 billion.
34. The name of the Financing Corporation recalls the Reconstruction Finance Corporation which helped to refinance failed banks, factories and farmers during the Depression era.
35. There are some similarities between this package and the proposal to resolve the Mexican Debt crisis. The Mexican government plans to issue $10 billion of marketable bonds, which will be exchanged for the existing $15–$20 billion of Mexican debt to US banks. The principal on the Mexican bonds will be collateralised by a purchase of $2 billion in zero-coupon US Treasury bonds payable in 20 years. However, the interest payments on the new Mexican bonds will depend upon 'the full faith and credit' of the Mexican government. See Jeffrey Sachs, 'Mexico plan a model for other debtors', *Wall Street Journal*, 19 January 1988, p. 30.
36. Citing a statement by the Shadow Financial Regulatory Committee concerning the refinancing of the FSLIC through the Financing Corporation, Lindley Clark emphasises this point, 'The Treasury could sell such bonds and at a lower interest cost [than the Financing Corporation] – $100 million a year lower'. Lindley H. Clark, 'Financial rules: the shadow seeks answers', *Wall Street Journal*, 25 November 1987, p. 14.
37. C. P. Kindleberger, *Mania, Panics and Crashes: A History of Financial Crisis* (New York: Basic Books, 1978).

38. See Douglas W. Diamond and Philip H. Dybvig, 'Bank runs, deposit insurance and liquidity', *Journal of Political Economy*, 3, 1983, pp. 401–19 for a discussion of deposit insurance as a public good.

20 Deregulation in Banking: Lessons from the Italian Case

Marco Onado

INTRODUCTION

All financial systems currently exhibit an urgent need to redefine their overall framework. Some years ago the prevailing climate of opinion and the attitudes of politicians seemed to favour a general deregulation, but now this line is apparently supported only by those directly operating in the financial and industrial sectors, and by no means necessarily a majority of these.

The preoccupation recently expressed by almost all central banks, and for many years by eminent scholars (Revell, 1978), with the growing potential instability of financial systems associated with the process of innovation and transformation of financial systems has shown results. What is now demanded is a so-called re-regulation or, to use a more elegant expression, a genuine reform of structures and institutions.

This is the first time that all the leading countries, despite their differing situations, have simultaneously reached the point where reform of their credit institutions is necessary. If it is not the first time, it happened previously only during serious international crises, the main example being that of the 1930s.

Since the financial integration of various countries has increased during recent years – and appears likely to increase still further in the near future – the various lines of reform cannot be pursued independently of one another. It is growing more and more difficult for a single country to adopt an institutional and legislative framework completely different from that of other countries. That which took place in the 1970s cannot be repeated. During the decade of the 1970s some banking systems underwent modifications aimed at increasing competition, but these were not co-ordinated with other regulatory systems. In other systems, Italy for example, the prevailing aim was to preserve rigidly the existing framework.

Discussion of the topic in Italy has been reflected in the enquiries carried out by the Commissione Finanze e Tesoro of the Chamber of Deputies. A substantial unanimity seems to obtain as to the need to intervene. The core of the discussion turns on the *general* and *special* criteria for such intervention. The differences of opinion on these points cannot be regarded as being of merely secondary importance; indeed, they are essential to the continuing debate. The following analysis will focus generally on Italian experience.

GENERAL CRITERIA

From the general debate over the evolution of the banking and financial systems and their framework, five general criteria can be singled out. These criteria should guide the corresponding process of reform in Italy, and they may be summarised as follows:

(A) *Regulation and supervision of intermediaries should be applied over a broader area.*

This criterion represents a *leitmotiv* in the revision of norms already carried out in leading countries and expected in further countries over the next few years. It rests on two basic hypotheses:

1. The barrier between banking and non-banking activities has been eroding everywhere. In the field of traditional banking, deposits and loans are increasingly substitutable with other intermediaries' liabilities and assets. Thus the principle – that of alleged 'uniqueness' – by which banks alone were subject to normative controls and supervision no longer holds in its original 'strong form'.
2. The growth of share portfolios held by families has dissolved the distinction between conscious and unconscious saving. It has also cast doubt on the need for a twofold control regime under which the role of safeguarding (or 'functional regulation') is applied mainly to the second form of saving, with more rigorous controls envisaged for the respective intermediaries.

For years this distinction between conscious and unconscious saving existed alongside a clear separation between forms of supervision belonging to the first type of saving (controls of transparency based on the principle of *caveat emptor*) and those belonging to the second type (more rigorous and thorough supervision).

As long as the flow of savings to intermediaries on the one hand, and to the market on the other, derived from different sources, the distinction remained a plausible one. Nevertheless, one might wonder how many conscious savers in the nineteenth and first half of the twentieth century, whose savings were eroded by financial crises and devaluations, were actually capable of evaluating risk in advance? Today, however, each saver's portfolio contains both deposits and shares (private shares or government bonds) held directly or indirectly through investment institutions. Also, among shares held directly by individuals there is a continual increase in the proportion managed by banks and other operators under trust agreements.

Thus the distinction, regarding the respective form of supervision, between primary securities and secondary securities also weakens. Control cannot be carried out exclusively based on the general distinction between savings or on the abstract features of financial activities. It must involve the entire range of financial intermediation and accord with a principle that represented an inspired intuition on the part of the authors of the 1936 banking legislation in Italy and which accounts for the long life of that law.

The 1936 law was comprehensive in scope. It covered all three areas of intermediation available at that time: banks, long-term institutions and the financial market. Here we find genuine foresight, not just regulation of something already in existence. Recent years have witnessed the growth of areas of intermediation only partly covered by regulation. To adjust what has come into being since 1936 would mean a return to the spirit in which the law was originally promulgated – and that law has proved its overall validity and vitality over fifty years of application. Of course, this would not involve purely and simply 'putting the clock back', but, rather, a complex process of reform that would have to take account of the far-reaching changes of the last few years and the new requirements of operators.

(B) *Preservation of rigorous barriers (also based on specialisation) between the various categories of intermediary is becoming more and more difficult, and contrasts with the opportunities offered by innovation in the field of finance.*

On the one hand, this innovation is breaking down the traditional barriers between the various categories of intermediary. On the other hand, greater competition leads each intermediary to modify (normally to expand) the range of products offered. The problem is becoming an especially urgent one for the banks as they are everywhere undergoing intense disintermediation.

Far from constituting a protection for intermediaries, the specialisation norms may lead to unfair competition by favouring uncontrolled intermediaries. As we shall see shortly, the result is not total despecialisation, but there certainly does occur a weakening in the rigid barriers that survived the changes in recent years.

Banks, in particular, or at least certain categories of banks, may be adversely affected if these strict barriers are retained.

(C) *The area to be supervised must be extended in such a way as to guarantee neutrality of regulation of the various categories of intermediary when the same activities are performed. This means 'levelling off the playing field' or, in other words, allowing the various operators to work under equal competitive conditions.*

As we have seen, financial innovation tends to erode the lines of demarcation between historical segments of the system. If, therefore, we see fit to extend the area of supervision, we must also safeguard neutrality in the rules of the game, giving all participants competitive equality. Once again, the guiding criterion for supervision must be the essential feature of the financial activity performed, and not the abstract structure of the intermediary.

How should supervision be conducted? It must be emphasised that in the field of banking, as with other intermediaries, where structural controls based on discretional authorisation once prevailed, there has been a gradual shift toward prudential controls to be applied to all operators. As segmentation has faded and the nature of the risks banks may incur have altered, so the need to strengthen these prudential controls makes itself felt.

(D) *Within the micro-organisational structure of intermediaries it must be recognised that the increasing integration between the various forms of intermediation is leading to the establishment of finance groups.*

These are taking on a central role in all countries. They are either based on the expansion of shareholdings in the various financial fields, as in the establishment of financial conglomerates in Great Britain and banking-financing groups in Italy, or on operating and organising agreements, as in the case of the *archipels* in France.

New problems of regulation have emerged from the growth of these groups. Supervision has become necessary on a consolidated basis and the question of 'separateness' between bank and company appears in a new light. Lastly, it is necessary to specify the areas of competence and the forms of coordination among the various supervisory authorities.

(E) *The problems to be tackled come together in the equilibrium between traditional supervision based on the institutions involved, and supervision based on the type of activity undertaken.*

Traditional control divides the various intermediaries into types. On the one hand there are those sanctioned by law for a specific function and thus endowed with a sort of monopolistic power. On the other hand, the same kind of activity may be performed by intermediaries regulated in a different fashion, or even by intermediaries of whom some are regulated while others are not. In both cases this has negative repercussions on standards of fair competition.

Regulatory norms must therefore be devised that bear on activities themselves, independently of the body undertaking these activities. This is the general criterion to follow in integrating control over intermediation and share dealing. For example, in the United Kingdom the Financial Services Act 1986 regulates all activities constituting investment business, which may be undertaken only by authorised operators.

SOME SUGGESTIONS FOR POSSIBLE LINES ON INTERVENTION

In the debate on the evolution of the system, and the framework of banking and finance, there would seem to be two essential points on which views differ. The first concerns whether or not to retain the principle of specialisation; the second concerns the regulation and supervision of non-bank intermediaries.

In our opinion, no evaluation at this point can neglect analysis of the experience of other countries (Pepe, 1986; Gualandri, 1987; Onado, 1987).

Specialisation

Specialisation – as a cardinal principle rather than a deliberate choice and mode of operation – can be defended on two grounds, namely:

1. the validity and relevance of the economic goals of specialisation in 1936;
2. the control of risks and, thus, the safeguarding of the stability and efficiency of the system, operated by separating credit into short-, medium- and long-term.

As far as point 1 is concerned we can hardly avoid taking into account the changes that have come about in the economic sphere during the last fifty years, and especially since the 1970s. In the view of several experts and scholars in this field, the main reason for introducing specialisation no longer exists: we refer to the employment of medium- and long-term as substitutes or surrogates for real capital (on all aspects of this, see Arcuti, 1987). The 1980s have witnessed the abandonment in Italy of the 'financial road to development', based on the association of long-term credit institutions with credit subsidies; this is concurrent with the new ability on the part of enterprises to finance themselves, and the use of direct financing through the stock market.

Inflation, as well as changes in the actual situation of enterprises and thus in their financial requirements, has largely undermined the reasons for separating credit into short- and medium/long-term as required by the banking law of 1936 (Sarcinelli, 1987; Onado, 1987).

In Italy, as elsewhere, there has been a growing similarity between the activities of banks and those of special institutions. It has, however, been shown (Onado, 1987) that in Italy the competition between these two categories is less marked than in other countries. During the same period the French banking system, first with the Debré reform (1966–7) and then with the 1984 banking law, has moved progressively towards despecialisation and broadening the range of activities in all maturity (short, medium and long-term) bands. In Italy, on the other hand, the boundary between the activities of the two categories of intermediary is still as promulgated in 1963, in compliance with the law of 1936.

The argument in favour of specialisation is substantially founded on the reduction of financial risks: a result of the equilibrating of credit terms and loan characteristics, and the need to maintain an arm's-length relationship between banks and industry. The 1936 law aimed 'to avoid the recurrence, within the same institution, of undifferentiated management of commercial credit and personal credit, which was typical of the big Italian banks prior to the reform' (Ciampi, 1987); this was in order to prevent a return of the unstable situation of the 1920s and 1930s. Specialisation thus finds its *raison d'être* in its ability to protect the stability of the system of intermediaries, and especially to safeguard the 'separateness' of banks and industry.

The model put forward by Governor Ciampi does not hinder intermediaries from extending their activities, but it favours the group model (where each institution devotes itself to a specific segment of intermediation) rather than despecialisation pure and simple. From this point of view the difference would appear to be one of form rather than substance regarding the operational possibilities available to intermediaries. As far as supervision is concerned, the proposed design rests on the hypothesis that it is easier to operate prudential control, particularly control of capital adequacy, through separate intermediaries, even though they may belong to the same economic unit, rather than through an all-purpose intermediary.

It should be noted, however, that this principle can only be adopted under two conditions. Firstly, effective control must be guaranteed on the basis of consolidated supervision; it should be recalled that in countries other than Italy the 'right of inspection' is applied also to units, or firms, controlled by the single bank. Secondly, the supervision must be the same where both non-bank intermediaries are owned by a holding company and where a holding company (even a foreign one) also controls a bank.

The kind of banking that may emerge from a policy where the specialisation norms are relaxed does not necessarily lead to the universal bank, let alone the mixed bank. It is also not true that the universal bank represents a necessary outcome in the evolution of those norms analysed within this essay.

There are many reasons to suppose that even when the barriers between institutions have been relaxed and equal competitive opportunity between the various operators established, operational differences will remain. Barriers between intermediaries must be gradually eliminated in order to enable each operator to choose the mix of products desired as most suitable, but not to license everyone to have a finger in every pie. Elimination of the barriers between intermediaries must also be accompanied by regulations in support of greater vigilance. The imposition of prudential standards, diversified according to the riskiness of the various activities, does not run counter to the goal of offering equal competitive opportunities to all. In other words, to offer an ever wider range of financial products is not a mere right with no counter right to offset it, but rather a privilege carrying its own burdens and responsibilities.

The aim is therefore to do away with disparities of treatment deriving from the traditional forms of structural supervision that cannot outlast the process of innovation. At the same time, the goal cannot be to leave the process of redefining of financial structures simply to take its own course.

As far as the separation between bank and industry is concerned, specialisation appears no longer to be either necessary or sufficient. The objective should thus be to strengthen prudential controls (beginning with those relating to the concentration of risks) and any other measures that guarantee the autonomy of the banking subject.

Much more dangerous would seem to be an attitude that simply evades the problem since the very structure of banking groups may 'lead down the inclined plane to the mixed bank without one's noticing what is happening' (Sarcinelli, 1987).

THE STRUCTURE OF CONTROLS

The system of regulating financial intermediaries can be synthesized in a double-entry table, that can be defined as the 'control matrix'. The columns would be occupied by the various kinds of intermediaries: banks, non-bank credit intermediaries and market operators. The last category is subdivided (Costi, 1987) into intermediary producers of indirect securities, such as funds, and intermediaries concerned with the placing of and dealing in shares.

On the horizontal lines (or rows) can be placed the various types of control, divided into the two main categories: supervision of correct dealing and transparency, and prudential controls classified according to degree of intervention, namely requirements in terms of capitalisation, fractioning of risks, composition of assets and liabilities and so on.

All those involved in the discussion of banking law hold the first category to be necessary: the controls concerning correct dealing and transparency would aim to guarantee the efficient functioning of the financial market.

At this point, discussion of the control matrix turns on whether or not one considers the regulation of transparency to be sufficient *vis-à-vis* a series of operators whose importance, for social purposes and purposes of monetary regulation, is not such as to require the introduction of prudential controls.

Majority opinion, however, considers that 'fair play regulation' is not sufficient for any type of intermediary. The justification for having intermediaries subject solely to fair play regulation derives from the conviction that extending controls is expensive in terms of diminished competition and efficiency. Against that, the growing importance of non-bank intermediaries, the increasing importance of direct forms of financing and thus of markets, and the blurring of the distinction between conscious and unconscious saving, for reasons noted above, makes it doubtful that fair play regulation is capable alone of dealing with risks inherent in the evolution of the financial system.

It is not by chance that the British system, traditionally based on fair play regulation, shifted (with the Financial Services Act) towards extending prudential controls to cover non-bank intermediaries in general; and this even though the specific regulations will have to take into account the type of activity performed. In any case, the application of financial resource rules to all operators in the financial market would appear to be one of the essential points of the reform.

As and when it is decided to extend controls, however, it will be essential to avoid repeating the mistake of separate regulation by types. The Italian experience during the second half of the 1970s has clearly demonstrated how difficult it is to bring order into the new financial system by prohibiting the creation of securities unless these have been subjected to legislative separation into types (Costi, 1987). This procedure, while straitjacketing the process of innovation, risks offering no effective protection of savings by way of exchange, since financial innovation always proceeds faster than the controls aimed at regulating it.

In accepting a formulation that extends controls to all intermediaries, a basic minimum of prudential control for all operators emerges. To this must be added further controls graduated according to the various types of risk borne by intermediaries.

In support of this scheme, it should be kept in mind that the activity of regulated and unregulated intermediaries – in the context of a continual processing of financial instruments and a blurring of the lines of demarcation between segments – leads to unfair competition at a time when the two types of intermediary undertake identical activities. Secondly, there is the fact that as the range of intermediaries in direct competition with banks broadens, so the area of the system susceptible to control by banking regulations tends to shrink. In countries such as France and the United Kingdom, prudential controls have been extended to cover non-bank intermediaries.

On the other hand, controls must be graduated according to the risk inherent in the type of activity undertaken. It would be ineffective merely to extend the norms concerning the banking sector in a generalised and indiscriminate fashion to the entire system. It should therefore be possible to devise prudential controls for leasing and factoring companies, taking into account the variations in mean maturing terms of assets as against liabilities (Bianchi, 1987), and for management of trust accounts, merchant banks, and so on.

To sum up, there are several problems to be tackled, but this debate has helped to identify the various points of view and the respective ways of dealing with the problems in the context of institutions and techniques. The question is how to translate these solutions into law. In a sense it is necessary to return to 'the principles of 1936' as regards the internal consistency with which that reform was launched.

References

Arcuti, L. (1987) 'Indagine conoscitiva sull'evoluzione del sistema e dell'ordinamento bancario e finanziario', *Camera dei Deputati*, Rome.

Bianchi, T. (1987) 'Disciplina diffusa con un unico organismo di sorveglianza', *Parabancaria*, no. 1.

Ciampi, C. A. (1987) 'Indagine conoscitiva sull'evoluzione del sistema e dell'ordinamento bancario e finanziario', *Camera dei Deputati*, Rome.

Commissione Fracanzani (1987) *Commissione di studio per l'Aggiornamento dell'Ordinamento Creditizio e per la Disciplina degli Intermediari Finanziari Non Bancari*, Ministero del Tesoro, Rome.

Costi, R. (1987) 'Nuova finanza richiede un giusto ordine', *Parabancaria*, no. 1.

Fazio, A. (1986) *Controllo dell'Attivitá Bancaria e dell'Intermediazione Finanziaria*, Relazione alla Commissione Fracanzani, 23 settembre.

Forestieri, G. (1987) 'Stabilità, efficienza e un efficace governo della moneta', *Parabancaria*, no. 1.

Gualandri, E. (1987) *Sistemi Finanziari e Normative di Vigilanza: Gran Bretagna, Francia e Italia*, Giuffrè, Milan Onado, M. (1987) 'Laissez-faire? No, grazie', Micromega.

Pepe, R. (1986) *Riflessioni e Confronti in Tema di Separatezza*, Banca d'Italia Temi di Discussione n. 76, ottobre.

Piga, F. (1987) 'Indagine conoscitiva sull'evoluzione del sistema e dell'ordinamento bancario e finanziario', *Camera dei Deputati*, Rome.

Revell, J. (1978) *Competition and Regulation of Banks*, Bangor Occasional Papers in Economics, Bangor, University of Wales Press.

Sarcinelli, M. (1987) 'Indagine conoscitiva sull'evoluzione del sistema e dell'ordinamento bancario e finanziario', *Camera dei Deputati*, Rome.

21 Prudential Regulation of Large Loans in the Italian Banking System

Francesco Cesarini

INTRODUCTION

The control of large loan exposures is a field of prudential regulation in which Italian banks are subject to rules far more permissive than those usually applied in other industrial countries. In this chapter we shall analyse the structure and rationale of the regulations in force, with a view to measuring how they match the standards set out in the EEC Recommendation of 22 December 1986, to which Italian regulators are expected to comply within a relatively short period of time.[1] We shall also examine extensively the several sets of available data on large loan exposures in order to get an idea of the dimensions of the concentration problem and of its intrinsic riskiness. Finally we shall suggest some of the interim steps that the banking authorities may take in order to restore the effectiveness of the controls on large exposures in forms that are consistent both with the EEC principles and with their changing attitude in operating prudential regulation.

EVALUATION OF RULES ON LARGE LOANS

In the Italian experience, the basic limit on the size of a loan to an individual borrower was established at one-fifth of the bank's gross capital funds (that is a definition of capital resources which includes loan loss reserves integrally) by the banking legislation of 1926, which also stated that loans for higher amounts may be granted provided that the bank has obtained a prior authorisation from the regulatory authorities on a case-by-case basis. Such limits and procedures remained in force for almost fifty years until, in 1973, their revision was prompted by the desire of the regulatory authorities to cut down drastically the growing number of requests for authorisation they had to handle as a consequence of the general reduction in the importance of capital funds relative to total funds administered by banks.

The new rules allowed each bank to grant individual loans in excess of the old basic limit of one-fifth of capital funds, but not larger than the total gross capital funds of the bank itself ('excess' loans), provided that their aggregate amount was not higher than 25 per cent of total customer deposits. Subsequently, in 1976, as a part of a general revision of rules aimed at inducing banks to achieve higher capital ratios, the ceiling on aggregate 'excess' loans was lifted to different levels, proportional to the capital adequacy of each bank, up to a maximum of 40 per cent of customer deposits for those banks which could exhibit a ratio of capital funds to customer deposits of at least 8 per cent. The need for authorisation was therefore restricted to loans of an amount higher than the bank's total capital funds, which thus became the relevant large exposure for regulatory purposes, and to loans in excess of one-fifth of capital funds when their extension would bring the bank beyond its ceiling on aggregate 'excess' loans.

Through this modification of policy regulatory authorities aimed at divesting themselves of most of the administrative burden and of the implicit responsibility of directly authorising the breaching of the principle of risk spreading. And in fact authorisations went down drastically in number, although they by no means entirely disappeared: in 1978, for instance, 2308 authorisations were still granted to 425 banks.[2] As Table 21.1 shows, their number declined still further in the period 1982–7. Most of the authorisations are presently requested by branches of foreign banks and by unlimited liability Raiffeisen co-operative banks: the former must respect a specifically designed individual loan limit fixed at three-fifths of their gross capital funds without being subject to an aggregate ceiling; the latter have the maximum amount of individual loans decided each year by the general meeting of members.

Table 21.1 Authorisations of loans in excess of the legal limit granted by Italian regulatory authorities 1982–7 (number of authorisations)

Category of banks	*1982*	*1983*	*1984*	*1985*	*1986*	*1987*
Branches of foreign banks	805	1029	1013	982	1123	868
Raiffeisen co-operative banks	693	507	316	172	201	162
Other banks	416	384	413	250	199	209
Total	1914	1920	1742	1404	1523	1239

Sources: Banca d'Italia, *Relazione annuale 1984*, p. 250; Banca d'Italia, *Relazione annuale 1987*, p. 288.

It is apparent that the authorisation procedure, in its present form, tends to become progressively less meaningful as an instrument for the control of large exposures. As a matter of fact, the recent increase in capital ratios of the various categories of banks largely above the parameters adopted in 1976 (see Table 21.2) has had the effect of reducing the need for a prior authorisation in two important respects: the higher the amount of gross capital funds of the bank, the larger is the maximum size of the individual loans it may make autonomously; at the same time, the higher the ratio of gross capital funds to customer deposits, the larger will be the aggregate ceiling on 'excess' loans that the bank must respect. As far as this latter point is concerned, in December 1980 48 banks out of 342 were allowed an overall ceiling on 'excess' loans barely equal to the minimum level of 25 per cent of customer deposits.[3] At the end of 1986 only a handful of banks were in that situation, whereas for the great majority (over 60 per cent) of the banks the aggregate ceiling was set at the 40 per cent level. Not surprisingly, only very few banks had sought and obtained an authorisation to exceed their ceiling.

It must be emphasised at this point that the present situation is radically different from that prevailing in the 1970s: the regulations on large loan exposures are *de facto* applied to a relatively small number of loan requests and, in addition, they have the paradoxical effect of legally permitting a degree of loan concentration which seems thoroughly inconsistent with sound banking practice.

To clarify this point, it is sufficient to point out that a hypothetical bank having a capital funds to customer deposits ratio of 10 per cent and a loan to deposit ratio of 50 per cent – that is, ratios similar to the average values for the entire credit system – would be able to concentrate almost all of its lending capacity on only four individual loans, each of the maximum allowed amount, without violating any formal rule established by the authorities and even without the obligation of asking for their prior

Table 21.2 Average ratio of capital funds to customer deposits (percentage) by groups of banks 1982–6

	1982	*1983*	*1984*	*1985*	*1986*
Larger banks	7.33	9.14	9.59	10.41	11.71
Smaller banks	8.51	10.50	10.86	11.37	12.55
Co-operative banks	10.95	13.11	14.00	13.95	14.27
Savings banks	5.41	6.87	7.73	8.61	9.47
Banking system	7.51	9.30	9.94	10.61	11.60

Source: Banca d'Italia, *Relazione anno 1986*, Appendix, p. 216.

authorisation. In fact, its limit on individual large exposures would be 10 and its ceiling on 'excess' loans would be exactly equal to 40 per cent of customer deposits.

The opinion that the regulations in force are extremely liberal is supported also by the fact that for the computation of the aggregate ceiling only the cash portion of outstanding 'excess' loans is considered. In addition, existing rules refer only to the loan exposure of *individual* borrowers, without taking account of the fact that they may belong to a given industrial or financial group. Consequently they do not efficiently prevent an excessive concentration of credit risk.

The actual degree of loan concentration which Italian banks show on their accounts is obviously significantly lower than the limits theoretically permitted by the regulations in force. On the wider dimensions of the phenomenon there exist several pieces of published information which it is worthwhile reviewing.

STATISTICAL EVIDENCE

According to Banca d'Italia's statistics, at the end of 1988 cash loans of an amount in excess of one-fifth of capital funds were on the books of 239 banks out of the 350 units (excluding foreign banks and Raiffeisen co-operative banks) which form the Italian banking system. In the case of 119 banks the aggregate amount of such 'excess' loans was less than 5 per cent of customer deposits, and for an additional group of 60 banks they comprised between 5 and 10 per cent of customer deposits. On the other hand, there were also 15 banks for which the ratio was over the 25 per cent level.[4]

In Table 21.3 we have gathered and analysed the available data on the aggregate size and on the distribution of 'excess' loans with reference to the end of 1982 and of 1986, and to the major categories of banks.

The absolute size of 'excess' loans, that is of loans exceeding each bank's limit of one-fifth of gross capital funds, is reported in lines (B) in terms of overall cash and non-cash exposures and in lines (C) with reference only to the cash portions of the exposures themselves. It is immediately noticeable that if the notion of large exposure is constructed in such a way as to include all forms of non-cash credit (such as loan commitments, loan guarantees, contingent liabilities, off-balance sheet obligations, and so on), the figures involved would be almost twice those reflecting cash loans alone. This is a clear indication of the difficulties that Italian banks will be facing in complying with the EEC Recommendation, which adopts an extensive definition of large exposure.

The fact that in the period 1982–6 aggregate 'excess' loans have remained fairly stable in absolute terms (26 074 billion lire in 1982 and

Table 21.3 Loans in excess of one-fifth of the banks' capital funds by category of banks as of year-end 1982 and 1986 (billion lire)

	Public law banks	*Banks of national interest*	*Joint stock banks*	*Co-operative banks*	*Savings banks*	*Total*
1982						
(A) Number of borrowers	61	56	1208	749	1071	3145
(B) Aggregate 'excess' cash and non-cash exposure	13769	17186	11801	3683	12192	57912
(C) Aggregate 'excess' cash loans	5777	5557	4491	1901	8348	26074
(D) Cash loans extended to all borrowers	27139	21914	40377	18895	28654	136980
(E) Average amount of 'excess' cash loans (C/A)	94.70	99.20	3.70	2.50	7.80	8.30
(F) = C/D (%)	21.28	25.36	11.12	10.06	29.13	19.03
1986						
(A) Number of borrowers	44	21	664	413	505	1647
(B) Aggregate 'excess' cash and non-cash exposure	13768	11245	8979	2987	14785	51764
(C) Aggregate 'excess' cash loans	6551	4346	5203	1633	10494	28227
(D) Cash loans extended to all borrowers	51241	37376	68298	41201	64941	263057
(E) Average amount of 'excess' cash loans (C/A)	148.90	206.90	7.80	3.90	20.80	17.10
(F) = C/D (%)	12.78	11.63	7.61	3.96	16.16	10.73

Source: *Bollettino della Banca d'Italia – Vigilanza sulle Aziende di Credito*, no. 83, p. 242, and no. 99, p. 160.

28 227 billion in 1986) may be explained by the already mentioned sustained growth of the parameters adopted for their definition, which also caused the sharp decline, from 3145 to 1647, in the number of borrowers involved. Borrowers to whom 'excess' loans are booked are heavily concentrated in three categories of banks of relatively smaller size. Savings banks, in particular, seem to show a propensity to grant 'excess' loans, since in 1986 they accounted for about 30 per cent of the number of borrowers and for 38 per cent of the aggregate cash exposure in monetary terms, with a significant increase over 1982.

The figures for the largest banks of the system (public law banks and banks of national interest), on the other hand, indicate that they extend credit beyond their basic limit in a relatively small and decreasing number of cases, and that the average size of their 'excess' loans is several times larger than for the other categories of banks.

By comparing the aggregate amount of 'excess' cash loans with the total amount of outstanding cash loans, we can obtain fairly precise information on the quantitative importance of the phenomenon, on its distribution among banks and on its trend in recent years.

Line (F) of Table 21.3 shows that for the entire banking system 'excess' loans represented 10.73 per cent of total outstanding cash loans at the end of 1986. Although significantly reduced in respect of the level reached at the end of 1982 (19.03 per cent), the concentration of bank loans, as measured by this particular standard, is a phenomenon of great importance for the Italian banking system. Surprisingly enough, in both years the ratio of 'excess' loans to total loans at savings banks is much higher than either the average for the entire system or the correspondent ratio for the largest banks. Public law banks and banks of national interest, in fact, have greatly reduced the relative importance of their 'excess' cash loans, and their ratios at the end of 1986 were only 1 or 2 points above the average.[5] The lowest figure (3.96 per cent) is to be found in the case of co-operative banks, which seem to have obtained a better control of their large exposures as a by-product of their traditional ability in obtaining capital funds in large amounts from their shareholders.[6]

Among the several factors which explain the significant decline of the ratio for the entire system between 1982 and 1986, mention should be made of the administrative ceilings imposed on bank lending by the monetary authorities, which have compelled banks, especially the larger ones, to reorientate their lending policy to the advantage of small and medium size borrowers, and of the extremely abundant amount of funds raised by large listed companies and financial groups on the stock market during the period 1984–6. More generally, in recent years large companies have become more careful in the management of their financial position. They have diversified their sources of funds and have shown, on the whole, a lesser degree of dependence on bank lending.

The information provided in Table 21.3 is based on the definition of large exposure currently adopted for regulatory purposes and illustrates the position of the banking system in respect of the rules in force.

An entirely different approach to the investigation of the large exposure problem is followed in Table 21.4, which focuses on the relative importance of cash loans granted by each individual bank to its first twenty largest borrowers (irrespective of whether or not they exceed the basic limit of one-fifth of the bank's capital funds) and is based on a sample with reference to both institutional categories of banks, thus making with preference to both institutional categories of banks, thus making comparisons possible with the data shown in Table 21.3, and to size groups as defined in official statistics published by Banca d'Italia.

The table indicates that at the end of June 1987 the entire sample of 59 banks had extended loans to their twenty most important individual borrowers that totalled 14.19 per cent of their total cash loans outstanding at the same date. The most numerous group, formed by thirty-one banks and including the majority of joint stock and of co-operative banks, belongs to the 10–15 per cent class, while the second largest group (fifteen banks) falls in the immediately higher class.

An analysis by institutional groupings indicates that the average ratio for savings banks (16.27 per cent) is 2 points higher than the average for the entire sample, with a majority of them showing a ratio of 15 per cent or higher. Such evidence seems to support our preceding analysis which indicates that this category of banks tends to concentrate its loan portfolio on a relatively small number of borrowers of large size.

According to the figures set forth in the lower part of Table 21.4, the size of the lending bank does not appear to be an important factor in explaining the concentration of loans to the first twenty most important individual borrowers. There is, however, some slight evidence of an inverse correlation between the two variables: the average ratio for very large banks (13.79 per cent) is, in fact, 0.40 points lower than the average for the entire sample, while the group of small banks has the highest average ratio. It is also important to point out that the ratio shows rather wide variances among the banks within the sample: from an absolute minimum of 5.84 per cent (at a large joint stock bank) to a maximum of 32.22 per cent (at a public law bank of a medium-classified size). This may indicate that loan concentration tends to depend on bank management choices as to the level of risk to be taken rather than on the specific institutional framing of the activity or on the size of the bank as such.

Table 21.5 shows data of the same type and format with reference to loans extended not only to the twenty largest *individual* borrowers (as in Table 21.4) but also to companies and entities with which they are connected from a juridical and economic point of view. The interest for this sort of analysis lies in the fact that it can contribute to clarifying another

Table 21.4 Classification of a sample of 59 Italian banks with reference to the relative importance of outstanding cash loans to the 20 most important individual customers by size of loan as of 30 June 1987

By category of banks Cash loans to the first 20 customers as percentage of total cash loans of the bank	*Public law banks*	*Banks of national interest*	*Joint stock banks*	*Co-operative banks*	*Savings banks*	*Total*
5–9.99	1	1	4	1	–	7
10–14.99	3	1	13	7	7	31
15–19.99	1	1	2	3	8	15
20–24.99	–	–	1	–	4	5
over 25	1	–	–	–	–	1
Total	6	3	20	11	19	59
High	(32.22)	(16.15)	(21.94)	(18.14)	(21.60)	(32.22)
Low	(9.96)	(9.95)	(5.84)	(8.16)	(10.11)	(5.84)
Average	(15.70)	(13.49)	(12.68)	(12.72)	(16.27)	(14.19)

By size of banks	*Very large*	*Large*	*Medium*	*Small*	*Total*
5–9.99	1	3	1	2	7
10–14.99	5	3	9	14	31
15–19.99	3	1	3	8	15
20–24.99	–	–	2	3	5
over 25	–	–	1	–	1
Total	9	7	16	27	59
High	(18.14)	(19.52)	(32.22)	(21.94)	(32.22)
Low	(9.95)	(5.84)	(8.92)	(8.16)	(5.84)
Average	(13.79)	(11.49)	(14.03)	(14.35)	(14.19)

Source: Elaboration of data from *Bancaria*, no. 10, October 1987.

Table 21.5 Classification of a sample of 59 Italian banks with reference to the relative importance of outstanding cash loans to the 20 most important customers (including their affiliates) by size of loan as of 30 June 1987

By category of banks

Cash loans to the first 20 customers (including affiliates) as percentage of total cash loans of the bank	*Public law banks*	*Banks of national interest*	*Joint stock banks*	*Co-operative banks*	*Savings banks*	*Total*
5–9.99	–	–	1	1	–	2
10–14.99	2	–	7	3	5	17
15–19.99	3	2	6	5	5	21
20–24.99	–	1	5	2	7	15
25–29.99	–	–	–	–	2	2
over 30	1	–	1	–	–	2
Total	6	3	20	11	19	59
High	(33.86)	(20.80)	(33.38)	(23.60)	(26.04)	(33.86)
Low	(14.06)	(16.29)	(9.04)	(8.16)	(10.44)	(8.16)
Average	(19.80)	(18.57)	(17.01)	(1.04)	(18.98)	(17.83)

By size of banks	*Very large*	*Large*	*Medium*	*Small*	*Total*
5–9.99	–	1	–	1	2
10–14.99	1	2	5	9	17
15–19.99	5	2	4	10	21
20–24.99	3	1	5	6	15
25–29.99	–	1	1	–	2
over 30	–	–	1	1	2
Total	9	7	16	27	59
High	(23.60)	(26.04)	(33.86)	(33.38)	(33.86)
Low	(14.53)	(9.04)	(12.56)	(8.16)	(8.16)
Average	(18.99)	(16.47)	(19.39)	(16.86)	(17.83)

Source: Elaboration of data from *Bancaria*, no. 10, October 1987.

important dimension of the problem of loan concentration for Italian banks, and on the intense effort that they will be called upon to make in adapting their loan policies to the new rules to be followed after the enactment of the EEC Recommendation, which adopts a consolidated notion of large exposures. In addition, the data summarised in Table 21.5 are the only piece of published information concerning bank lending to groups of companies so far available.

When loans to connected companies are added to those booked to the twenty largest individual borrowers, the characteristics of the distribution change somewhat. While the average ratio for the entire sample increases by 3.64 points to 17.83 per cent, the same ratio calculated for very large banks grows much more (5.20 percentage points) indicating that they have a stronger propensity to lend both to large borrowers and to their satellite companies. On the other hand, smaller banks, co-operative banks and savings banks, especially those which operate on a regional or local basis, are more likely to finance only a few companies of each group, with which they sometimes maintain only indirect relationships, such as through the acquisition of a sizeable portion of a syndicated loan organised and managed by one of the large banks or finance companies. It is also worth mentioning that, according to this more precise parameter, the level of risk concentration appears to be fairly high in the upper portion of the distribution, where four banks have more than 25 per cent of their total outstanding loans concentrated in only twenty individual borrowers and their connected companies.

Published information would permit the measurement of loan concentration with reference to the first thirty and fifty borrowers with or without their satellite companies, but there is no point in overburdening the analysis with pedantic details. It is preferable, therefore, to treat the available data with a view to providing at least a tentative answer to this question: how much would the concentration ratio increase if account is taken of lending to the next thirty most important individual borrowers?

Table 21.6 shows that for the entire sample of banks the aggregate size of this additional group of individual borrowers amounts to 6.99 per cent of total outstanding loans; in other words the concentration grows by nearly 50 per cent when the relevant number of large individual borrowers is increased from twenty to fifty. This second layer of large customers seems to be relatively more important for public law banks (7.76 per cent) and, once again, for savings banks (7.20 per cent). This result tends to confirm the indication emerging from the previous analysis of 'excess' loans which shows that savings banks are the category with the highest concentration of loans and presumably the one which will encounter more problems in adapting to a less liberal set of rules designed to control large exposures.

Table 21.6 Classification of a sample of 59 Italian banks in respect of the difference (in percentage points relative to total cash loans) between the loan exposure to the 50 and to the 20 most important individual customers as of 30 June 1987

Difference (percentage points of total loans)	*Public law banks*	*Banks of national interest*	*Joint stock banks*	*Co-operative banks*	*Savings banks*	*Total*
2– 4	–	–	1	–	2	3
4– 6	1	1	5	3	5	15
6– 8	2	2	10	5	6	25
8–10	2	–	3	3	3	11
10–12	1	–	1	–	3	5
Total	6	3	20	11	19	59
High	(10.84)	(7.14)	(11.08)	(8.15)	(10.66)	(11.08)
Low	(5.17)	(4.96)	(3.17)	(5.51)	(3.47)	(3.17)
Average	(7.76)	(6.37)	(6.73)	(6.85)	(7.20)	(6.99)

Source: Elaboration of data from *Bancaria*, no. 10, October 1987.

COMPARISONS WITH THE EEC (DECEMBER 1986) RECOMMENDATION

The preceding analysis appears to leave no doubt that regulations currently in force for the control of large exposures of Italian banks would need to be revised even if it were to be the case that no obligation in that sense would stem from the EEC Recommendation of 22 December 1986. The regulations are, in fact, exceedingly liberal and allow for an unduly high and uncontrollable concentration of loans, even when the capital structure of the bank is well below the average ratio for the system. In addition, given the rather wide margins already afforded by standard regulations, the number of exceptions authorised each year (see figures for 'other banks' in Table 21.1) are to be considered disproportionately high. In his Report to the general meeting of shareholders for the year 1986 the Governor of the Bank of Italy has publicly admitted that the rules under consideration have lost much of their effectiveness and he has announced that in their revision useful suggestions would be drawn from the EEC Recommendation on large loans.[8]

The variance between present rules and those suggested in the EEC document is rather large and finds its origin in the definition of the phenomenon to be controlled. In the EEC Recommendation large exposures are defined according to the so-called 'double consolidation' principle: on the one hand, consideration must be given not only to loans granted by the bank itself, but also to those extended by credit and finance companies affiliated with or controlled by the latter, such as special credit institutions, leasing and factoring companies, and so on; on the other side of the credit arrangement, so to say, it is the borrowing group as a whole that must be taken into account by adding loans to the parent company together with those booked in the name of all other companies under its control.[9]

Italian discipline, as it is presently applied, falls short on both counts. While banks are generally already equipped for the reporting of their aggregate lending to groups or to connected companies, the consolidation on the side of lenders is greatly complicated, for example, by the fact that special credit institutions, most of which are controlled by a bank, must respect an individual lending limit of their own, which appears to be already rather large[10] and which must in any case be co-ordinated with that established for the controlling bank itself.

Another divergence of a qualitative nature can be found in the fact that the EEC Recommendation does not admit any administrative procedure for derogating from the standard rules on lending limits while, as has been seen, the Italian system relies heavily on such procedures and consequently gives regulatory authorities vast discretionary powers to determine the actual level of loan concentration for specific banks. It is important that this should not turn out to be a deterrent to adopting the EEC discipline since Italian regulatory authorities have already inaugurated a different attitude towards the exercise of prudential controls, which calls for a lower degree of discretionality and a greater reliance on general instruments apt to be used in an automatic and impersonal way. A definite and, possibly, irreversible step in that direction was taken last year when two ratios of capital adequacy were imposed on all banks irrespective of their size, type of ownership and specific financial situation.[11]

The most important problem that the Italian authorities will have to face in revising and adapting their rules is quantitative in character and stems from the disparities in the level at which both relevant and maximum large exposures are set. Leaving aside the problems related to the different coverage of the definition from a technical point of view, which may in itself cause some practical difficulties (especially with reference to the treatment of off-balance sheet transactions), attention should be drawn to the fact that, according to the EEC Recommendation, the relevant level of a large exposure is established at 15 per cent of the lending institution's consolidated capital funds (as against 20 per cent of gross capital funds in the Italian case), while the maximum lending is set without exceptions at 40 per cent of the same aggregate (as against 100 per cent in current Italian regulations). In other words, the EEC standards are much more stringent than the Italian ones, particularly as they are to be put into effect on a consolidated basis.

The evidence produced in Table 21.5 with reference to lending to the first twenty groups, although rather scanty, seems sufficient to support the opinion that an unabridged adoption of the EEC standard limits would put several Italian banks under considerable pressure to curtail their loans to large customers.

No problems should arise, on the other hand, from the introduction of the ceiling on the aggregate amount of all large exposures, which is also contemplated by the EEC Recommendation and which is established at eight times the consolidated capital funds of the lender: in fact, such an aggregate ceiling is substantially higher than the one to which Italian banks are now subject which is 40 per cent of customer deposits in most cases.

The situation is such that Italian authorities will undoubtedly need a certain amount of time so that the new rules consistent with the EEC principles may be phased in properly. In the meantime, however, they should urgently take some specific measures in order to resume control of a regulatory instrument to which the banking authorities of most industrial countries are paying renewed attention.[12]

We would suggest as an interim step that they reduce the lending limit on individual loan exposures to three-fifths of the bank's net capital funds (gross capital funds less earmarked loan loss reserves, which is the same parameter used with reference to other regulatory instruments) and, at the same time, that they suspend the authorisation procedure that can be followed by banks which want to exceed the limit itself.

A more accurate definition of the capital base and the termination of discretionary powers of making exceptions to the standard limits on a case-by-case basis would be consistent both with the principles of the EEC Recommendation and with the changes in the philosophy and in the technique of prudential controls that the authorities themselves have initiated recently. In addition, the new temporary flat lending limit proposal would put all the banks operating in the Italian market on an equal footing, thus removing a competitive disadvantage for the branches of foreign banks that has apparently forced regulatory authorities to avail themselves too frequently of their powers of granting discretionary authorisations in this delicate area of prudential regulation.

Notes

1. A thorough investigation of the matter has been announced by Banca d'Italia in its *Relazione annuale 1986*, pp. 304–5.
2. It may be interesting to note that 100 authorisations were aimed at derogating both the capital funds limit and the aggregate ceiling on 'excess' loans (1510 authorised loans of an amount higher than total capital funds) while the remaining 696 authorisations concerned loans in excess of one-fifth of capital funds which resulted in the bank exceeding its aggregate ceiling.
3. E. D'Andrea, 'L'autonomia delle aziende di credito nella concessione di fidi "eccedenti": un'analisi retrospettiva', *Bancaria*, no. 8, 1981, p. 810.
4. 'Bollettino della Banca d'Italia – Vigilanza sulle Aziende di Credito', no. 107, January-March 1986, p. 199. The corresponding figures at the end of 1982 showed that more banks were in the high loan concentration groups.
5. Figures for 1986 on line (B) show, on the other hand, that they have increased their importance in respect of non-cash lending to borrowers of large size.
6. F. Cesarini, 'Equity financing by banks in the Italian market: the 1980–84 experience and the new trends', *Journal of Bank Research*, no. 1, 1986, pp. 28–39.
7. The data are taken from a half-yearly information sheet submitted by banks to Associazione Bancaria Italiana and published by *Bancaria*, which covers some important aspects of their financial and economic situation.
8. Banca d'Italia, *Relazione annuale 1986*, pp. 306–7.
9. This principle has been adopted for the first time in the revised rules on lending to subjects which directly or indirectly own more than 5 per cent of the bank's voting stock (see CICR decision of 20 March 1987 and Banca d'Italia regulations issued in February 1988).
10. It has been fixed in an amount equal to 100 per cent of capital funds of the special credit institution in Law no. 23 of 10 February 1981 and Ministerial Degree of 22 November 1981.
11. F. Cesarini, 'Note sull'applicazione di coefficienti patrimoniali alle banche italiane', in F. Parrillo (ed.) *Efficienza e stabilità dei sistemi finanziari; un raffronto internazionale* (Rome, 1988).
12. R. M. Pecchioli, *Prudential Supervision in Banking* (OECD), 1986, pp. 74–7 and Annex VII.

22 Capital Adequacy: The Italian Experience

Cesare Bisoni

BACKGROUND: THE ROLE OF CAPITAL

Economic doctrine has dealt extensively with the capital of credit institutions, emphasising its importance from various points of view, according to the different functions it fulfils. Already at the beginning of this century some economists, while not ascribing any significant role to capital in the conduct of business, pointed out its importance for maintaining the public confidence in credit institutions and for protecting creditors.[1]

It is hard to imagine that capital can cover all debts if a bank becomes insolvent, but its importance as a guarantee to creditors is universally recognised. This derives from the need to protect depositors, who are not usually capable of evaluating the riskiness of their investment, as well as from the need to avoid a situation where a crisis of the institution may produce such a lack of confidence as to bring about a general demand to withdraw deposits.

At the same time an adequate amount of capital is a requisite for correct management of the bank, as well as a means for offsetting the negative repercussions of unanticipated losses that may occur in times of difficulty. In this connection, an important role is played by earnings, which represent both the first line of defence against losses incurred and the internal means of strengthening the capital of the institution.[2]

SUPERVISORY ISSUES AND RATIO TECHNIQUES

Capital, therefore, thus has a leading part to play in guaranteeing liquidity, solvency and, as a result, the continued working of the bank. This condition is essential for the stability of the credit system and, more generally, for the orderly working of the economy.[3]

Because of this the supervisory authorities in various countries have sought suitable instruments to ensure that credit institutions maintain their capital at levels adequate to this purpose. According to the different aims of banks and authorities, capital requirements may lead to a capital structure which can differ significantly from what is deemed optimal by the management.[4]

One line taken by the authorities consists of establishing ratios between the capital of the bank and some aggregate of assets or liabilities: the ratios are then used to monitor the management of the bank, or the bank itself may be required to respect fixed minimum values.

The earliest examples of this kind of regulation involved introducing ratios which were not particularly sophisticated as regards their calculation. A case in point was the capital to deposits ratio set (as far back as 1914) by the US Comptroller of the Currency; this was later modified by substituting deposits, first with total assets, then with risky assets. Another case was that of Belgium where the ratio was capital to debts. This was subsequently modified when it was decided to take account of the specific riskiness of each asset category in order to determine the rating percentage of capital to debts. The indicators more recently introduced by the Bank of England belong to the same type: they set capital against deposits and risky assets. The first of these can be fairly easily assessed by consulting the balance sheet of the individual banks: the authorities intend that it should enable the public to judge the bank's capital adequacy.

Nonetheless, there has been a debate among economists and supervisory authorities as to whether these indicators can correctly determine the amount of capital that should be considered adequate for a particular bank. Doubts concern those ratios having deposits as a reference parameter, as well as those taking into account particular assets or their overall volume.[5]

The most frequent criticisms are concerned with:

1. the fact that the value obtained refers to a specific and unrepeatable moment in the life of a bank, with all the limitations that this view involves;
2. the possibility of measuring capital adequacy while neglecting important aspects of a qualitative nature in the management of the bank;
3. the correctness of establishing compulsory minimum values common to all banks, given their individual peculiarities and their different risk potentials;
4. whether freedom of decision on the part of management should be restricted when there is no certainty that this will markedly enhance control of risk. In this connection, it has been correctly pointed out that the presence of the above-mentioned ratios significantly affects the decisions of banks. For instance, they are induced to regard portions of the existing capital as unusable for absorbing losses; they may pursue a policy on interest rates aimed at increasing profits at the expense of keeping down costs of intermediation;[6] bank corporate growth itself may be adversely affected when the inability to increase capital forces management to limit the corresponding volume of assets.

To the above remarks may be added a more general one concerning the impossibility of defining minimum values of the ratios and, consequently, the levels of capital adequacy valid at any moment. It is thus not out of place to state that 'the answer to the question of how much capital is adequate is "as much as the regulators insist upon" '.[7] The debate that has developed around this topic has also led to several attempts to refine the ratios.

Intervention by the supervisory authorities in various countries has essentially aimed at guaranteeing a more accurate representation of the precise degree of risk assumed by banks.

Notwithstanding the variety of procedures chosen – especially in defining the values to be used for the variables included within the ratio – the basic criterion generally adopted is a differentiated weighting of the various categories of assets based on the differing degrees of riskiness of these categories, along the lines drawn up in the 1950s by the US authorities in the Federal Reserve Form ABC (Analyzing Bank Capital) System. The goal is to define more accurately the capital cushion necessary to absorb losses the banks may incur as a result of their portfolio strategies.[8]

These sophisticated ratios manage to assess banks' exposure to risk in a more precise way, even though the value by which this is expressed depends on the risk weights adopted and is therefore the result of a subjective evaluation by the supervisory authorities of the riskiness to be ascribed to the various classes of assets. Doubts remain due to the fact that even these aforesaid indicators take no account of the qualitative elements in bank management; not to mention problems as to how to define the required 'crisis level' of capital adequacy. Moreover, the ratios may operationalise a link between supervision policy and management decisions by banks: for instance, the need to conform to fixed minima may lead management to modify the composition of assets or even of loan portfolios.

The foregoing remarks should have highlighted the problems and uncertainties encountered by supervisory authorities in various countries when using capital ratios to guarantee the solvency of banks. In this connection, the experience of the United States may be taken as emblematic: following the initial formulations and the subsequent, progressive refinements of the ratios, the mid-1970s witnessed the decision to give up the Form ABC System owing to the impossibility of achieving a general consensus on the minimum levels of capital adequacy required. For some years the authorities relied almost solely upon moral suasion; after which they resumed a very simple ratio (primary capital to total assets). Recently the US authorities, in agreement with the bank of England, have returned, though not without some new adjustments, to ratios that take account of the risk profile of assets.[9]

ITALIAN DEVELOPMENTS

Italian banking law provides for possible intervention by the supervisory authorities with regard to the quantitative ratios between capital and assets or liabilities. But in the past they have refrained from imposing compulsory ratios of the sort described above. Capital has only been adduced in order to determine, for each individual bank, the amount of compulsory reserve; the limit of credit allowed to the single customer; the possibility of lending beyond the short term; the volume of bankers' acceptances that can be issued; the maximum amount of investments in real property and shareholdings. Thus, only the desire to expand operations in these areas could provide a stimulus to increase net worth.

There were two reasons for this attitude by the authorities. On the one hand, it was unsuitable to introduce compulsory capital ratios in the presence of a credit corset and with public banks encountering problems in raising equity capital; on the other hand, it was difficult to define the level of capital adequacy, given each bank's specific situation. The authorities therefore confined themselves to introducing, in 1981, the ratios envisaged in the first EEC directive, but this was limited to a group of banks and was intended only for the purpose of observation.

March 1987 saw a substantial change in the attitude hitherto taken by the Bank of Italy, when it imposed two compulsory minimum ratios described below.

1. Ratio related to the riskiness of assets

This ratio requires the bank to restrict the total loans and financial guarantees granted through branches in Italy and abroad, and weighted so as to take account of different degrees of risk: the ceiling must not exceed 12.5 times the capital.

Table 22.1 lists the accounts involved in calculating the ratio, with their respective risk weights. Some remarks are useful here:

1. the category 'public sector' (items 1, 2, 10, 14) comprises public administration bodies; public non-financial enterprises; state participation holdings (IRI, ENI, EFIM);
2. the category 'international bodies' (item 3) comprises bodies such as the International Monetary Fund, the Bank for International Settlements, the European Investment Bank, the World Bank;
3. the threshold between short and middle/long-term loans (items 4, 5) stands at eighteen months;
4. the category 'other subjects' (items 7, 11, 12, 15) includes all debtors to the bank not accounted for otherwise; this means, basically, the ordinary customers;

Table 22.1 Ratio related to the riskiness of assets

Accounts	*Risk weights*
1. Bonds issued by public sector bodies	0.250
2. Other claims on public sector bodies	0.500
3. Bonds issued by international bodies	0.250
4. Short-term loans to credit institutions	0.125
5. Medium-/long-term loans to credit institutions	0.250
6. Bonds held by foreign branches, issued by the central government of the country concerned in local currency	0.250
7. Loans to other subjects	1.000
8. Bad debts	2.000
9. Financial guarantees in favour of credit institutions	0.125
10. Financial guarantees in favour of public sector bodies	0.250
11. Financial guarantees, related to commercial operations, in favour of other subjects	0.250
12. Financial guarantees, related to financial operations, in favour of other subjects	1.000
13. Other risks with credit institutions	0.125
14. Other risks with public sector bodies	0.250
15. Other risks with other subjects	0.500
16. Estimated losses (minus)	2.000

5. 'bad debts' (item 8) are those loans whose recovery has necessitated legal action, and those loans to customers whose serious and lasting economic and financial difficulties are such as to induce legal action, even though there may be special reasons from refraining from such an action;
6. the category 'other risks' (items 13, 14, 15) includes all risks not otherwise accounted for, especially those relating to off-balance sheet operations.

In addition:

7. notes and coins; claims on the Bank of Italy, the Italian Foreign Exchange Office and foreign central banks; government securities; deposits with the Treasury, the Cassa Depositi e Prestiti and the Post Office Savings Banks; all these constitute assets deemed to be risk-free and are thus not considered in calculating the ratio;
8. the various categories of loans should include all financial relations, in whatever technical form adopted, even if transferred *pro-solvendo*;
9. the amount of securities should be taken as net of provisions for depreciation included in the liabilities.

The highest risk weights are obviously assigned to credits to ordinary customers. In particular, loans and guarantees linked to operations of a financial nature are assigned full value, whereas bad debts are ascribed double their value. Estimated losses – that is those portions of bad debts and loans which the bank has good reason to regard as probable losses – are also given a 2 weighting, but with a minus sign. This is in order to take account of the fact that they are also included in the capital base as calculated for supervision purposes (see Table 22.2).

Table 22.2 Capital base as calculated for supervision purposes

Positive elements
1. Equity capital
2. Ordinary reserve
3. Federal guarantee reserve (only for savings banks)
4. Reserve for monetary revaluation
5. Other reserves
6. Provisions for loan losses
7. Provisions for other operational risks
Negative elements
1. Due from shareholders
2. Previous years' deficits
3. Negative differences deriving from mergers
4. Estimated losses
5. Own stock of shares in portfolio

The total amount resulting from the algebraic sum of all the weighted assets represents the term of reference for comparison with the capital aggregate. The latter is determined as follows: from the capital base as calculated for supervision purposes, and comprising the costs and revenue of foreign branches, the shareholdings in Italian credit institutions are subtracted; the result is multiplied by 12.5; from this amount the value relating to the other shares and holdings in the bank's portfolio is deducted.

2. Ratio related to the volume of business

This ratio requires the bank to restrict the total of loans granted through Italian branches to an amount not exceeding 22.5 times the capital.

The aim of this ratio is to link the growth of the volume of business to that of capital; this explains the different ways of calculating this ratio as compared to the risk ratio. It may be useful to underline the differences:

1. credit aggregate (see Table 22.3) includes government securities (item 1) and all accounts in the category 'other financial assets' (item 9), such as claims on the Bank of Italy and the Italian Foreign Exchange Office; deposits with the Treasury, the Cassa Depositi e Prestiti, and the Post Office Savings Banks; cash items in process of collection; current accounts with foreign branches;
2. the aggregate excludes all financial guarantees, loans granted through foreign branches and foreign currency securities held by foreign branches;
3. all asset accounts are used in the calculation at their full value;
4. in determining capital aggregate no account is taken of the costs and revenue of foreign branches.

Table 22.3 Ratio related to the volume of business

Accounts	
1.	Government securities
2.	Bonds issued by public sector bodies
3.	Other claims on public sector bodies
4.	Bonds issued by international bodies
5.	Short-term loans to credit institutions
6.	Medium-/long-term loans to credit institutions
7.	Loans to other subjects
8.	Bad debts
9.	Other financial assets
10.	Estimated losses (minus)

Every quarter, banks are required to notify the Bank of Italy of the above data. When making decisions the managing bodies must bear in mind the need to respect these ratios at all times. In so doing, they will need to evaluate the fluctuations that may occur in the volume of assets. It is also up to them to take prompt decisions, which will be submitted to the Bank of Italy, in order to guarantee that capital requirements are respected when exceptional events threaten otherwise.

When the ratios were introduced, a maximum time limit of four years was laid down within which to conform to the new discipline. In addition those banks that have yet to comply with the established minimum levels are required to notify the supervisory body of the means by which they envisage meeting these requisites. The central bank may also, if necessary, require individual banks to observe ratios higher than those established for the system as a whole.

The Governor of the Bank of Italy has explained the change of attitude in the following terms:

> The recent measure introducing mandatory minimum capital ratios for banks is in response to the need to buttress stability in a phase of growing competition. It became possible to adopt these provisions, which give binding force to indicators that were already in use, after a period devoted to building up banks' capital and reserves, developing the share market and making the changes required to enable public sector banks to have access to it . . . The capital adequacy requirements will intensify the stimulus for banks to improve their efficiency and enhance their entrepreneurial skills.[10]

There can be no doubt of the significance of this introduction of capital ratios into the Italian banking system. It is consistent with the change of attitude over the past few years towards supervision and monetary policy which has had the aim of affording more scope to the market.

The chance in monetary policy has led to direct control of credit being progressively loosened, especially with regard to administrative constraints, and to an increasing reliance on open market operations.

As far as supervision is concerned, a start has been made by reducing entry controls, particularly as regards the opening of new branches. At the same time the aim has been to assign the task of evaluation over a wider range of analysts and other interested parties, especially the investors, in the dual guise of depositors and shareholders. Relevant in this connection, for instance, are the initiatives aimed at securing a larger and qualitatively better flow of information, not only relating to the accounting side, from banks to outsiders.

The introduction of capital ratios is an important step in supporting this new direction of allowing a greater role for the market in influencing banking resources allocation decisions.

EVOLUTION AND IMPACT

These indicators contain some highly subjective elements, which can be criticised as follows.

There is room for argument over the values selected for defining the capital multiple (12.5 for the risk ratio and 22.5 for the volume of business ratio), since these represent a crucial element in determining the status of a bank between those undercapitalized and those having excess capital. These values probably derive from evaluations made by the supervisory authorities on the basis of empirical investigations based on previous conditions. They take account of the need to place these values at lower levels than the banks would fix themselves, and of the impact of the regulation on first application. From a retrospective analysis carried out by the Bank of Italy, the overall theoretical requirement of capital would appear to be 3900 billion lire; this is determined both by the needs of certain large public banks and by the capital shortcomings of several small banks. Against this sum must be set capital surpluses in the remaining banks, totalling 13 600 billion lire.[11] Various analyses have emphasized the strengthening of capital that has developed in the banking system in recent years as a result, among other things, of a greater ability to raise funds on the market. The application of compulsory capital ratios should help to speed up this process and, above all, encourage it to spread and become homogeneous.

As for the risk weights assigned to the various categories of assets, these derive from a subjective judgement and are therefore questionable. The suggested values do gauge the various degrees of riskiness of the assets, but it would be possible to establish different relations between the accounts even while following the same criterion.

Other elements involved in computing the ratios may be open to question. Among these are:

1. the choice as to which security qualifies for which risk ratio. On the basis of different levels of issuer risk it is hard to justify the exclusion of government securities while including other securities, such as those issued by public or international bodies, with a 0.250 weight;
2. the decision to deduct shareholdings, but not property holdings, from the capital. Property holdings do not always have a marginal value; moreover, there is a long-standing rule that the sum of property holdings plus shareholdings cannot exceed the net worth;
3. the different treatment of shareholdings according to whether they involve banks or other types of company; the first are deducted from capital, the second from the capital multiple. This may lead to situations of inequality among banks, especially when the shareholdings are in credit institutions such as those dealing in special credit; where these are concerned, a degree of risk may be envisaged comparable to that of banks. This rule may also affect decisions about company expansion, since it tends to favour processes of internal growth: on one hand this is because the purchasing prices of share parcels are normally higher than what would be calculated on the basis of the balance sheet values of the company involved;[12]and on the other hand because, *ceteris paribus*, a purchase of this kind involves renouncing loans to an amount equal to 22.5 times the funds thus invested.

Whatever the situation, the introduction of capital ratios is bound to have significant effects on the behaviour of individual banks and on the banking system as a whole. It is one extra factor that bank management must bear in mind when taking decisions.

Above all, these ratios affect decisions on the structure of assets in the balance sheet, both as regards the relation between investments in securities and investments in loans, and as regards the composition of the respective portfolios. Shareholdings have already been mentioned. The nil weighting assigned to government securities may make them more attractive than other kinds of securities. This phenomenon may occur, in particular, when the risk ratio is very high or when there is a more pressing need to create scope for credit activity.

As far as credits are concerned, the economic aspect of the decision takes on greater importance. The high weighting assigned to loans to ordinary customers requires that more care be taken in judging the suitability of introducing into the portfolio loans of high amount and poor remuneration, such as those of so-called 'hot money'.

Since the lack of precise regulation allows banks ample freedom to make their own decisions as to bad debts, the double weighting assigned to these may lead management to limit the transfer from loans to this category in order not to increase the risk ratio. Similar behaviour may occur where estimated losses are concerned. Underestimating these makes capital appear higher. In fact the decrease in loans, as a result of the quantifcation of estimated losses, is more than offset by the opposite effect produced by the reduction in the capital aggregate.[13]

In addition, more attention must be given to the bank's ability to generate profits, not only because profits represent the most direct means of strengthening capital, but also because they are the necessary condition for raising capital on the market; the feasibility of development programmes ultimately depends on this latter element. Where the banks concerned have been established as limited companies, decisions taken in the matter of dividends are important. Policies in this connection must be consistent with the financial strategy; for the reasons stated above, the need to offer a competitive return on capital involves finding the best combination between return on assets and financial structure.

The presence of capital ratios brings in set standards to which management must necessarily refer in strategic planning. This becomes more important as entry controls are reduced and the system of authorisations is progressively abandoned, thereby limiting the Bank of Italy's freedom of discretion.

At banking system level, the introduction of ratios confers privileges on those banks having wider capital margins: they can compete more aggressively on the market when offering both products and prices, thus causing problems for the marginal banks. This argues in favour of a greater concentration of the market, with the aim of increased efficiency; a target that the Bank of Italy has been determinedly pursuing for some years now.

Lastly, capital ratios help to bring Italian supervisory regulation closer to that of other European countries. This is an important step, in view of the objective, recalled in the recently passed second EEC directive, of harmonising legislation relating to capital and solvency ratios.

Notes

1. M. Pantaleoni, *La Caduta della Società Generale di Cre-dito Mobiliare Italiano*, 1st edn (Rome, 1895), reprinted (Milan, 1977) p. 56; J. G. Courcelle-Seneuil, *Les Opérations de Banque: Traité Théorique et Pratique* (Paris, 1920) p. 168.
2. J. R. S. Revell, 'The solvency of banks', *The Banker*, January 1975, p. 28.
3. A. Ferrari, 'La liquidità e la tesoreria', in P. Mottura (ed.), *La Gestione della Banca* (Milan, 1981) pp. 606–7.
4. M. Onado, *Aspetti Economici e Tecnici del Capitale Proprio delle Banche* (Milan, 1982), p. 5.
5. J. R. S. Revell, *Solvency and Regulation of Banks* (Bangor, 1975) p. 99.
6. E. P M. Gardener, 'Legal rules versus "vicarious participation" in bank prudential regulation', in J. R. S. Revell (ed.), *Competition and Regulation of Banks* (Bangor, 1975) p. 39.
7. H. D. Crosse, 'Capital adequacy revisited', *The Bankers Magazine*, Summer 1975, p. 82.
8. E. P. M. Gardener, *Capital Adequacy and Banking Supervision* (Bangor, 1981) p. 19.
9. 'Convergence of capital adequacy in the UK and US. Agreed proposal of the United States Federal Banking Supervisory Authorities and the Bank of England on primary capital adequacy assessment', *Bank of England Quarterly Bulletin*, February 1987; J. M. Moulton 'New guidelines for bank capital: an attempt to reflect risk', *Federal Reserve Bank of Philadelphia Business Review*, July/August 1987; Banca dei Regolamenti Internazionali, Comitato per la Regolamentazione Bancaria e le Procedure di Vigilanza, *Proposte er la Convergenza Internazionale della Misurazione del Capitale Proprio e dei Coefficiente Patrimoniali Minimi*, December 1987.
10. Banca d'Italia, Ordinary General Meeting of Shareholders, Abridged Report for the Year 1986 (Rome, 1987) p. 181.
11. Banca d'Italia, *Relazione per l'anno 1986* (Rome, 1986) pp. 313–15.
12. F. Cesarini, 'Note sull'applicazione di coefficienti patrimoniali alle banche italiane' (typescript), p. 11.
13. R. Locatelli, 'L'introduzione di coefficienti patrimoniali per le aziende di creditor italiane', *Note finanziarie*, 1987 (n. 21), p. 12.

John Robert Stephen Revell: List of Publications

Books and monographs

(with John Moyle)(1966) *The Owners of Quoted Ordinary Shares: A Survey for 1963* (London: Chapman & Hall).

The Wealth of the Nation: The National Balance Sheet of the United Kingdom, 1957–61 (1967) (London: Cambridge University Press).

Changes in British Banking: The Growth of a Secondary Banking System (1968) Hill, Samuel Occasional Paper no. 3 (London: Hill, Samuel).

Financial Structure and Government Regulation (1972) (London: Inter-Bank Research Organisation).

The British Financial System (1973)(London:Macmillan). (with C. R. Tomkins (1974) *Personal Wealth and Finance in Wales* Cardiff: HMSO for Welsh Council).

Solvency and Regulation of Banks (1975) Bangor Occasional Paper no. 5 (Cardiff: University of Wales Press).

Flexibility in Housing Finance (1975) (Paris: OECD).

Savings Flows in Europe (1978) (London: Financial Times).

Rischio e Solvibilità delle Banche (1978) (Milan: Banca Commerciale Italianà, Italian translation of part of *Solvency and Regulation of Banks).*

Competition and Regulation of Banks (ed.) (1978) Bangor Occasional Paper no. 14 (Cardiff: University of Wales Press).

Inflation and Financial Institutions (1979) (London: Financial Times).

Costs and Margins in Banking: An International Survey (1980) (Paris: OECD).

A Study of the Spanish Banking System (1980) (Bilbao: Banco de Vizcaya).

A Study of the Spanish Banking System: Some Additional Comments (1982) (Bilbao: Banco de Vizcaya).

Banking and Electronic Fund Transfers (1983) (Paris: OECD).

Changes in Spanish Banking (1984) (Bilbao: Banco de Vizcaya).

Costs and Margins in Banking Statistical Supplement (1985) (Paris: OECD).

Mergers and the Role of Large Banks (1987) IEF Research Monographs in Banking and Finance no. 2 (Bangor: Institute of European Finance, University College of North Wales).

(with E. P. M. Gardener) (1988) *Securitisation: History, Forms and Risk,* IEF Research Monographs in Banking and Finance no. 5 (Bangor: Institute of European Finance, University College of North Wales).

Internal research reports

United Nations Economic and Social Council, Statistical Commission (1969) 'The proposed balance sheet and revaluation accounts of the system of national accounts (SNA)' (E/CN.3/398).

Inter-Bank Research Organisation (1974) 'Solvency and liquidity ratios for credit institutions'.
HM Treasury and Central Statistical Office (1977) 'Committed and discretionary saving'; later published in Sue Toland, 'Committed and discretionary saving', *Economic Trends*, no. 337, November 1981, pp. 109–35.
Royal Commission on the Distribution of Income and Wealth (1977) 'Property missing from Inland Revenue capital statistics'.
HM Treasury (1983) 'The turnover of assets'.
Office of Fair Trading (1984) 'Competition in banking'.

Articles and reprinted seminar papers

'Who owns ordinary share capital?'; *The Times*, 23 June 1960 (with C. H. Feinstein).
'A survey of the holders of local authority debt', *Local Government Finance*, vol. 64, no. 7, July 1960, pp. 164–8 (with G. C. Hockley).
'Holders of local authority stocks and bonds', *Local Government Finance*, vol. 64, no. 12, December 1960, pp. 282–6 (with G. C. Hockley).
'Settled property and death duties', *British Tax Review*, May-June 1961, pp. 177–82.
'Trustee holdings of gilt-edged stocks', *The Times*, 11 July 1961.
'Building societies and the Common Market', *Building Societies' Gazette*, vol. 94, no. 1117, June 1962, pp. 421–4.
'Assets and age', *Bulletin of the Oxford University Institute of Statistics*, vol. 24, no. 3, August 1962, pp. 363–78.
'Insurance company investments', *Policy Holder*, vol. 82, 9 January 1964, pp. 40–42.
'The wealth of the nation', *Moorgate and Wall Street*, Spring 1966, pp. 57–89.
'A secondary banking system', *The Banker*, vol. 118, no. 511, Sept. 1968, pp. 798–804; reprinted in H. G. Johnson (ed.) *Readings in British Monetary Economics* (Oxford: Clarendon Press, 1972) pp. 422–31.
'A "crawling peg" for bank lending', *Bankers' Magazine*, vol. 212, no. 1548, July 1971, pp. 10–13.
'National balance sheets and national accounting: a progress report', *Economic Trends*, no. 211, May 1971, pp. 1–8 (with A. R. Roe).
'Trends in the financing of companies', *Stock Exchange Journal*, vol. 24, no. 4, December 1974, pp. 12–17.
'UK building societies', in *Housing Finance: Present Problems* (Paris: OECD, 1984).
'Financial centres, financial institutions and economic change', in H. G. Johnson (ed.), *The New Mercantilism* (Oxford: Basil Blackwell, 1974) pp. 74–89.
'The solvency of banks', *The Banker*, vol. 125, no. 581, January 1975, pp. 27–31.
'Liquidity and solvency management for banks', in R. Brealey and G. Rankine (eds.), *European Finance Association: 1975 Proceedings* (Amsterdam: North-Holland, 1976) pp. 375–89.
'Improving the solvency and liquidity of various financial institutions', in J. E. Wadsworth *et al.* (eds), *The Development of Financial Institutions in Europe, 1956–1976* (Leyden: Sijthoff, 1976) pp. 203–13.
'Reforming UK bank supervision', *The Banker*, vol. 126, no. 607, September 1976, pp. 1021-3.
'Housing finance in Europe', *Three Banks Review*, no. 114, June 1977, pp. 61–77.

'Housing finance in Europe', *In Touch* (Netherlands–British Chamber of Commerce) September 1977, pp. 33–7, and Oct 1977, pp. 47–53.
'La situation actuelle du controle des banques au Royaume-Uni', *Banque*, no. 364, July–August 1977, pp. 780–82.
'International comparisons of financial statistics', in *Statistics Users Conference on Financial Statistics: Report of Proceedings* (London: Bank of England, 1977) pp. 93–8.
'Competition and regulation of banks', evidence to Committee to Review the Functioning of Financial Institutions; reprinted in J. Revell (ed.), *Competition and Regulation of Banks*, Bangor Occasional Paper No. 14 (Cardiff: University of Wales Press, 1978) pp. 48–63.
'The London clearing banks' evidence to the Wilson Committee', *Bankers' Magazine*, vol. 222, no. 1610, May 1978, pp. 21–3; reprinted in J. Revell (ed.), *Competition and Regulation of Banks*, Bangor Occasional Paper No. 14 (Cardiff: University of Wales Press, 1978) pp. 64–7.
'Liquidità e solvibilità delle banche: concetti e misure', in Francesco Cesarini and Marco Onado (eds), *Struttura et Stabilità del Sistema Finanziario* (Bologna: Il Mulino, 1979) pp. 119–41.
'More flexibility for European housing finance institutions and instruments', in L. Mühlhaupt and H. Wielens (eds) *Die Internationalisierung der Wohnungsbaufinanzierung* (Frankfurt am Main: Fritz Knapp, 1980) pp. 27–45.
'The regulation of banks and the new English banking law', *Bancaria*, vol. 36, no. 5, May 1980, pp. 463–75 (in Italian).
'Towards a microeconomic theory of financial institutions', *Bancaria*, vol. 36. no. 10, October 1980, pp. 1011–24 (in Italian); *l'Industria*, n.s., vol. 1, no. 4, Oct.-Dec. 1980, pp. 463–83 (in Italian).
'The complementary nature of competition and regulation in the financial sector', *Revue de la Banque*, 1/1980.
'The complementary nature of competition and regulation in the financial sector', in A. Verheirstraeten (ed.), *Competition and Regulation in Financial Markets* (London: Macmillan, 1981) pp. 16–34.
'The effects of electronic fund transfers on the structure of banking systems', *Bancaria*, vol. 37, no. 8, August 1981, pp. 774–83 (in Italian).
'The regulation of banks and the new English banking law', *Revue de la Banque*, 1/1981.
'Lessons to be learned: a book review', *Credit*, vol. 23, no. 2, June 1982, pp. 43–7.
'The OECD report on costs and margins in banking', in D. E. Fair and F. Léonard de Juvigny (eds) *Bank Management in a Changing Domestic and International Environment* (The Hague: Martinus Nijhoff, 1982).
'Electronic fund transfers and monetary policy', *Banche e Banchieri*, vol. 9, nos. 7–8, July–August 1982, pp. 609–17 (in Italian).
'Consequences of electronic fund transfers', *Norwegian Commercial Banks*, vol. 56, no. 2, 1982.
'Reciprocity in banking', *World of Banking*, vol. 1, no. 1, January/February 1982.
'Electronic fund transfers and monetary policy', *Bancaria*, vol. 38, no. 11, November 1982, pp. 1268–70 (abridged version in Italian).
'Costs and margins in savings banks', *Banca, Impresa, Società*, vol. 2, no. 3, December 1983, pp. 367–85 (in Italian).
'Banking supervision in the United Kingdom', *Banca, Impresa, Società*, vol. 2, no 3, December 1983, pp. 397–410 (in Italian).
'Capital adequacy, hidden reserves and provisions', *Bancaria,* vol. 39, no. 4, April 1983, pp. 346–56 (in Italian).

'The public policy issues of payment system regulation', part 1, *Issues in Bank Regulation*, vol. 7, no. 2, Autumn 1983, pp. 11–15; reprint of part of *Banking and Electronic Fund Transfers* (Paris: OECD, 1983).
'Efficiency in the financial sector', in David Shepherd *et al.* (eds), *Microeconomic Efficiency and Macroeconomic Performance* (Oxford: Philip Allan, 1983) pp. 137–70.
'The likely shape of payment systems in the next decade', *World of Banking*, vol. 2, no. 5, September–October 1983, pp. 12–15; reprint of part of *Banking and Electronic Fund Transfers* (Paris: OECD, 1983).
'Trends in banking markets', *Parabancaria*, vol. 2, no. 4, December 1983, pp. 56–61 (in Italian).
'The new technology and financial institutions: editorial commentary', *Managerial Finance*, vol. 10, no. 1, 1984, pp. 1–5.
'The public policy issues of payment system regulation', part 2, *Issues in Bank Regulation*, vol. 7, no. 3, Winter 1984, pp. 20–4; reprint of part of *Banking and Electronic Fund Transfers* (Paris: OECD, 1983).
'International financial centres', in Velo, Dario (ed.), *Sviluppo della Finanza Internazionale e Interdipendenza dei Sistemi Finanziari: in Onore di Riccardo Argenziano*, Collana di Diritto ed Economia no. 7 (Milan: Giuffrè Editore, 1984) pp. 125–38.
'Building societies and money transmission' ('How societies could deal with the banks on equal terms'), *Building Societies' Gazette*, vol. 116, no. 1410, July 1984, pp. 832–6.
'The relationship of capital, hidden reserves and loan loss provisions', *World of Banking*, vol. 3, no. 5, September–October 1984, pp. 19–22, and vol. 3, no. 6, November–December 1984, pp. 19–24.
'Capital adequacy, hidden reserves and provisions', *Osterreichisches Bank-Archiv*, vol. 32, no. 10, October 1984, pp. 343–55 (in German).
'International comparisons of bank costs and profits', *The Banker*, vol. 135, no. 707, January 1985, pp. 25–30.
'New forms of competition and new competitors', *Revue de la Banque*, vol. 49, no. 2, February 1985.
'Banking and the international corporate customer', *World of Banking*, vol. 4, no. 3, May–June 1985, pp. 11–13; reprint of part of *Banking and Electronic Fund Transfers* (Paris: OECD, 1983).
Articles on 'Banking' and 'Credit' in Adam Kuper, and Jessica Kuper (eds), *The Social Science Encyclopaedia* (London: Routledge & Kegan Paul, 1985).
'Home Banking', *Banking World*, vol. 3, no. 6, June 1985.
'Progress with electronic banking', *Irish Banking Review*, 3/1985.
'Rischio bancario e assicurazione dei depositi', *Banca, Impresa, Società*, vol. 4, no. 3, December 1985, pp. 375–89.
'The complementary nature of competition and regulation in the financial sector', and 'Capital adequacy, hidden reserves and provisions', in Edward P. M. Gardener (ed.), *UK Banking Supervision: Evolution, Practice and Issues* (London: Allen & Unwin, 1986).
'Implications of new technology for financial markets', in Donald E. Fair (ed.), *Shifting Frontiers in Financial Markets* (Dordrecht, Netherlands: Martinus Nijhoff for SUERF, 1986).
'Banking structures in Great Britain: changes and future aspects', *Oesterreichisches Bank-archiv*, 1986.
'The structures of the credit systems: concentration and fragmentation', *Review of the Economic Conditions in Italy*, no. 3, September–December 1985, pp.

393–411; Italian translation in *Economia Italiana*, no. 3, Ottobre–Dicembre 1985, pp. 427–47.
'Effects of new technology on the operations of financial institutions', Research Paper 86/3, Institute of European Finance, Bangor 1986.
'Effects of new technology on the operations of financial institutions', *World of Banking*, vol. 5, no. 5, September–October, 1986, pp. 26–30.
'Recent developments and prospects in banking', Research Paper 86/4, Institute of European Finance, Bangor, 1986.
'Technology and capital markets', Research Paper 86/13, Institute of European Finance, Bangor, 1986.
'Technology and capital markets', *Revue de la Banque*, vol. 51, no. 1, January 1987, pp. 39–44.
Introductory essay to Italian translation of C. P. Kindleberger, *A Financial History of Western Europe* (Milan: CARIPLO, 1987).
'The impact of technology on bank operations and bank marketing', *International Journal of Bank Marketing*, vol. 5, no. 4, 1987.
'International financial markets and the impact of new technology', *Journal of Foreign Exchange and International Finance*, vol. 1, no. 4, October 1987, pp. 386–90.
'Efficiency and risk: the UK example', Research Paper 87/9, Institute of European Finance, Bangor, 1987.
'Towards a microeconomic theory of financial institutions', Research Paper 87/10, Institute of European Finance, Bangor, 1987.
'Comparative concentration of banks', Research Paper 87/13, Institute of European Finance, Bangor, 1987.
'Comparative concentration of banks', *University of Wales Business and Economics Review*, no. 2, Winter 1987, pp. 49–54.
'Effects of new technology on the operations of financial institutions', *Bulletin de l'IDATE*, vol. 4, no. 29, 1987.
'Uno Studio comparato della concentrazione bancaria' *Banca Impresa Società*, vol. 6, no. 3, December 1987.
'Aspetti della storia finanziaria più recente', *Rivista Milanese di Economia*, no. 24, October–December 1987, pp. 127–33.
'The future of the large Spanish banks', *International Correspondent Banker*, March 1988.
'Mergers among banks and other financial institutions in Europe', *FT Mergers and Acquisitions*, 1988.
'Impact on banks on small countries', *World Banking*, vol. 7, no. 6, November–December 1988.
'Shake-out in Spain', *Banking World*, vol. 6, no. 10, October 1988, pp. 30–33.
'Bank preparations for 1992: some clues and some queries', Research Paper RP 88/17, Institute of European Finance, Bangor, 1988.

Index